AF593966

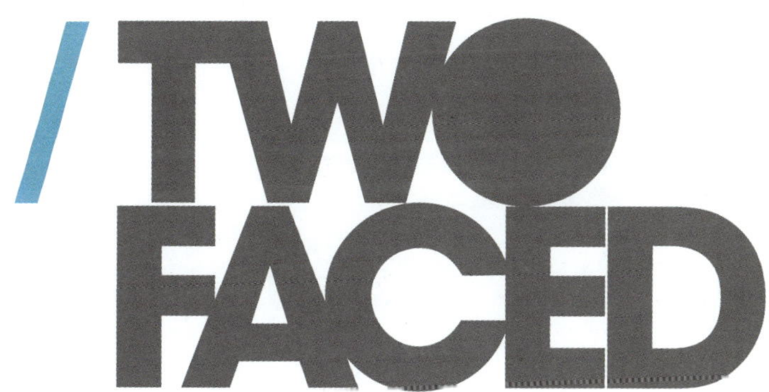
/ TWO
FACED

/ TWO FACED

The Changing Face Of Portraiture

'THE PERSON PORTRAYED AND THE PORTRAIT ARE TWO ENTIRELY DIFFERENT THINGS'

Jose Ortega Y Gasset

Timothy Saccenti

01 / Danger Doom.
Photograph.
Original size_20" x 30"

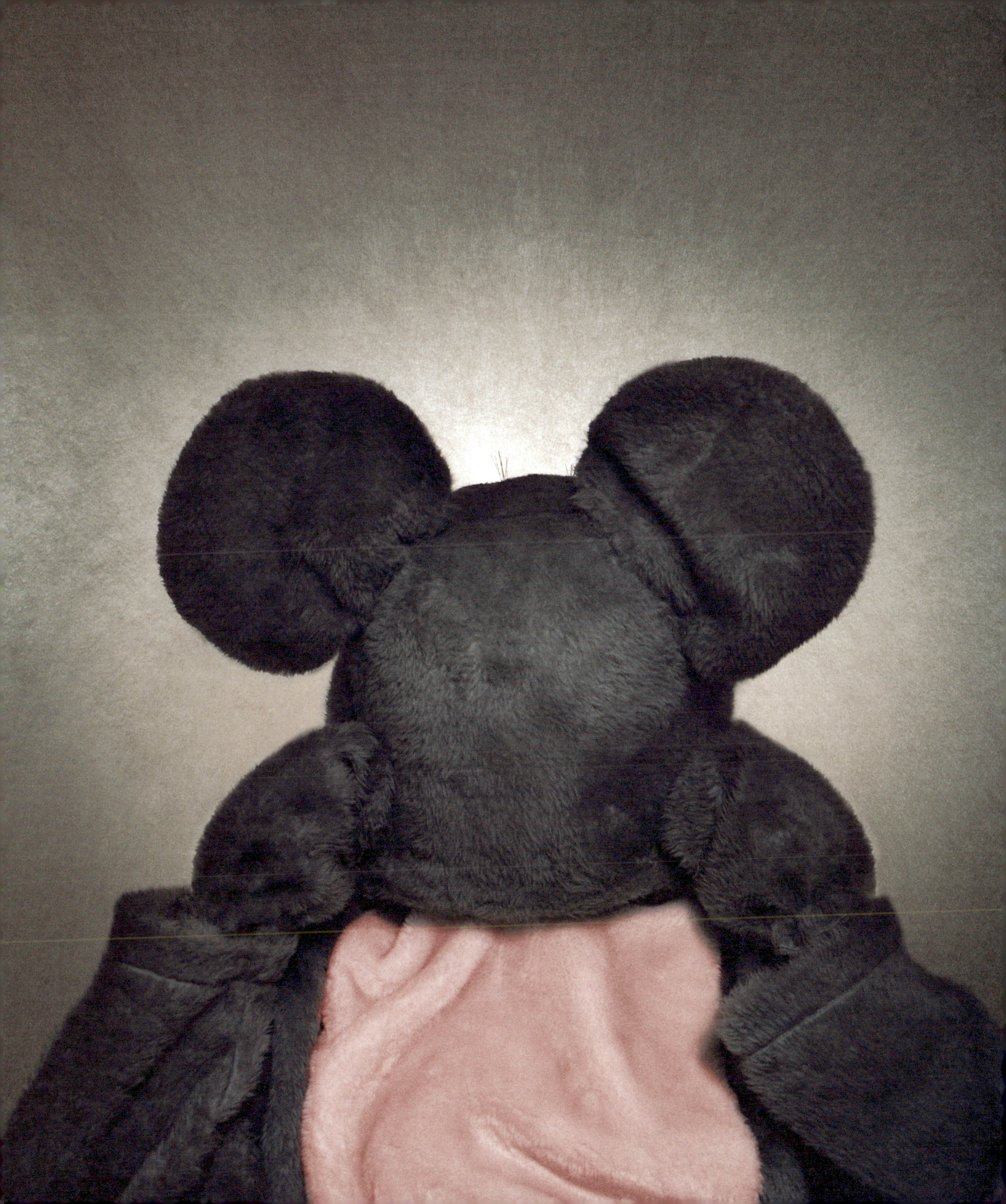

ONE / FOREWORD

By Gavin Lucas_Creative Review

It used to be that image makers were an elite group of skillful craftsmen who plied their trade to those who could afford to employ their particular skill sets. Today we are all image makers. With our mobile phone/camera/web-roaming gadgets permanently at the ready, we can shoot (in the photographic sense) anyone we like, including ourselves, whenever we like. Thousands upon thousands of freshly snapped images of friends and family are put up on websites such as Flickror MySpace on a daily basis or sent in messages on mobile phones – or simply deleted from our digital tools. In short, image making has become everyday, commonplace – throwaway even. But while most of us have or have access to image making tools, not all of us have an eye for compositional perfection or indeed any other skill associated with the professional image maker.

Despite the increase in the number of ways we can capture likenesses in the last hundred years or so, the role of the portrait artist remains the same: Portrait taking or making is the art of capturing the sitter's physical likeness and imbuing that likeness with his or her personality.

"TWO FACED", then, is a celebration of portraiture in the 21st century – split into two sections. The first is dedicated to showcasing a selection of contemporary portraiture produced in various mediums by a host of well known photographers and artists such as Rankin, Simon Henwood and Stella Vine.

In the second section, Firth has assembled and paired up leading image makers to produce each other's portraits. And these are not necessarily specialist portrait artists. Rather, Firth has selected a range of creatives who work across a variety of media to contribute to "TWO FACED". Illustrators such as Marion Deuchars and David Shrigley who work primarily with pencils and pens; graphic designers like Michael C Place and eBoy who produce vector based graphics on their macs; artists including Ian Wright and Paul Willoughby who might use spray paints, brushes, tape and a range of other materials to create their work; and even filmmakers Shynola are among the creatives who have produced portraits for this book. So how did each image maker respond to their subject and to their task? What will each image reveal about the sitter and also about the artist responsible?

"TWO FACED" thus, is not simply a collection of snapshots, or images to be downloaded and subsequently discarded, but an art project that celebrates the notion of cultural exchange as well as the talents of some of the most in-demand image makers of our time.

TWO / CONTENTS

THREE

/ PORTRAIT OF THE DESIGNER

By Adrian Shaughnessy

I've always believed that our faces are guides to our inner beings. A face is like a good guidebook to a city we are unfamiliar with: it doesn't tell us everything, yet it tells us most of what we need to know. But how reliable are faces as a guide to personality? Are our faces maps of our psyches, or are they random arrangements of flesh and muscle predetermined by DNA and the amount of alcohol we consumed the night before? Can you have a sweet and smiley face and yet be miserable inside? Can you have a sour face and still be a happy human being?

Our faces are our signatures: something that is indelibly us. Try swapping Elvis Presley's face with Michael Jackson's face: can't be done. Both of these iconic figures are defined by their faces. Yet faces are paradoxical: we can easily misread them. We must beware of shallow, impulsive readings, or over-reliance on immediate impressions. A pretty face, with regular features, might, on closer inspection, reveal an inner cruelty. A clumsy, irregular- featured face, may, with careful study, reveal intelligence and vision. To be viewed as accurate guides to the minds of the individuals they 'represent', faces require close and informed scrutiny. The ability to 'read' faces – to discern their inner meanings – is the core skill of the portrait maker.

In daily life, we learn to read faces in the same way a portrait artist prepares to make a portrait. We look for signs and hidden meanings. We scan continuously for indications of concealment, for signs of warmth, for hints of aggression. The smallest facial tick sends out a signal. We may not know what that signal is telling us, but we note it and file it in a complex system of mental folders that we use to build up a psychological profile of the people we meet. Of course, the face isn't the only way we

‘Our faces are our signatures: something that is indelibly us. Try swapping Elvis Presley’s face with Michael Jackson’s face: can’t be done.’

create an understanding of someone: language, gesture, posture, movement, even personal hygiene, all reveal essential components of a persona. But the face reveals the most. This is why at an early stage in our development as human beings we learn the importance of controlling our facial muscles. It’s a pivotal moment in the growth of an individual when he or she takes full control over the previously autonomous zone of the face. I was a late developer in this area: I was a teenager before I discovered that I could control the muscles in my face. I realised – slowly – that I didn’t have to reveal what I was thinking. But I could achieve this only if I was able to retain control of my facial expressions.

The ability to dissemble is an essential life skill: if we can conceal our innermost thoughts, we can gain many advantages, especially in the competitive domain of business. Yet in other spheres, we gain advantage by allowing our inner feelings to flood our faces: when we wish to show a lover our emotions, or when we want to show a child that we are pleased with them, we let our inner selves, to use Violet Leduc’s word, ‘irradiate’ our faces. But because we know that so much is written in our facial expressions, it is essential that we learn to control our faces. It is a basic survival mechanism. It is often said that some so-called primitive societies believe that if you photograph them you will capture their souls.

This doesn’t sound primitive to me. It sounds sophisticated. Just think of today’s celebrities; they live only to be photographed and catalogued in magazines and on TV. They have no life beyond the life encapsulated in the images of themselves: if they stop appearing in the glossy mags and the luminous dazzle of TV screens, they cease to exist. If this isn’t forfeiting your soul, I don’t know what is.

The pictures of celebrities that deluge our culture are portraits of a sort. But they are not portraits with any ambition to reveal psychological truths. In fact, they seek to do the opposite. Like much of the great formal portraiture of the past (paintings of aristocrats and royalty), they trade in falsehood and hype. Their defining characteristic is that they are driven by the subject, not the image-maker.

And it appears that we can divide portraits into one of two categories: there are those that are made to glorify or idealise the subject: and there are those that are made to objectify the subject. Most portraits – especially photographic ones – deal with the former. They exist to flatter the sitter. They connive with the sitter to project the image the sitter wants to project. Even so, the truth sometimes slips through. In the supermodel’s beautiful features we sometimes glimpse cruelty and self-obsession, or, conversely, modesty and intelligence.

The other sorts of portraits are those that are made with sensitivity and psychological insight: these portraits, usually done by artists, eloquently reveal the inner reality of their subjects. Who tells a deeper truth: the painter Francis Bacon, or a celebrity photographer with an arsenal of Photoshop filters and a team of stylists? Bacon seems to tell a deeper truth, perhaps because he has no interest in flattering his sitters. It’s almost as if he is not looking at the face but peering into his subject’s soul: you find the same psychological penetration in Picasso’s cubist portraits.

So – with this in mind, why would anyone turn to a graphic designer (not to mention commercial photographers and illustrators) to make a portrait of another human being? Isn't it a bit like asking a person to write a symphony just because they can whistle a tune? Graphic designers have opposite skills to most portrait makers. Graphic designers are problem solvers, or message carriers, or organisers of visual and textual information. They are rarely, at least in their work, concerned with psychological truth. After all, graphic design is the art of the surface. It is about instant communication: it is about now-ness and immediacy. And even when graphic designers claim that their work is about 'ideas', along comes commercial reality and demands that these ideas are instantly comprehensible. There must be no ambiguity or mystery. Graphic design is the art of the obvious.

But some graphic designers have a different view of graphic design; an alternative view that allows for ambiguity and mystery. Increasingly, designers are turning away from the traditional role of the designer – a conveyor of other people's messages – and looking within themselves to find ways to use their skills and vision to create graphic work that no longer conforms to the purely commercial view of graphic design. In order to pursue these ideas of graphic authorship, they require either a supportive client or the strength and vision to write their own briefs.

This is being done at a time when design is under greater pressure than at any time in its short history to be the mute servant of rampant commercialism. Many graphic designers no longer call themselves graphic designers. They prefer to be called branding consultants. Big design groups have eradicated the 'D' word from their vocabulary with Stalinist ruthlessness. Design in the marketplace increasingly looks as if it comes from a universal template: uniformity and blandness are the most desired qualities in graphic communication.

Hardly surprising then, that a growing band of thoughtful designers are questioning this one-size-fits-all approach and turning to more meaningful modes of expression. Hardly surprising then, that a new generation of graphic designers and image makers can happily, and with such enjoyable results, turn their hands to portrait making, as the work in this book amply demonstrates.

Johnny Hardstaff

By Eboy

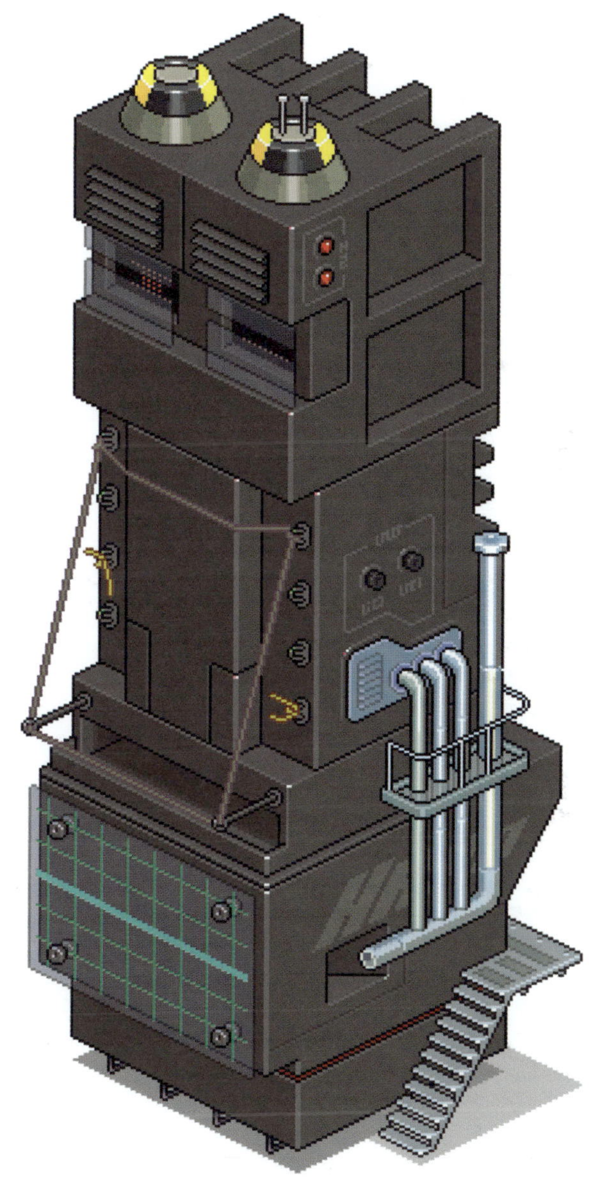

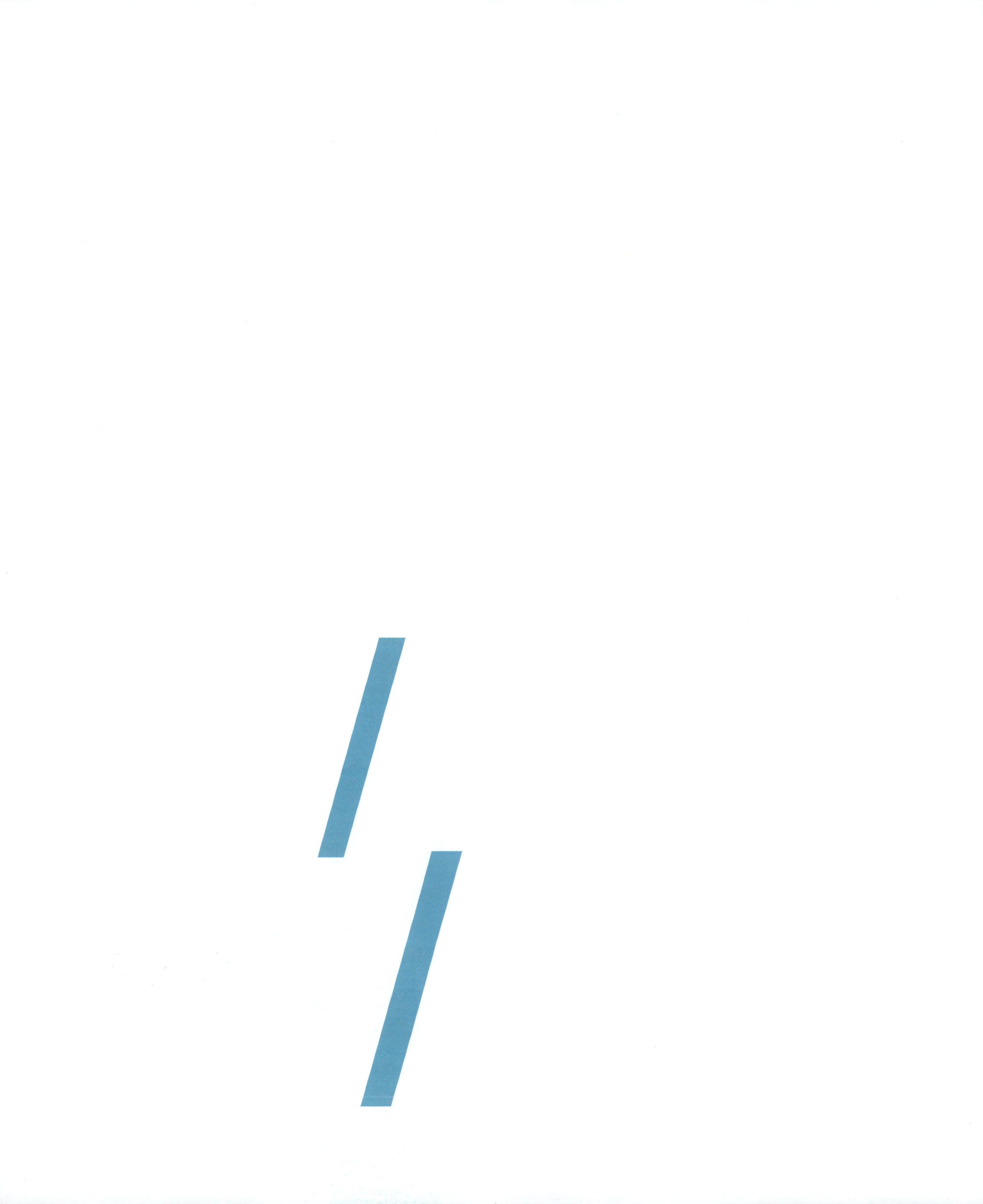

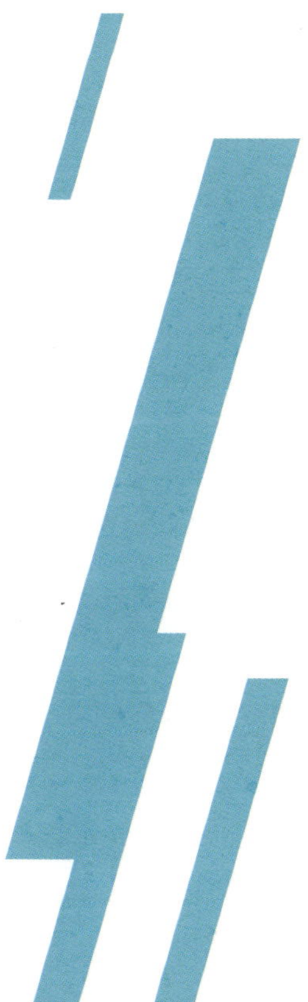

START

04 / Pages 17 to 124

FOUR / SHOWCASE

A collection of work, showcasing both traditional and experimental portraiture, produced by a host of well known international creatives from across the globe.

_Illustration 79 / 93

—

SHOWCASE

LARGEST PORTRAIT
_ 72" X 72"
SMALLEST PORTRAIT
_ 0.8" X 9.5"
/ 93 PORTRAITS
SUBMITTED

_Photography 07 / 93

_Other 08 / 93

Hellovon /

01 / Bob Dylan.
Indian ink on paper.
Original size_8" x 11.5".

bob dylan

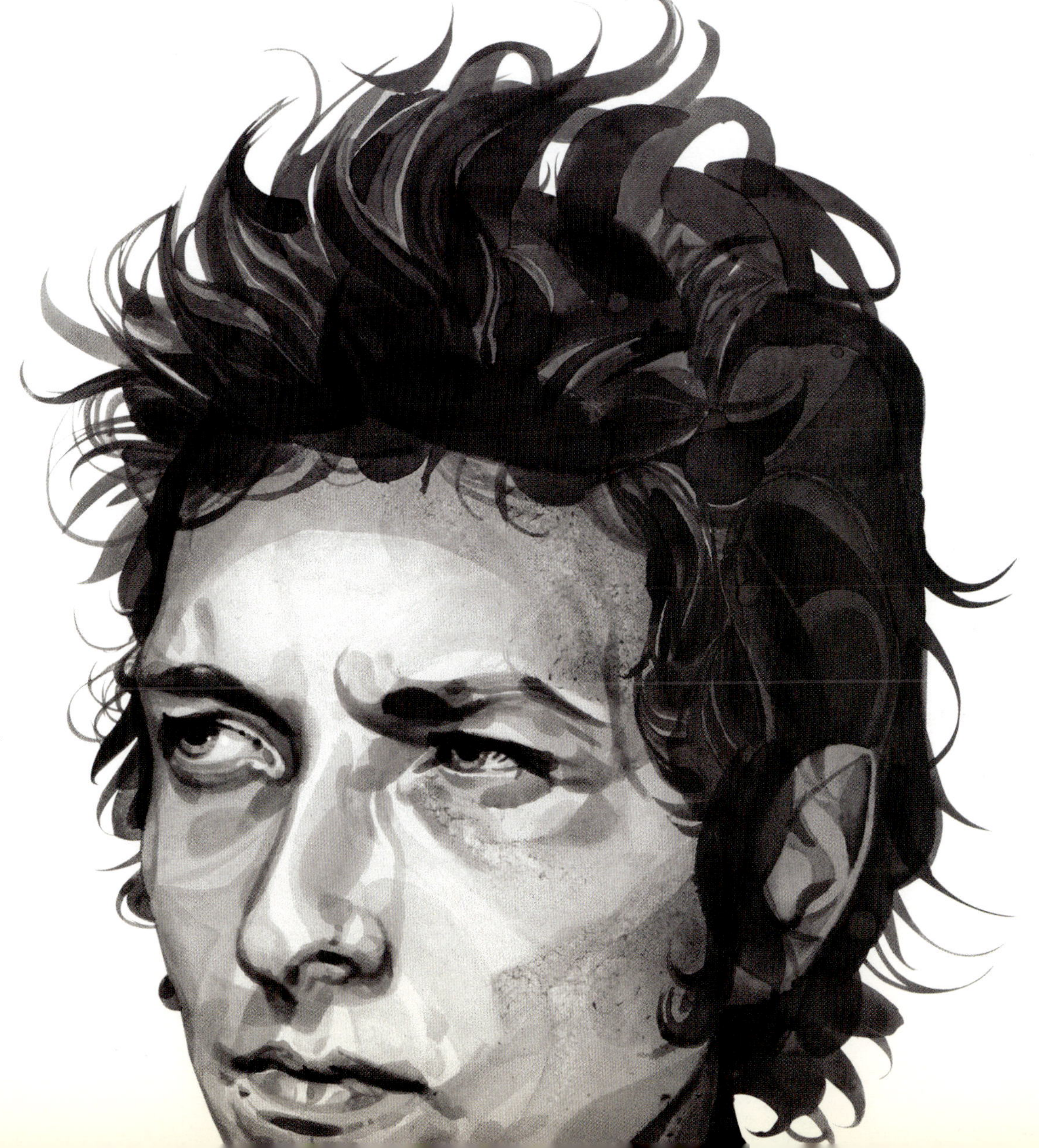

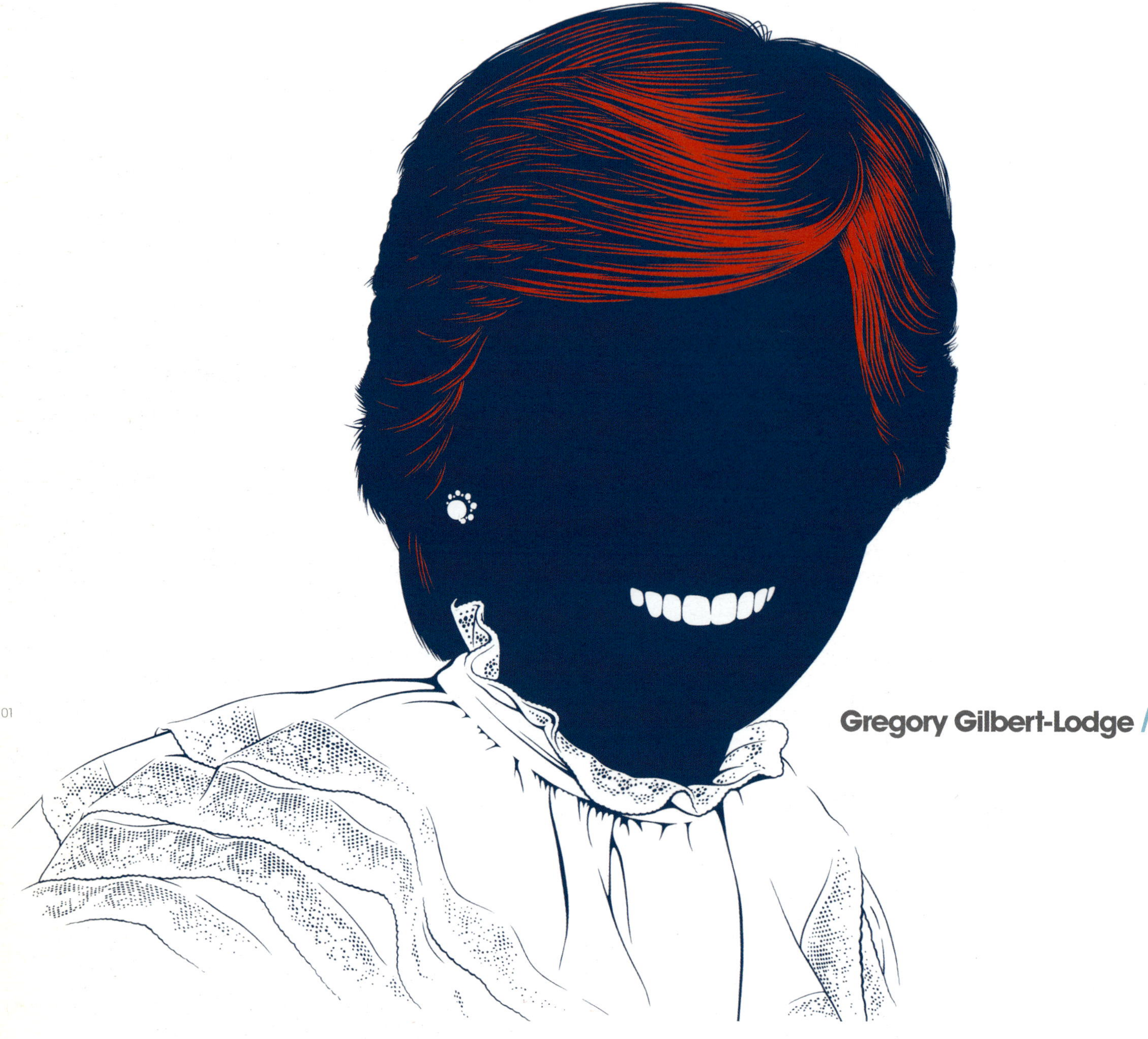

01

Gregory Gilbert-Lodge /

02

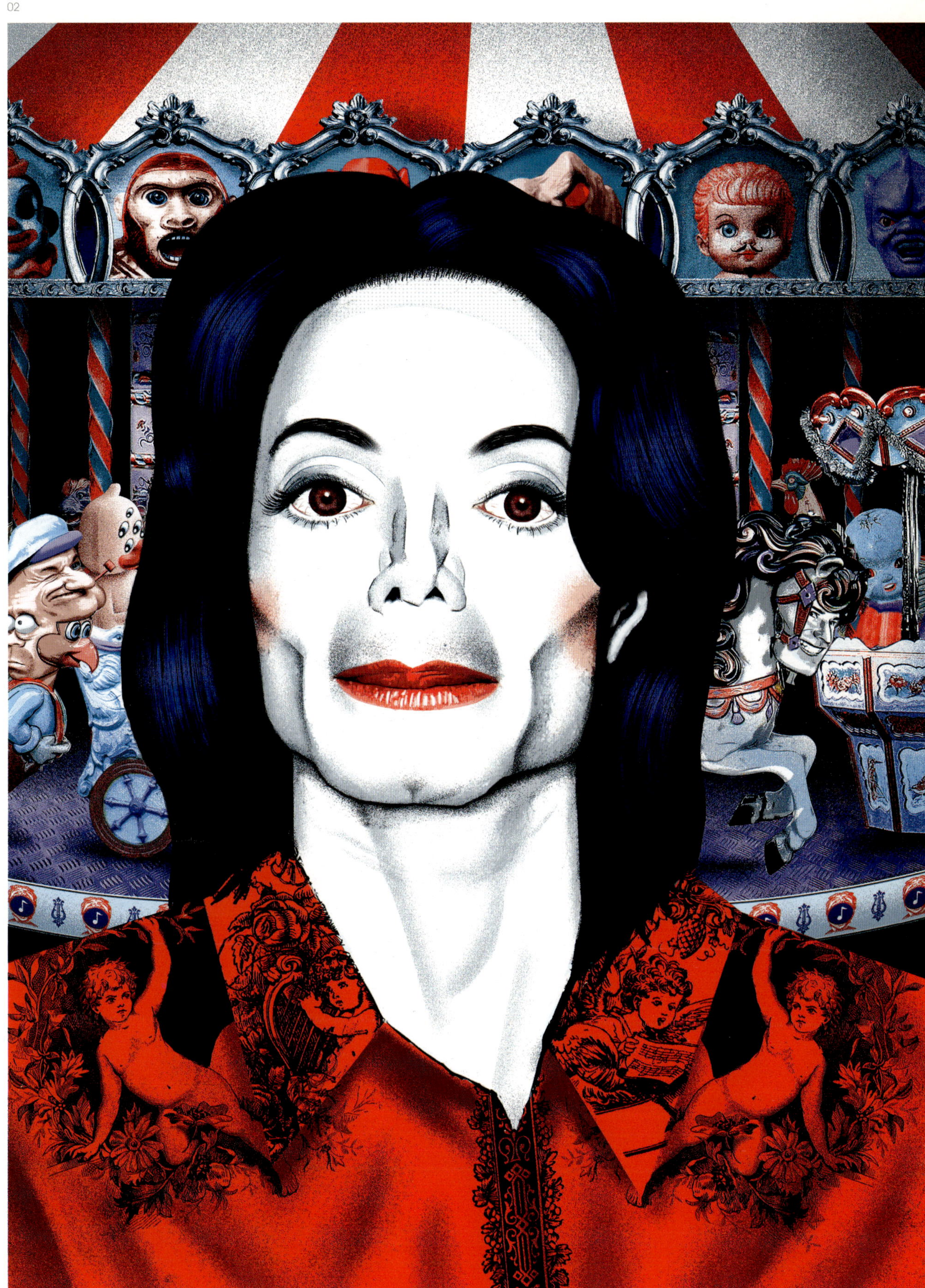

01 / Diana.
Felt pen on paper, Photoshop.
Two colour screen print.
Original size_22.5" x 22.5"

02 / Michael Jackson.
Photoshop.
Original size_7.7" x 12.2"

Eboy /

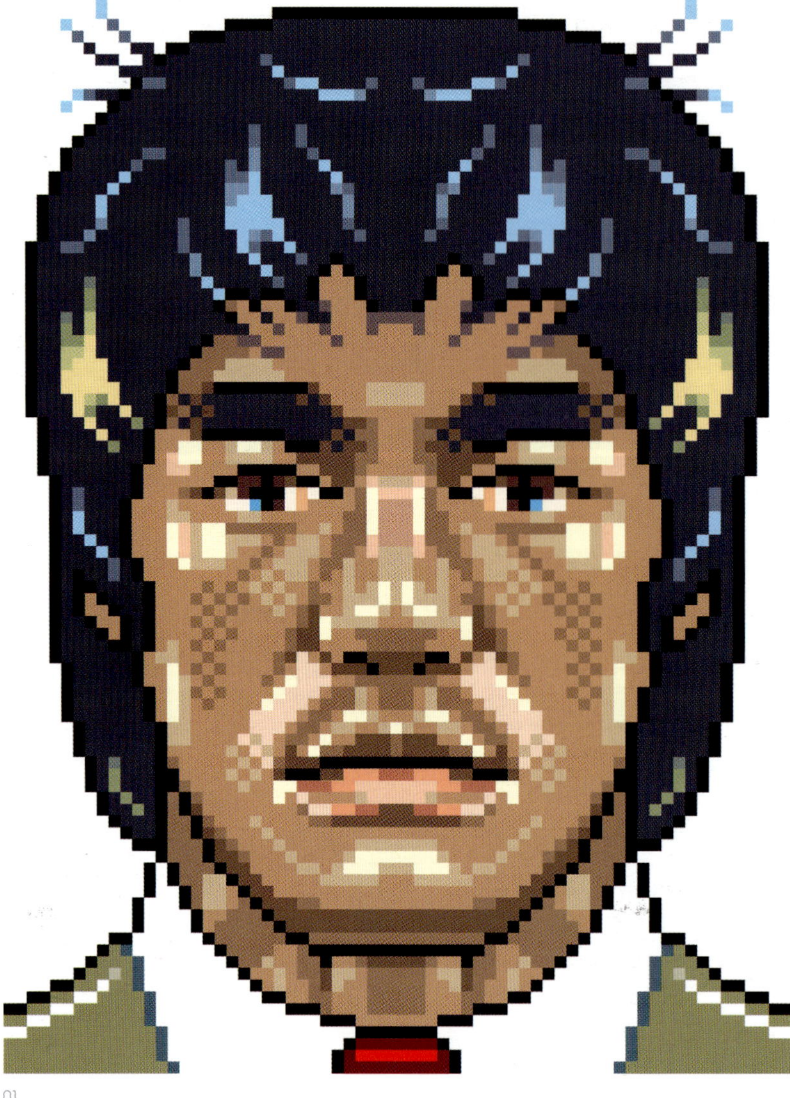

01

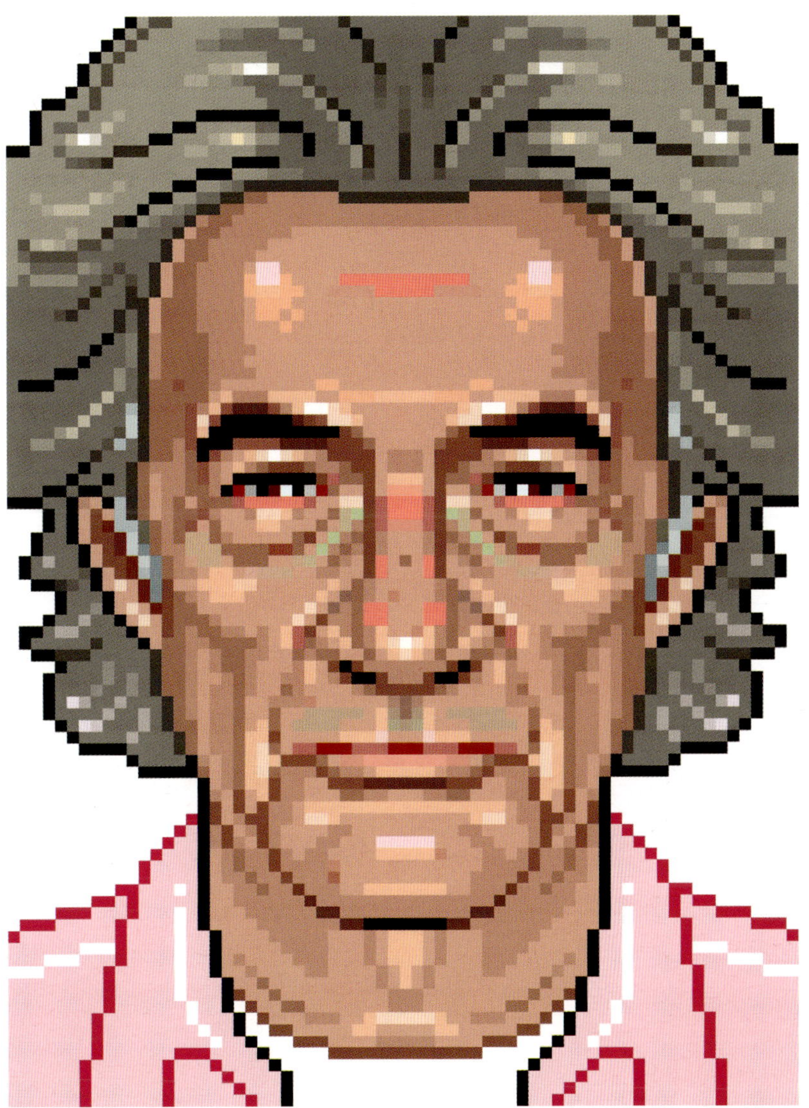

02

01 / Bruce Lee.
Pixel art.

02 / Paul Smith.
Pixel art.

01 / Promise Broken.
Oil on panel.
Original size_24" x 24"

Kris Lewis /

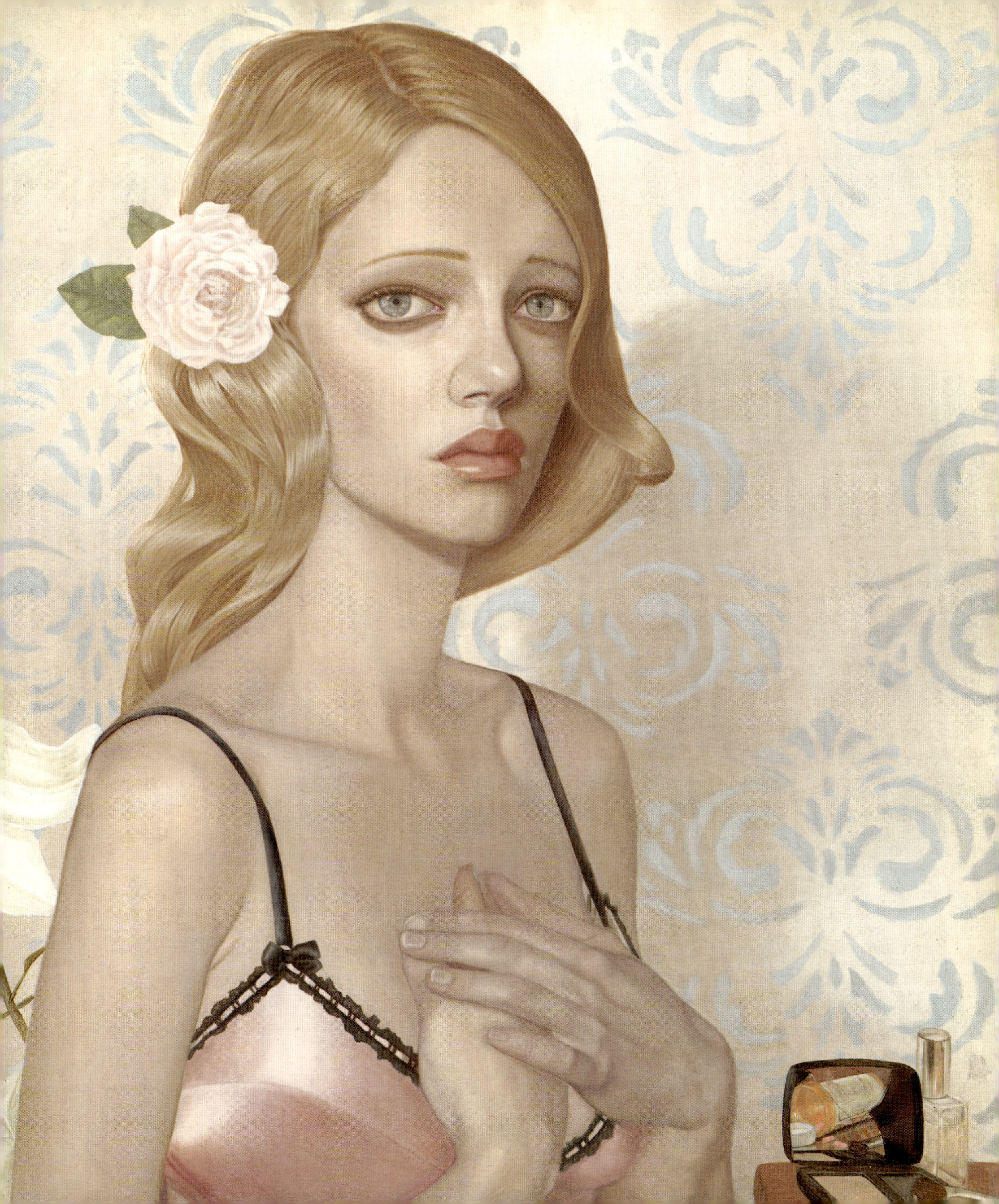

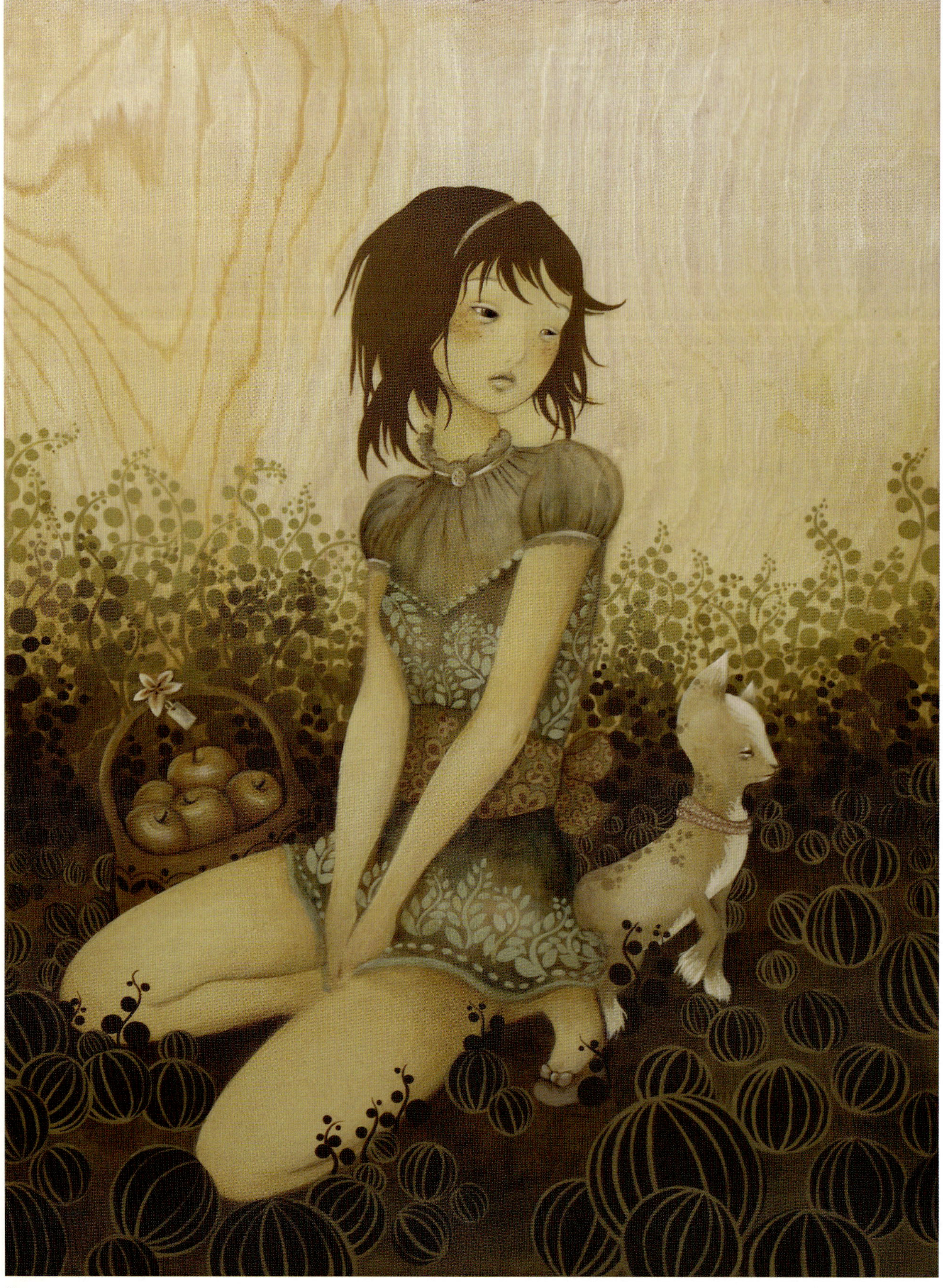

01

Amy Sol /

01 / Waiting in the Melon Vines with Nala.
Acrylic on wood.
Original size_16" x 11"

02 / Nest Hair.
Paint on wood.

03 / Isabelle.
Paint on wood.

02

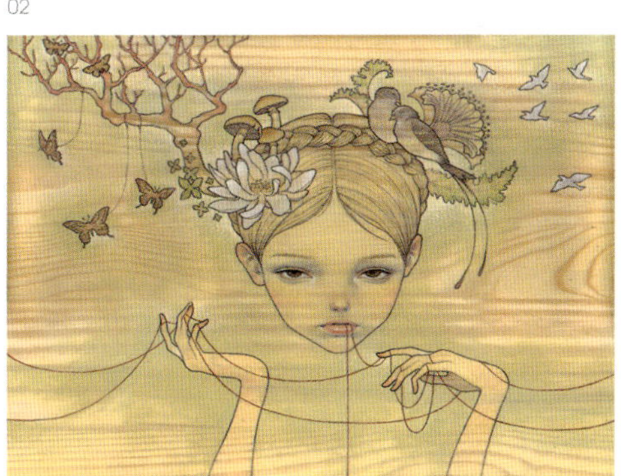

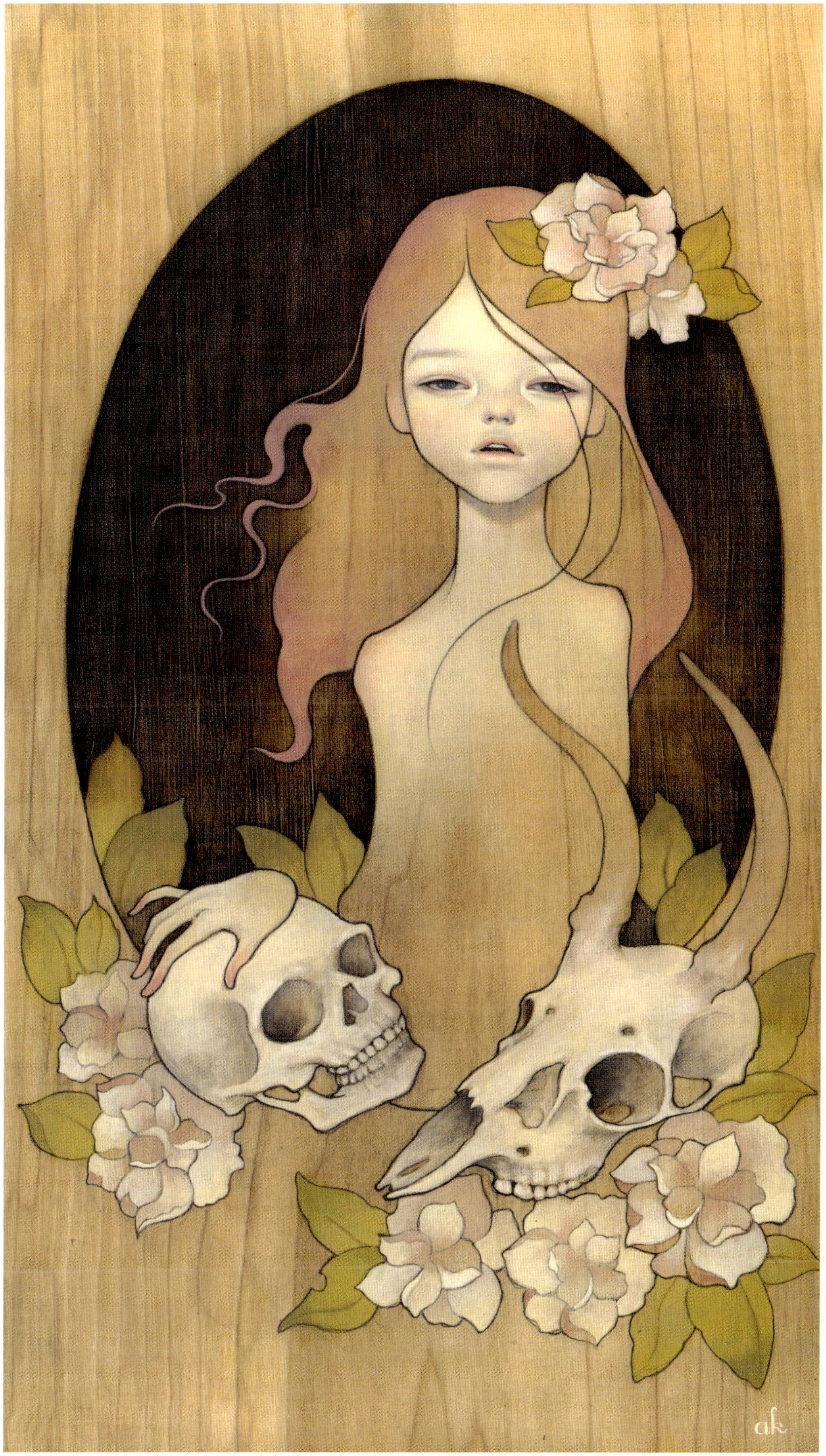

03

Audrey Kawasaki /

01 / Jay Dee.
Inkblot collage.
Original size_8.3" x 11.7"

Mr Ian Wright
__Q&A/01

What or who inspired you to become an artist?

I had an office job when I left school, and spent a lot of time drawing at my desk, doodling on the blotter. A couple of people there thought I should pursue it, and I went to evening classes locally, at Goldsmiths College of Art. Through the encouragement of the tutor, Tessa Adams, I applied for the foundation course.

That's where it started.

I was 21.

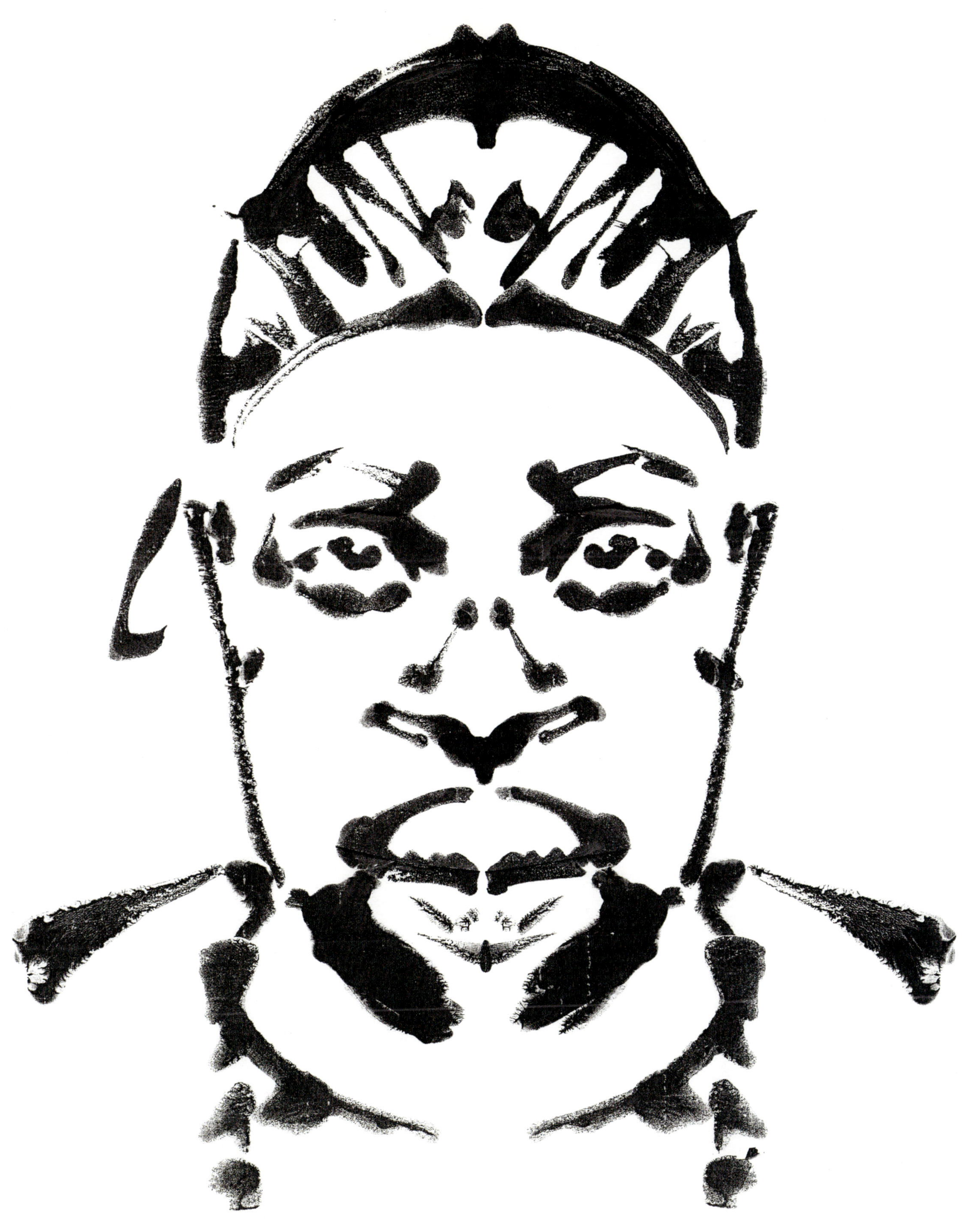

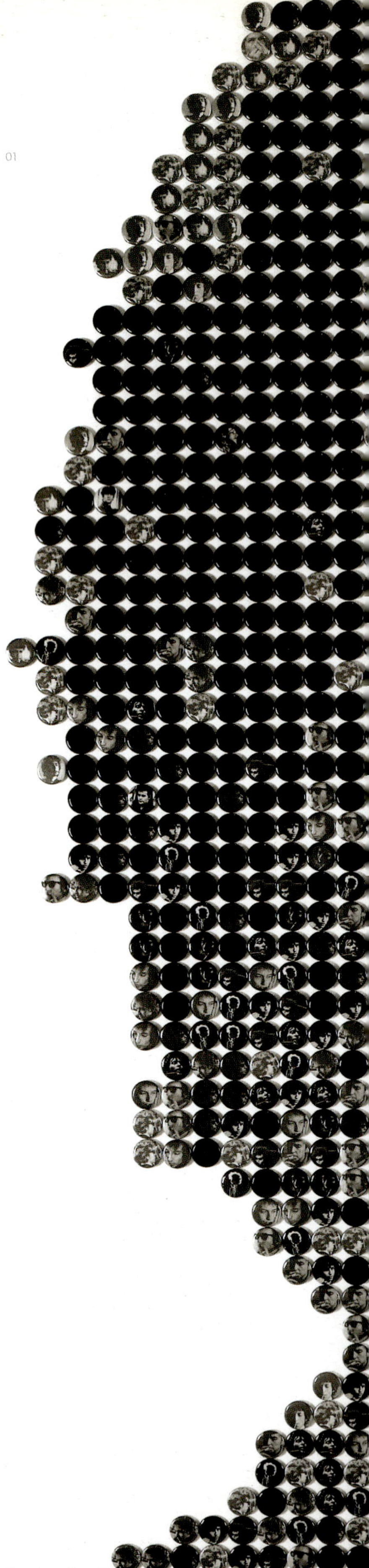

01

Q&A / 01

Give us a brief history of your career.

Goldsmiths Foundation in 1975, then a frustrating time on the Graphics course at the (then) LCP. I couldn't wait to leave. I assisted designer / illustrator George Hardie for a year, while working on my own stuff. It's been the same ever since.

Your style is very specific, how did this take form?

Is it? I'm still working on it. I like to play, experiment, make mistakes. I want to make quite iconic images, mainly portraits. I want to push my work somewhere new for me.

You seem to use a lot of raw materials in your work, from beads to badges. What influences you to use these materials and is there a specific process in picking a material for a particular piece?

Again, it probably goes back to the weekly portrait I made for the *NME*, on the album review pages. I wanted to think about materials other than paint, usually because my idea about the subject enabled me to explore other mediums.

Do you use much technology in your work? Pre or post-production?

I've always liked process, whether through a photocopier or a computer. I'm interested in the process of using digital media, but I want the final piece to be an one-off 'made' piece, not a digital printed image. I want to visually slow down digital methods of production away from the electronic area.

Portraiture plays a big part in your work, is there a story behind this?

I remember when I first started drawing for the *NME*, the space I was given was limited, and I needed to make my pictures punch out from a sea of newsprint type.

'I like to play, experiment, make mistakes.'

So I concentrated on the head, trying to make an iconic likeness, as well as thinking about how I saw that person and what they were about. As the paper was mainly full of photographic imagery, I was trying to bring a different experience of the person/musician, using drawing.

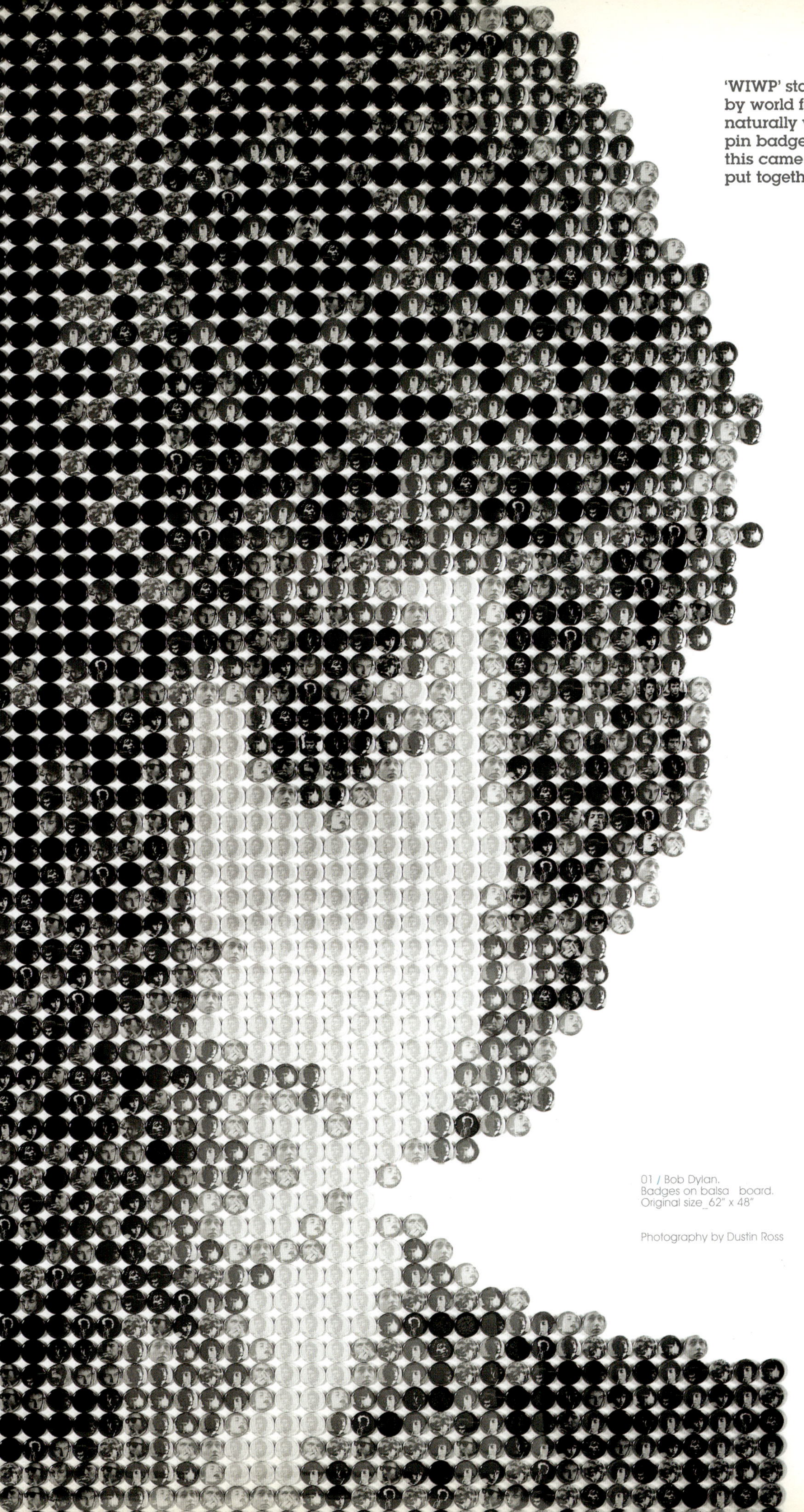

'WIWP' started out as a project producing unique badges by world famous designers and illustrators, so we are naturally very interested in your recent portraiture using pin badges. Can you tell us a little bit more about how this came about and how these particular pieces were put together?

I'm interested in continuing to explore the utilisation and changing context of the use of low value materials, such as the badge. I want to connect the portrait to the material used - the badge, and that which is communicated by the featured image.

It started with an idea of monochrome portraits: that led to thinking of the photographs I'd seen of Warhol in the 60s. He seemed to tie in with the badge idea, a material available in a multiple form, easily available and deliberately non-expensive. Edie Sedgwick was then an obvious choice. I discovered a story that Bob Dylan was given a Elvis print by Warhol, so that tied him in.

Hendrix represents the explosion of technicolour with which he arrived, making an impact both musically and visually.

I liked these people meeting in the same space again. Chuck Close was an obvious visual link, and that portrait dates from the same time period. It was a response to sometimes being asked,' Are you aware of the work of Chuck Close?" (Reply; 'Yes, there's one over there.....")

01 / Bob Dylan.
Badges on balsa board.
Original size_62" x 48"

Photography by Dustin Ross

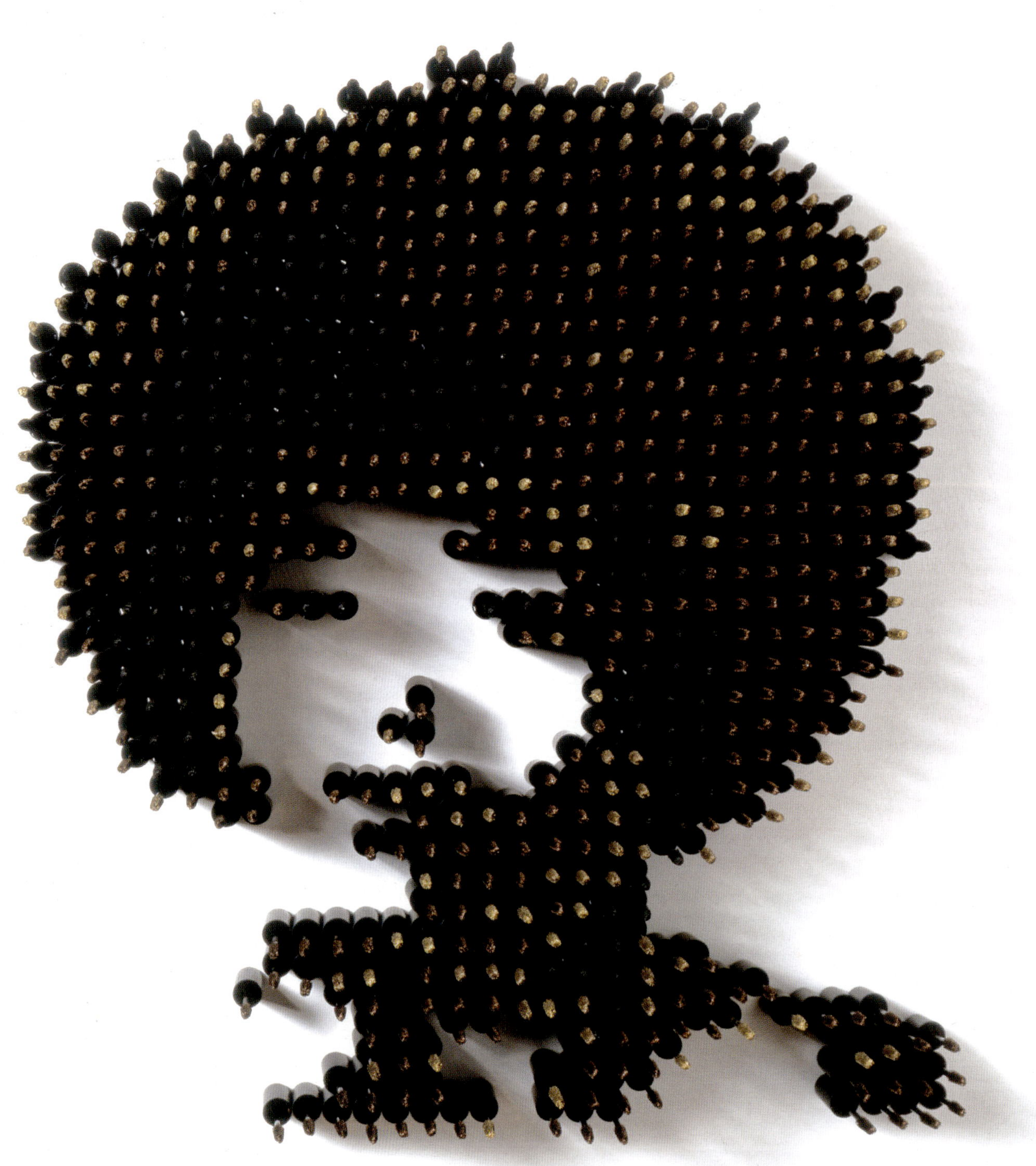

01 / Angela Davis.
Bottles.

Who was the first person you created a portrait of?

Big Daddy + Giant Haystacks!

What has been your most exciting project to date?

An installation at Issey Miyake in 2002 was a big turning point. I made a 'Ghost Gorilla', 22 feet high, from pointed paper cups, and a dog portrait, 'DogTag', from paper luggage labels. I used badges to make a bear head, 'Peace Bear'. It felt like the work I had been trying to do for a long time, in terms of scale and materials.

What is the longest period of time one of your pieces have taken to complete?

The recent badge portraits. It is difficult to be exact, but around 60 hours; I cut and made the badges myself, then worked with two assistants involved in the end stages, of laying out and gluing. I like to show the process, again the time element. It is important to me that my pieces look hand crafted, that the viewer is aware of the element of production involved, the process of making.

Which other creative people do you admire, past and present?

Far too many – I've always been a fan first and foremost. But still important to me are: George Hardie, Bush Hollyhead, Malcolm Harrison, Bob Lawrie, working together as NTA Studios, in the mid 70s. Tadanori Yokoo, Karl Wirsum + Jim Nutt of the Hairy Who, JC Leyendecker, William Roberts, Gary Panter, Charles Burns, Barry McGhee + Lee Perry the Upsetter, Jimi Hendrix, James Brown, The Beatles, John Peel and Gilles Peterson.

If you had to name a famous portrait from the past, which would immediately pop into your head?

Bob Dylan by Martin Sharp.

An image maker since 1978, Ian Wright has been working across art and design. He has recently been involved in producing large-scale modular installations for clients such as Issey Miyake, The British Museum, Brinkworth Architects, the Design Council; and a new Tony Bennett portrait for the 'Duets' CD release. This year saw his first solo show, 'Mass Production' at the Christopher Henry Gallery in Chelsea, NYC.

Using materials not immediately associated with picture making, Wright seeks to distance himself as far from the pencil as possible. Enjoying the unpredictability they offer, his unconventional use of materials has included salt, cassette tape, buttons, beads, paper cups and thumb tacks.

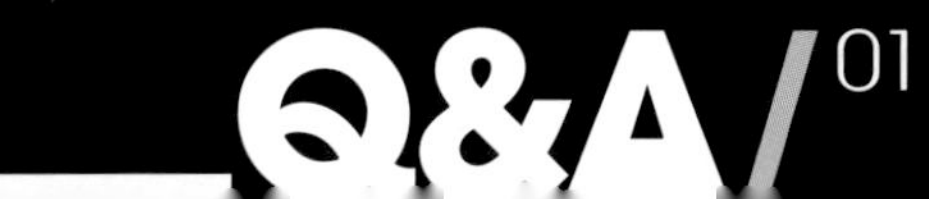

01 / Crowdsourcing.
Original drawing.
Graphite on bond.
Original size_8.5" x 11"

02 / Crowdsourcing.
Original sketch.
Blue pencil on grey paper.
Original size_15" x 22"

03 / Crowdsourcing.
Final piece.
Mixed media, digital.
Original size_15" x 22"

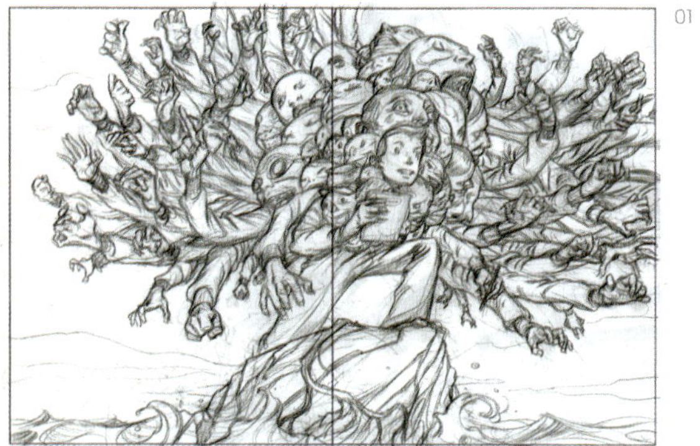
01

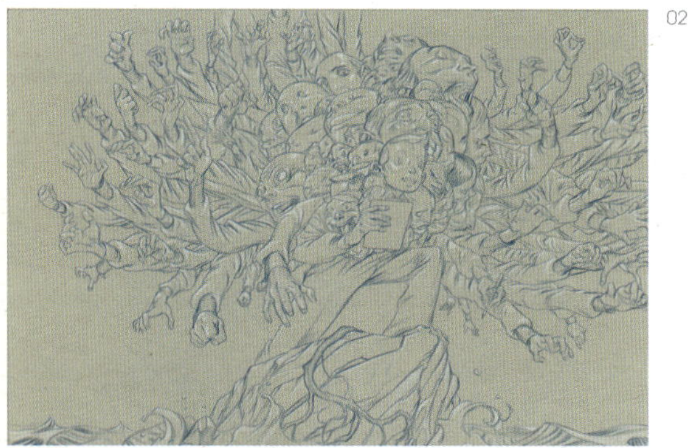
02

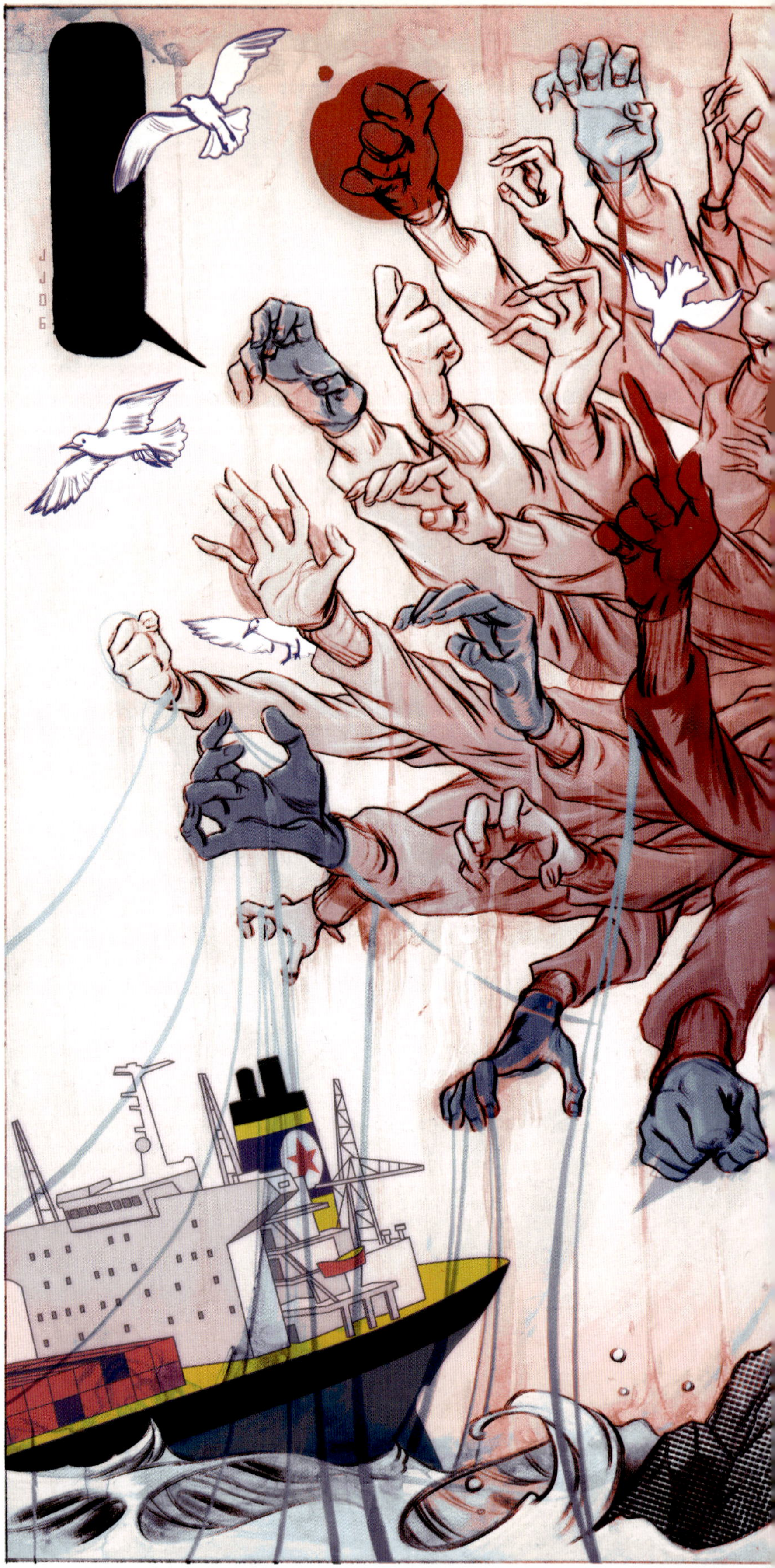

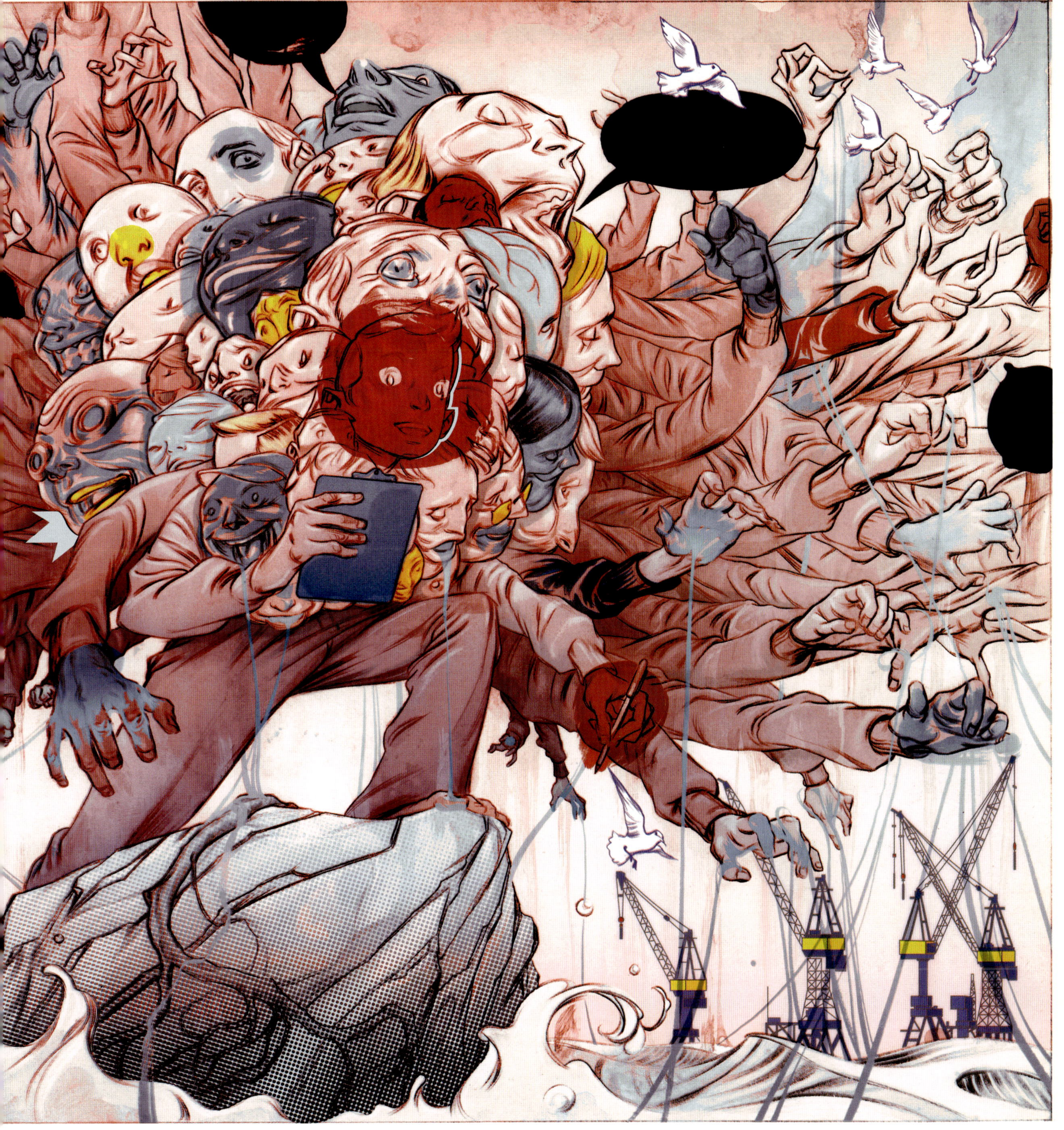

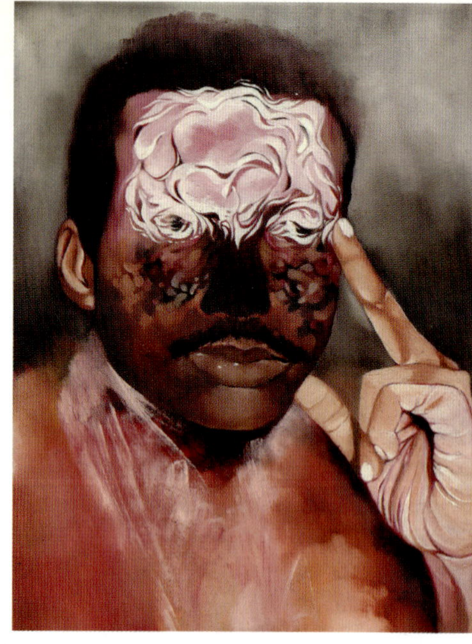

02

01 / Bau.
Oil on canvas.
Original size_9" x 12"

02 / Bau No 2.
Oil on paper.
Original size_9" x 12"

03 / Bau No 4.
Oil on canvas.
Original size_9" x 12"

Maureen Gubia /

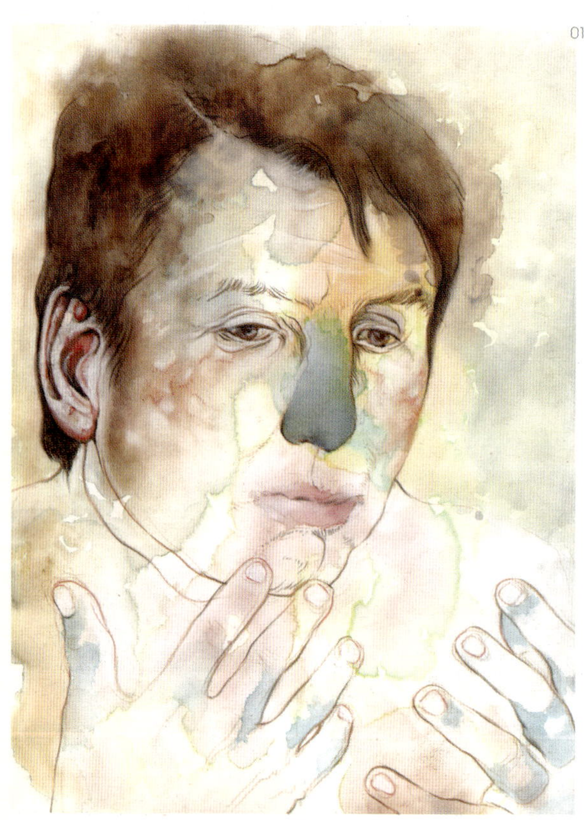

01

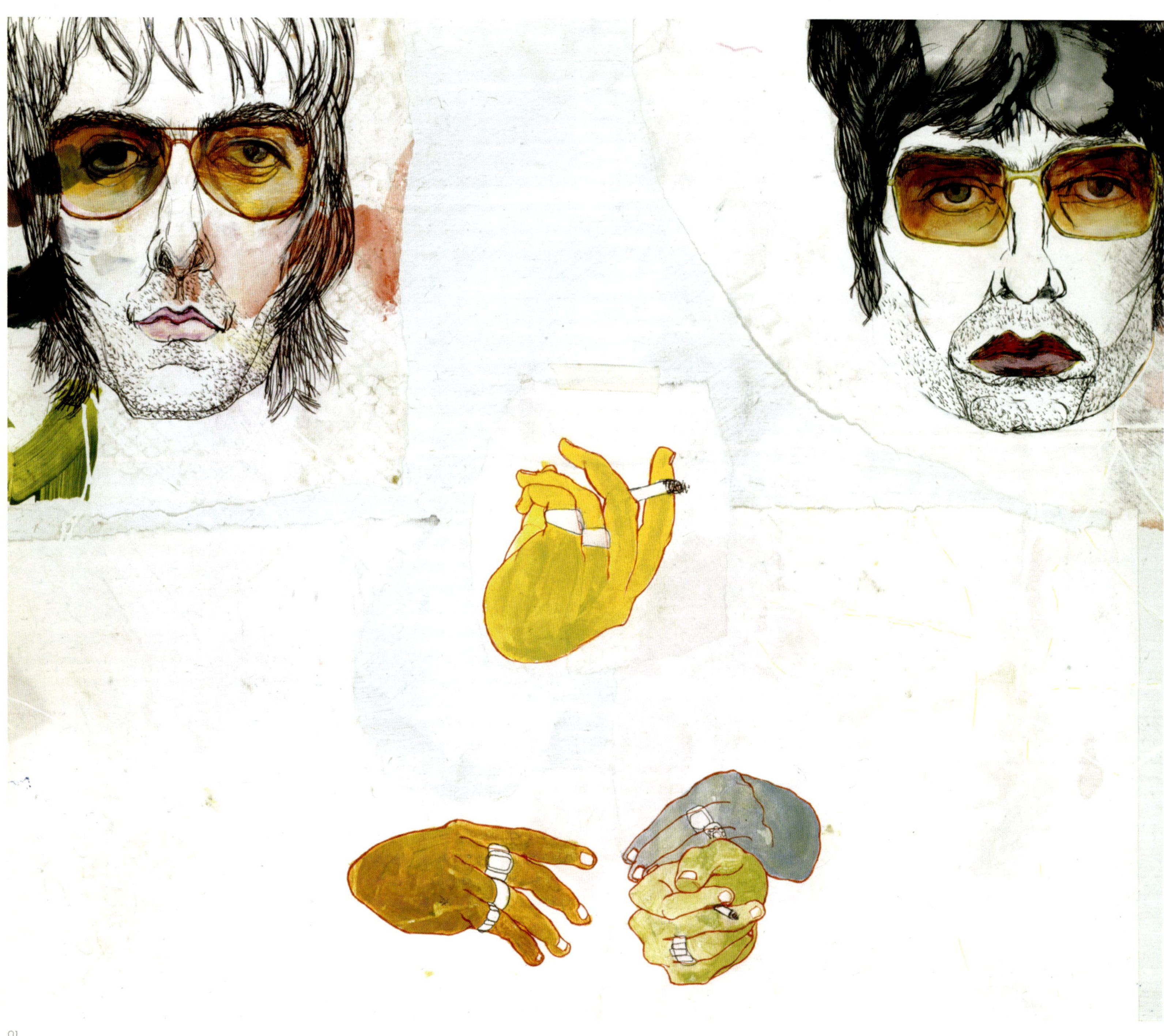

01

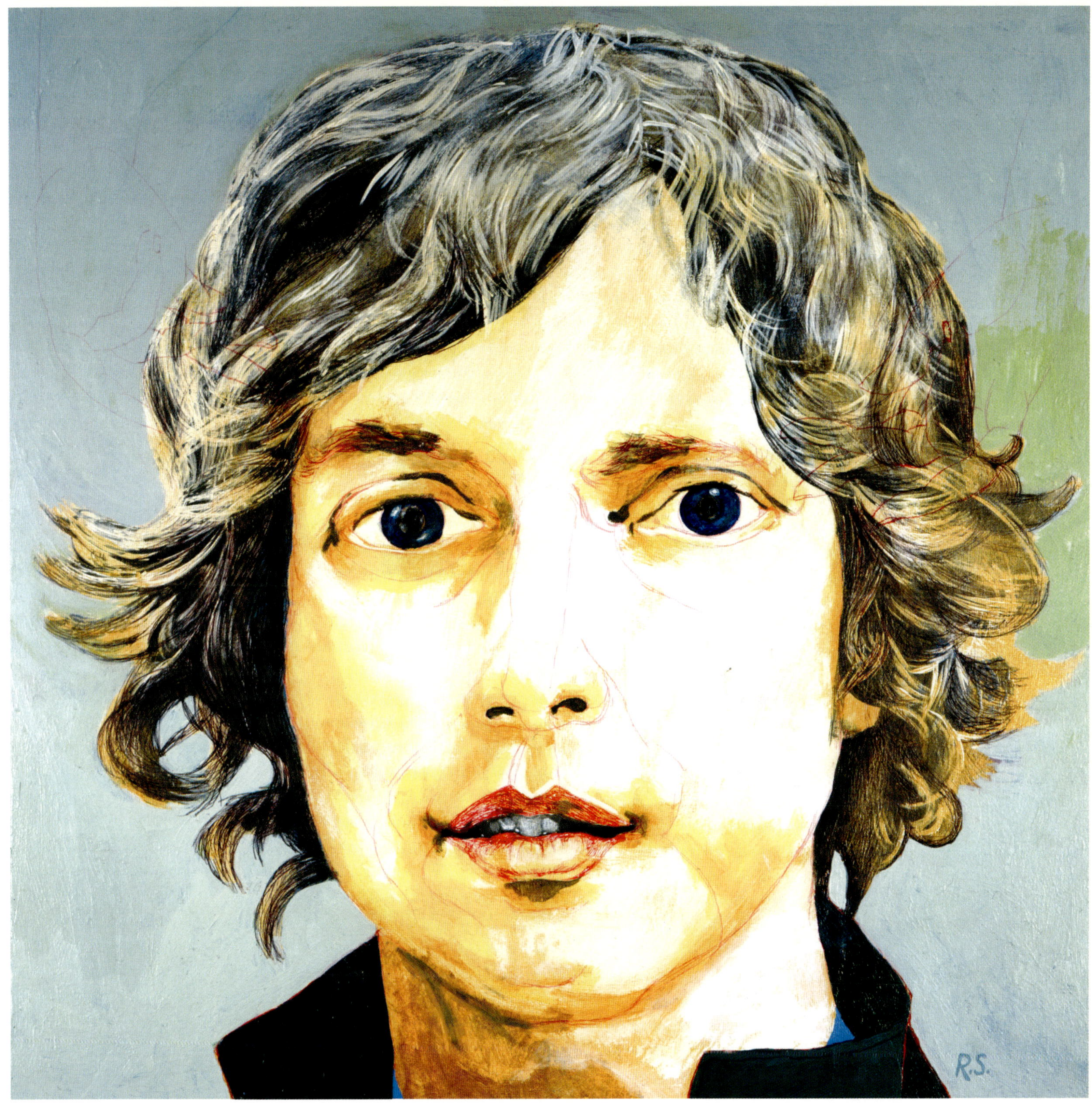

02

Rachel Salomon /

01 / Oasis.
Acrylic and pen.
Original size_17" x 23"

02 / Beck.
Acrylic and pen.

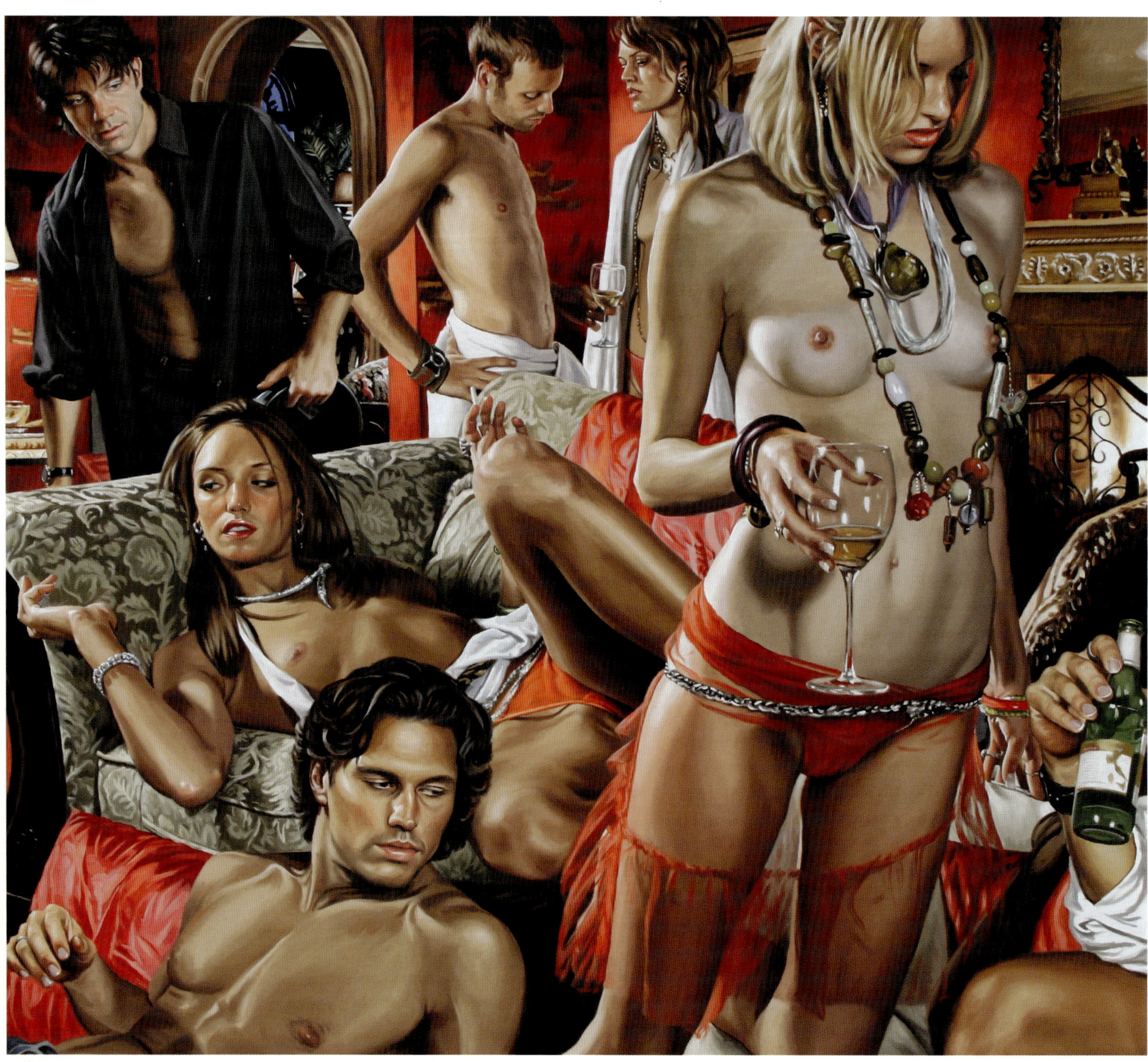

01

Terry Rodgers /

01 / The Fragility of Peace.
Oil on linen.
Original size_66" x 72"

02 / Sammy.
Oil on linen.
Original size_54" x 67"

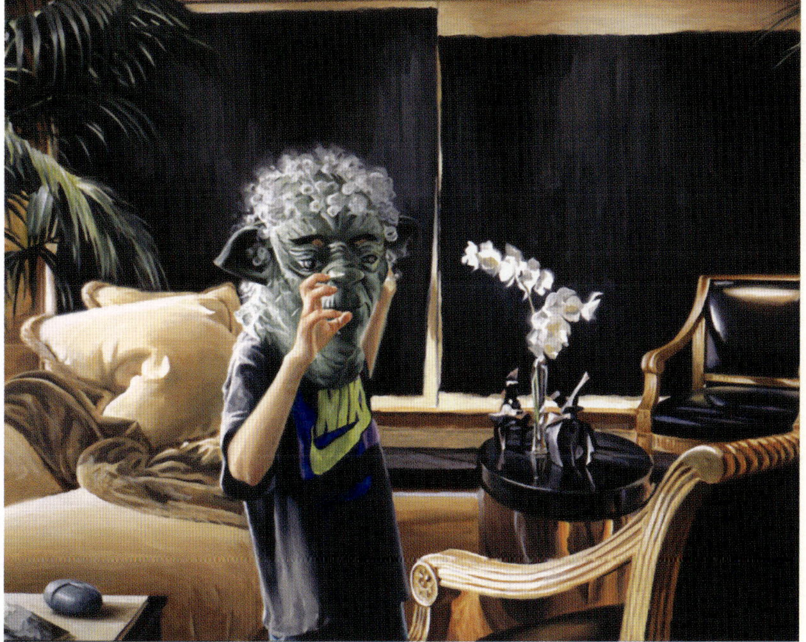

02

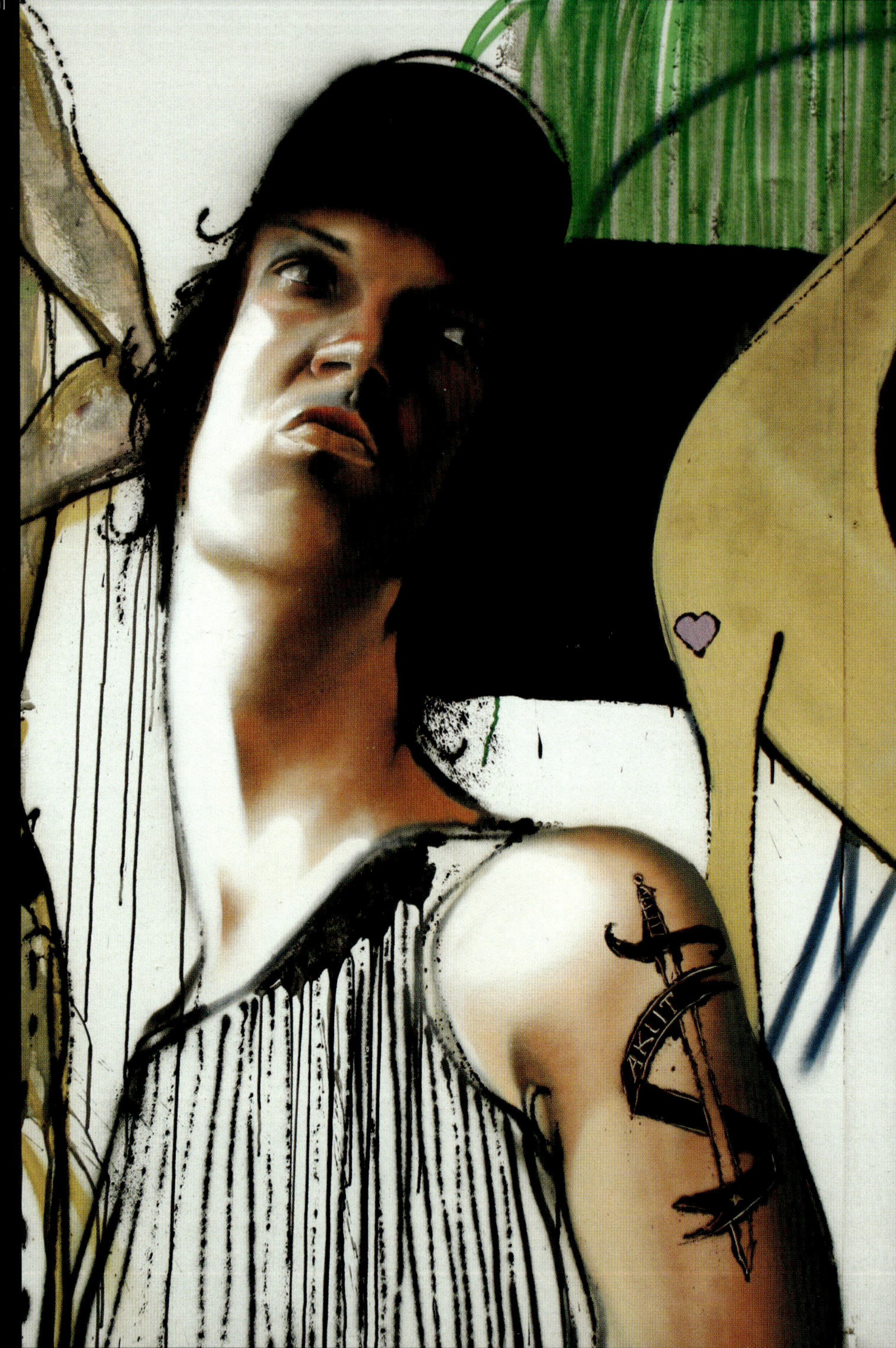
AKUT

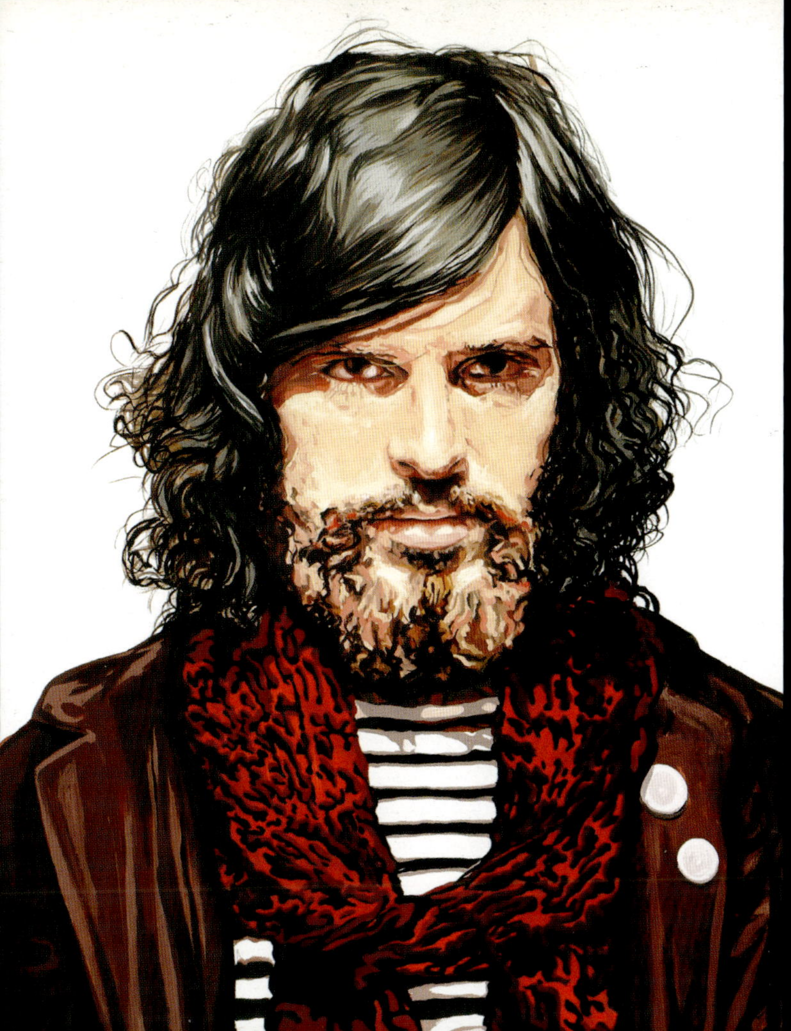

02

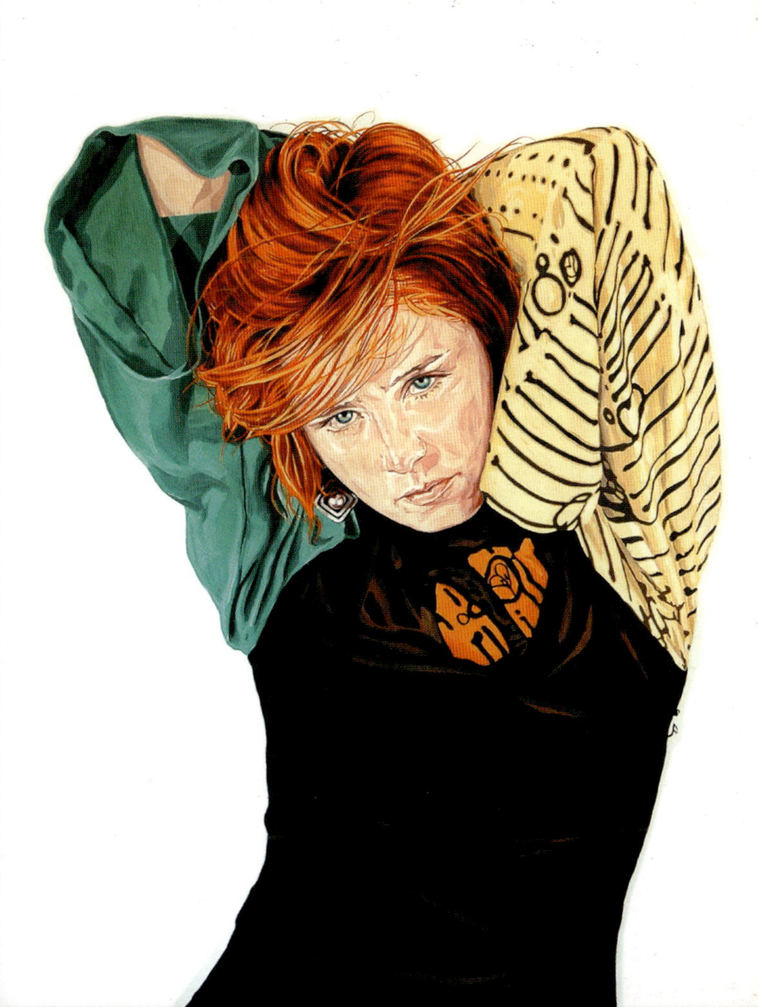

03

Simon Henwood /

01 / Zaragoza (Self Portrait).
Spray paint on wood.
Original size_1.5m x 1m

02 / Roisin Murphy.
Gouache on paper
Original size_54.7" x 39.3"

Simon Henwood /

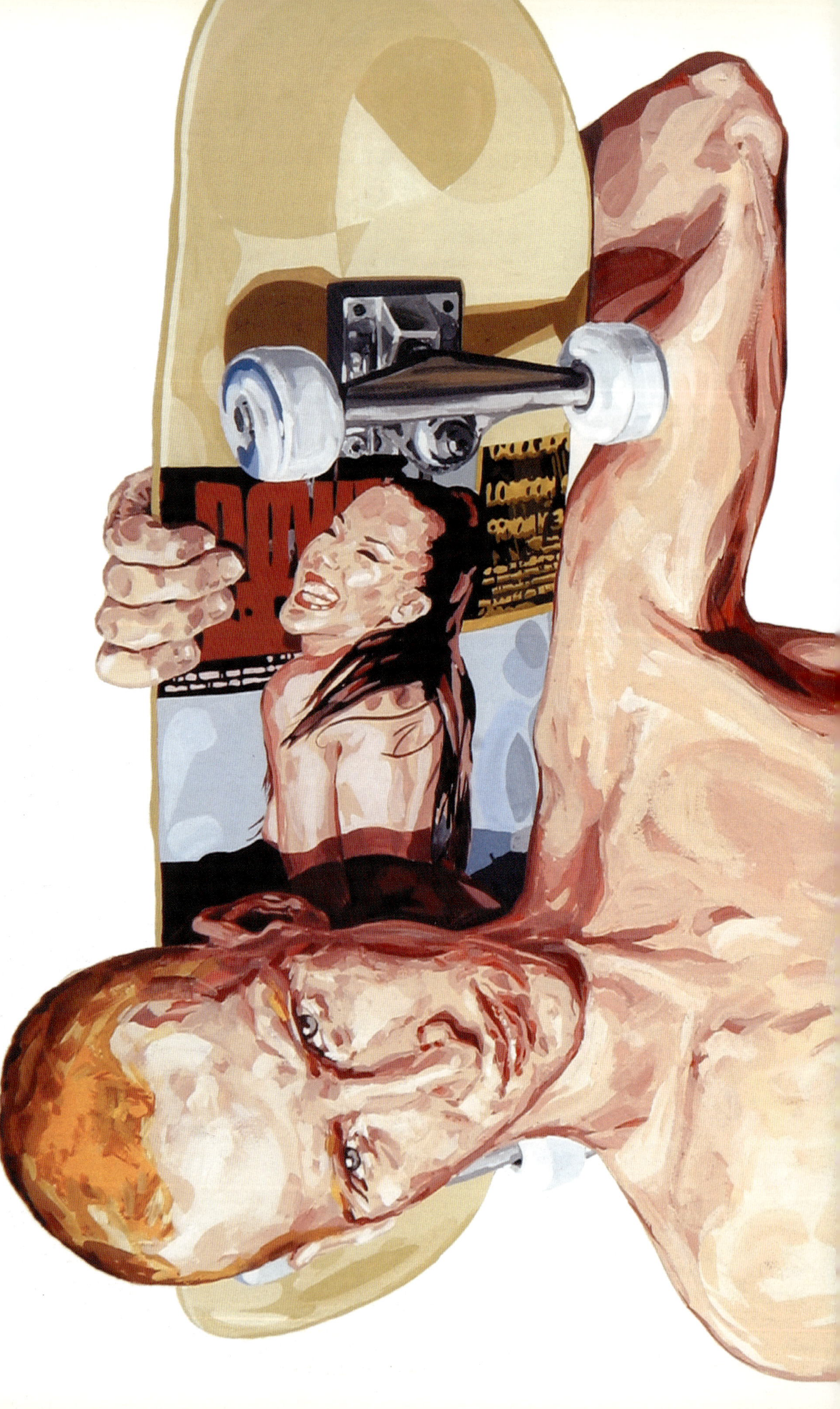

01 / Henry 20.
Gouache on paper.
Original size_54.7" x 39.3"

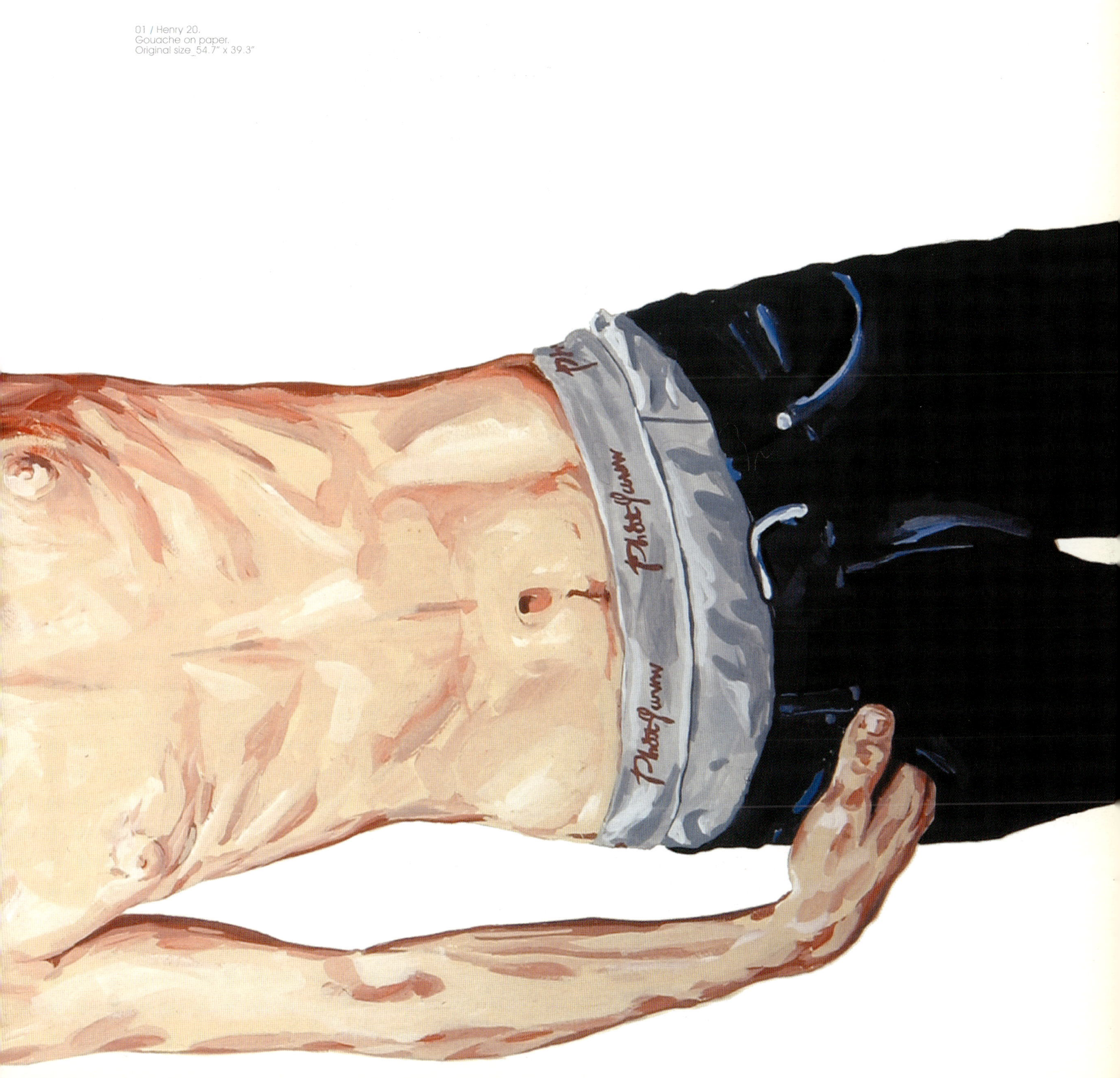

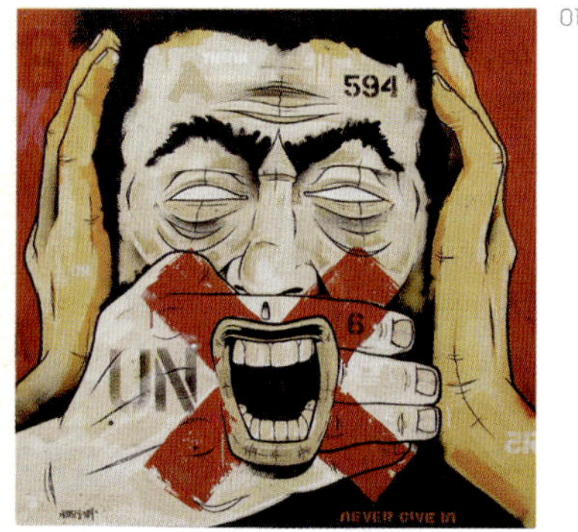

01

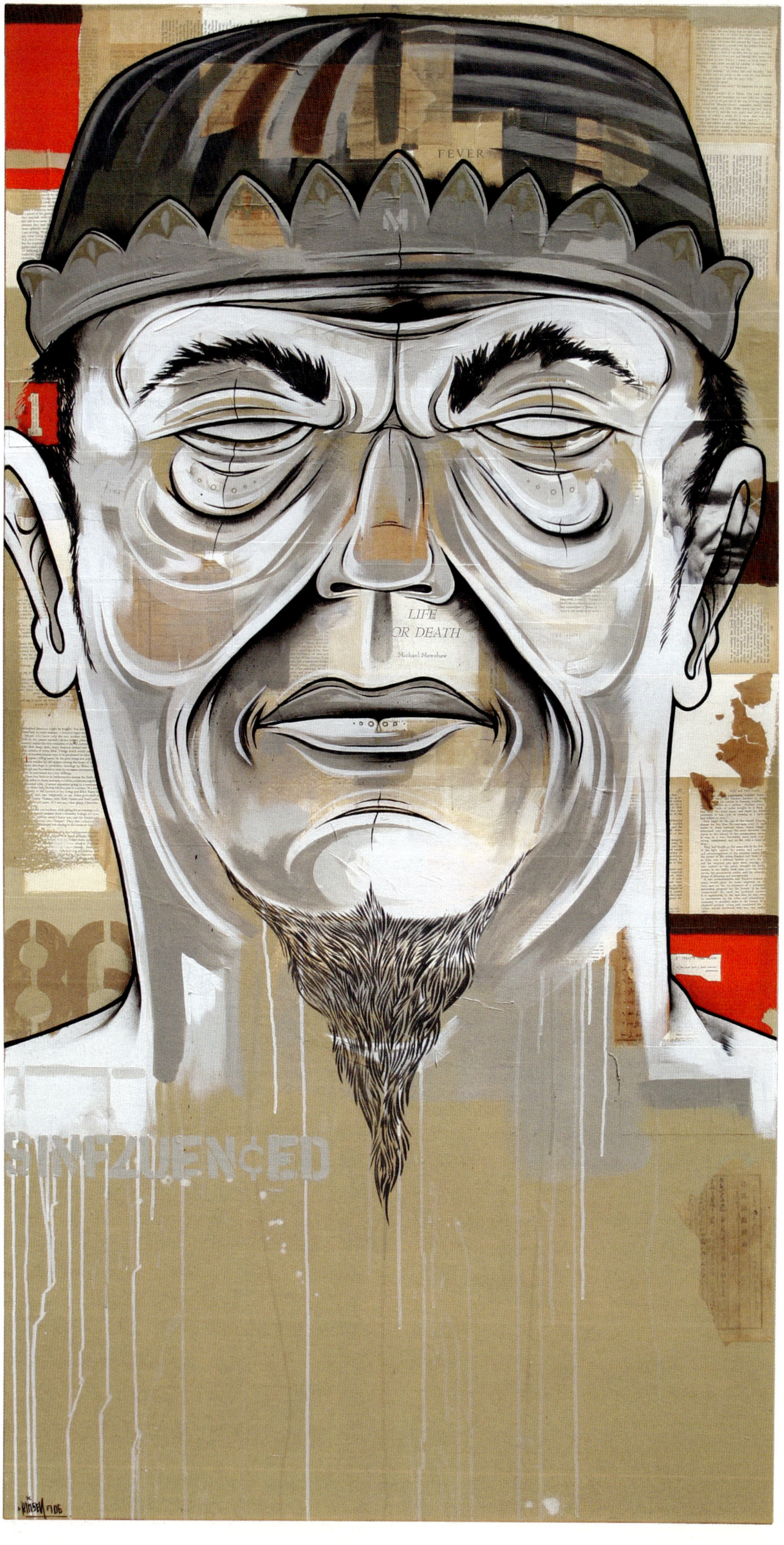

02

Kinsey /

03

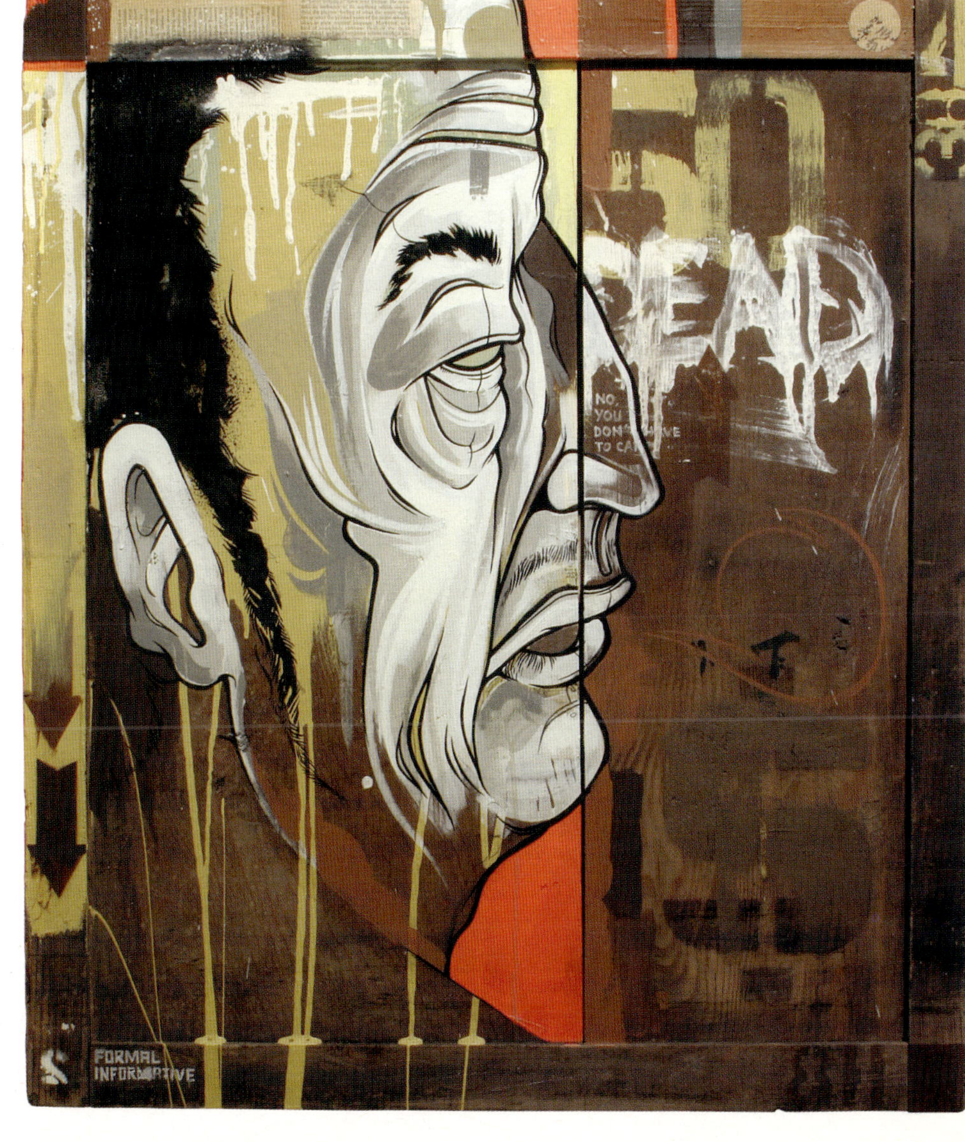

01 / Never Give In.
Acrylic and oil enamel on panel.
Original size_48" x 48"

02 / Sinfluenced.
Acrylic, ink, paper and oil enamel on panel.
Original size_72" x 36"

03 / 50 Dead.
Acrylic, ink and oil enamel on antique furniture panel.
Original size_34" x 28"

01

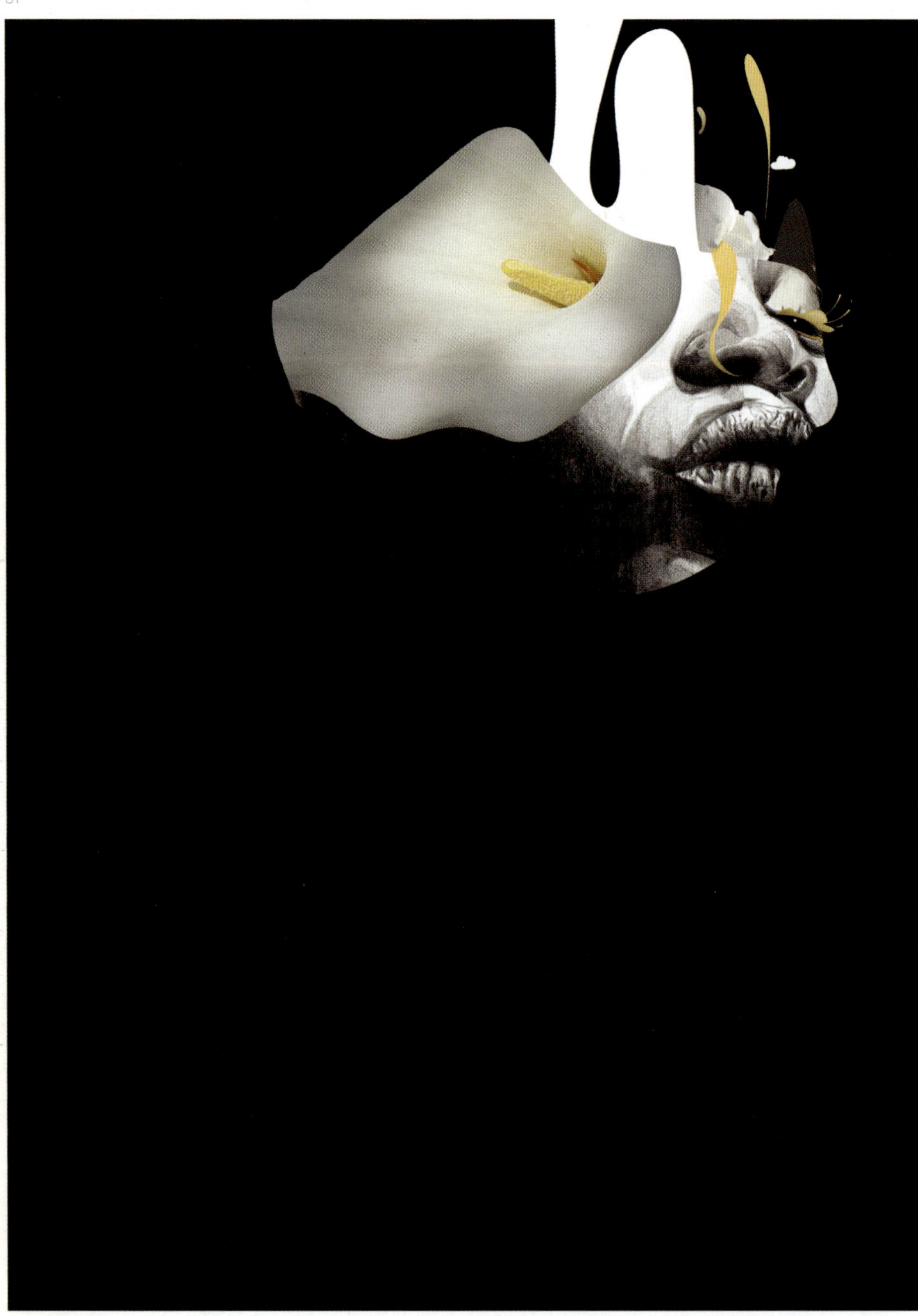

Hellovon /

01 / Sleep Two.
Mixed media on paper.
Original size_33" x 23.4"

02 / Sleep One.
Mixed media on paper.
Original size_33" x 23.4"

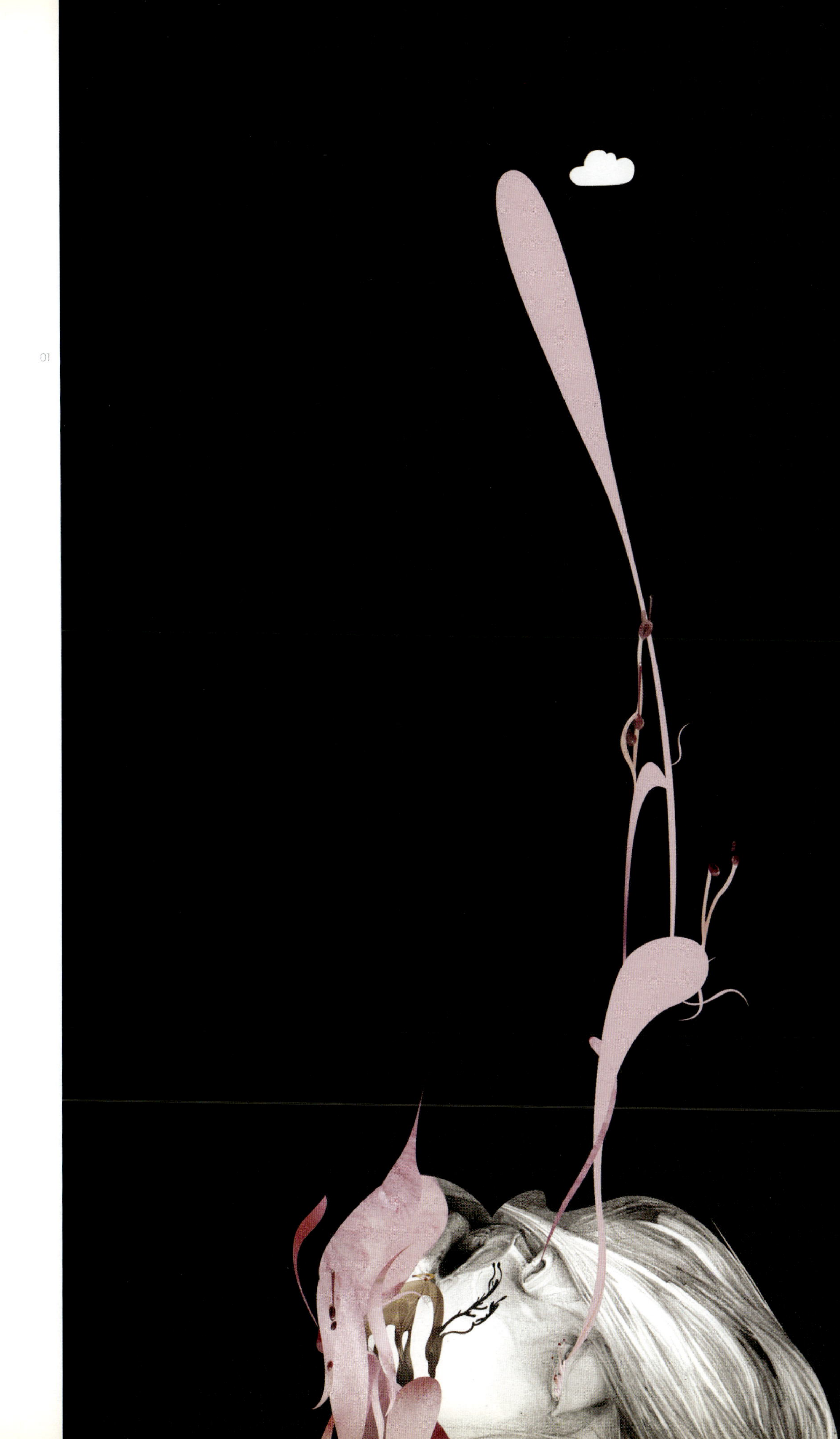

01

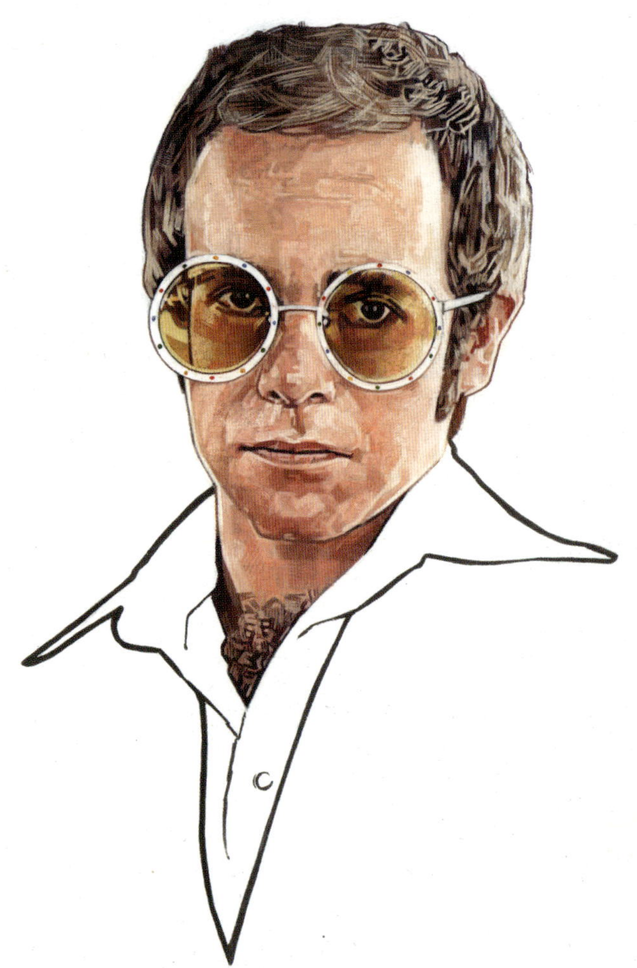

01 / Elton John.
Acrylic on paper.
Original size_63" x 67

02 / Gold Tooth.
Mixed media.

Buggy /

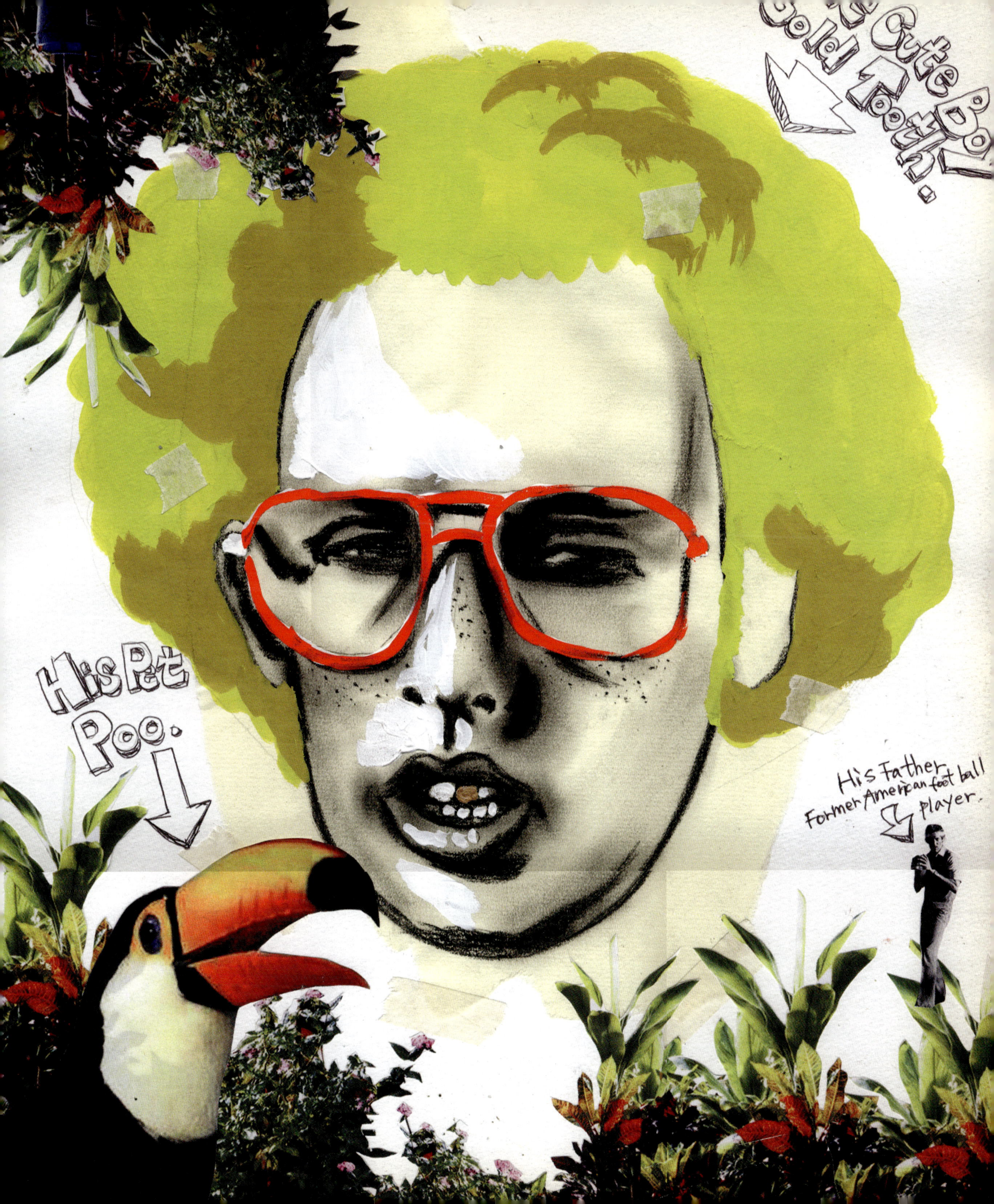
Cute Boy!
Gold Tooth.
His Pet
Poo.
His Father
Former American foot ball player

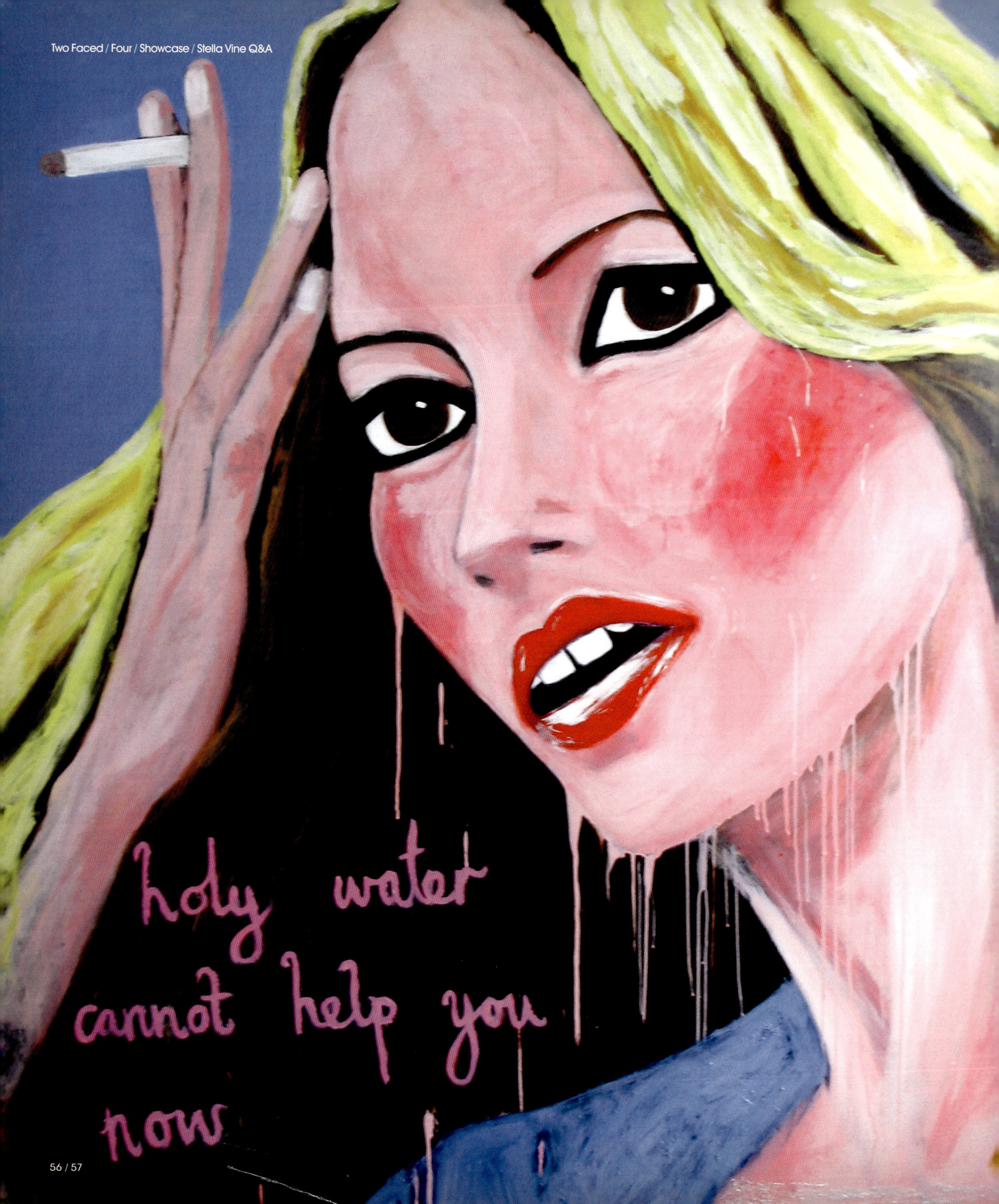
holy water
cannot help you
now

Stella Vine
Q&A / 02

Who was the first person you created a portrait of?

Three words: Robert Kilroy Silk. No, Romeo and Juliet, when I was a wee lass.

Your style is very specific, how did it materialize?

When I paint, I'll talk to the person I'm painting, as if they're in the room, "Come on Samuel" and snippets like that. My style is basically me trying to get as direct a route to my emotions as is possible, the emotion, the idea, the thing I'm trying to get across. My style is basically as close to me as I can get, if that makes sense.

Your work is usually topical and quite often controversial, are you ever in two minds about releasing any of your work into the public domain, in fear of how some people will react or perceive it? Is the controversial aspect intentional or is it just a case of painting subjects you are passionate about?

If I wanted my paintings to be controversal I think I'd just stroll into a gallery and start working away right on top of a Rembrant. I'd do a very quick painting of the security guards sprinting towards me. My work is sometimes topical, but certainly not always. Whatever grabs me, I'll paint. I did do a piece based on the London bombings recently, a bus painting, but in the end, decided to paint over it. It seems that most supposedly controversial artists in this country get treated as if they're just callous, thoughtless children beltching for attention. Of course, that's not the reality of the situation.

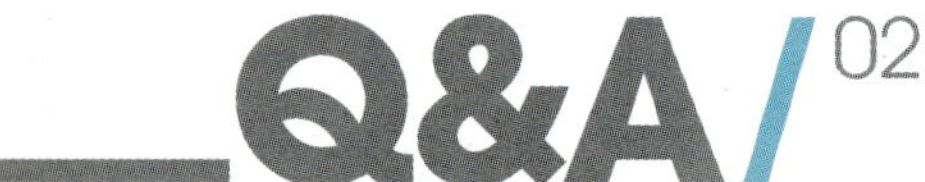

Out of all the people you have created portraits of, has any of them seen your work and made comments about it? Good or bad?

Yes! Robert Kilroy Silk was absolutely fucking livid. Only joking (I haven't painted him)! I found out recently that Chantelle and Preston are fond of my work, which really thrills me, as I adore them. I often paint people who can't really comment anymore, unfortunately.

Which portrait are you most proud of and why?

Mick Hucknall, squatting in a fog, with massive green tits glowing like a neon festival. It's just a very serene piece. No seriously, I think it might be this new one of my Mum, 'Ellenor Seaton Point'.

How do you pick the people you paint?

I have a huge backlog of images which I take from a wide, wide (a bit wider) range of magazines, books, pamphlets, cookery books, etc. These are images that startle me, people, pets, places, who I have a very close, intimate emotional connection with. Without that powerful connection, I just don't begin.

If you were approached by someone to create a portrait of them, who would be your perfect subject? Famous person? Musician? Artist? Etc

Do you know I can't do commissions, I just clam up, start tearing my hair out, it gets confusing. I like total freedom, not the pressure of pleasing people.

Are you, or have you ever been affected by public opinions and press coverage?

Yes, I'm only human! Good press, bad press, it all goes inside and clangs around. I'm communicating my emotions to people, that's my life.

It's refreshing to see a successful and established artist using current events and often tabloid topics in their work. Do you think this is what differentiates you from other artists and helps your work appeal to a wider audience?

I don't think that's really, ultimately, what differentiates me, as a whole host of wonderful artists (artists that I admire) use similar topical reference points. However, yes, some of my subjects are easier to immediately embrace than, say, a painting of Andrew Lloyd Webber's niece or something. I like to think that my work appeals to a large amount of people, from all different walks of life, because they can see the emotions I'm working with, and feel them for themselves. I think I present my subjects from my individual viewpoint, really quite fiercely my own, and it works.

'No, I don't ski.

01 / Kate / Holy Water.

02 / Pete_01.

03 / Ellenor.

What do you consider the perfect atmosphere/set-up, when creating your work? Day/Night?

Right now, while I paint, I like to listen to Peaches, in the daytime, in a ski suit. No, I don't ski. Occasionally I will eat a Ski yogurt as I paint, however that's not absolutely essential for a masterpiece, as Picasso proved time and time again.

Which other creative people do you admire? Past and present?

Karen Kilimnik, Jeff Koons, Sarah Lucas, Sophie Von Hellermann, Anna Bjerger, Cathy Lomax, Annabel Dover, Tracey Emin, Sophie Calle, Goya, Samuel Becket, PJ Harvey, John Currin, Joan Littlewood, Mike Leigh, Michael Crowe, Hal Hartley, Alex Gene Morrison, Eva Hesse, Powell and Pressburger, Picasso, Balthus, James Jessop, crikey it goes on and on...

If you had to name a famous portrait, which would immediately pop into your head?

A lady by Goya, can't remember her name, she's lying back in a yellow blouse.

Occasionally I will eat a Ski yogurt as I paint, however that's not absolutely essential for a masterpiece, as Picasso proved time and time again.'

02

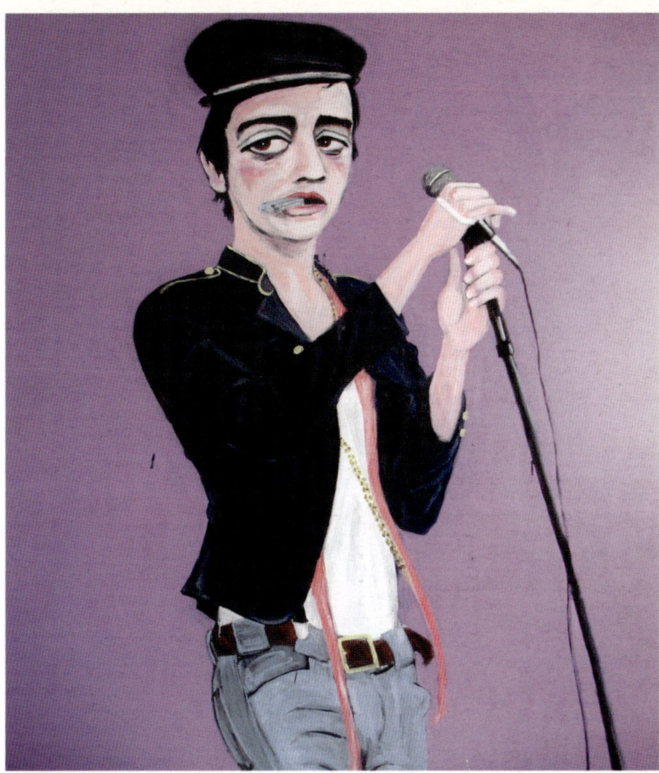

03

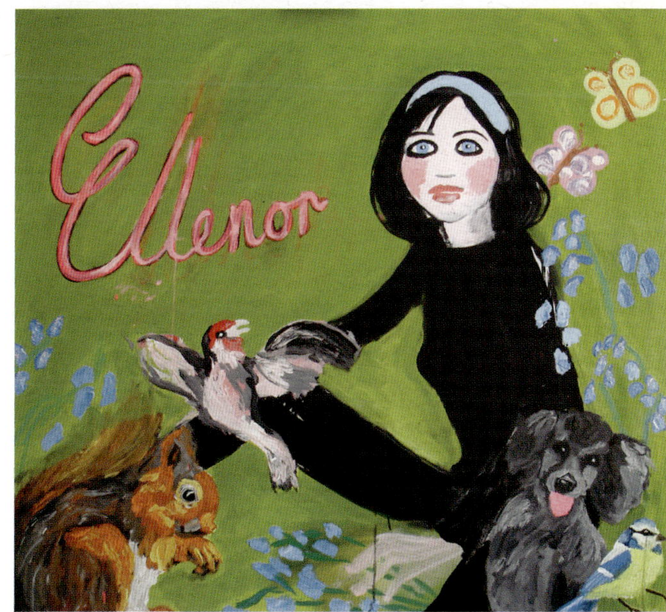

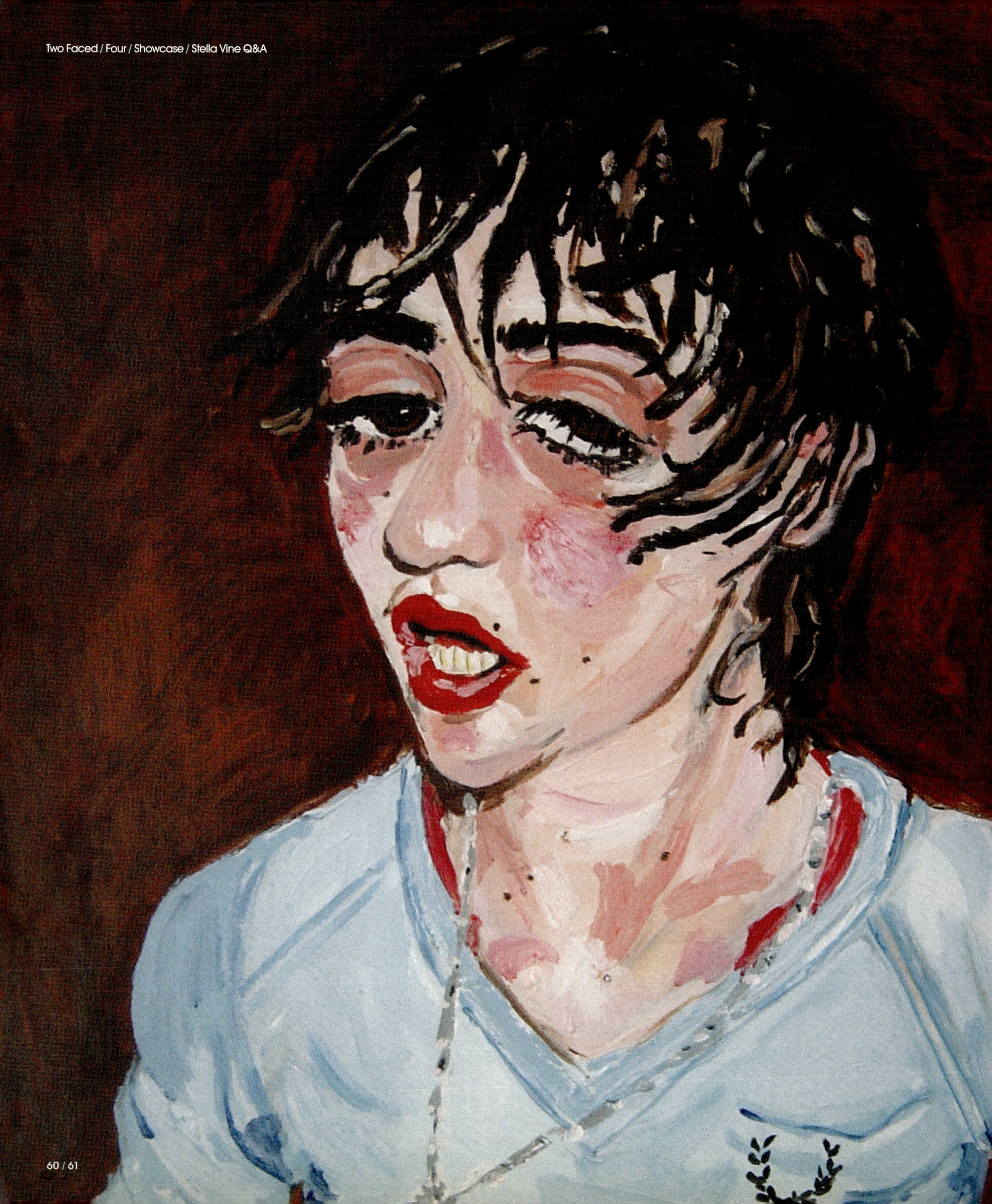

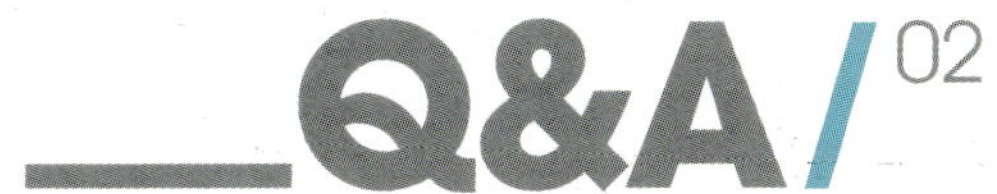

Stella Vine paints. Her family, her pets, her celebrities; her smouldering passions. The paintings are honest, kitsch and hauntingly direct. While showing in Transition Gallery's "Girl on Girl" exhibition, Charles Saatchi bought Stella's (now infamous) painting, "Hi Paul, can you come over...?" On the surface we see a fragile, human Princess Diana, wild eyed, dripping in makeup and blood. Before you could say "unintentional controversy," Stella's art was then the critical highlight of Saatchi's notorious "New Blood" show at County Hall, hurling Stella into the limelight, which intensified further with her subsequent painting of Rachel Whitear.

Stella's fiery passion for DIY creativity in writing, art and music has remained since she was 13 years old in Norwich, visiting the inspirationally anarchic Premises Arts Centre. By 1984 Stella was improvising with the National Youth Theatre of GB, and by 1987 she was attending The Academy of Live and Recorded Arts, obsessing over Mike Leigh and Joan Littlewood.

Stella was a cleaner for The Thomson Twins through Drama school, and was a waitress, a stripper and a night-club hostess, experiences which have fed into her intensely expressive art. In 1999 she took her son to the Hampstead School of Art, where it transpired that he didn't want to go, so Stella did instead, taking her first painting class as an adult with tutor Vincent Millner.

Now with her own unique style of skewed self portraiture, Stella creates from a huge range of eclectic, personal interests and makes her source materials of icons and inspirations her very own, seen in soloshows at Roberts and Tilton in Los Angeles in 2005, Alon Segev Gallery in Tel Aviv in 2004 and numerous group shows including 'chockerfuckingblocked' at Jeffrey Charles Gallery in London and several shows at Transition Gallery.

Stella has completed a number of artists talks, the most recent at Tate Modern, and will enjoy her first major museum show at Oxford Modern Art in September 2007. And, as if that wasn't enough, Stella Vine also runs her own independent project space, "Rosy Wilde," in Wardour Street, Soho, a beautiful space hosting solo shows to thrilling new artists.

01 / Pete_02:

01

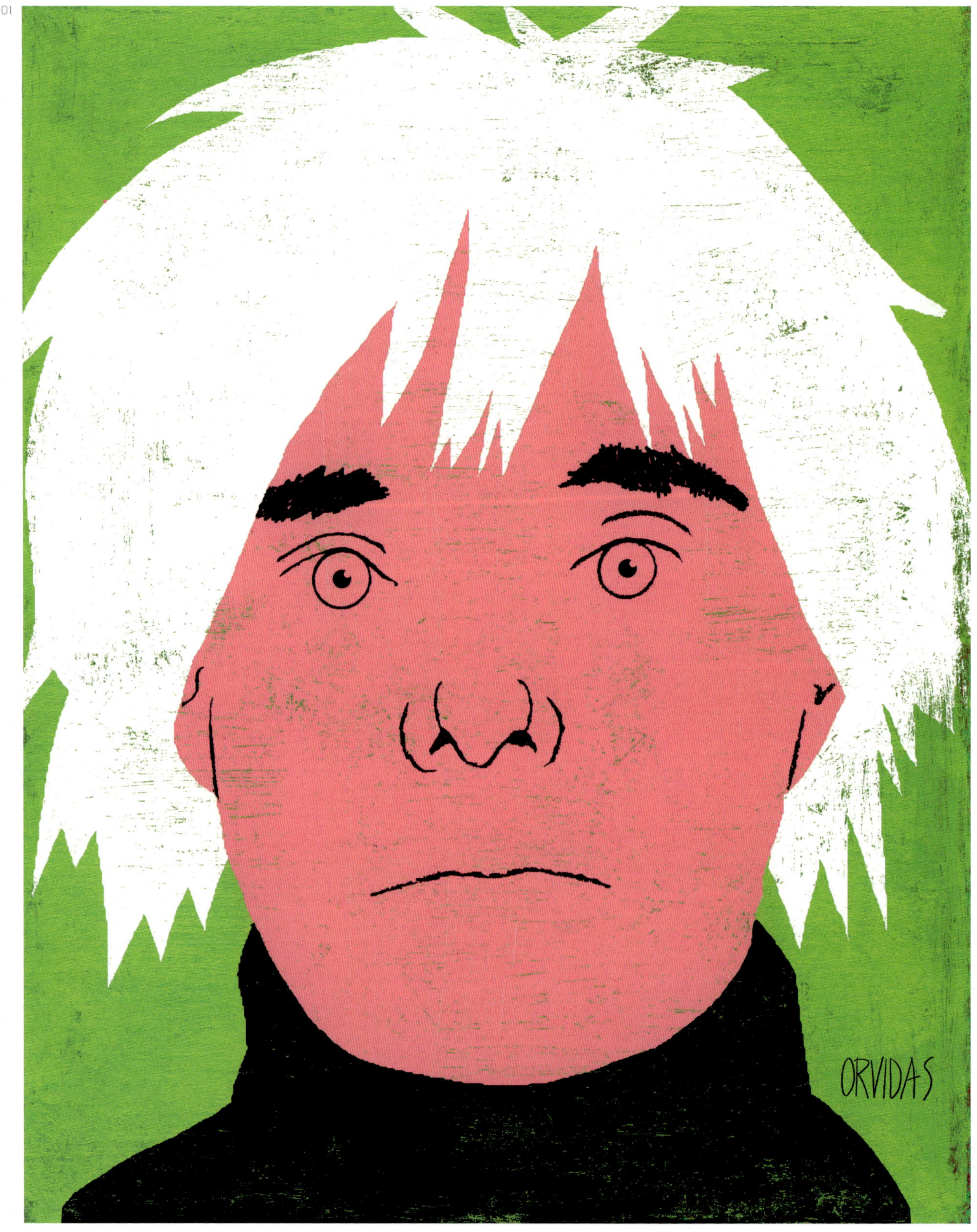

Ken Orvidas /

01 / Andy Warhol.
Digital, Photoshop.
Original size_8.5" x 11"

02 / Bowie.
Mixed media.
Original size_8" x 9.5"

02

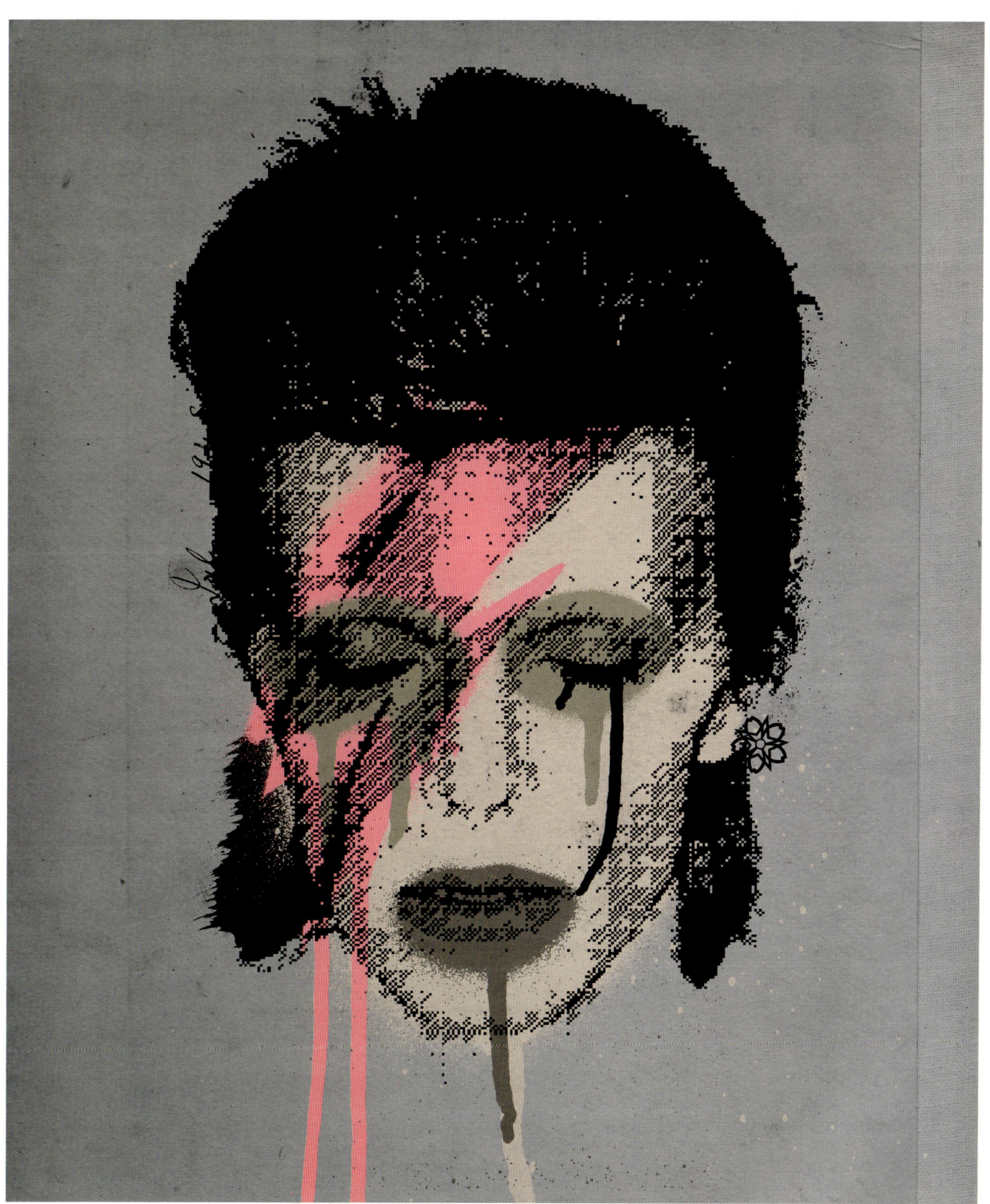

Paul Willoughby /

James Joyce /

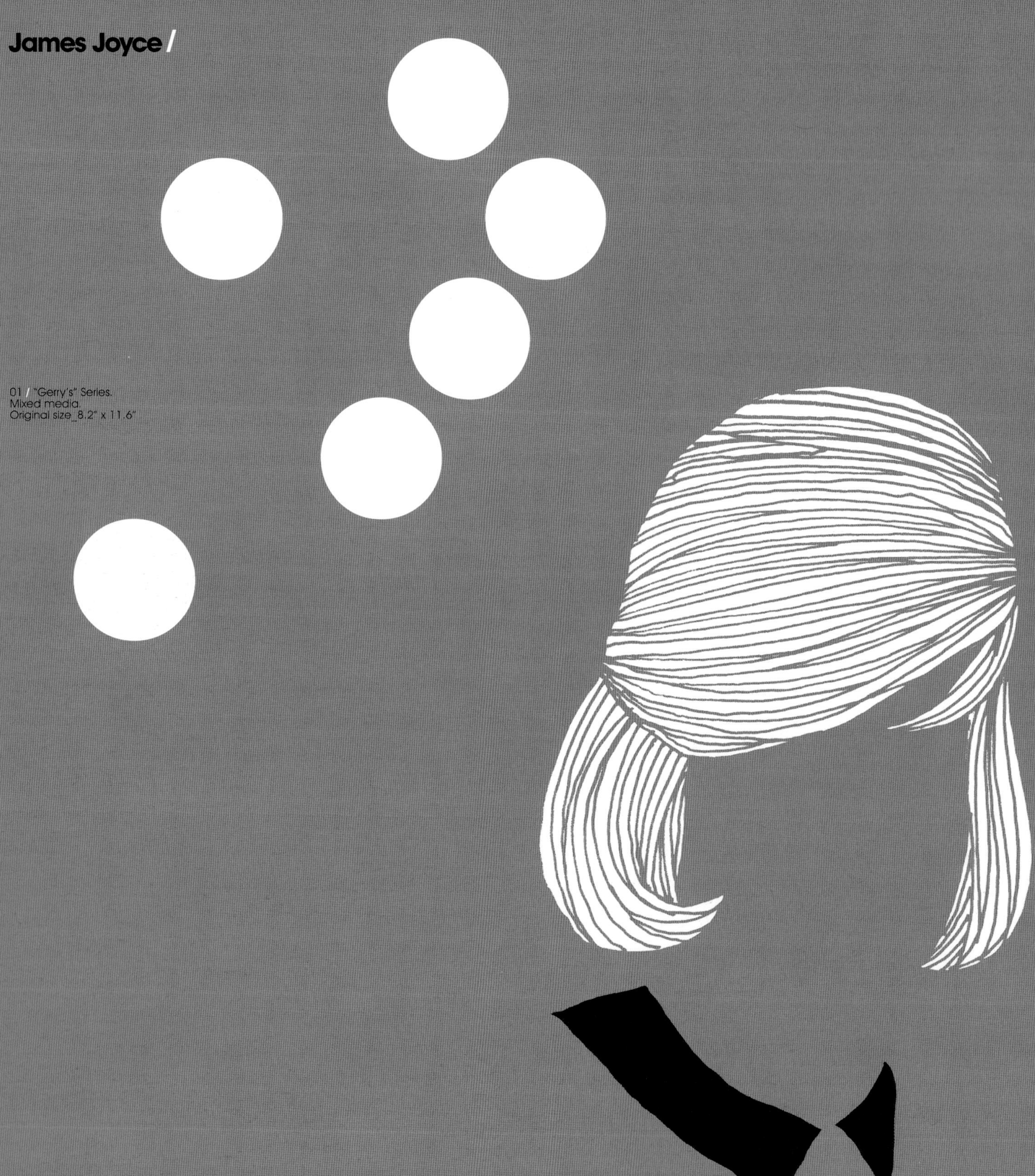

01 / "Gerry's" Series.
Mixed media.
Original size_8.2" x 11.6"

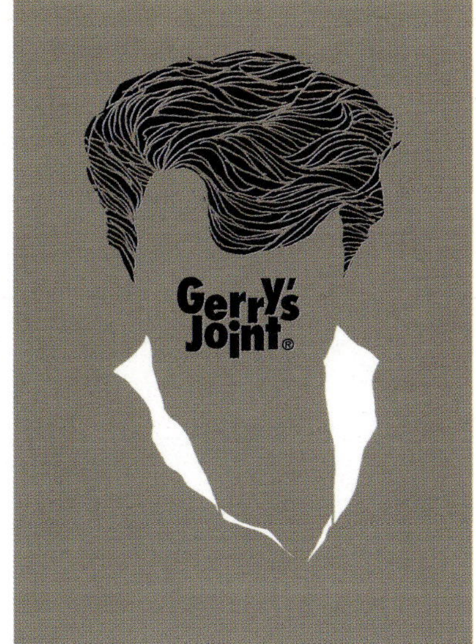

02

03

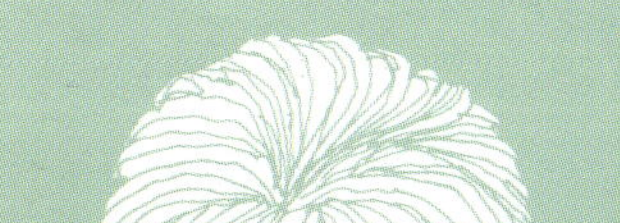
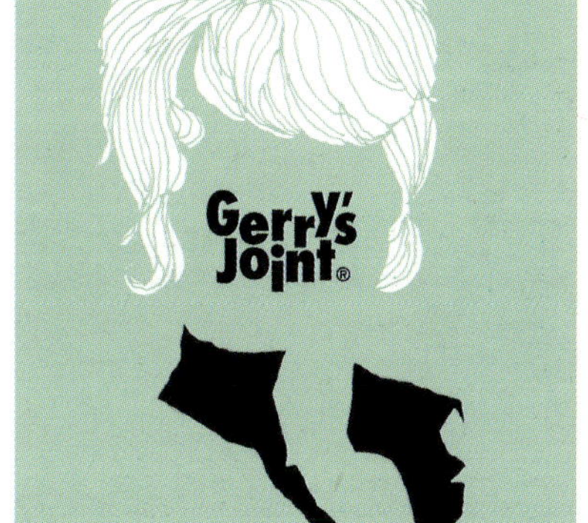

04

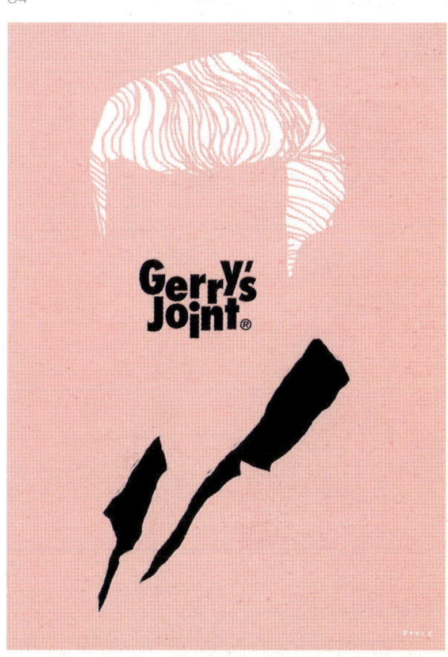

05

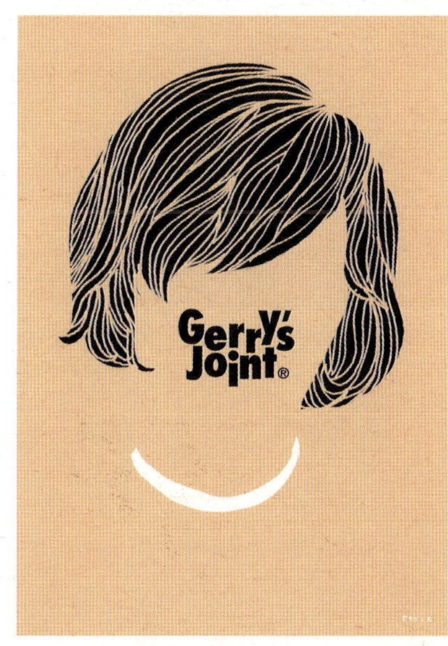

'THE PORTRAIT IS ONE OF THE MOST CURIOUS ART FORMS'

Henri Matisse

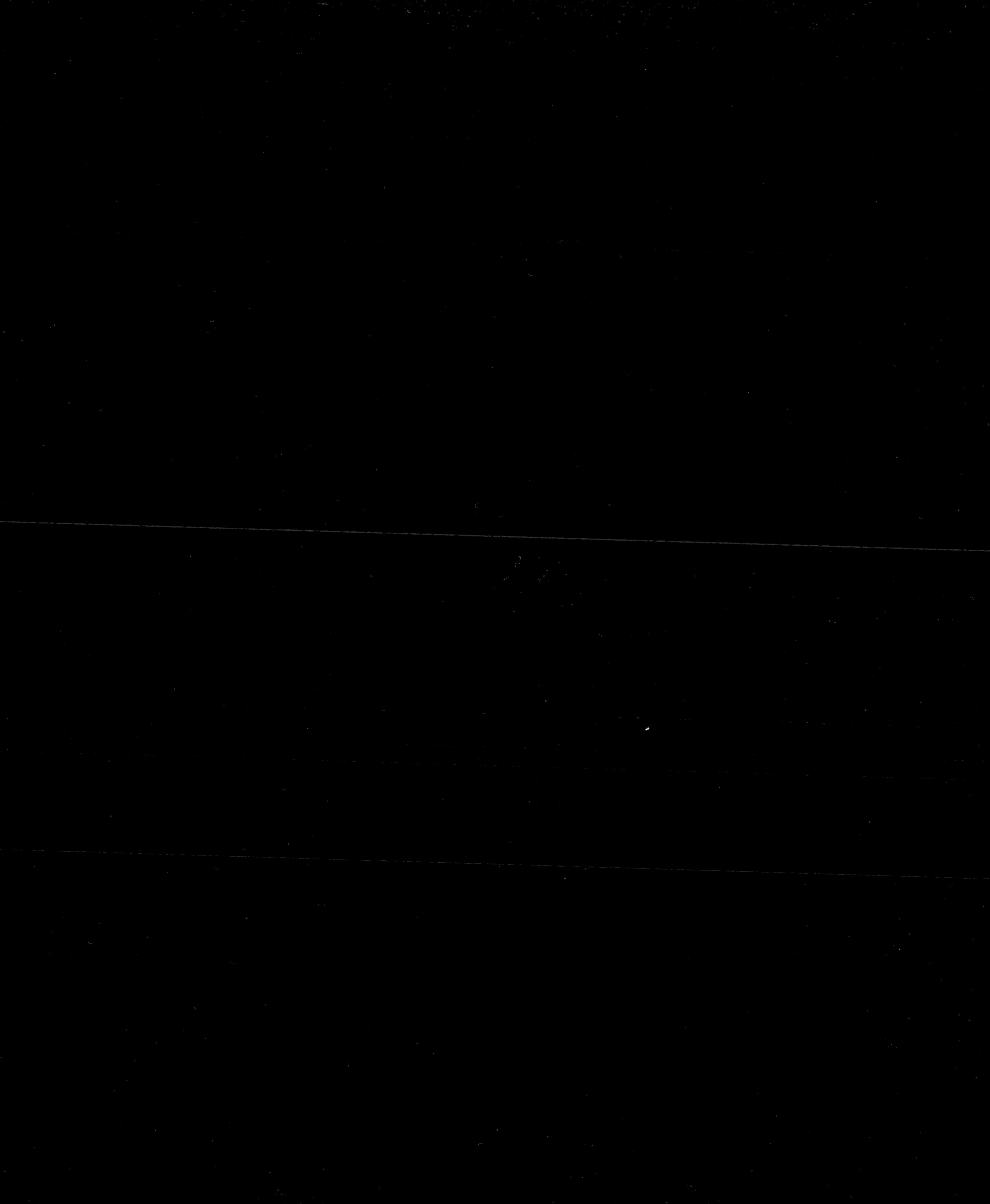

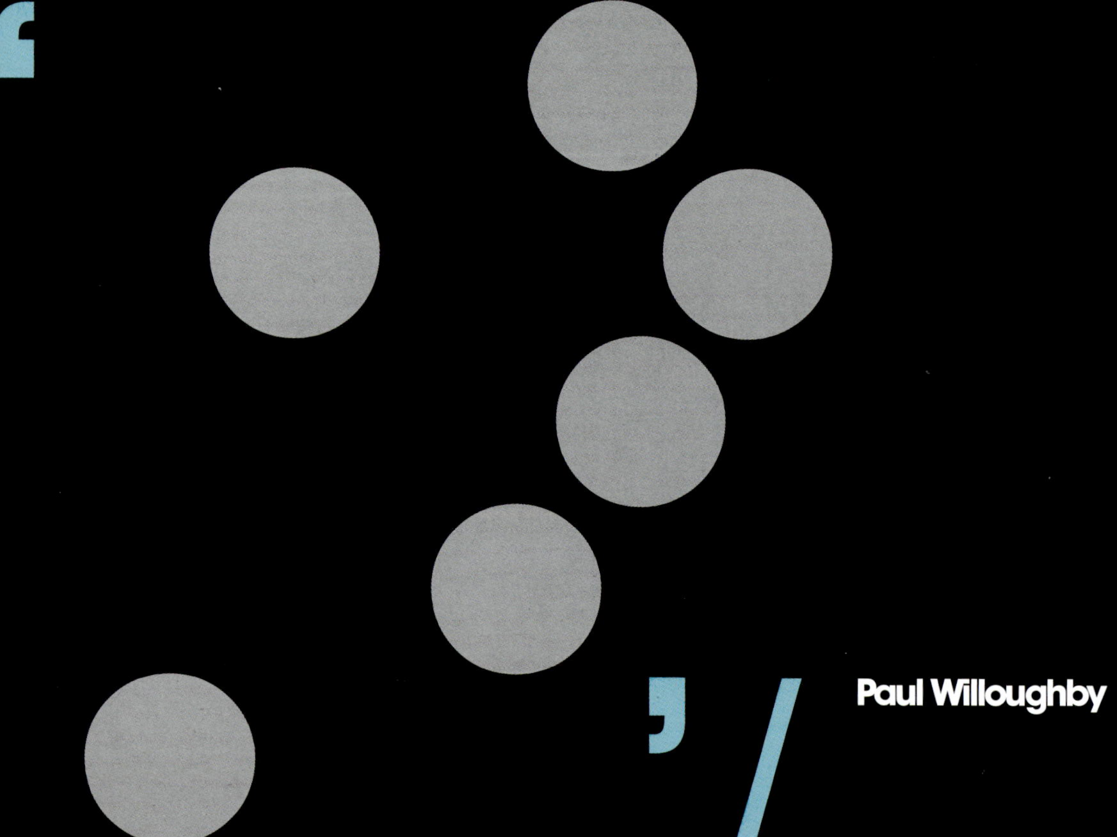

Paul Willoughby

01 / Romance and Cigarettes
Mixed media screenprint.
Original size_7.8" x 9.6"

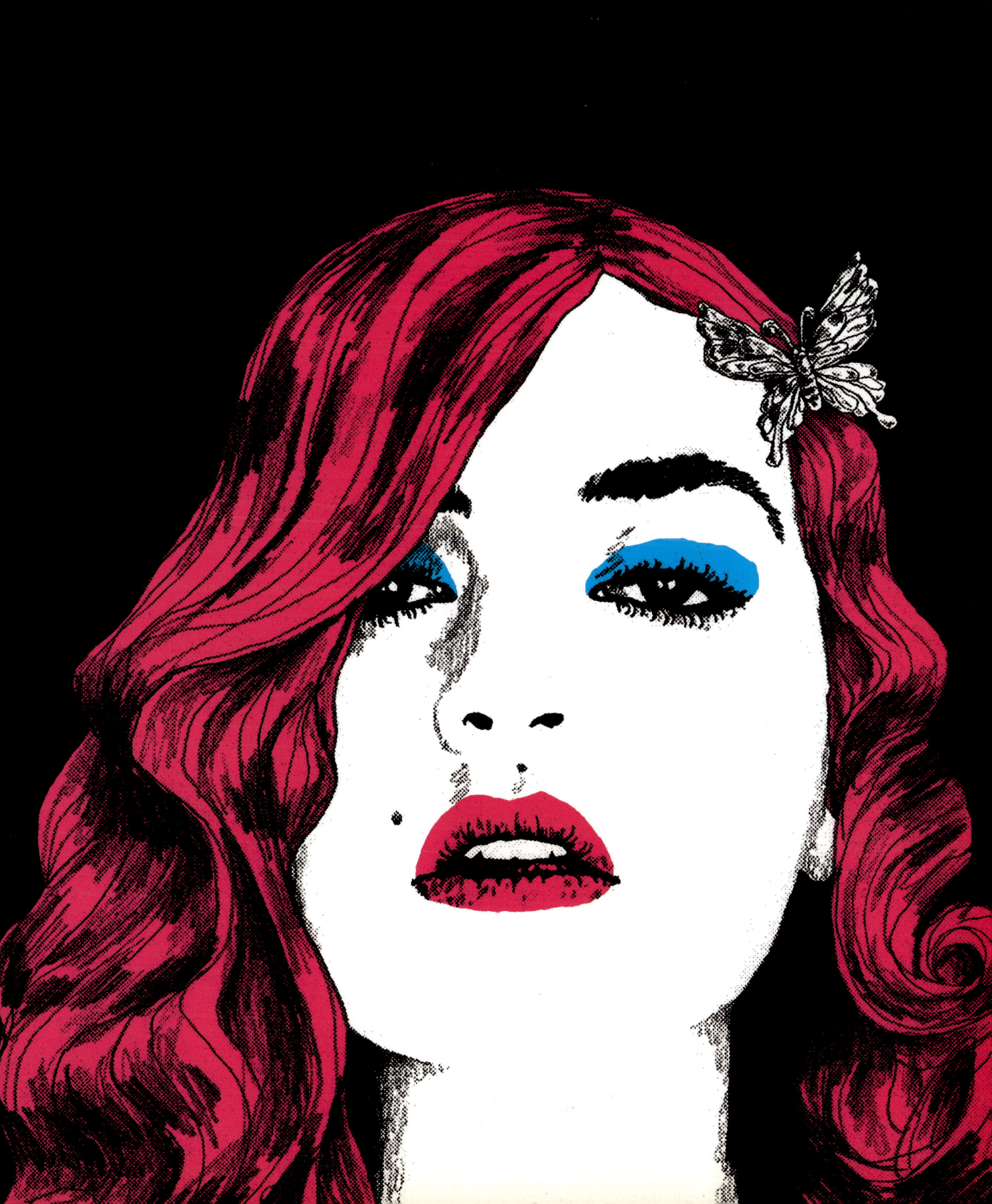

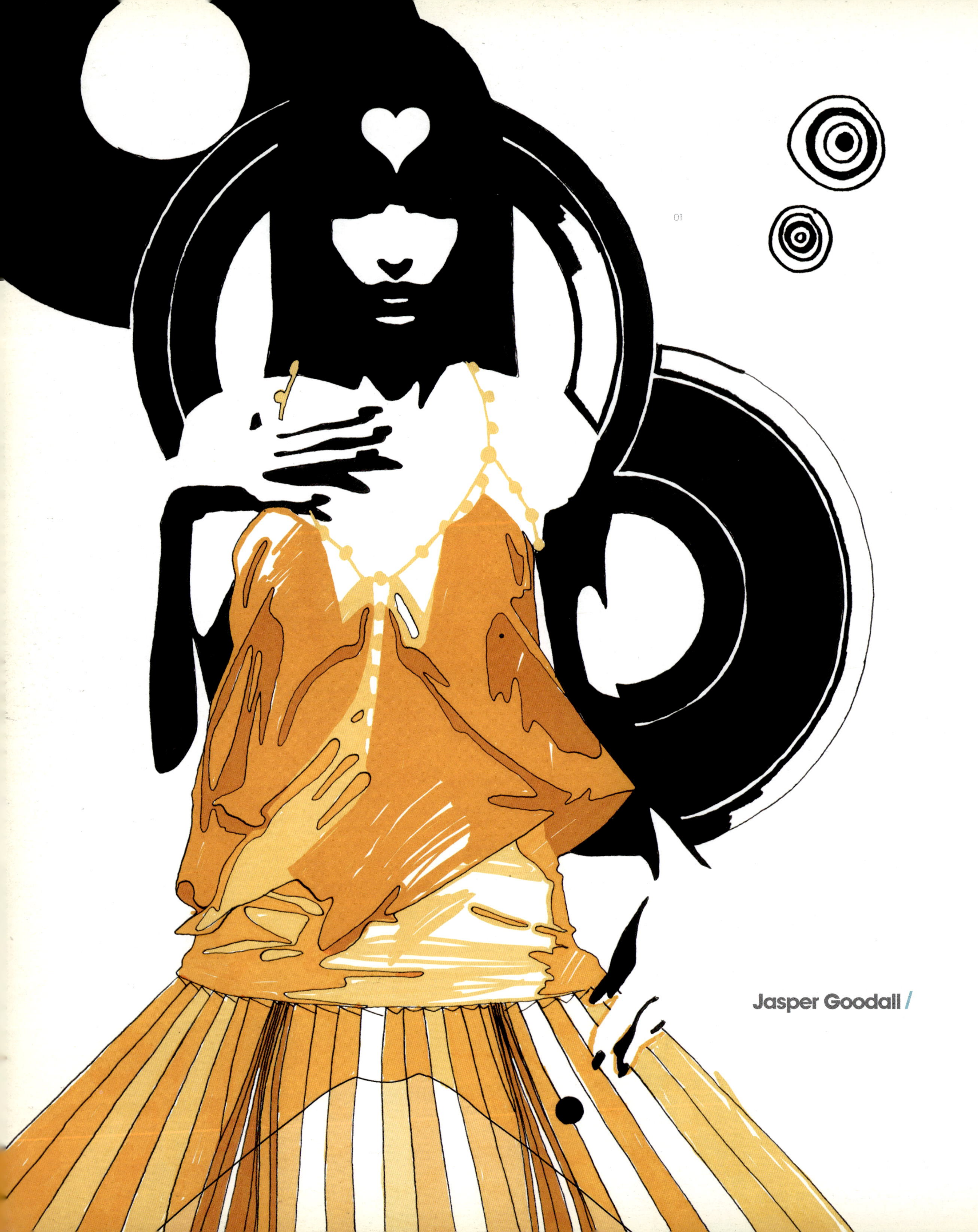

01

Jasper Goodall /

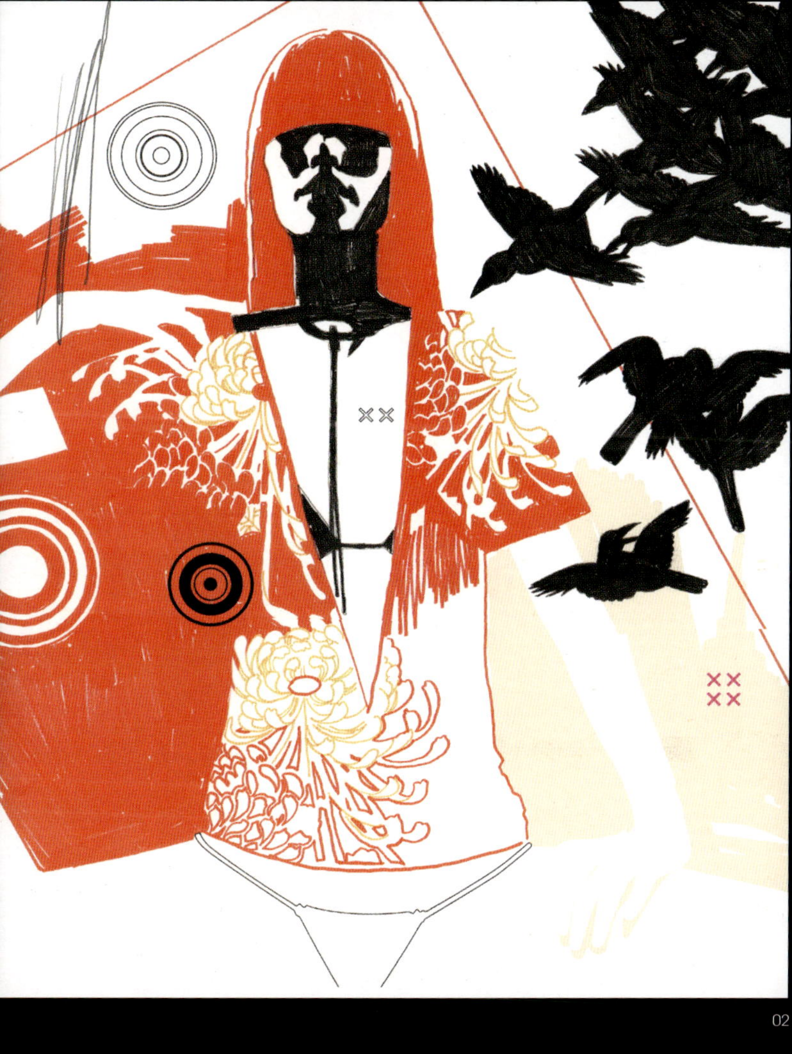

01 / Never Give In.
Acrylic on wood.
Original size 48" x 48"

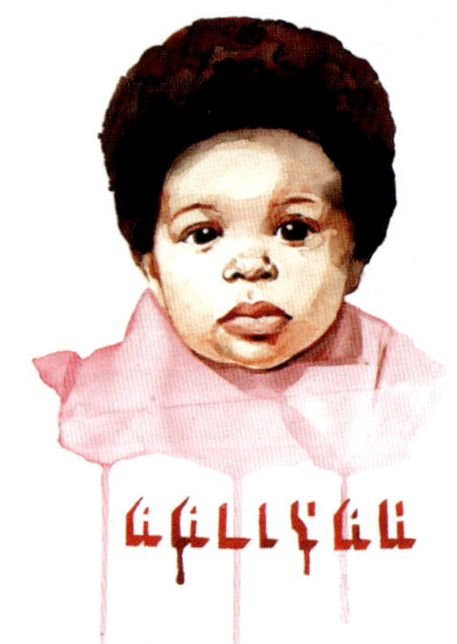

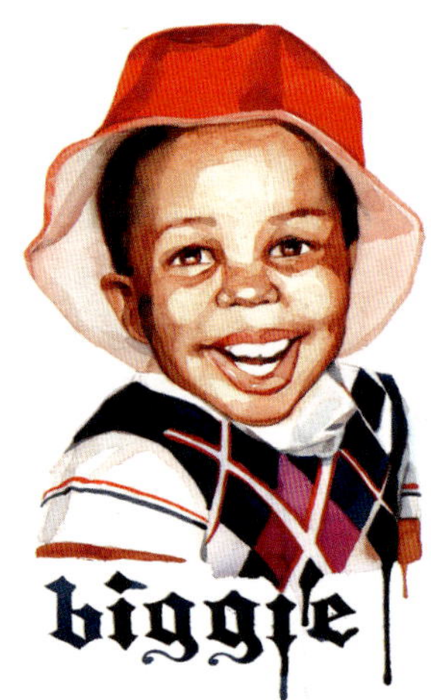
biggie

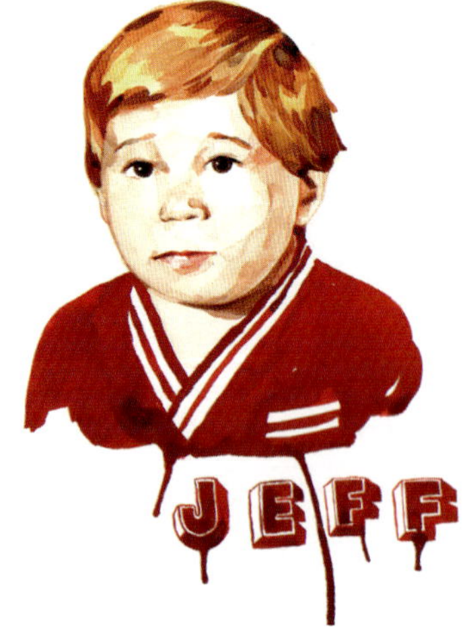
JEFF

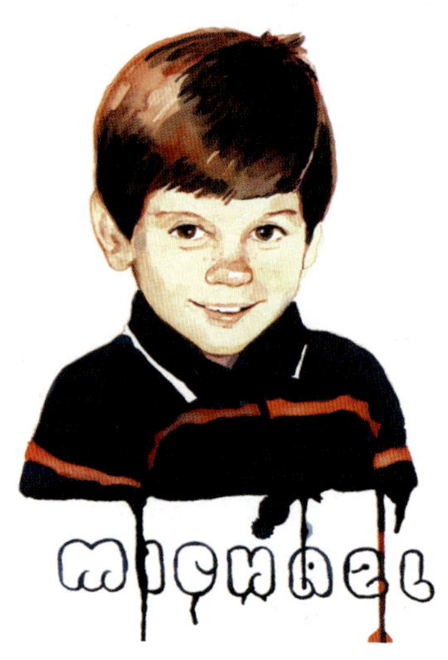
michael

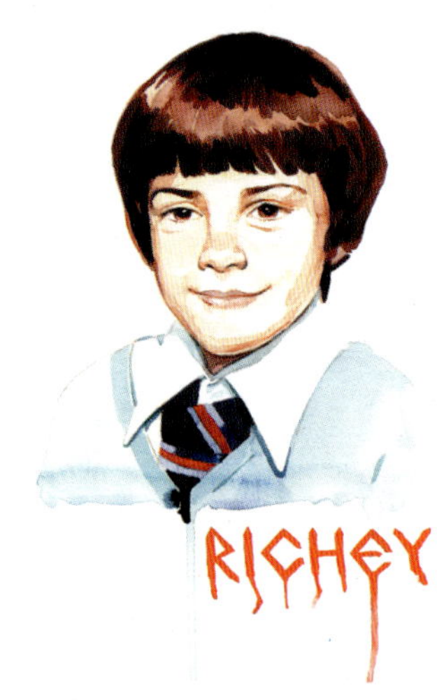
RICHEY

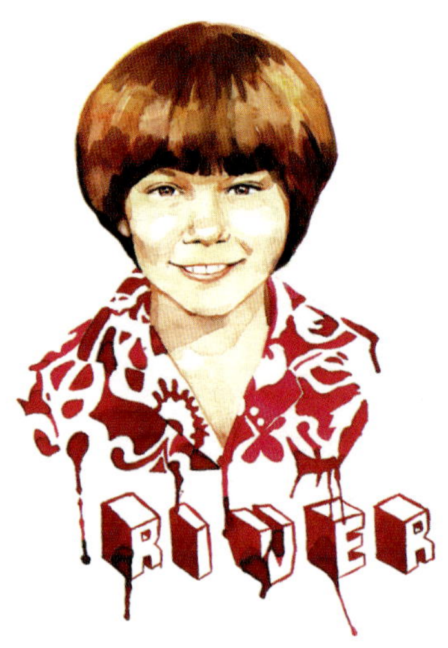
RIVER

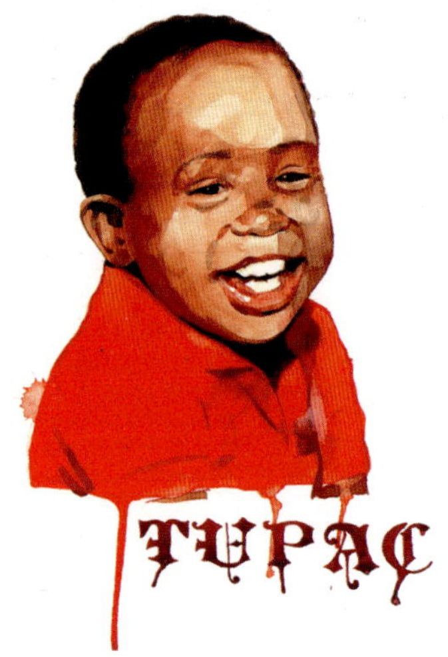
TUPAC

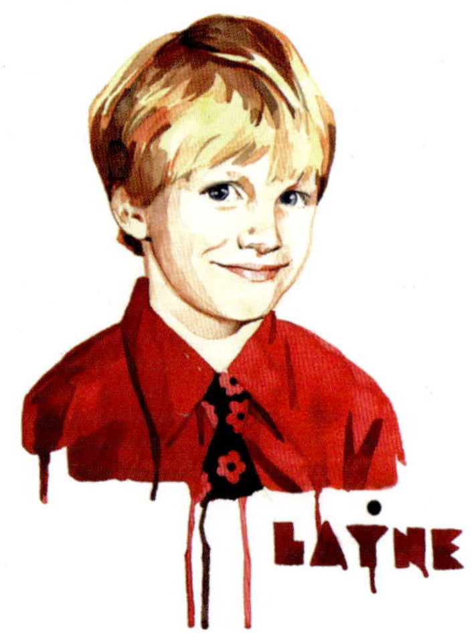
LAYNE

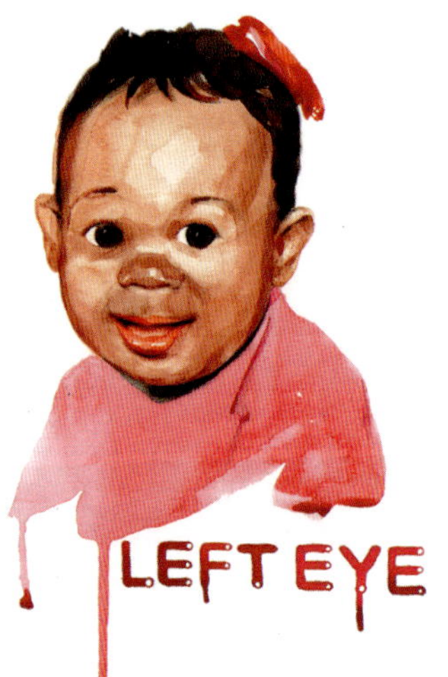
LEFT EYE

Michael Gillette /

01 - 10 / Little Angels.
Watercolour.
Original size_9" x 11"

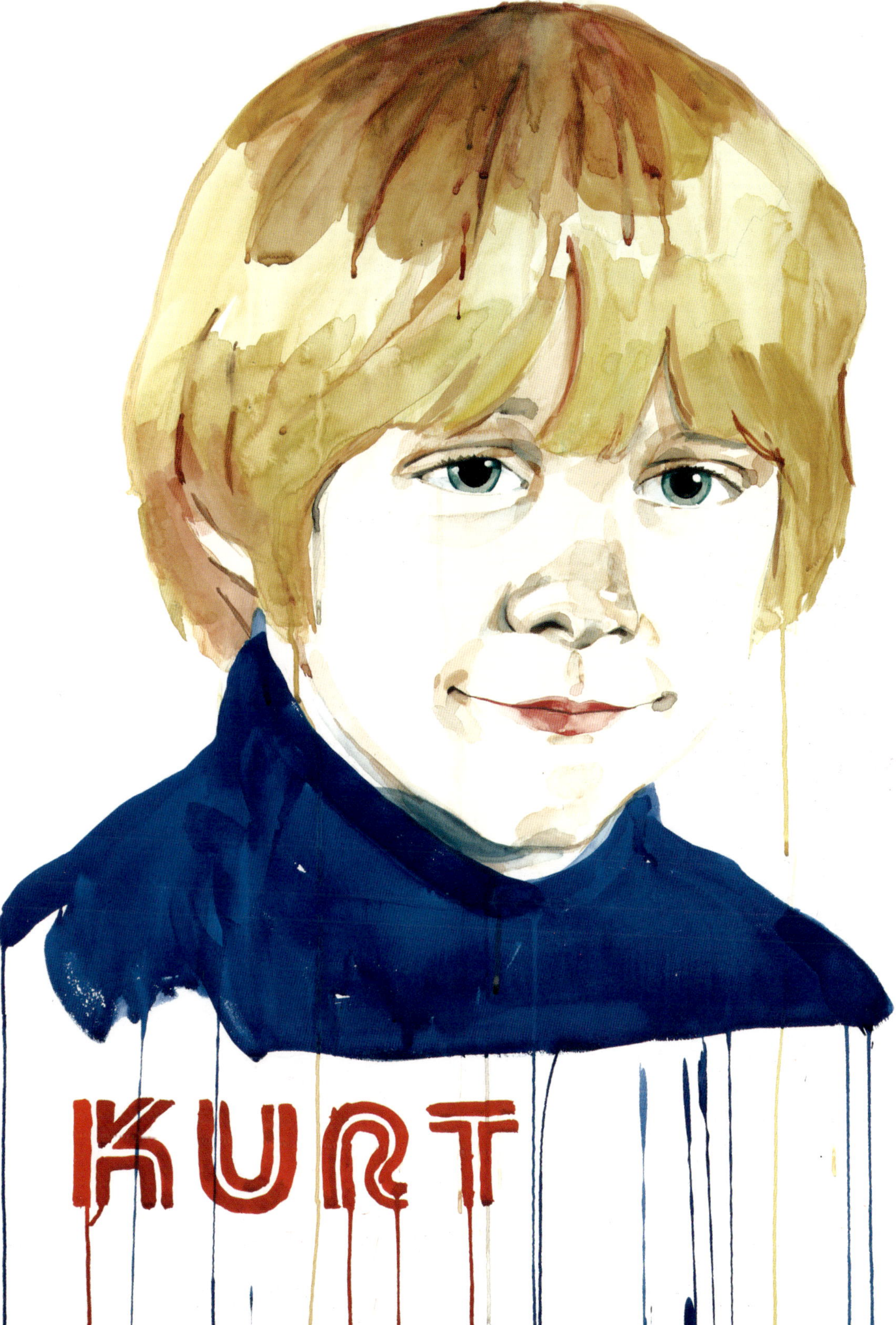

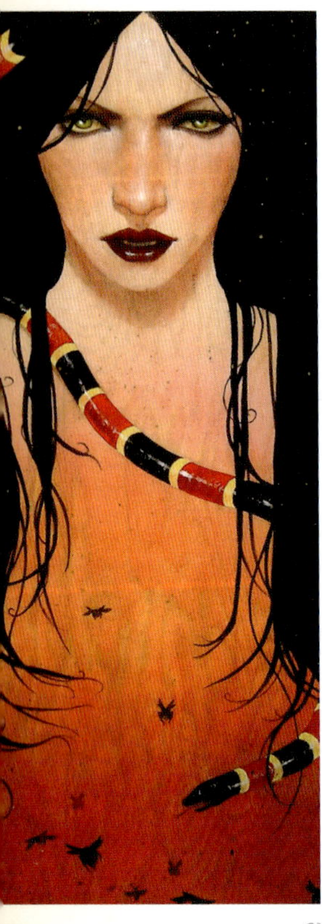

01

01 / Soul.
Acrylic on wood.
Original size_12" x 32"

02 / Fading.
Acrylic on wood.
Original size_24" x 16"

03 / Absolution.
Acrylic on wood.

02

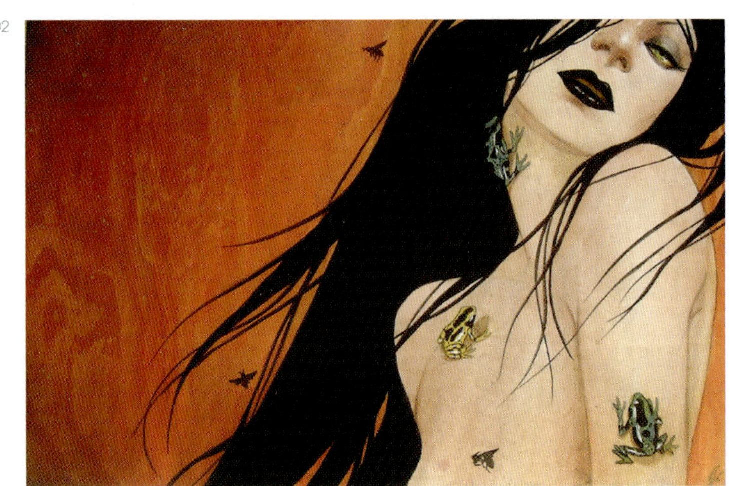

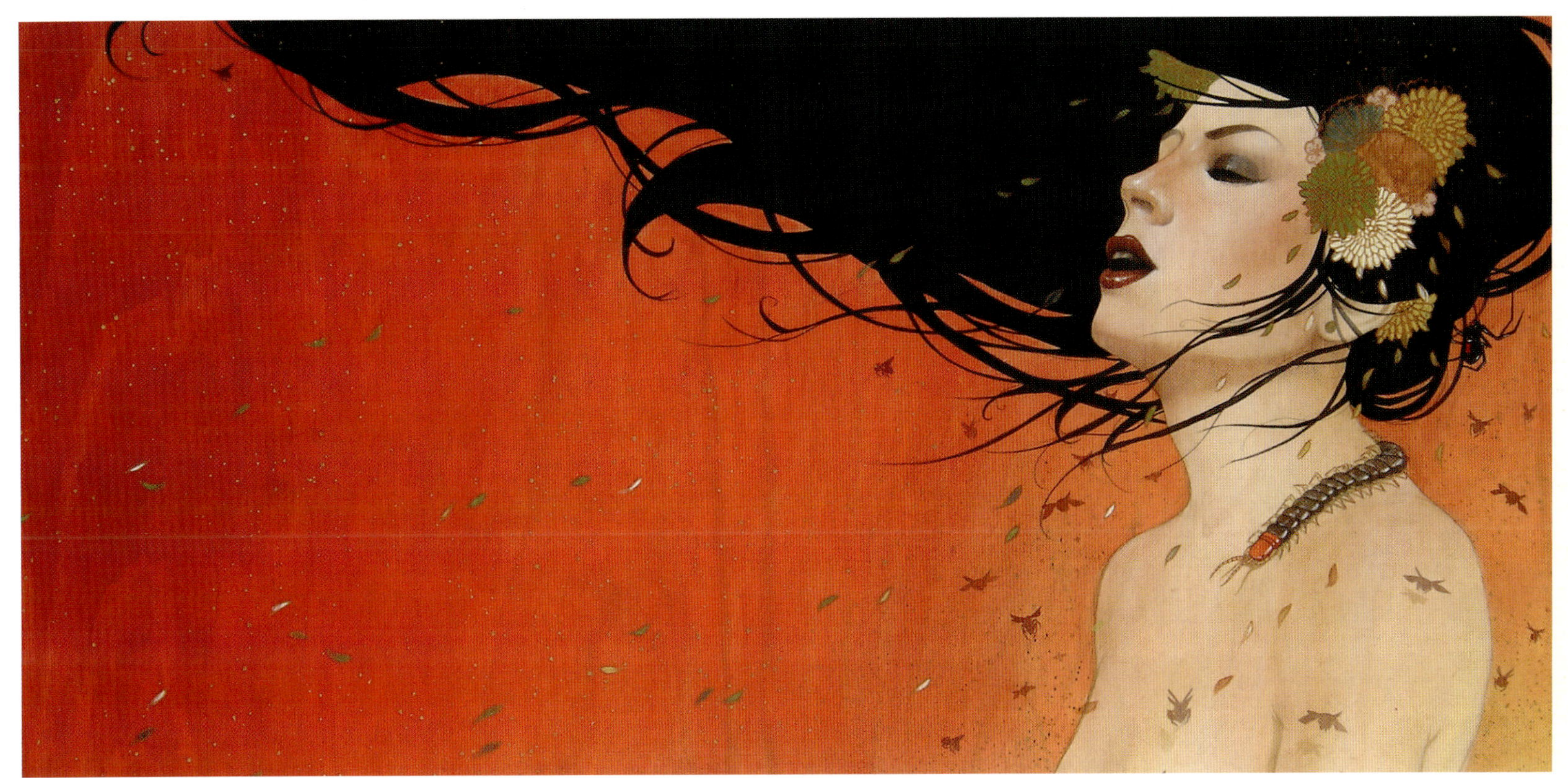

03

Sylvia Ji /

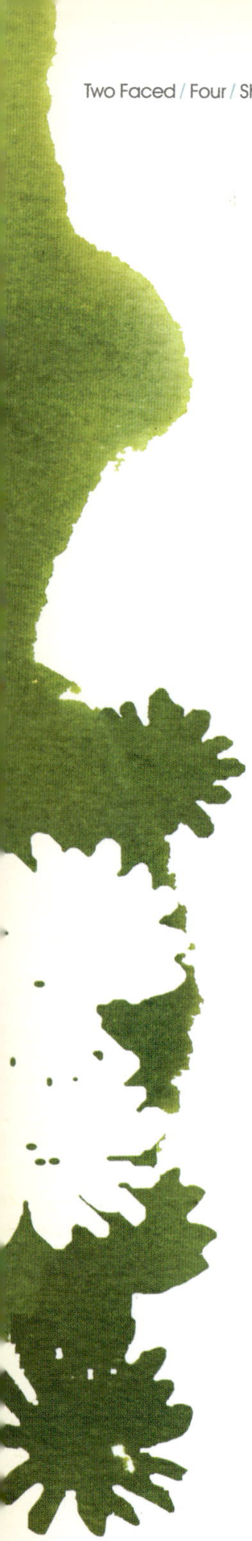

01

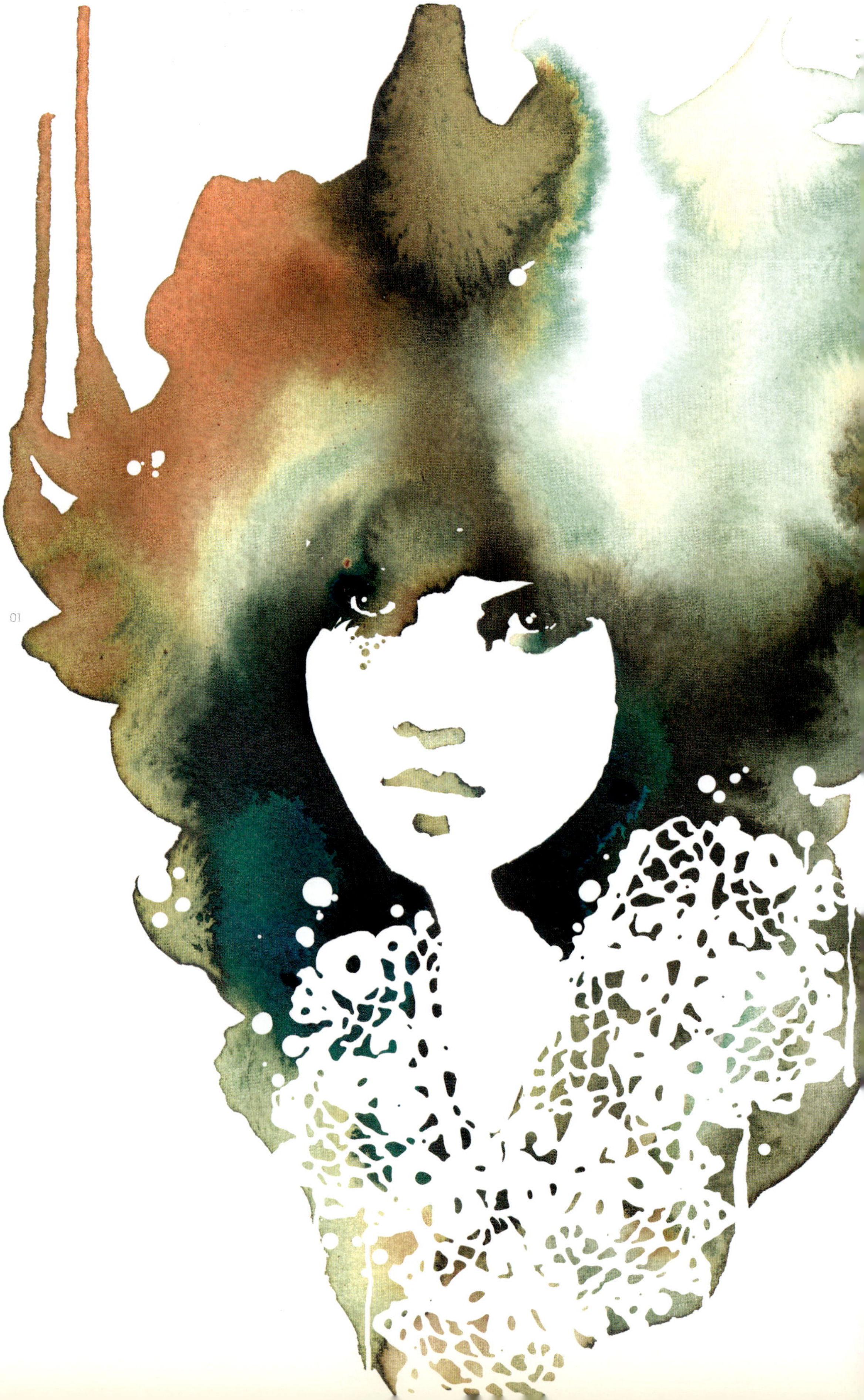

Stina Persson /

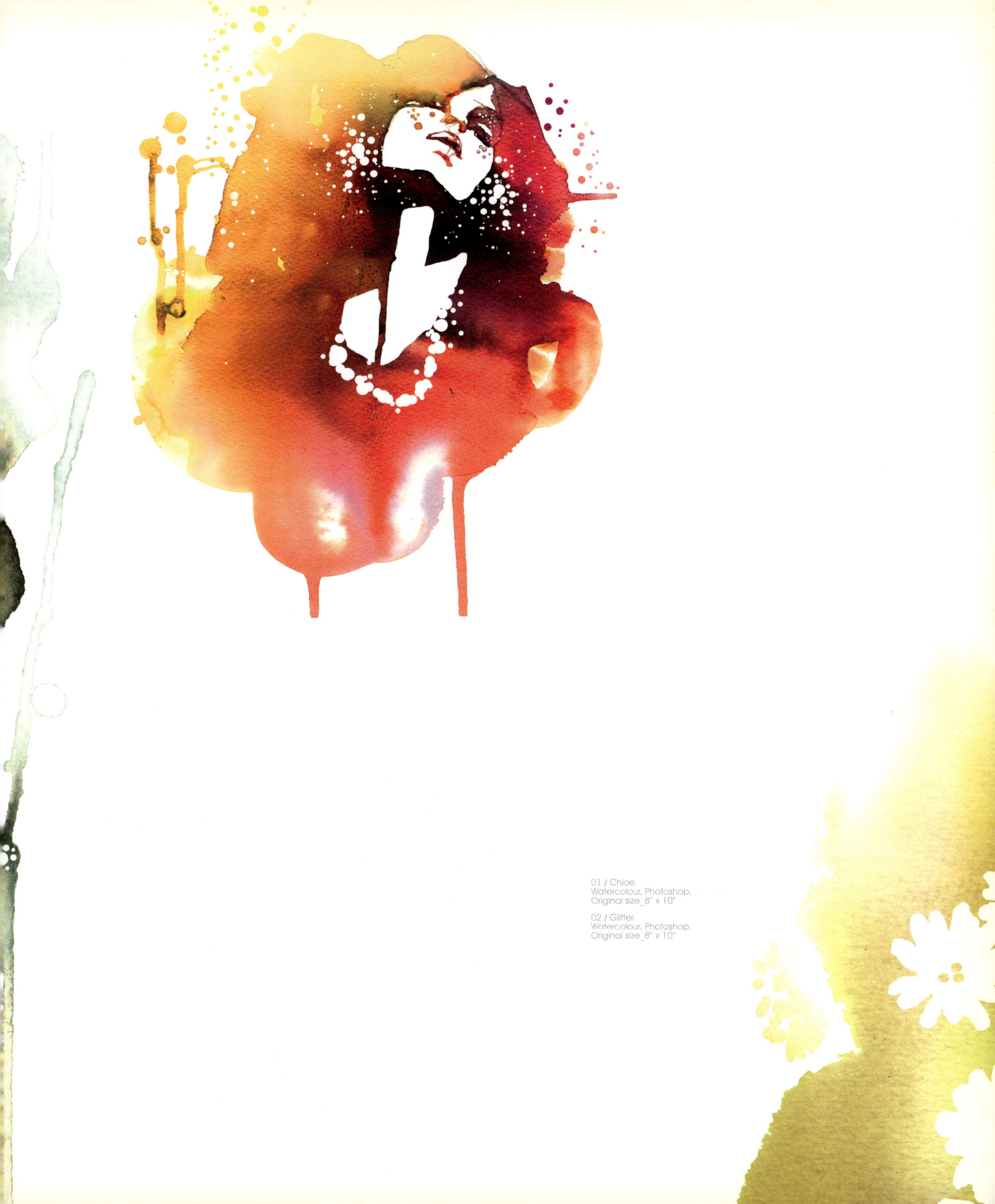

01 / Chloe.
Watercolour, Photoshop.
Original size_8" x 10"

02 / Glitter.
Watercolour, Photoshop.
Original size_8" x 10"

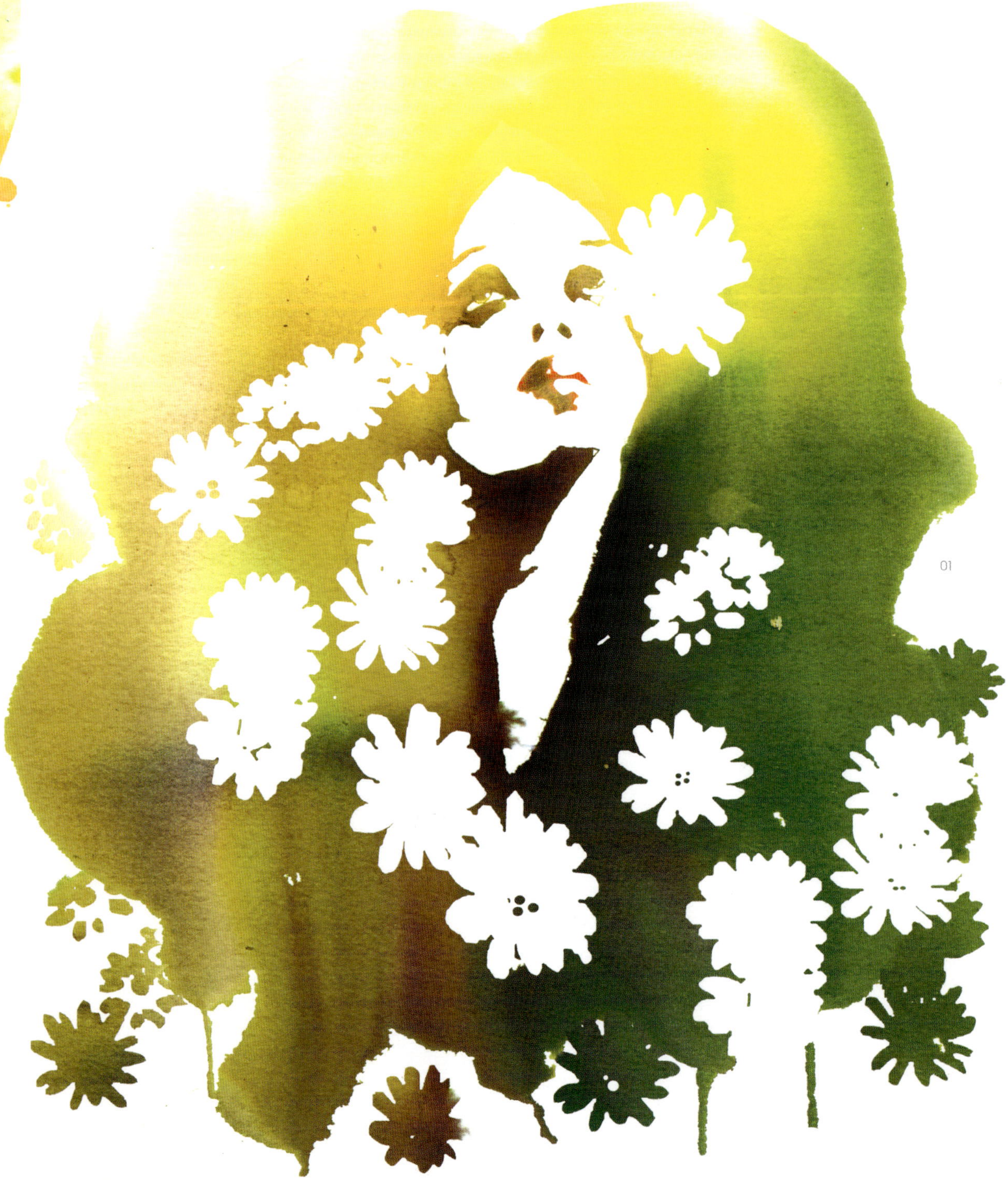

01

02

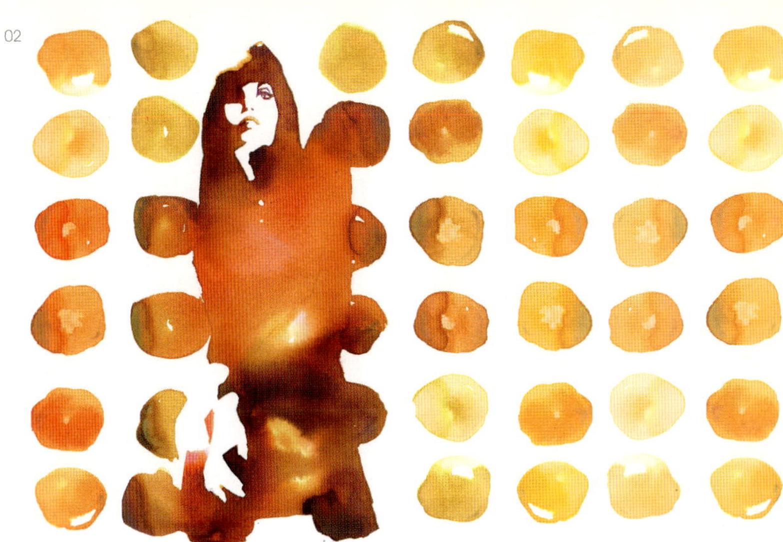

01 / Daises.
Watercolour, Photoshop.
Original size_10" x 12"

02 / Sixties.
Ink, coloured pencil.
Original size_11" x 14"

Represented by
c/o CWC International, Inc
www.cwc-1.com
Email: agent@cwc-i.com

Stina Persson /

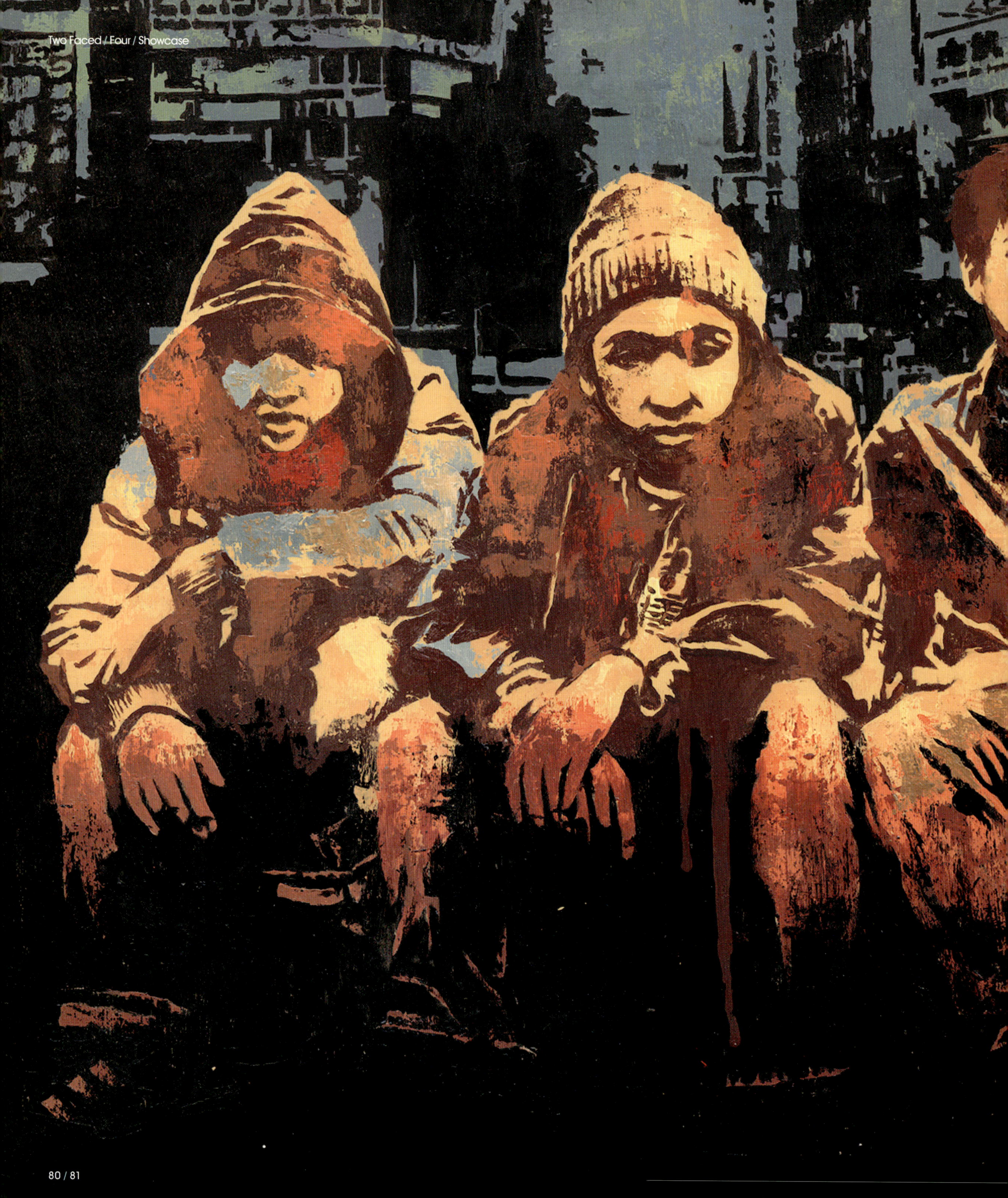

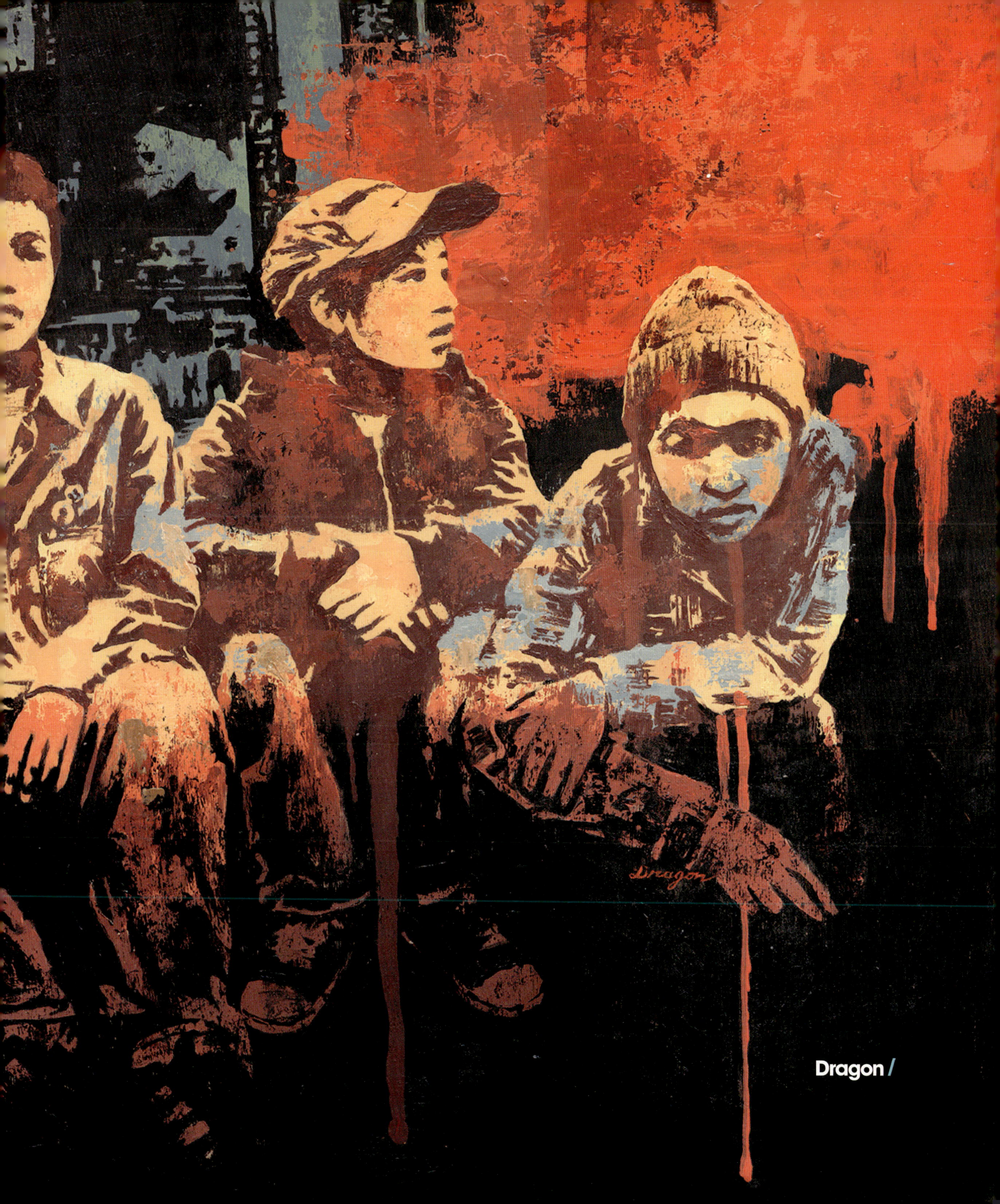

Dragon /

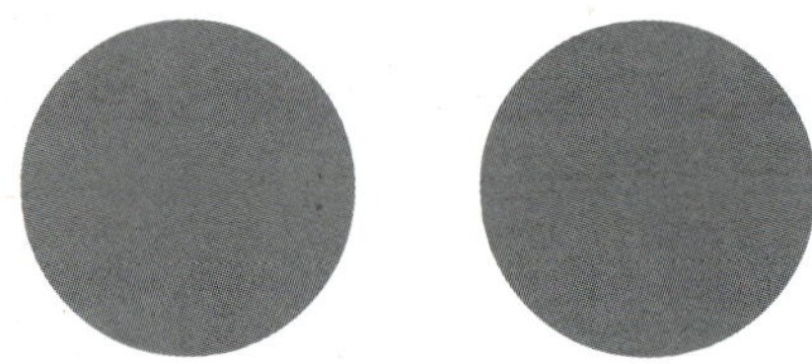

Olaf Hajek

01 02

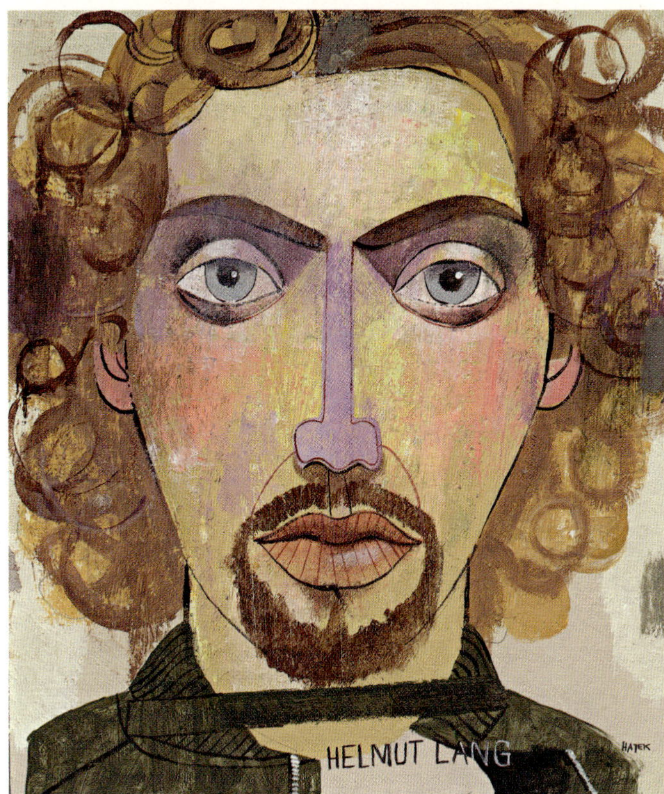

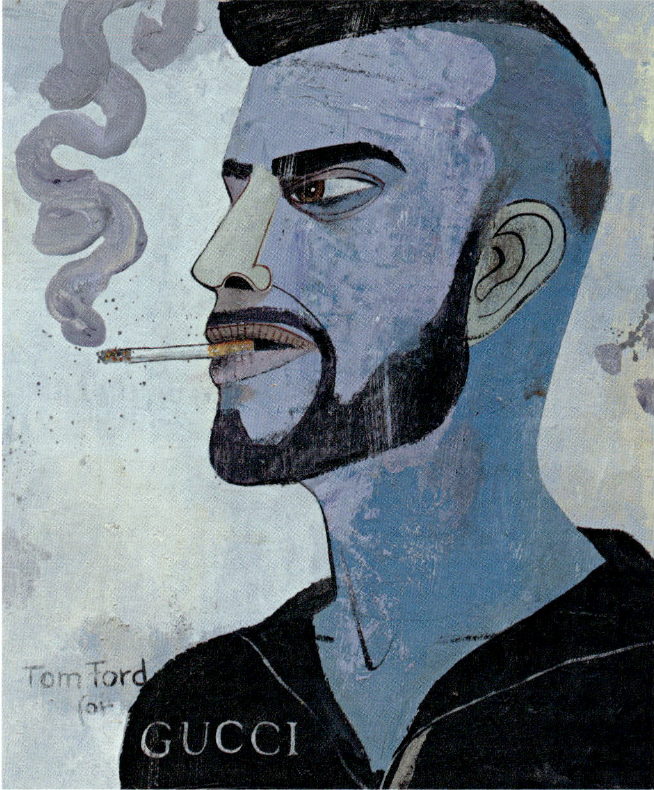

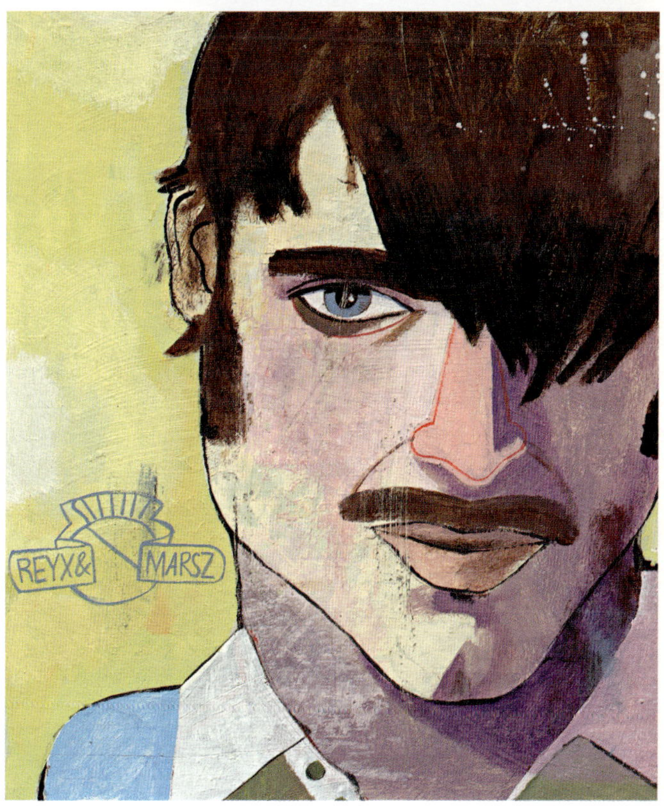

03

01 - 03 / Maxim Fasion.
Acrylic on cardboard.
Original size_8.3" x 11.7"

‘LIGHT MAKES PHOTOGRAPHY. EMBRACE LIGHT. ADMIRE IT. LOVE IT.’

George Eastman

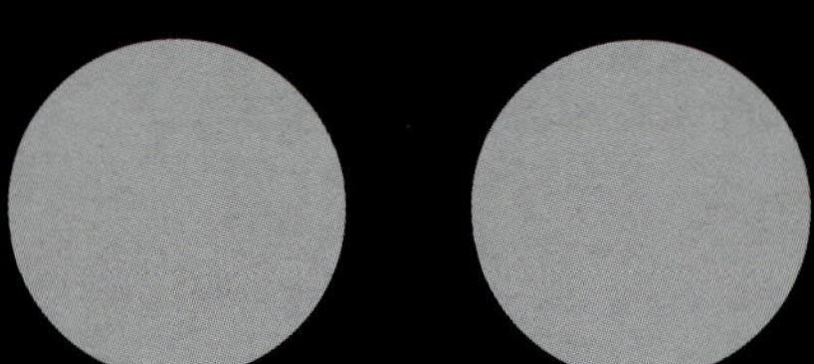

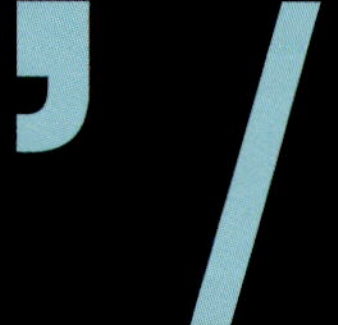

Timothy Saccenti

01 / Beans 1.
Photograph.
Original size_20" x 30"

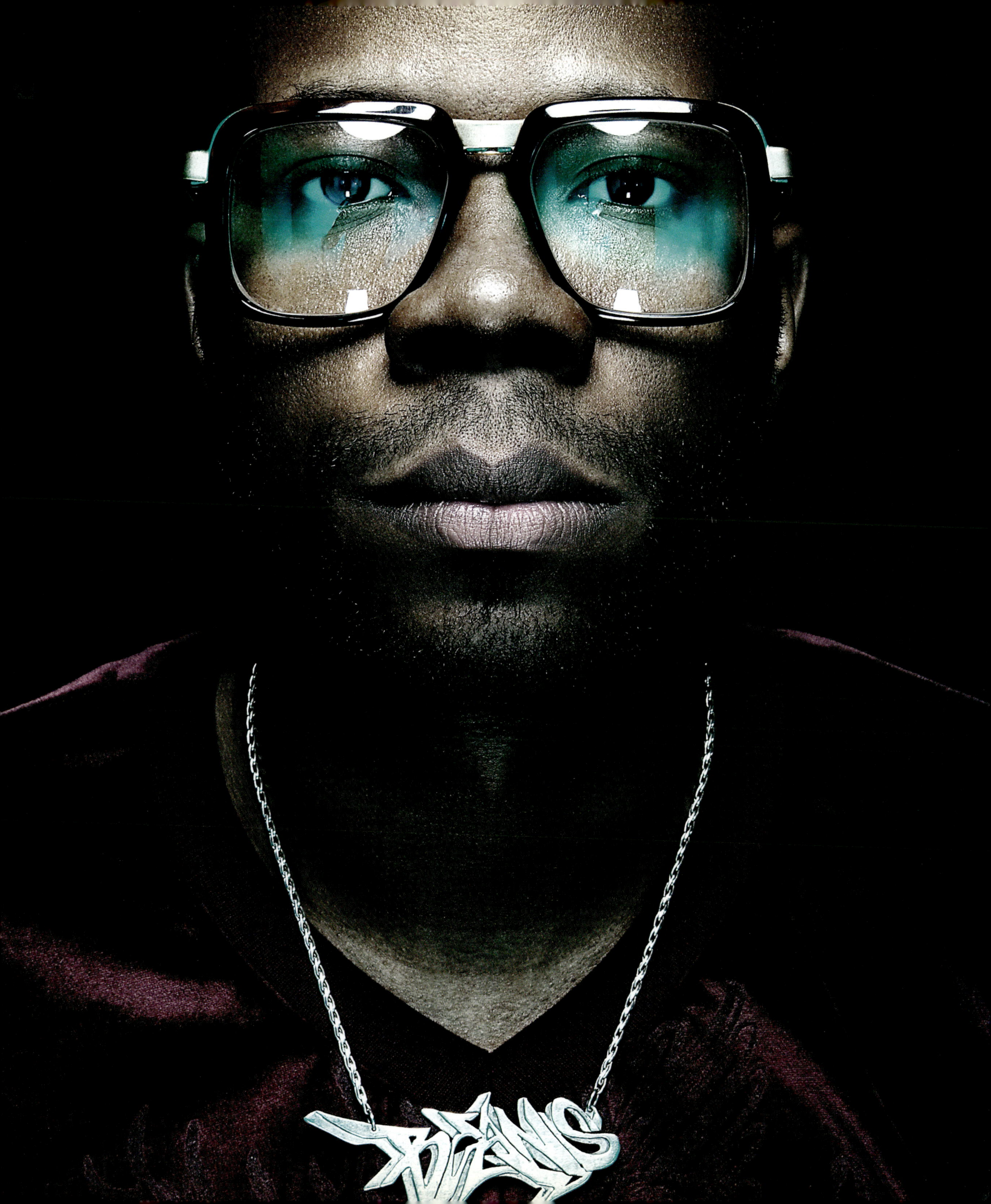

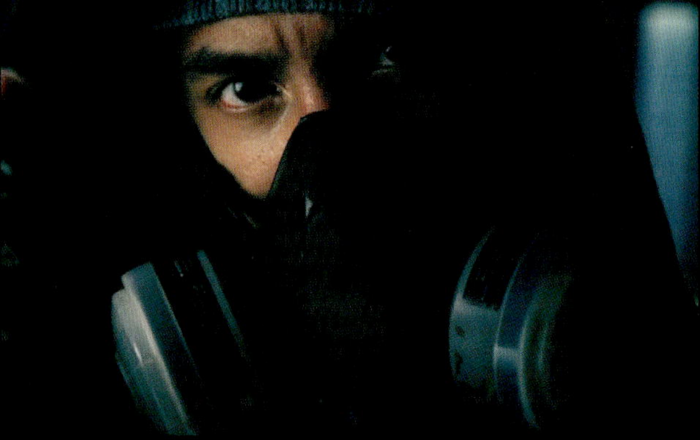

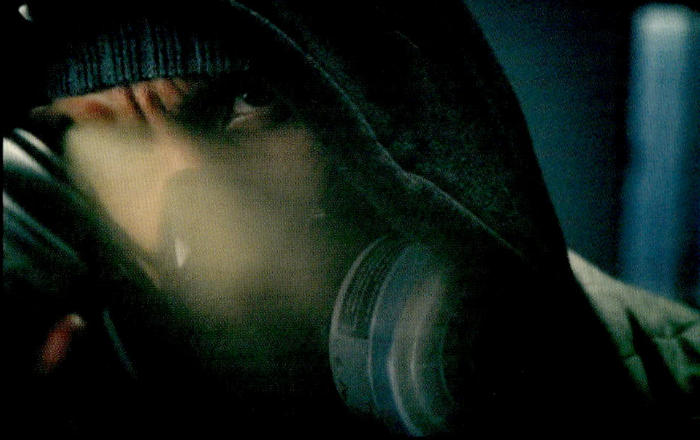

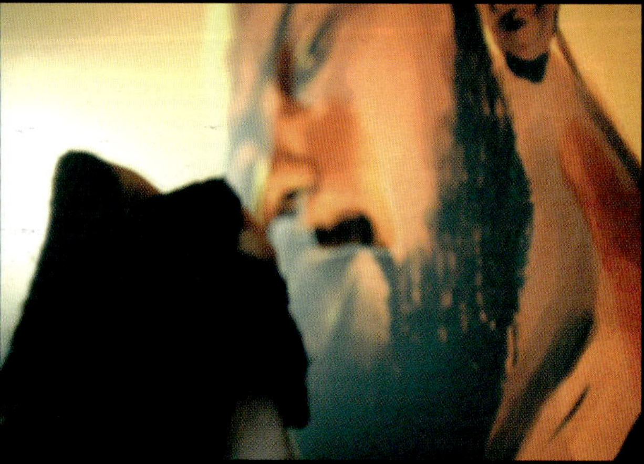

01

01 / Nu Classic Soul.
Video Stills.

02 / Nu Classic Soul.
Mixed media.
Original size_20" x 12"

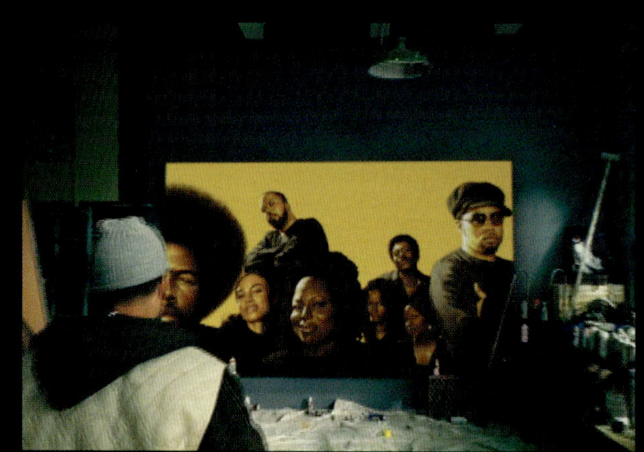

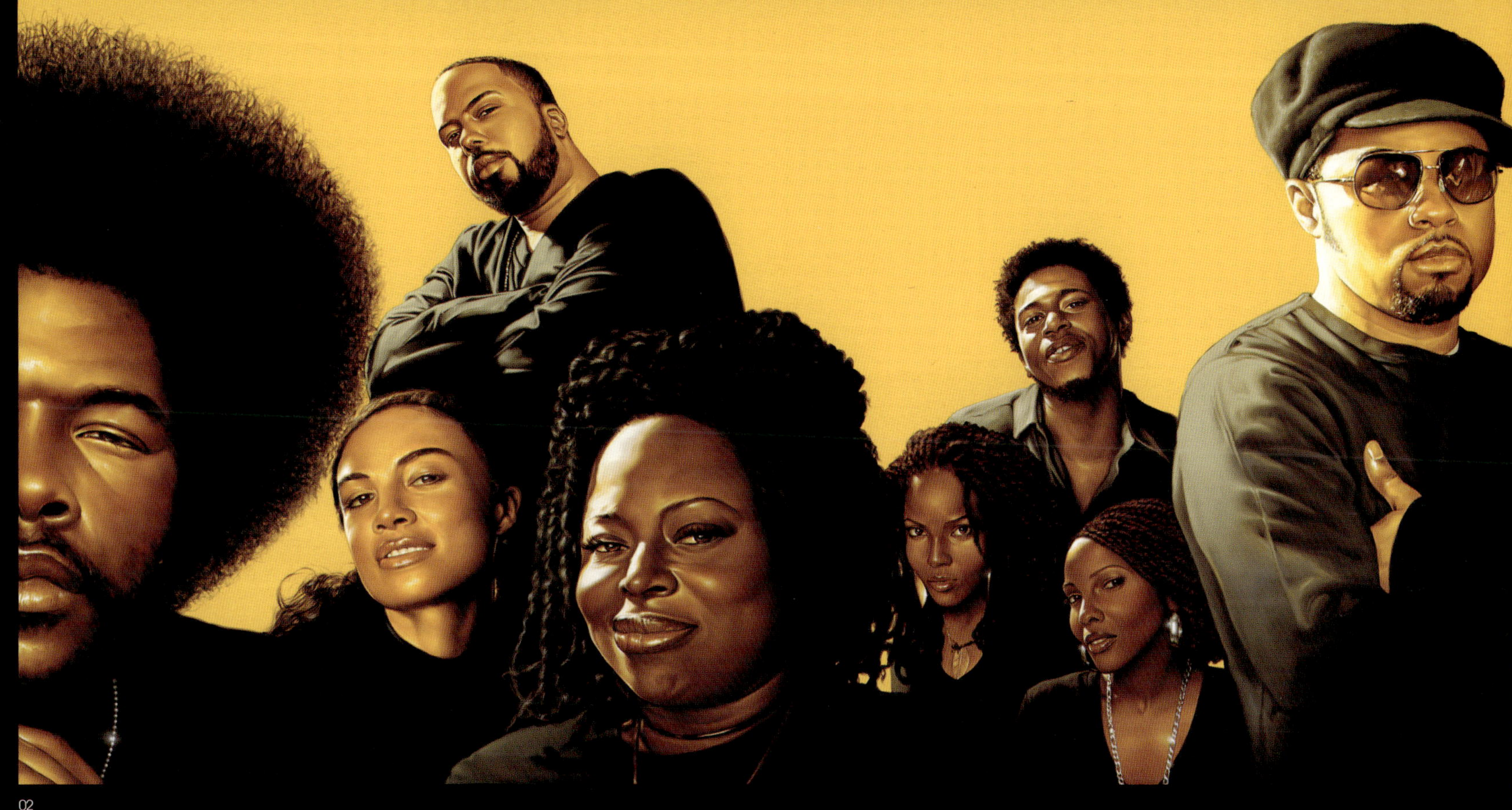

02

Mike Thompson /

01

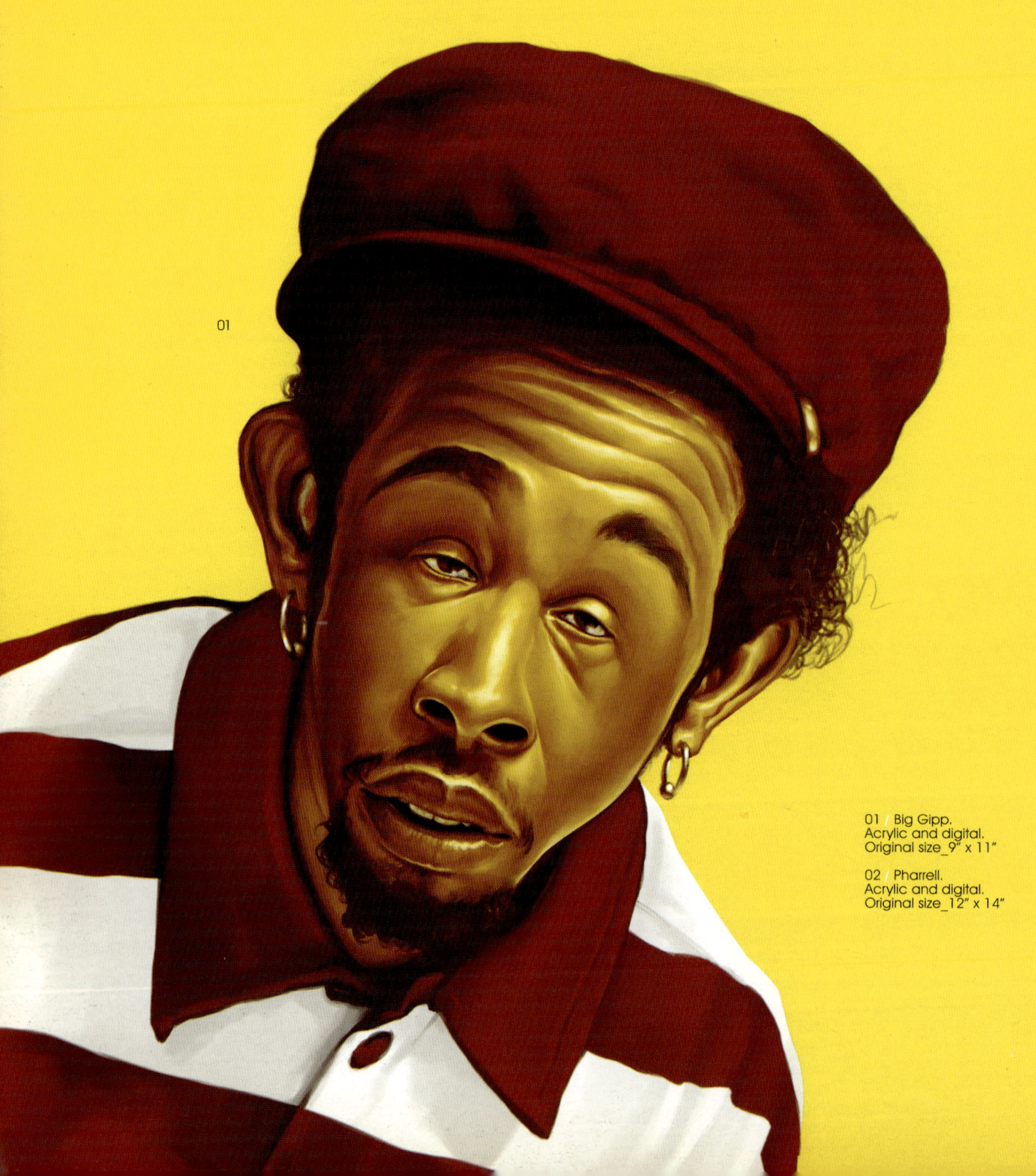

01 / Big Gipp.
Acrylic and digital.
Original size_9" x 11"

02 / Pharrell.
Acrylic and digital.
Original size_12" x 14"

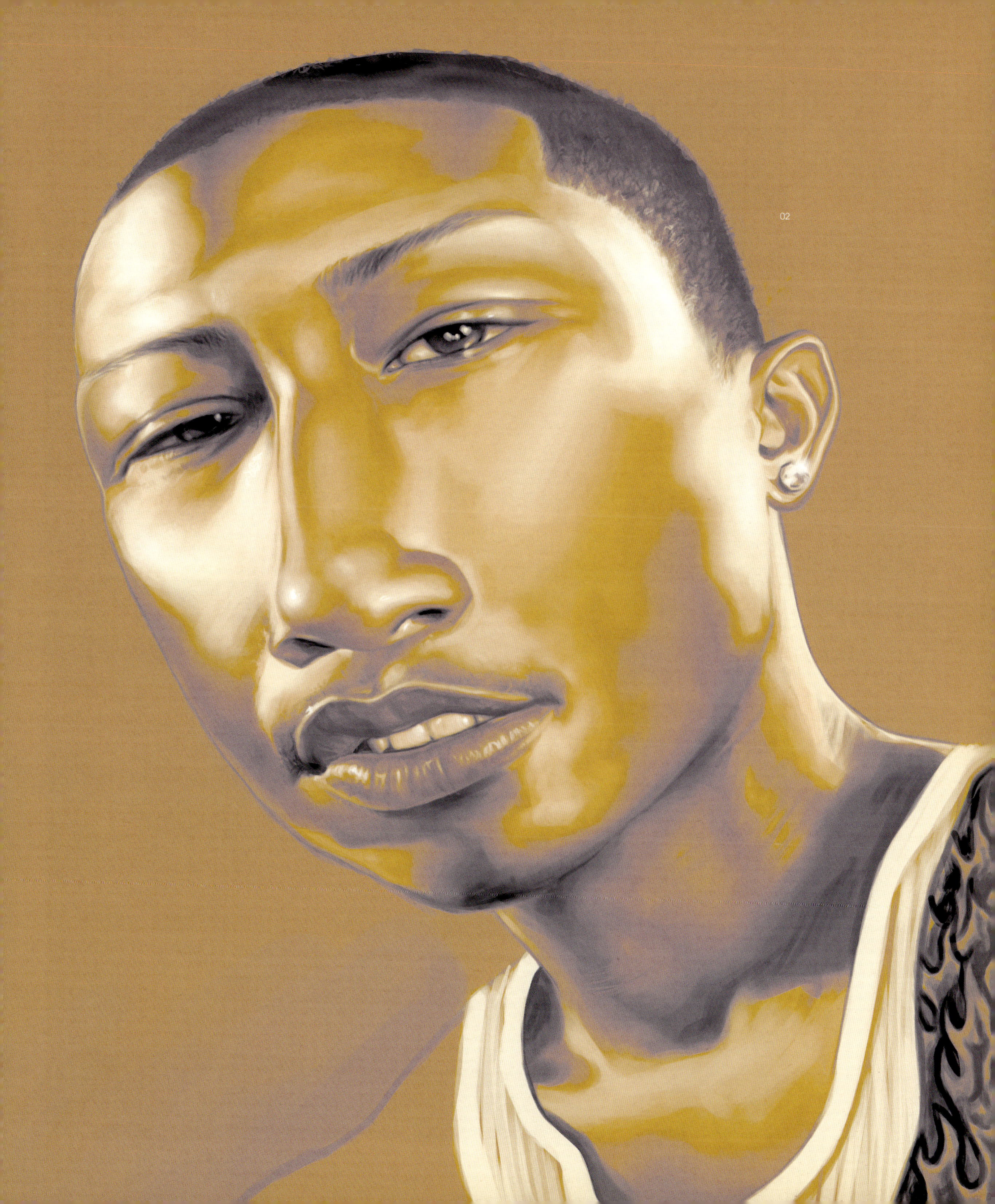
02

01

SAGMEIST
AIGA DETROIT
& CRANBROOK
ACADEMY OF ART
Style = FART
THURSDAY, FEB 25,
AT CRANBROOK
6:30 pm
AIGA MEMBERS FREE, NON-MEMBERS $5.-
DONATIONS:
SPONSORS:
NATIONWIDE PAPERS
STRIPS

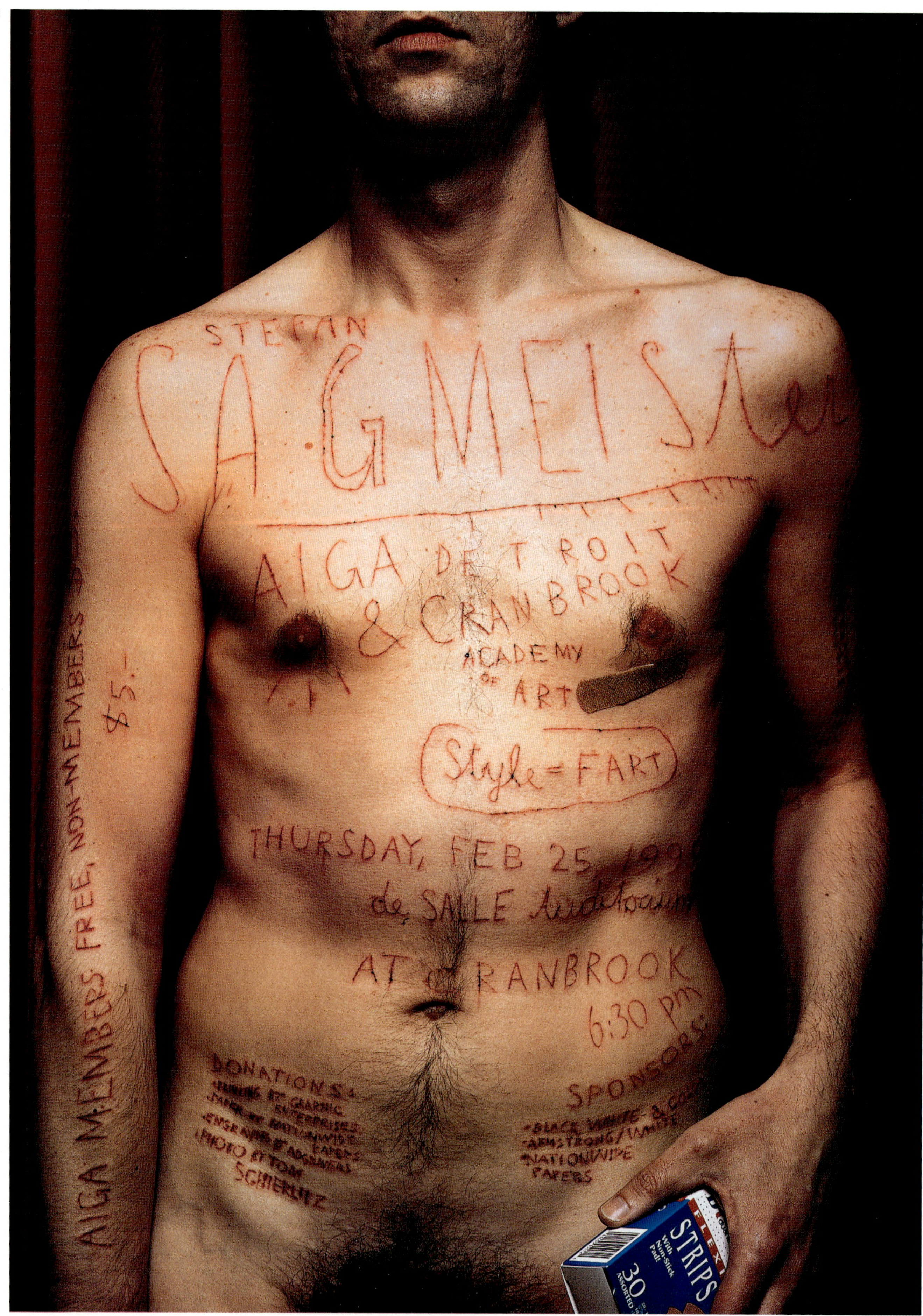

Stefan Sagemeister

Q&A/ 03

What or who inspired you to become an designer?

Like most design students at the time, I was enticed by album covers. I was also starting to work as a writer at a tiny little magazine and discovered that i actually preferred hand drawing the headlines to writing.

Did you experiment with portraiture when studying in your earlier years (uoaa / pratt institute)?

Not in any serious manner. We all had to do self portraits as part of a drawing from nature class, but this was for training purposes (and not for experimental ones).

What were your earliest design commissions?

A brochure for an Alfa Romeo dealership, a business card for my brother in law who was a badminton coach.

What is your favourite piece of your own work?

Our own book, *made you look*, because it a) contains a lot of work and b) created the most direct feedback of anything we ever designed.

You have used and experimented with portraiture in some of your client work, from Lou Reed to David Byrne. What was the thought process behind these? Was using portraiture a suggestion from the individual or self-initiated?

Obviously, in the music business, portraits of stars are a mainstay and it is a little challenge to come up with a direction that is not trite. For the two artists mentioned it was clear from the start that their portraits are going to play a central role.

You have used a kind of self portraiture in both client and personal work, for example the lecture poster for AIGA Detroit. Using yourself and your body in a client job is a pretty brave move for a designer, can you elaborate on this?

I do think that a more personal view can help communicate a message if appropriate.

In our case, all the jobs that showed myself or my body had my studio as the content, i.e. they were lecture posters, exhibition announcements etc. So in a way this is just the utilisation of the oldest advertising device, the package shot.

You have gone through personal bodily injury in the name of art. Was this a carefully thought out plan/idea or a spur-of-the-moment spark of creativity?

This was done in the name of design (not art).

And I tried it out first.

Yes, it did hurt real bad.

For the lecture poster for the AIGA Detroit we tried to visualize the pain that seems to accompany a number of our design projects. Our intern Martin cut all the type into my skin.

Which other creative people do you admire, past and present?

Tibor Kalman. Storm Thorgerson.

If you had to name a famous portrait from the past, which would immediately pop into your head?

Domenico Ghirlandaio's 1488 portrait of Giovanna degli Albizzi in Madrid.

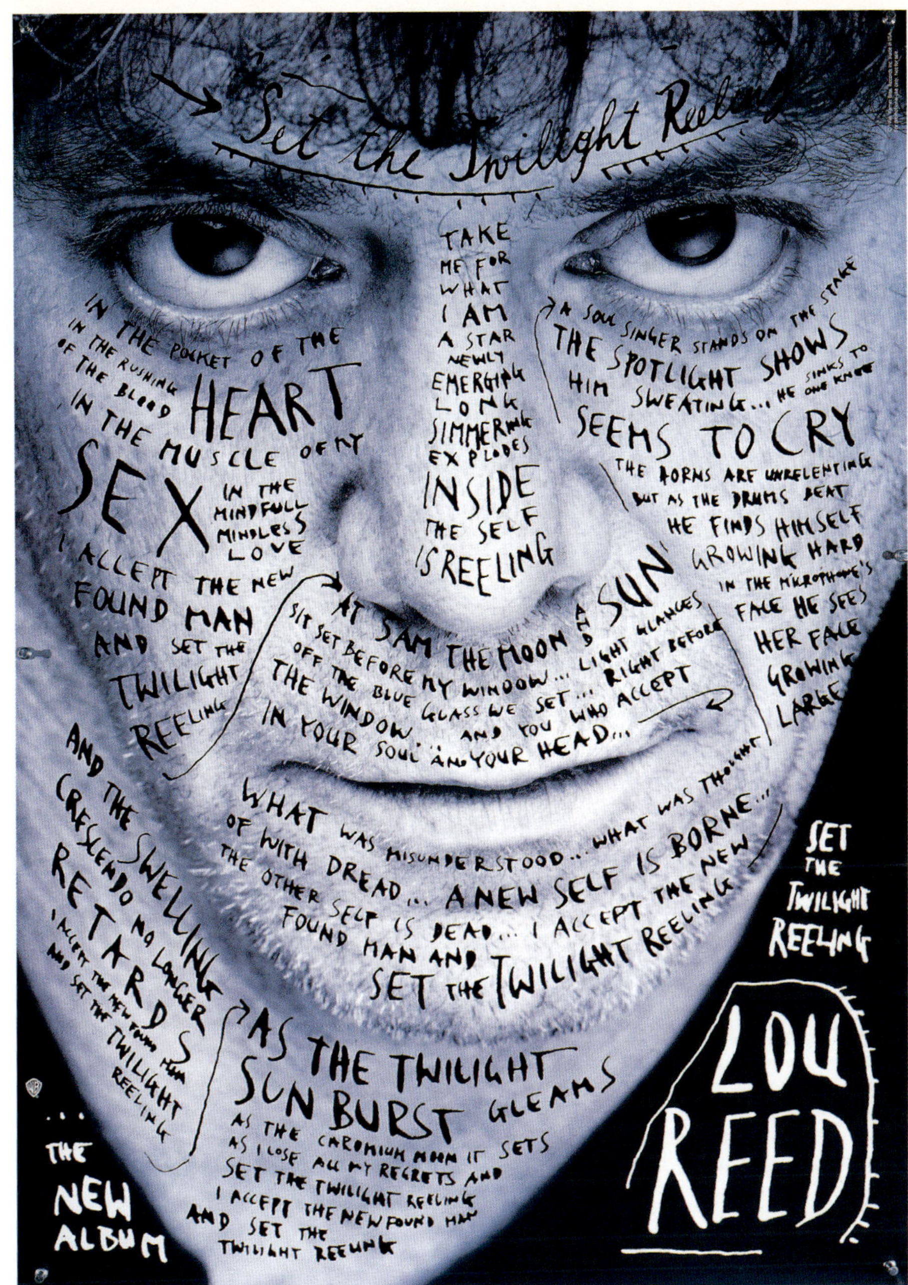

02

Stefan Sagmeister formed the New York based Sagmeister Inc. in 1993 and has since designed branding, graphics and packaging for clients as diverse as the Rolling Stones, HBO, the Guggenheim Museum and Time Warner. Having been nominated five times for the Grammies he finally won one for the Talking Heads boxed set. He also earned practically every important international design award.

In 2001 a best selling monograph about his work titled *Sagmeister, Made you Look* was published by Booth-Clibborn editions. Solo shows on Sagmeister Inc's work have been mounted in Zurich, Vienna, New York, Berlin, Tokyo, Osaka, Prague, Cologne and Seoul. He teaches in the graduate department of the School of Visual Art in New York and has been appointed as the Frank Stanton Chair at The Cooper Union School of Art, New York. He lectures extensively on all continents.

A native of Austria, he received his MFA in graphic design from the University of Applied Arts in Vienna and, as a Fulbright Scholar, a master's degree from Pratt Institute in New York.

01 / Aiga Detroit poster.
Photography, unretouched.
Original size_27.5" x 39"

02 / Lou Reed poster.
Ink on photography.
Offset print.
Original size_26.7" x 39"

01

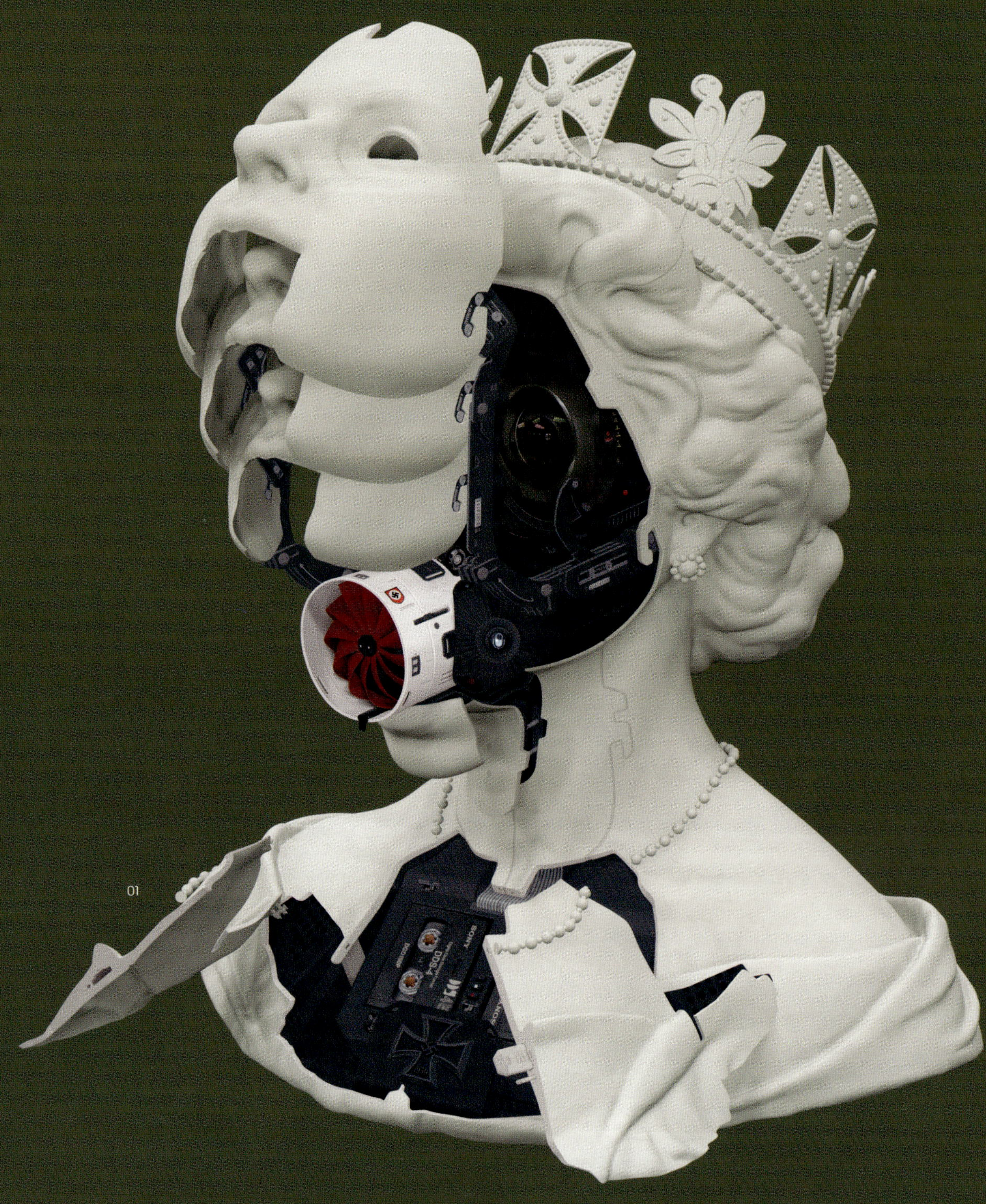

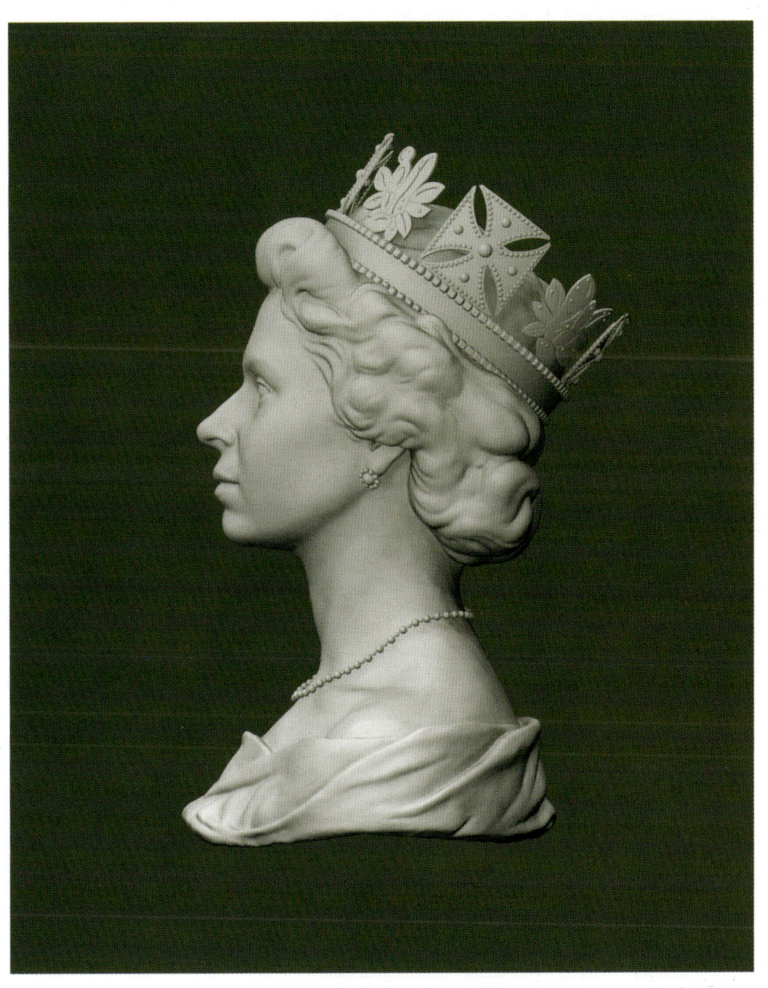

02

01 / 6MM Hate Head 01
3D scan of sculpture.
Digitally reworked.
Original size_12" x 32"

02 / 6MM Hate Head 02
3D scan of sculpture.
Digitally reworked.
Original size_24" x 16"

Johnny Hardstaff /

Adam Pointer /

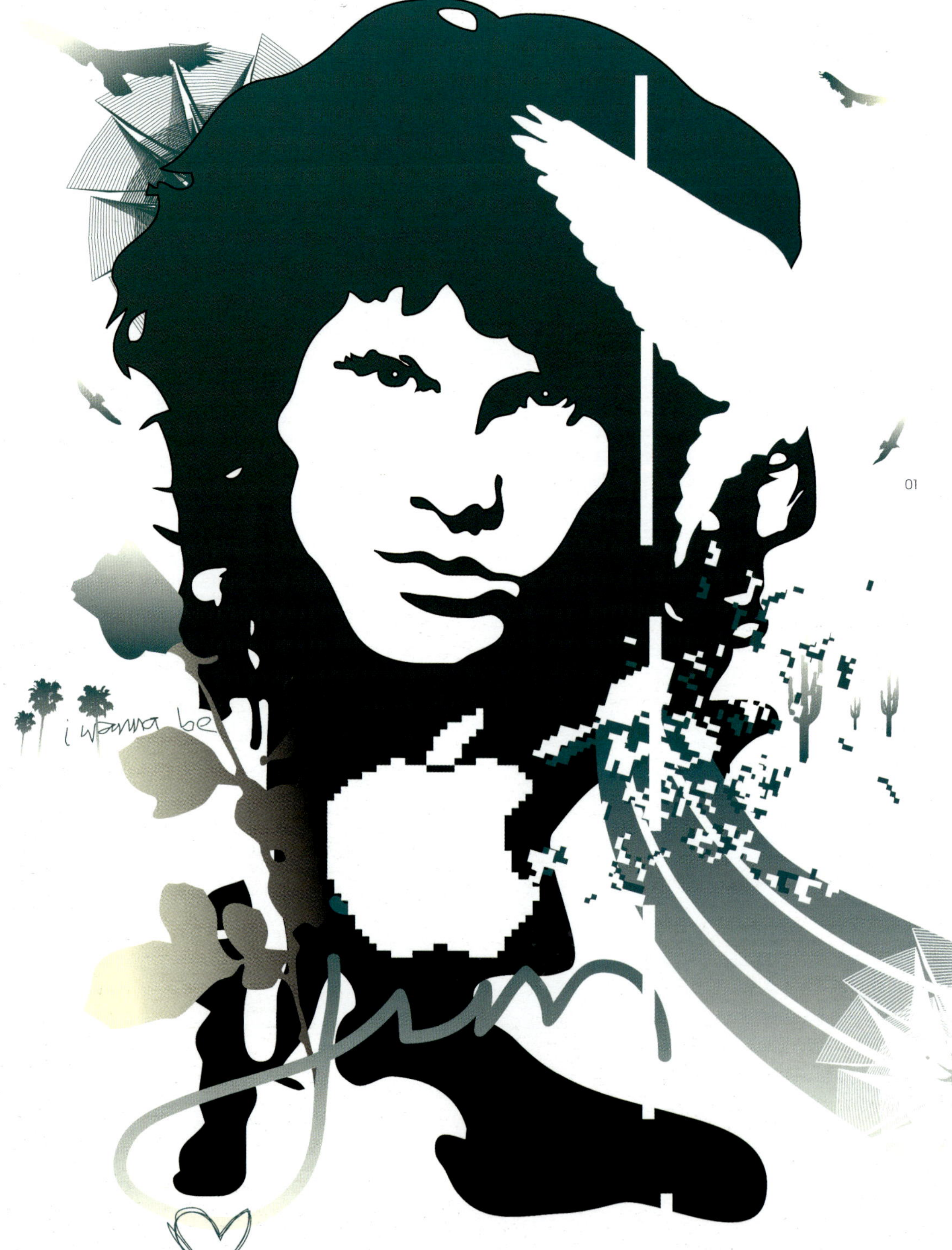

01

01 / Jim.
Vector.

02 / Koi Drop.
Vector.

Nico, Represented by
Dutch Uncle Agency

Nico /

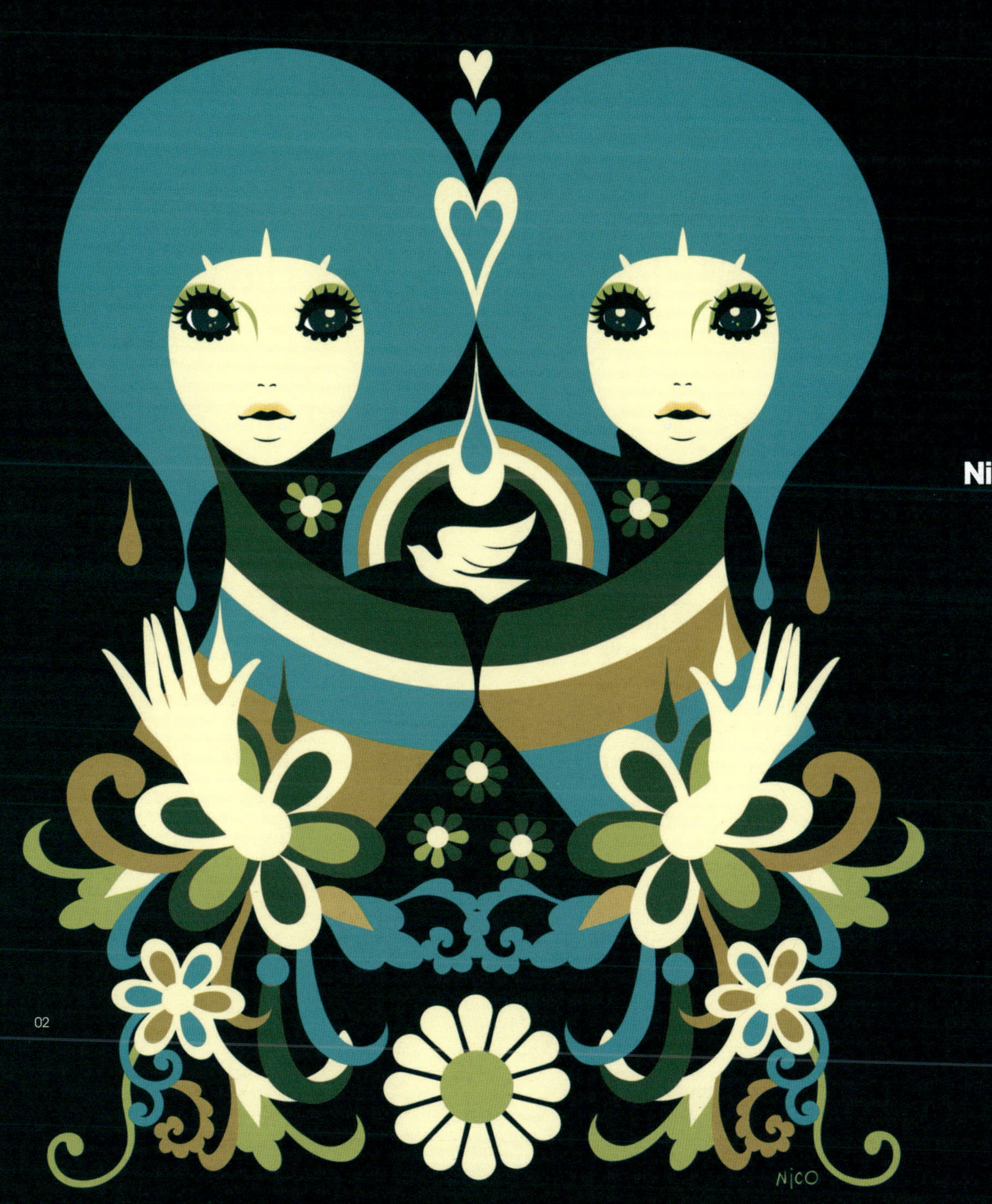

02

01

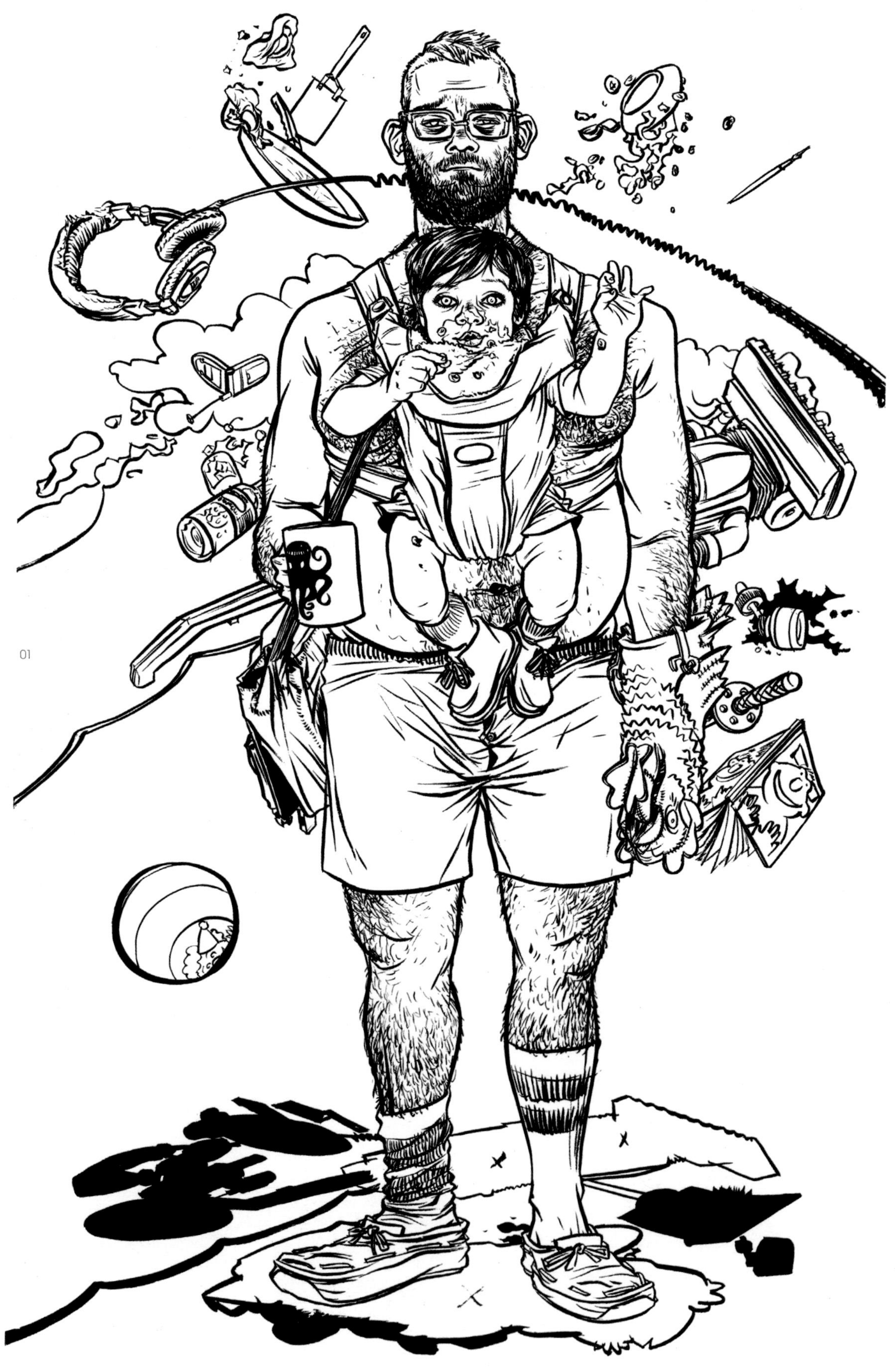

Nathan Fox

01 / Fatherhood.
Pen on paper.
Original size_12" x 32"

02 / Girl Shirt.
Pen on paper.
Original size_24" x 16"

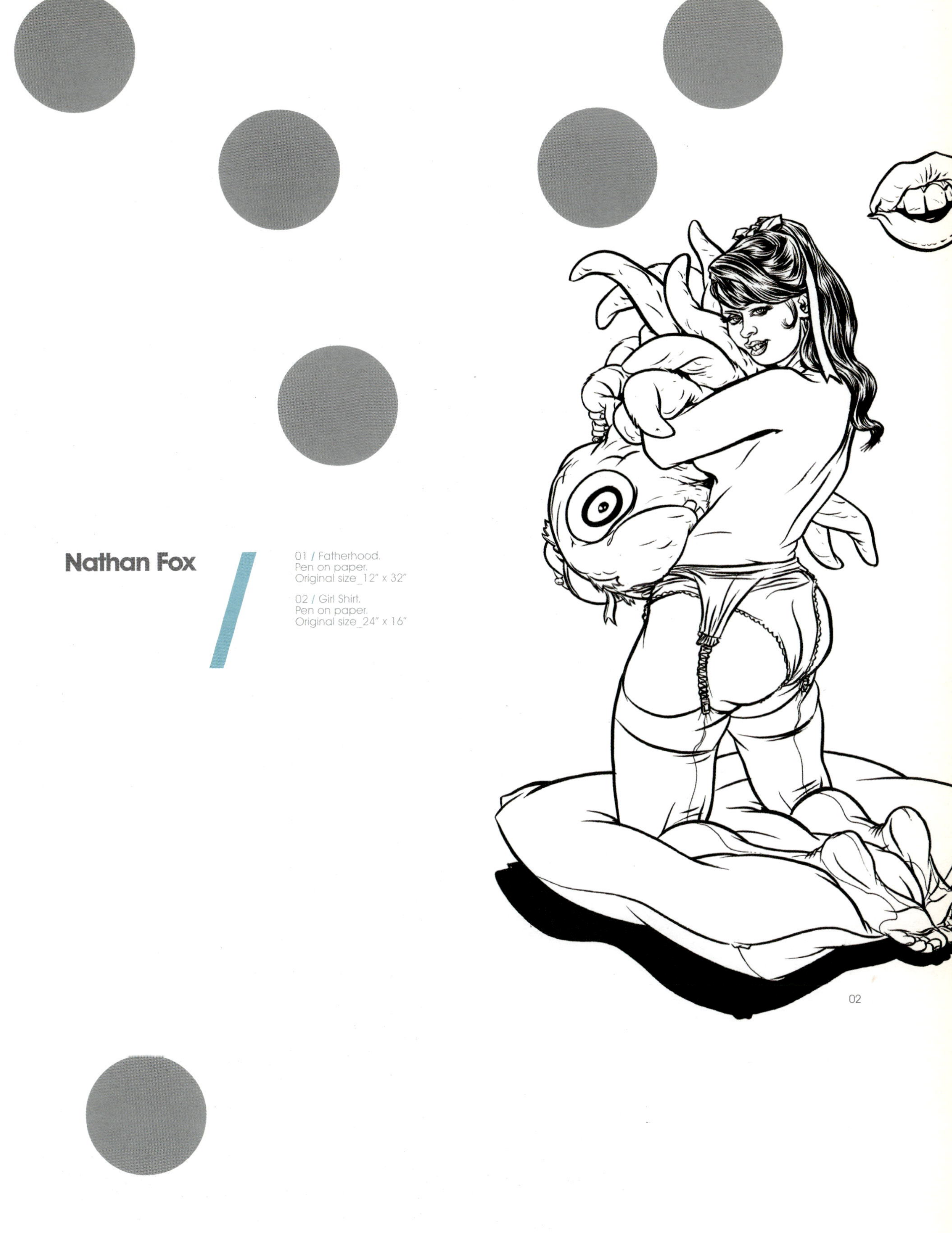

02

‘A PORTRAIT, TO BE A WORK OF ART, NEITHER MUST NOR MAY RESEMBLE THE SITTER,

ONE MUST PAINT ITS ATMOSPHERE’

Umberto Boccioni

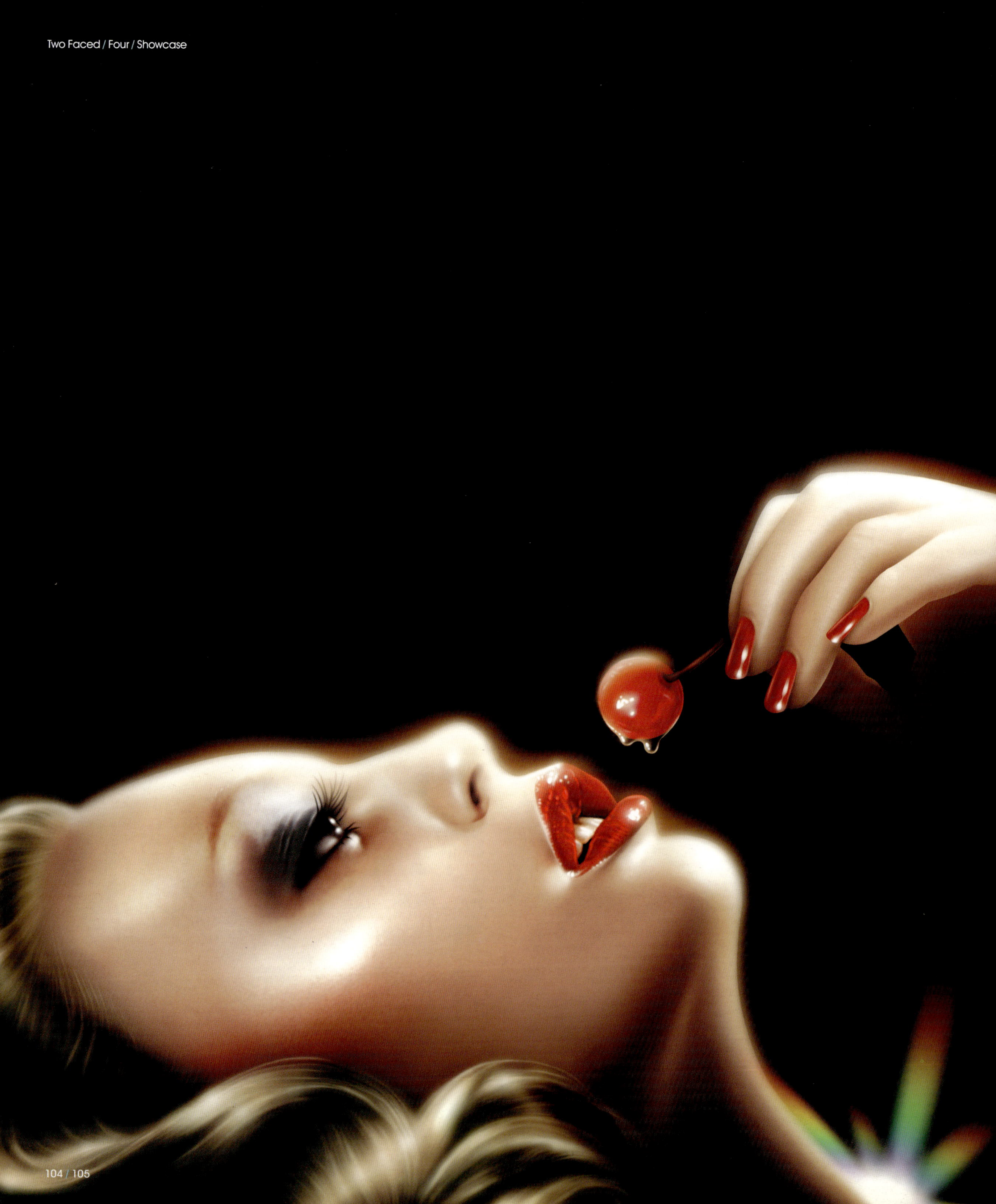

Arno

Cyan D /

Cyan D (aka M Edmonson) refers to her practice as a representation of painting rather than as being representational. Despite the overt use of faces as her source, she regards her work as neither figurative paintings or as portraits of people. Employing the momentary seduction of fashion photography to lure the viewer into the world of idealised beauty, her paintings mimic the styles and codes of the desire industry to question the values and obsessions of aspirational perfection.

Just as in fashion photography, where the model is a support for the product and contextualises it, such images also support and contextualise her paintings. Although seductive, the ideal they present becomes hyper-real: the image is devoid of identity, and paradoxically, an empty façade which is quickly consumed giving way to the anxiety and obsession that assert these paintings as paintings. Beyond the image which gives them their presence, what is being portrayed here is the question of aspirational perfection of painting itself.

As the viewer engages with these works and scans the surface, shifting their reading between fantasy and the tropes of modernist painting, the skin of the image and the skin of painted surface, these works become paintings of unattainable desire.

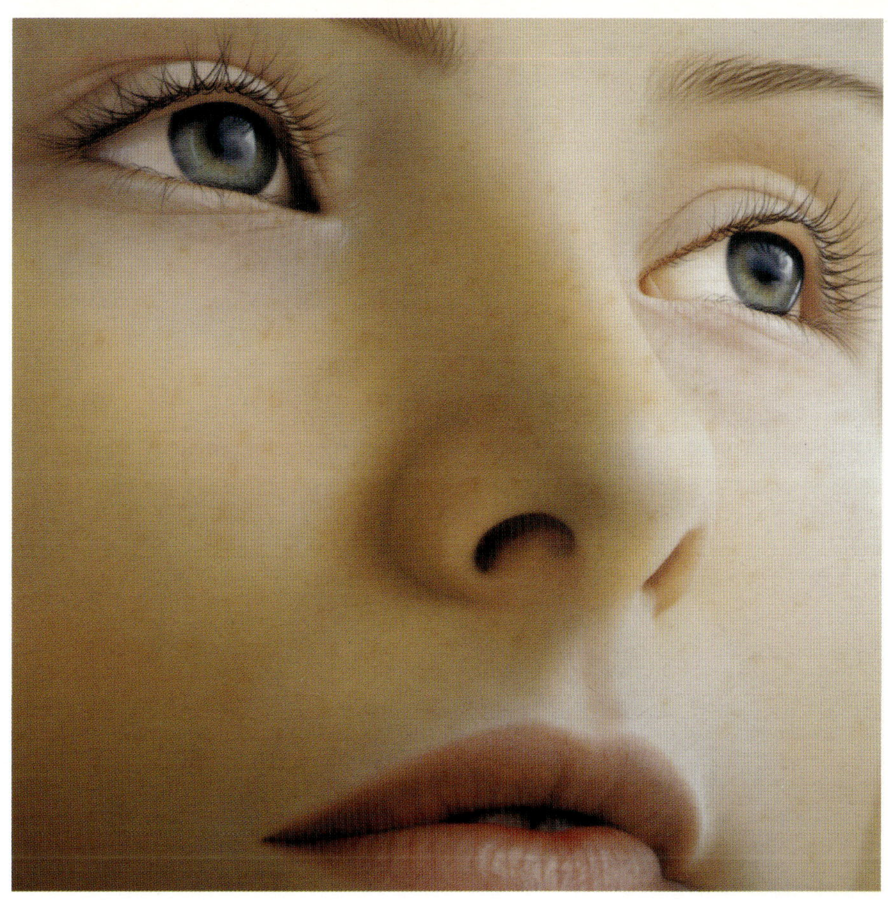

02

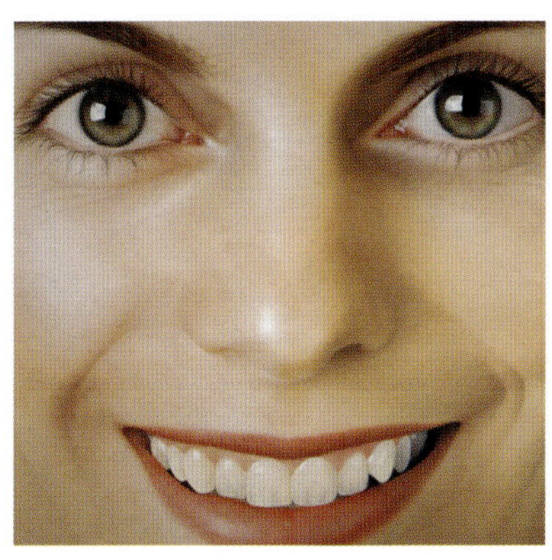

01

01 / Virtually Everything.
Oil on canvas.
Original size_72" x 72"

02 / Come Sail Your Ships With Me.
Oil on canvas.
Original size_72" x 72"

03 / I've Seen Your Seaside Eyes.
Oil on canvas.
Original size_72" x 72"

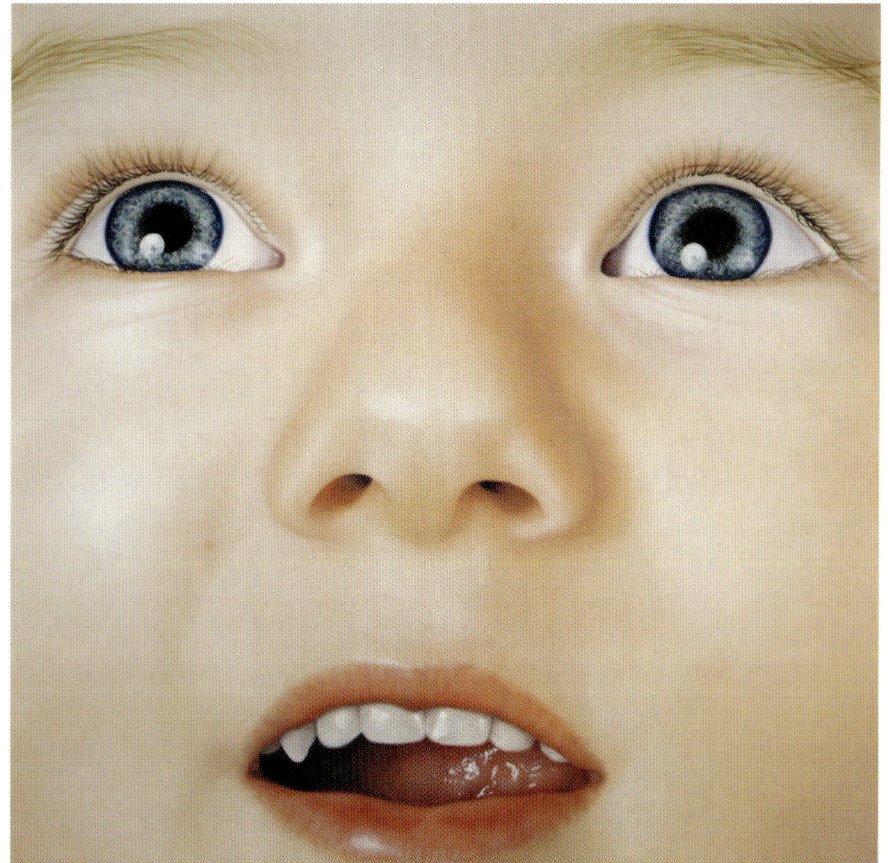

03

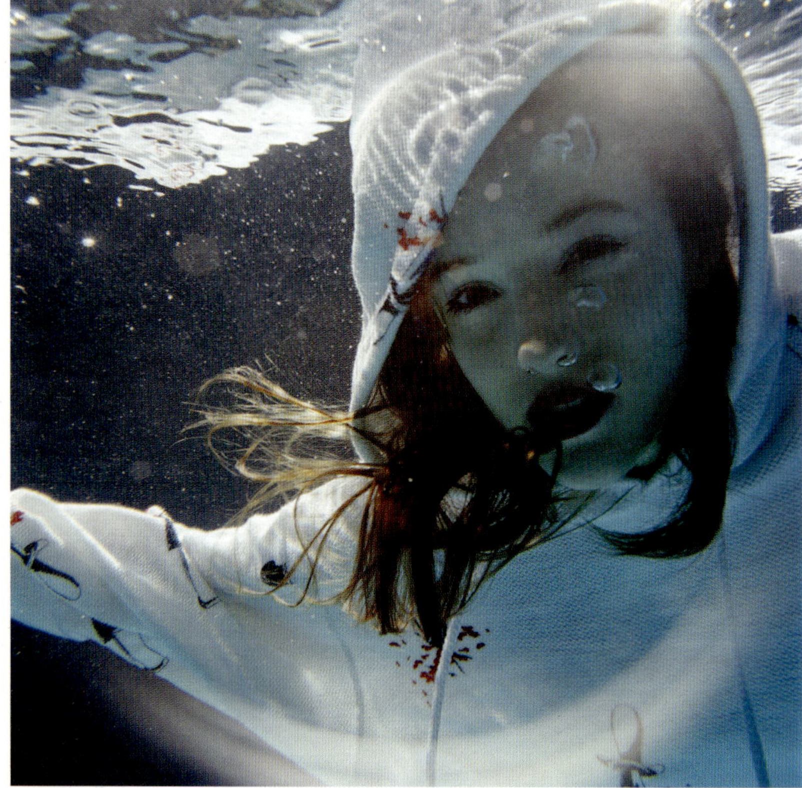

01

01 - 02 / I C'ant See What You Are Saying.
C-Type prints.
Original size_43.3" x 43.3"

Thymann /

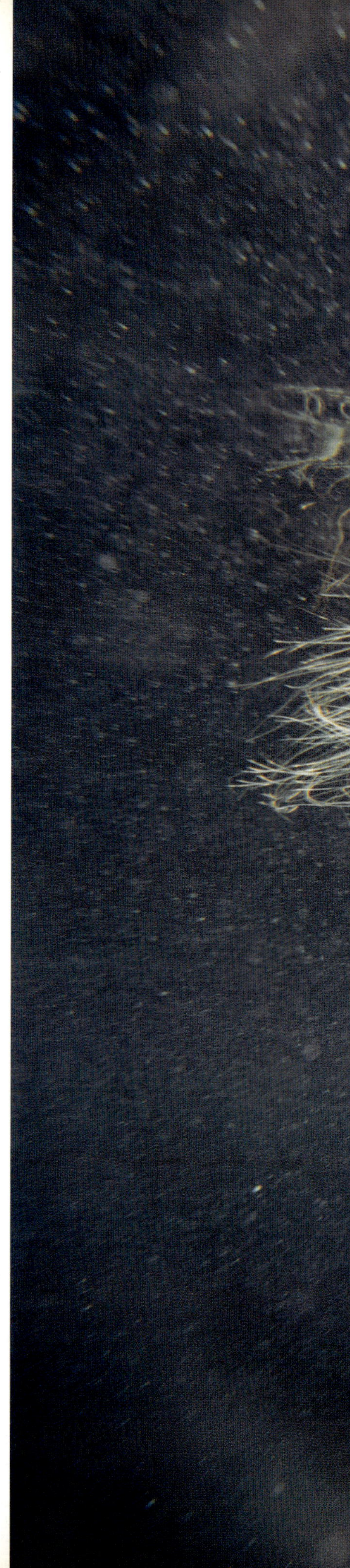

02

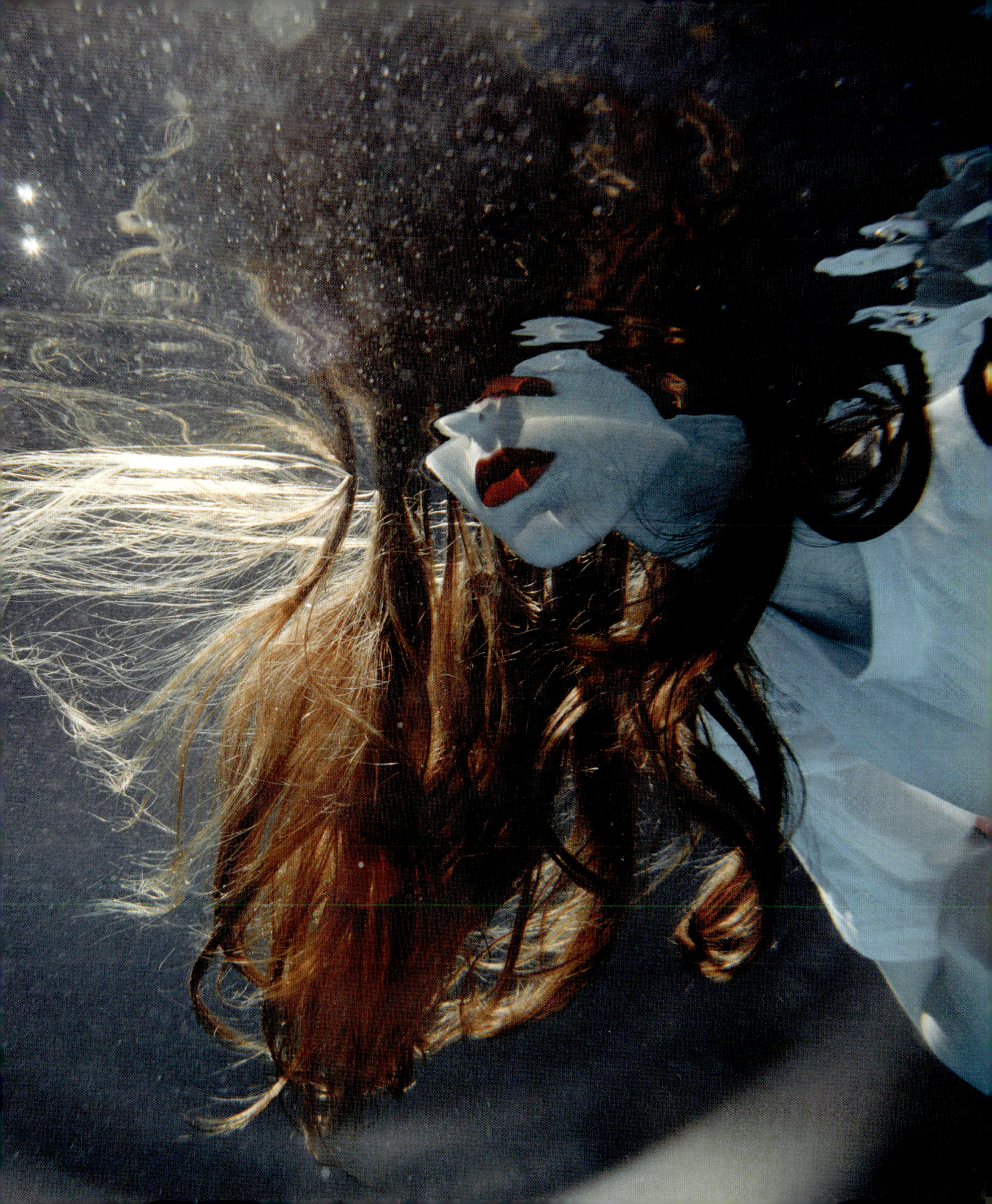

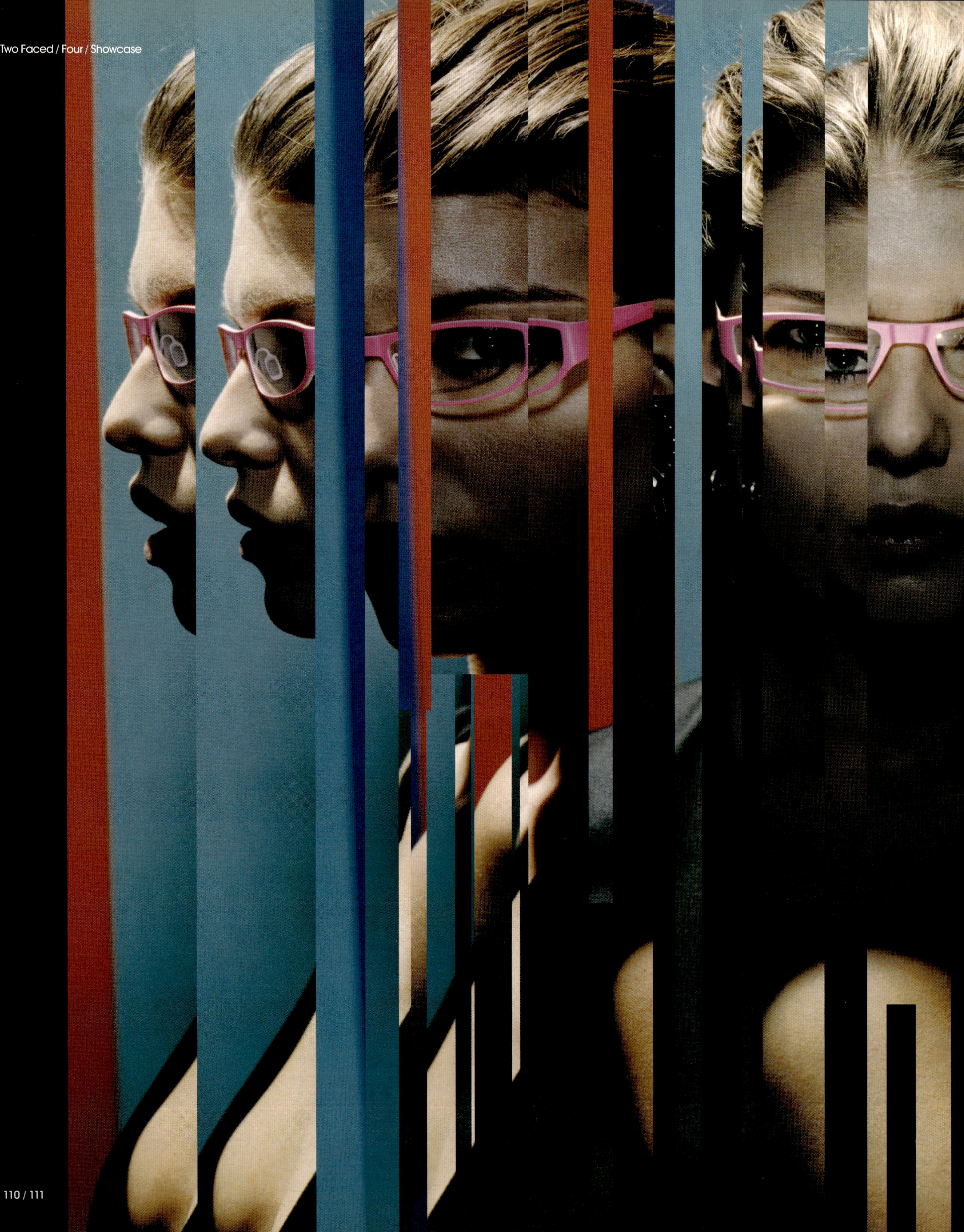

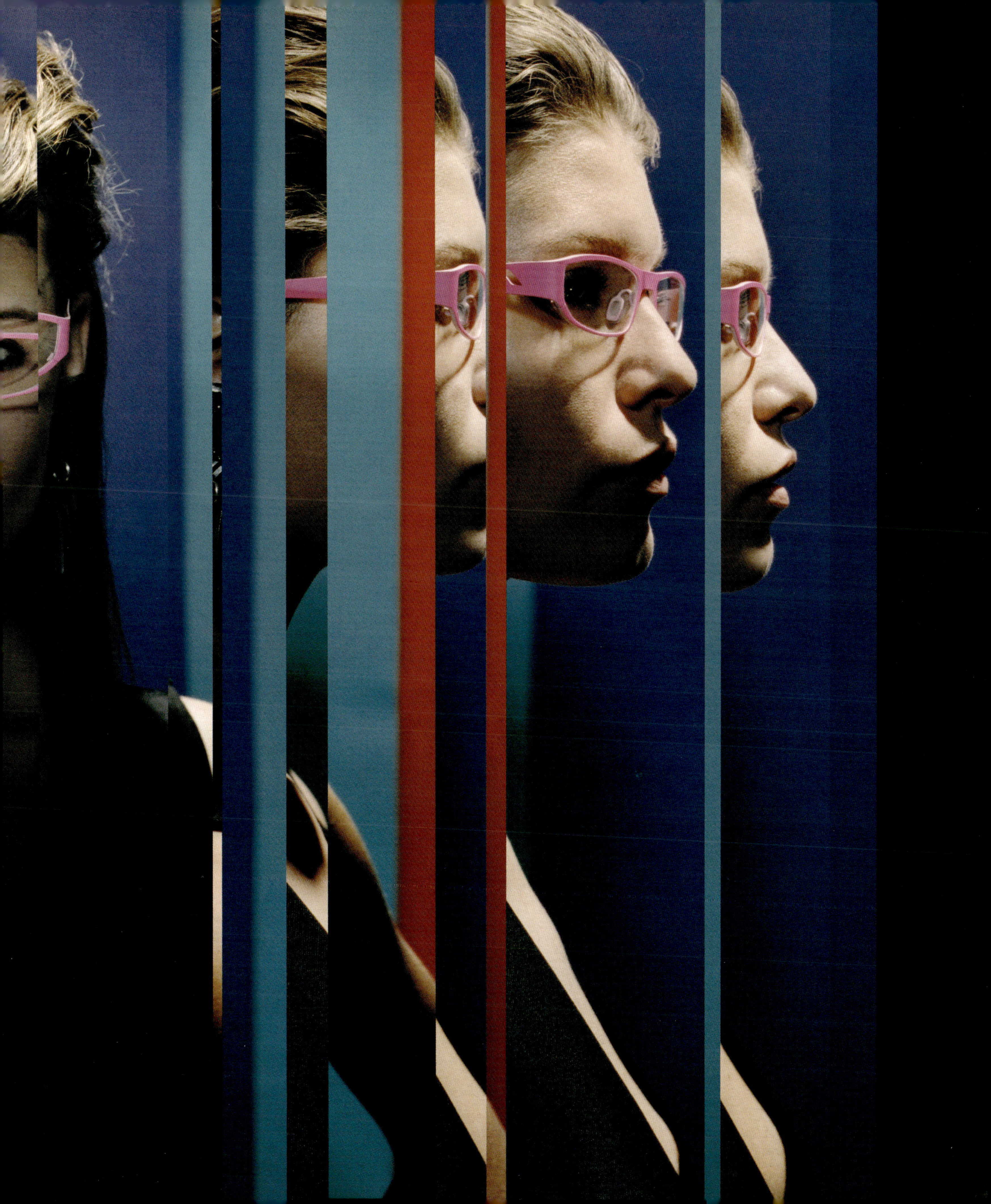

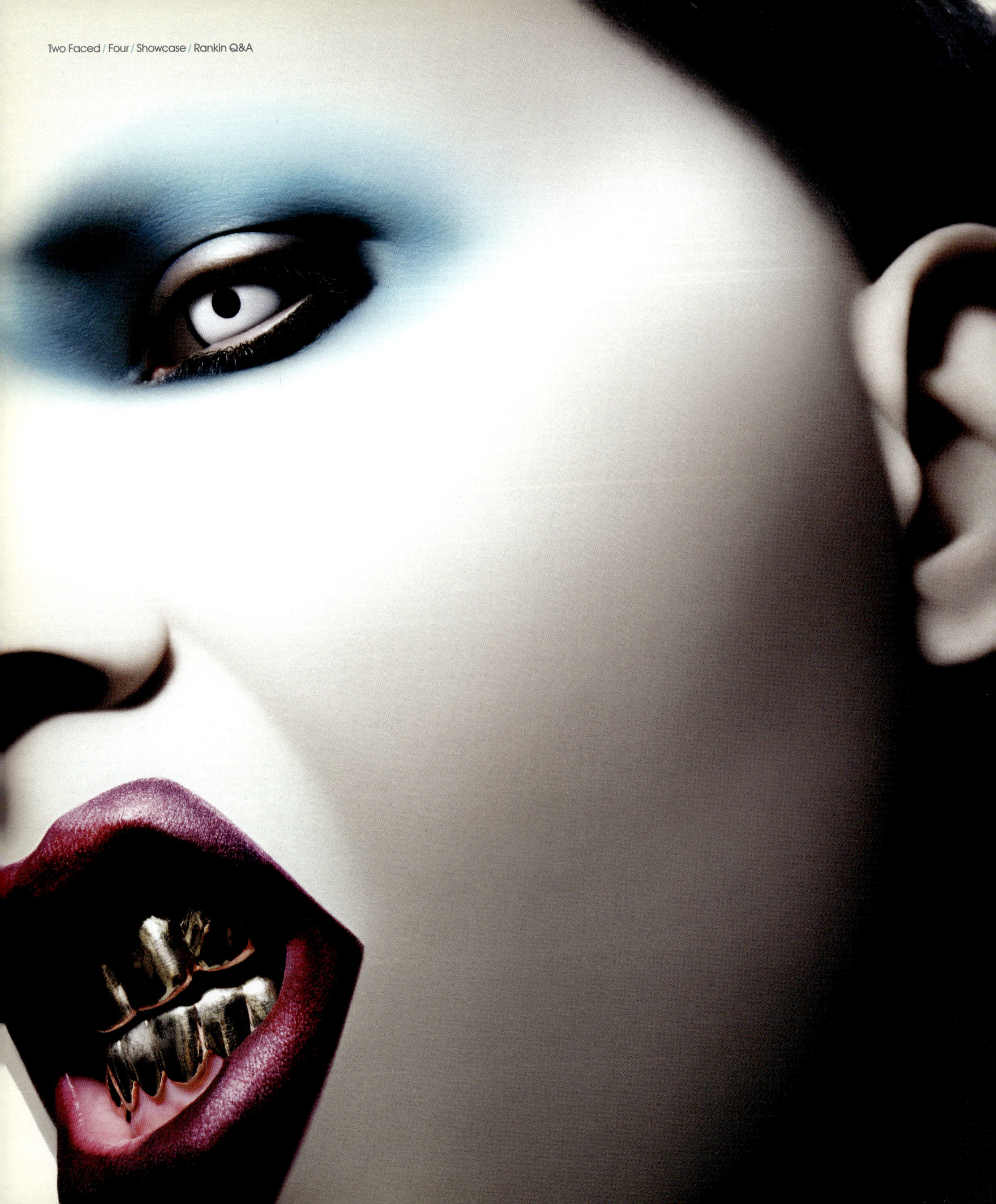

Rankin
_Q&A/ 04

At what point in your career did you have to stop searching for work and just relied on it coming to you?

That hasn't happened yet! Also I have to say I don't think you should ever do that in your career. If you do you're just resting on your laurels and the reality is you're only as good as the last job you do. If you want to create interesting work – you have to keep pushing yourself both within yourself and to other people!

Some people say I am too much of a self publicist, but I just love doing what I do and want people to see my work - so I can get the best work I can.

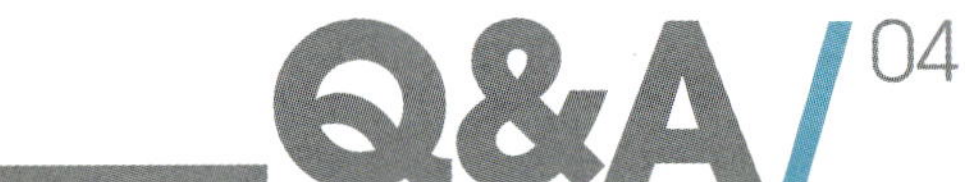

You have taken pictures of a large group of people, ranging from Arnold Schwarzenegger to Tony Blair. Do you have any particular favourites?

Not really – my job is loads of fun whoever I'm doing photos of. Although I have to say taking naked pictures of the world's most beautiful women is tough to beat.

What's the weirdest thing that's happened on a shoot?

A woman masturbated in front of me. It was for my female nudes project where the women came up with their own ideas. It was such a strange experience as I realised pretty quickly she was getting off on me watching and taking the pictures. Each time I released the shutter she would moan.

I was literally on the floor and couldn't take my eyes away from the view finder in case I laughed. She climaxed in exactly 18 frames. I mean honestly I'm good but NOT that good.

Very unusual.

Photographing people is what you have become famous for, have you ever been approached or had the desire to do abstract or landscape photography?

Yep I love doing things like that all of the time – it's very important for me to push myself! I'm always keen to do projects that are unusual or demanding.

How do you assess your work? Are you ever 100% happy with the final product?

No I'm never 100% happy with anything – I think it's important to be your biggest critic.

'She climaxed in exactly 18 frames....

From your collection of cameras, which is your favourite? If you could only keep one, which would it be?

The Mamiya RZ67 – I think it's the best camera in the world.

Are you interested in other creative mediums, rather than film and photography. As you branch out into other mediums do you still label yourself as a photographer?

Yea. I'd love to direct a play and a musical.

You were included in a short list of 10 photographers to take a portrait photograph of the Queen for her golden jubilee, how did you feel when you were approached about this?

Privileged – I honestly couldn't believe the Queen knew who I was or "the establishment" would be at all interested in me! The most unusual thing is that after I'd taken the portrait so many people asked if I'd got her nude!

How weird is that!

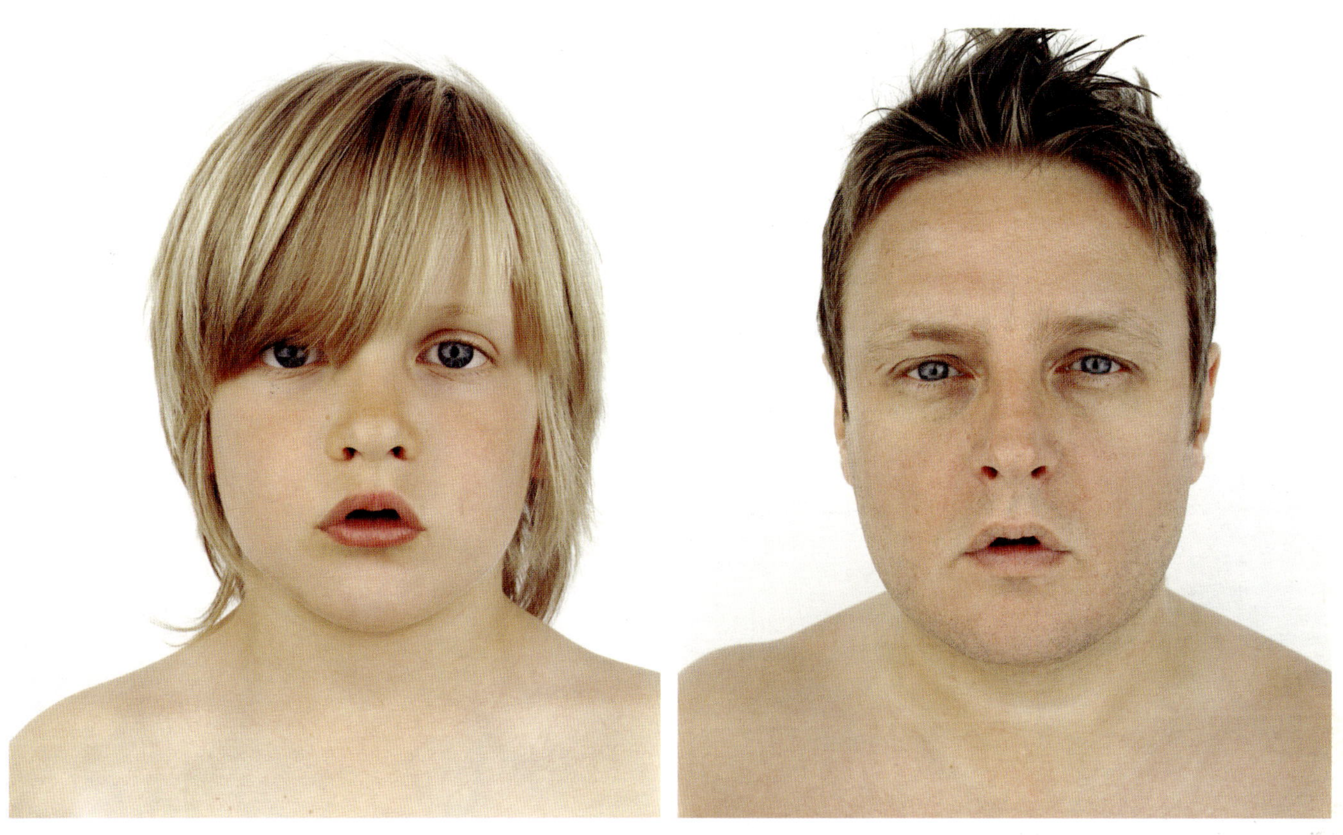

...I mean honestly I'm good, but NOT that good. Very unusual'.

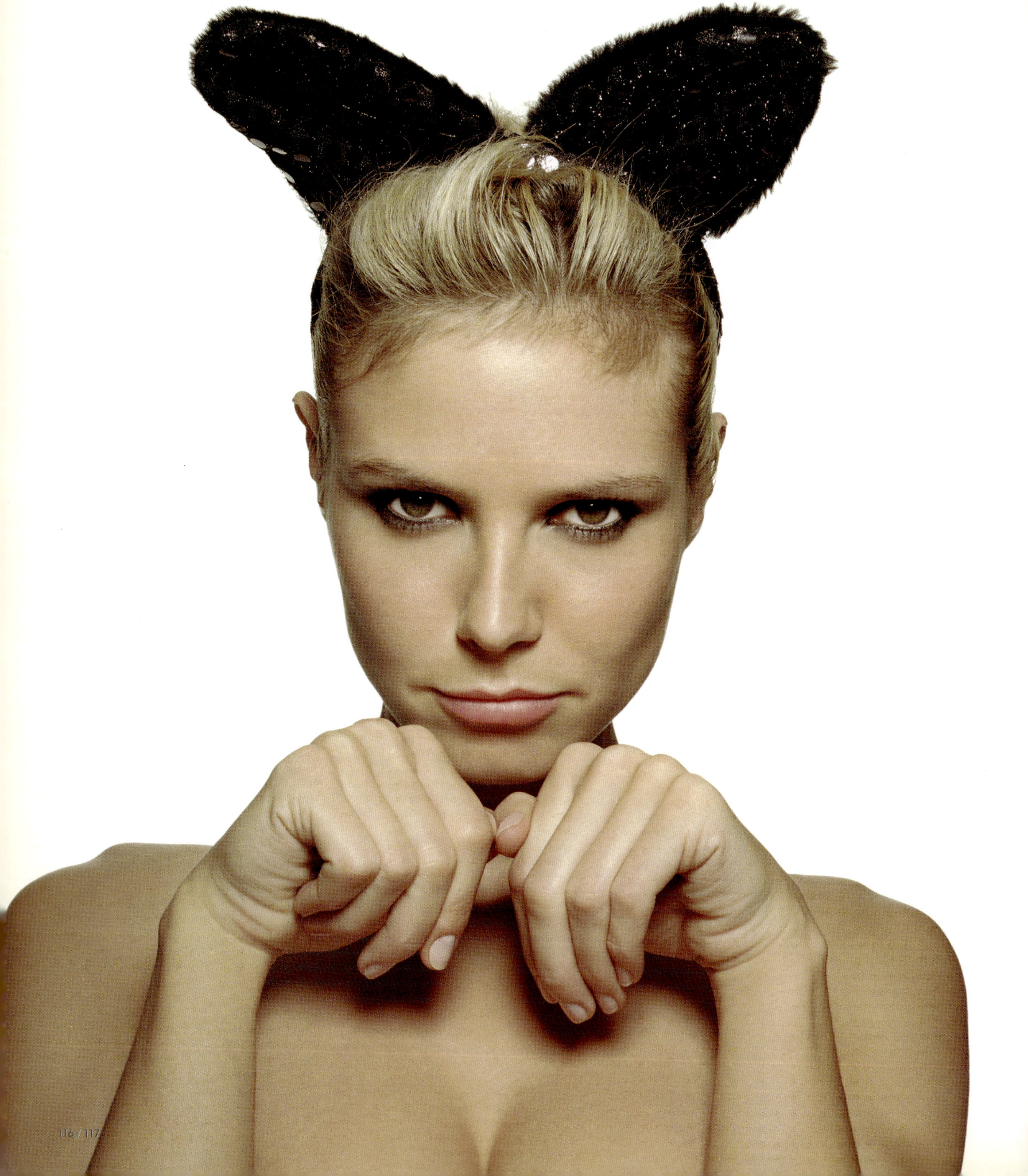

From his iconic shot of Kylie lying naked and prostrate, which graced a million bedroom walls, to the Queen smiling enigmatically in front of the red, white and blue, Rankin's iconic, intimate portraiture style, and his mischievous eye have gained him a reputation as one of the world's leading photographers.

Photographer, publisher, and most recently film director; Rankin established his reputation when he launched *Dazed & Confused* with his business partner Jefferson Hack in 1991. Completely new in its approach, the magazine fused the pair's editorial vision with Rankin's photographic talents to present the faces of the time in a less mediated way. Right at the heart of London's creative explosion that gave rise to the Britpop phemomenon with bands like Blur and Pulp and the accompanying fashion boom and stylists Katie Grand and Katy England and designers such as Alexander McQueen, who have gone on to dominate the industry, it is Rankin's commitment to publishing some of the most ground-breaking magazines of his generation and his support for young photographers that have further earned him a reputation as a leading cultural and trend opinion former. As well as magazines Rankin has produced a string of highly successful exhibitions, ad campaigns and books. He has shot front covers for German *Vogue, Harpers Bazaar, Arena* and *GQ*.

An infamous workaholic, Rankin has photographed subjects from Kate Moss to the Queen, from Tony Blair to Oasis. Looking at his body of work it is also clear that celebrity holds little allure for him, some of his most outstanding images are from a series of nudes featuring ordinary people who answered an advert in *Time Out* asking how they would like to be photographed. He consistently seduces with his images, by drawing out individual personality, while considering and commenting on broader ideas.

Rising to every challenge, Rankin has never shied from portraying difficult subject matters, addressing issues from domestic violence to body image in both his personal work as well as charity and commercial projects. He made headlines again with his campaign for Dove showing women who differed from the usual stick-thin advertising stereotype. He has shot charity campaigns for Amnesty International, Everyman, Special Olympics, Refuge, Women's Aid, and a recent project for breast cancer research amongst many others.

Not content with still images, he has turned his lens to filmmaking. The short film he directed for Film Four, 'Perfect', was one of the few shorts shown at the Los Angeles, Raindance and Edinburgh film festivals. His first feature film, 'The Lives of the Saints', a darkly comic morality tale written by Tony Grisoni ('Fear and Loathing in Las Vegas') and starring an all British cast. Distributed by Tartan films, the film has been shown in numerous festivals this year, winning the grand jury prize in Salento.

Rankin will be publishing several books of personal work this year. He lives in London and has a 10-year-old son, Lyle.

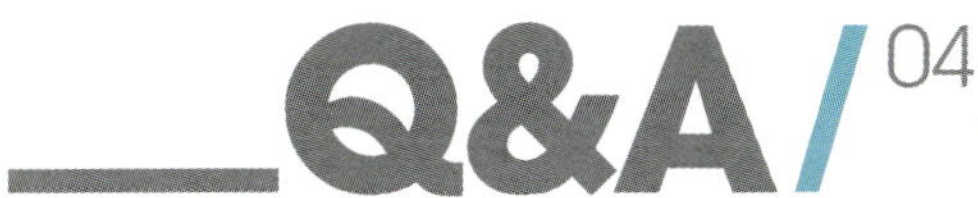

Who was your most difficult subject? Can you say?
Vinnie Jones – he just didn't want to be there!

Is there anyone you haven't shot yet, that you would love to get in your studio?
Sean Penn, Johnny Depp, and of course God.

If you could choose anyone to take a picture/portrait of yourself, who would it be?
Bailey

If you had to name a famous portrait from the past, which would immediately pop into your head?
The portraits by Avedon are legendary and incredibly memorable.

Arno /

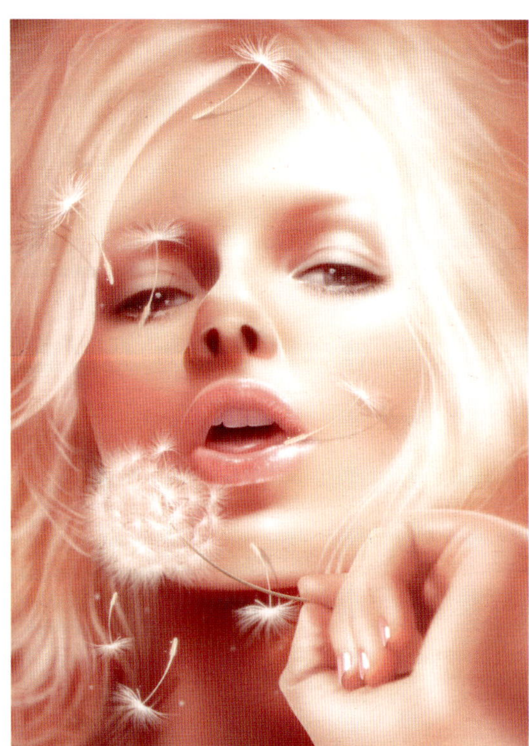

01

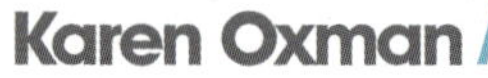

Karen Oxman /

01 / Pink.

02 / Sunburn.

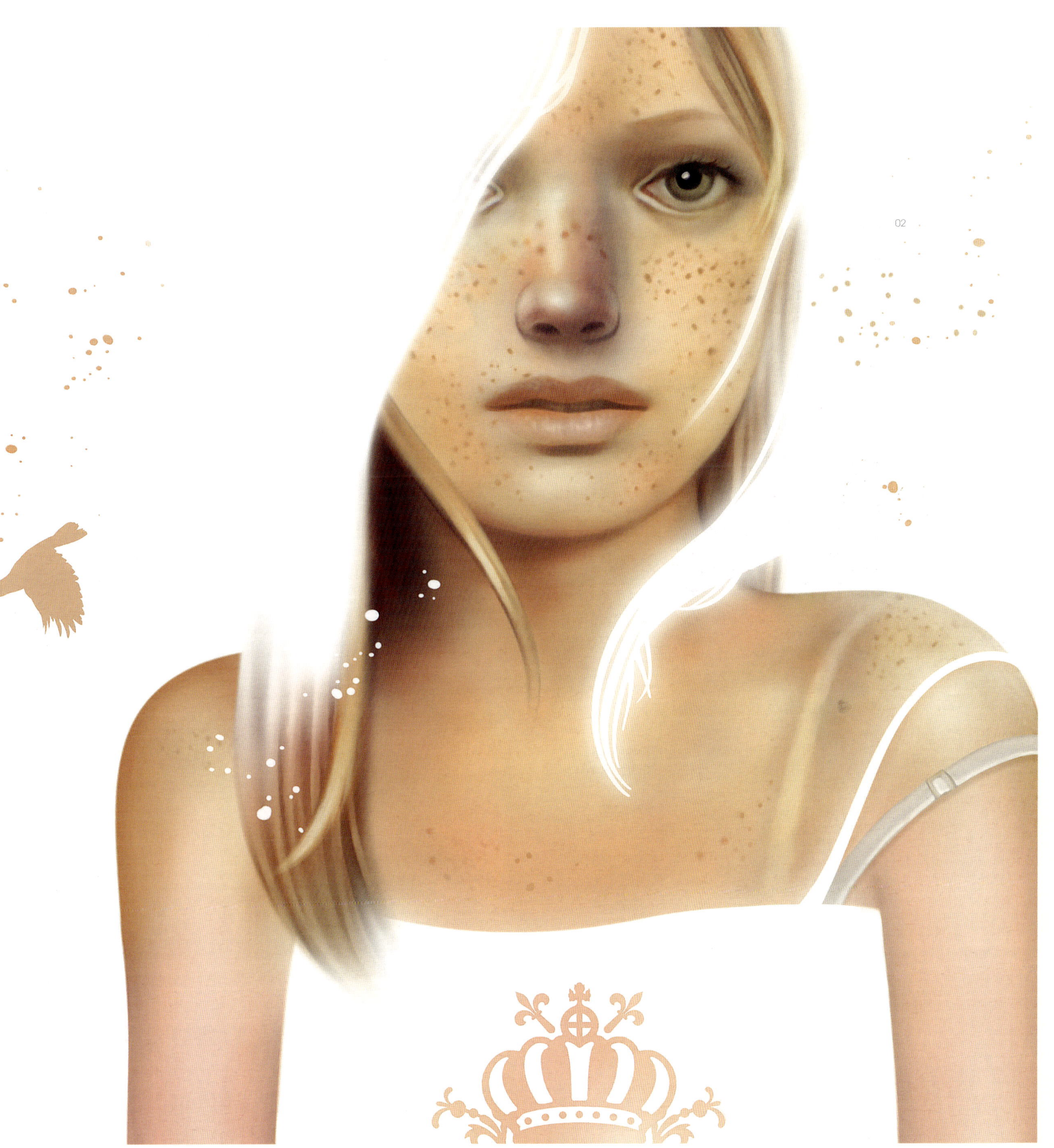
02

02 / Falling.
Photoshop, Painter IX,
Illustrator.
Original size_11.7" x 16.5"

02 / Downfall.
Photoshop, Painter IX,
Illustrator.
Original size_11.7" x 16.5"

Tom Bagshaw /

01

02

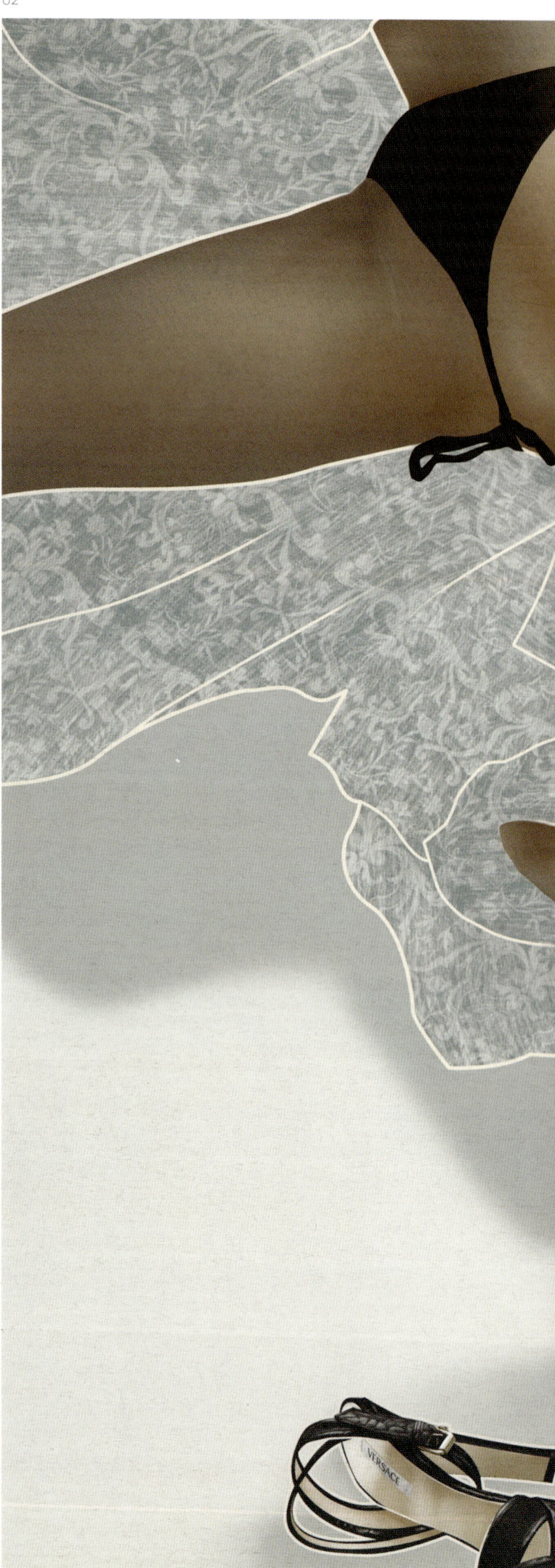

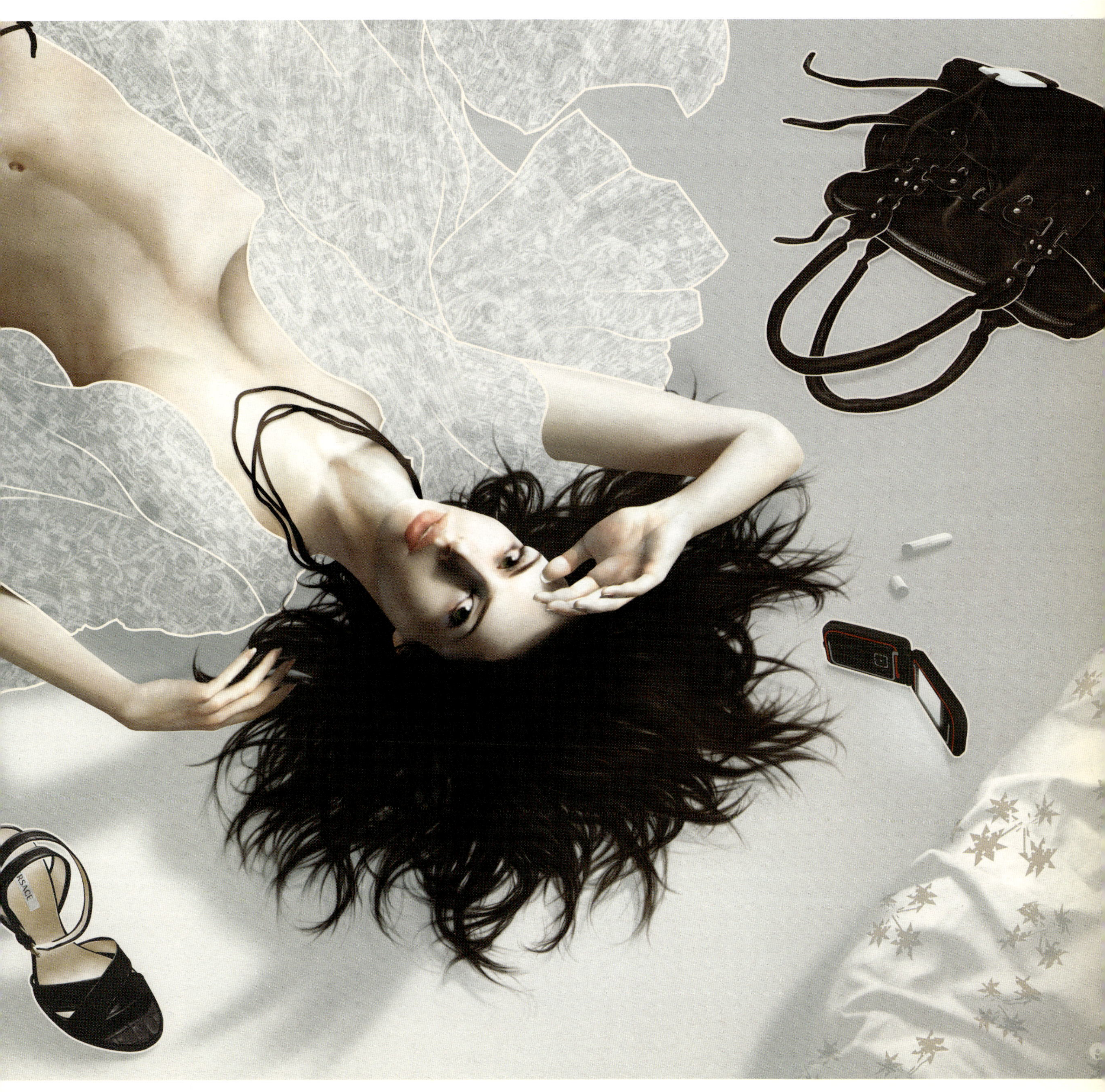

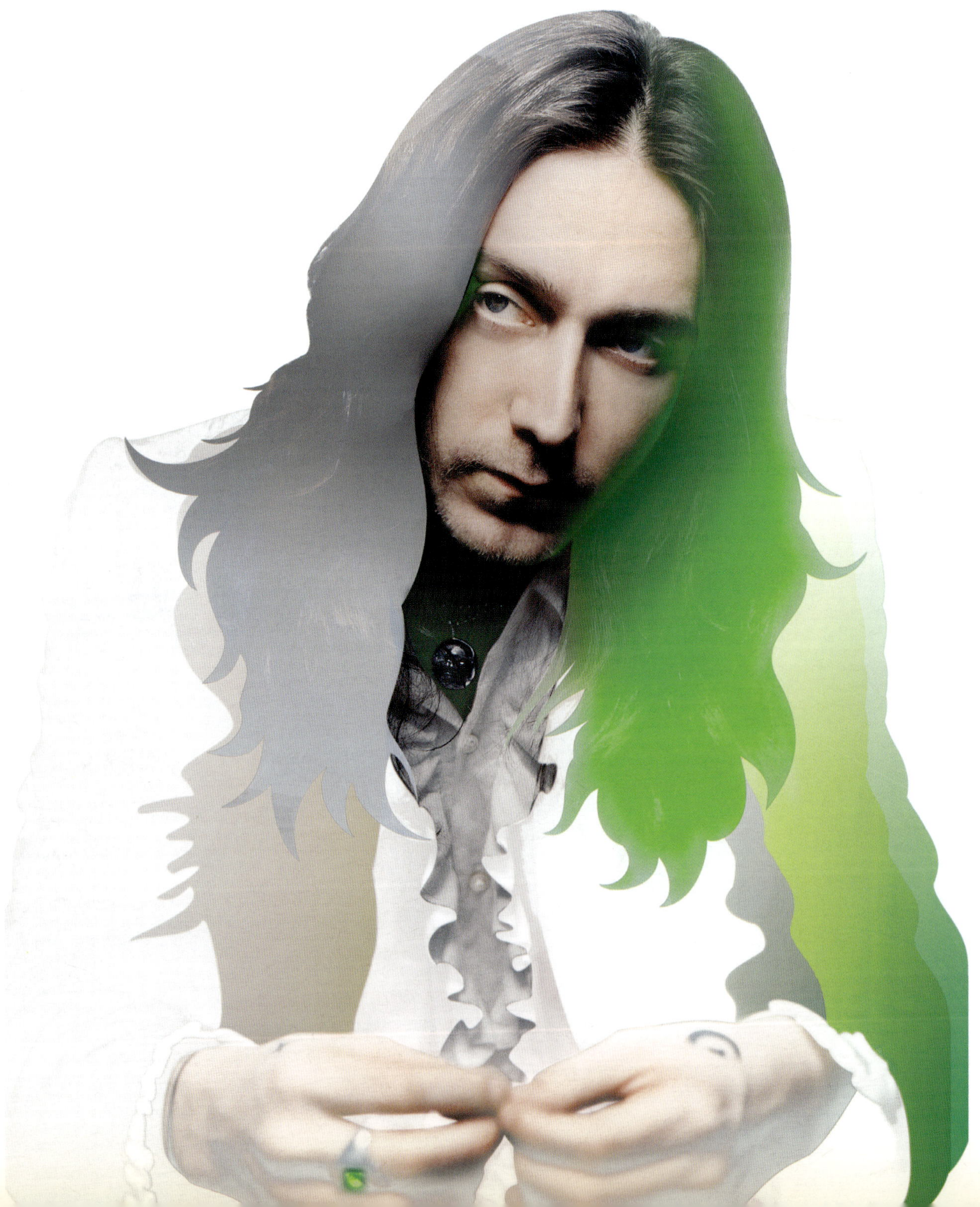

Mi - Zo /

01 / Black Crowes.
Photography, illustration.

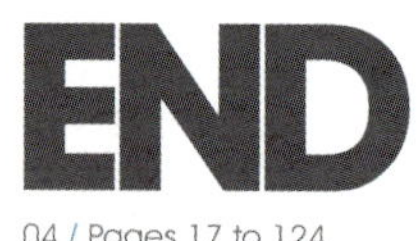

04 / Pages 17 to 124

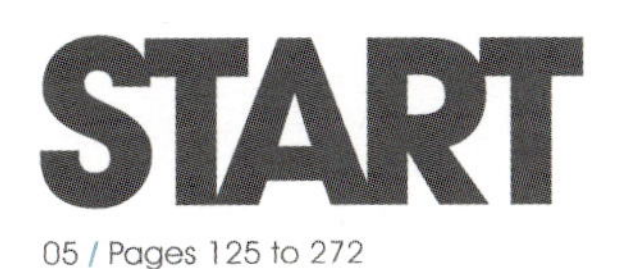
START
05 / Pages 125 to 272

FIVE / TWO FACED

First and foremost the "TWO FACED" project was set up to be an experiment; An experiment that would aim to challenge and push the boundaries of the portrait format. It wasn't a search to find specific individuals who could create immaculate figures or rereate the human form with precision detailing. Although people of this degree would naturally be involved, it was important that we had individuals/groups from as many different creative fields as possible, taking part.

Over a period of four months, WIWP approached a large variety of creative people ranging from toy designers to art directors, photographers to illustrators, artists to designers. We targeted creatives, whose varying styles and approaches would bring diversity to the group, from long established industry giants, to up-and-coming creative collectives and individuals.

The artists were paired off and given the task of creating a portrait of the person they had been teamed with, using their own style for which they have become renowned.

There were no strict rules concerning the creation of their portraits. They could be abstract or photo-realistic, hand-drawn or digitally composed and so on.

The results were as follows.

PROJECT COMMENCED
_ 01.04.06
TWO FACED
FIRST PORTRAIT
_ 23.06.06
LAST PORTRAIT
_ 28.09.06
/ 103 PORTRAITS
SUBMITTED

_Illustration 82 / 103

ARTISTS

_In Order of Appearance

_Pages 132 / 171

Ben Frost &
Paul Willoughby

Fons Schiedon &
Alexei Tylevich_Logan

Gregory Gilbert-Lodge &
Shirana Shabazi

Maureen Gubia &
Julia Sonmi

Rankin &
Mark Blamire

David Foldvari &
Andy Potts

FL@33 &
Antoine + Manuel

Tom Muller &
WeWorkForThem

Grandpeople &
Syrup Helsinki

Ian Wright &
Trevor Jackson

Tim Marrs &
Morten Laursen

Kinsey &
Ben Tour

Nathan Fox &
Scott Scheidly

Gabriel Suchowolski &
Trevor Van Meter

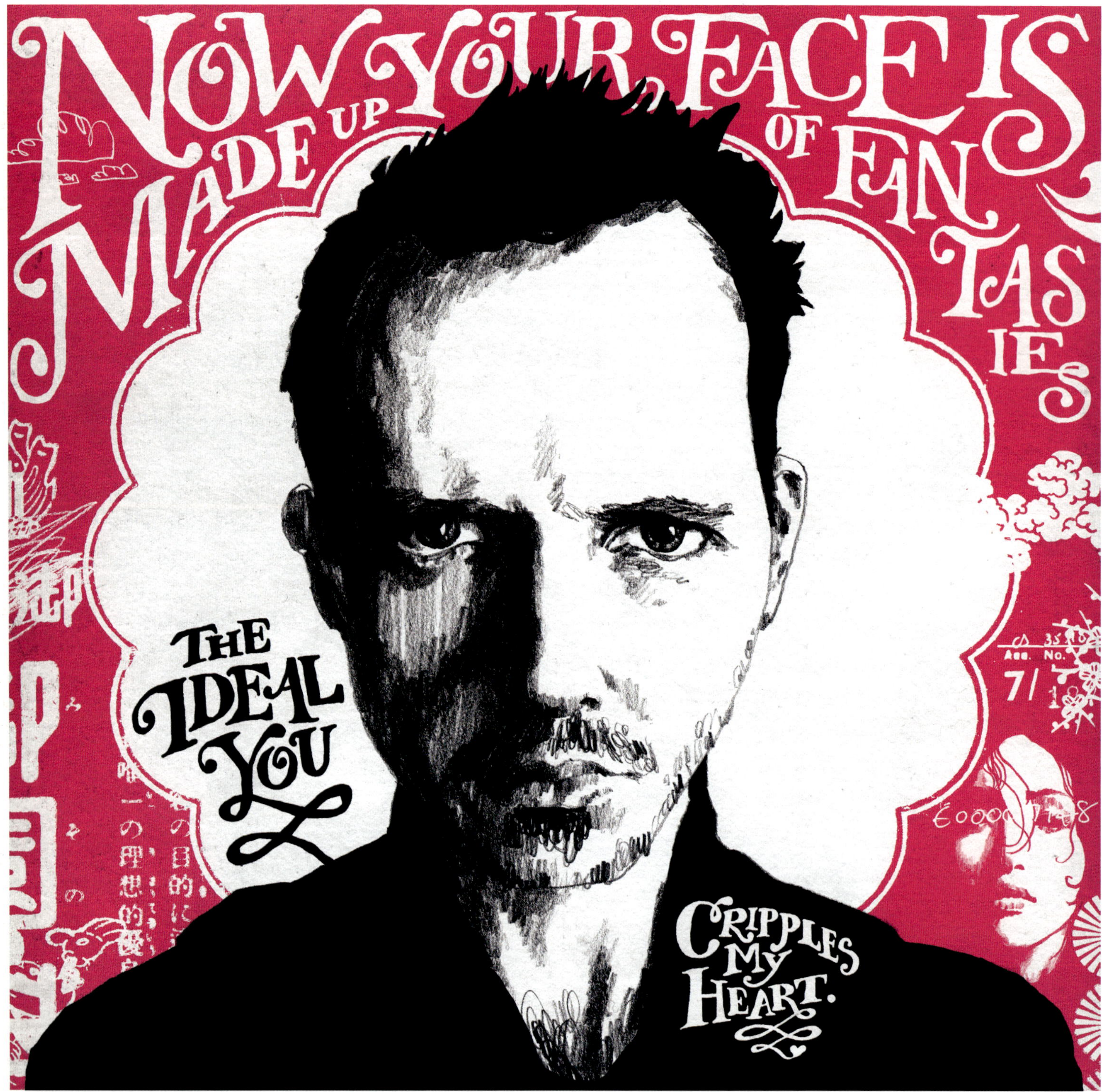

Ben Frost /
By Paul Willoughby

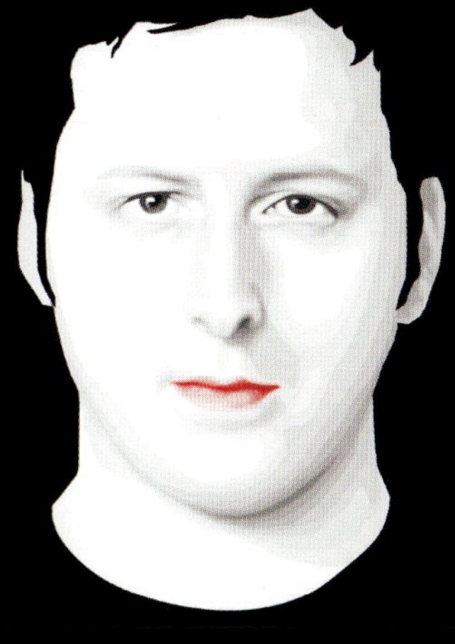

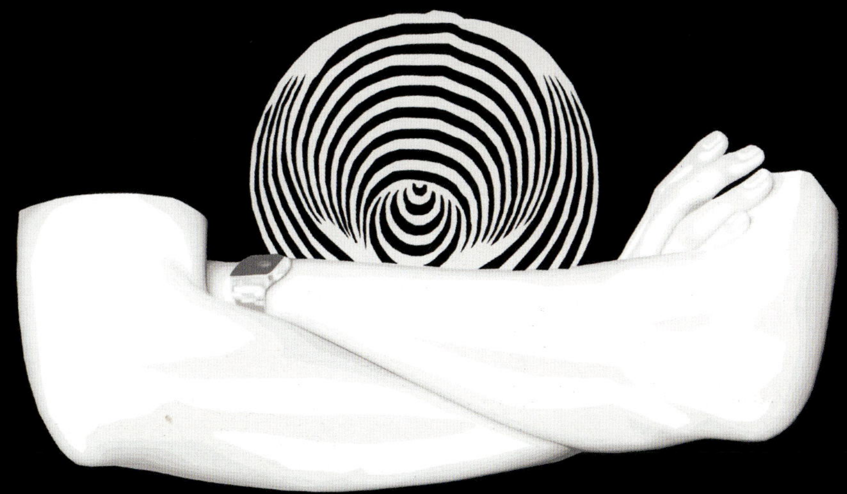

Paul Willoughby /

By Ben Frost

Fons Schiedon

By Alexei Tylevich_Logan

When I first met Fons in Amsterdam, I found his work incredibly refreshing. His visual language is futuristic, complex, sophisticated and funny. He samples the world with childlike wonder, which is a rare gift. The initial impression is absolute visceral overload. Closer inspection reveals layers of detail and finish-fetish. Hyperactive blend of techniques and forms lead the eye into constant cul-de-sacs and detours, yet the experience is somehow satisfying. The feel is strangely Japanese, but also distinctly European. Fons is doing some of the best work at the moment, casually inventing the future in the process.

Fons Schiedon works as a designer and director for print, websites, film and tv.

Since 2001 he has illustrated for a variety of magazines including *Esquire*, *Volkskrant Magazine*(NL) and *Park Avenue* (GER). He worked on a wide range of projects including the corporate identity for Submarinechannel.com, several other websites, principal designs for Peter Greenaway's online game Tulse Luper Journey and motion graphics for the 2004 documentary 'SNEAKERS'. He has worked on a number of interior projects and designed a museum exhibition. In 2005 he made a weekly political cartoon for one of the major Dutch newspapers, which was fun to do and sometimes fun to read.

As a director he delivered music videos, commercials and animated shorts, as well as channel id's for Nickelodeon and MTV ASIA. For many of these he was also animator and most of the other names on the end credits (except for the audio).

He writes and directs 'MobSquad', a biweekly animated series for MTV in South-East Asia and Australia (2006). This extremely short format mini series (45-80 sec) is distributed via TV broadcast and mobile phones and features three friends celebrating their dysfunctional lives.

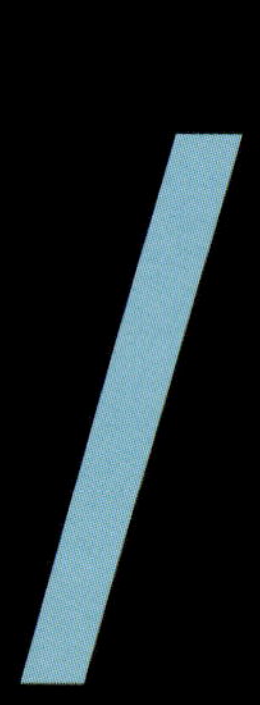

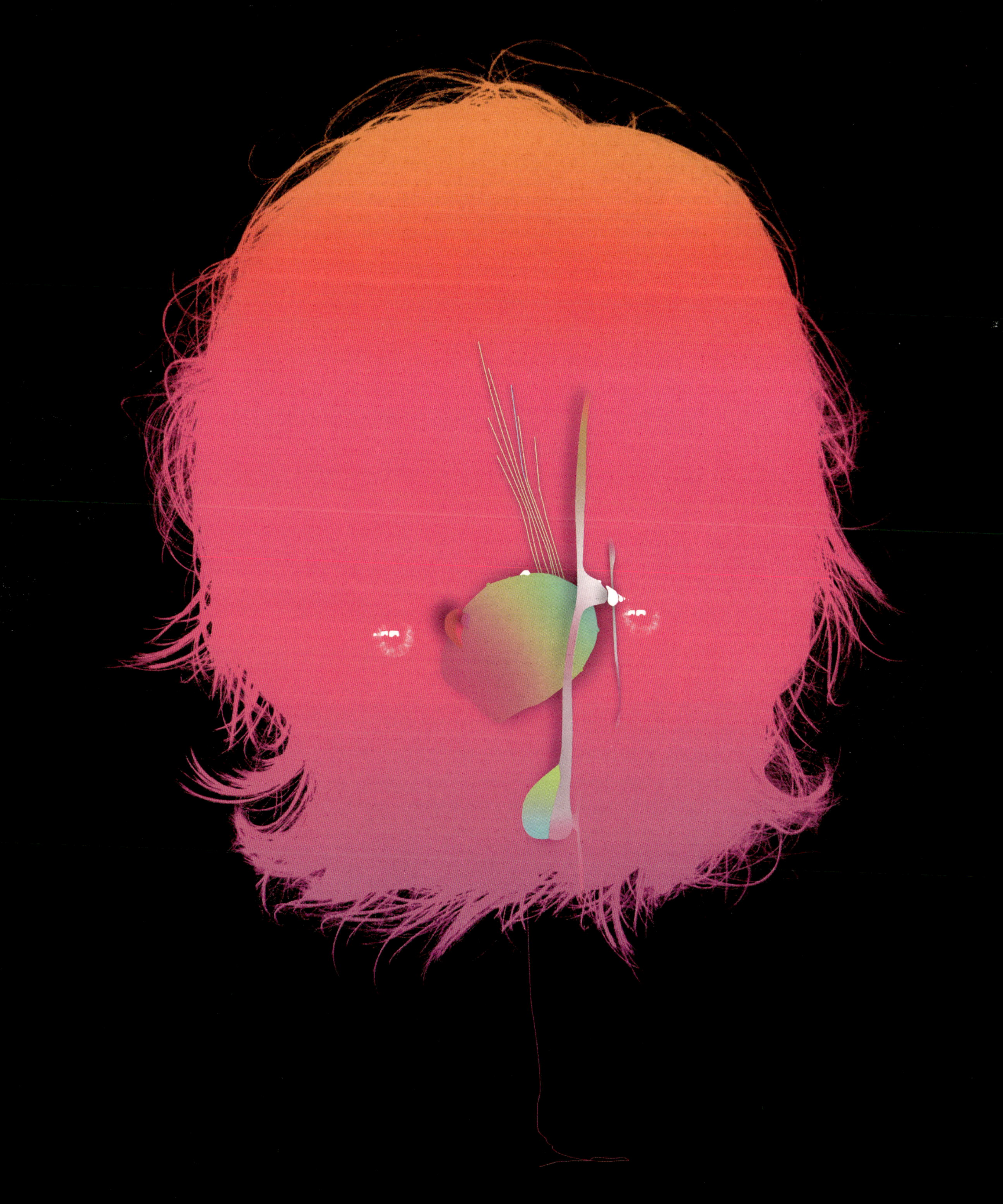

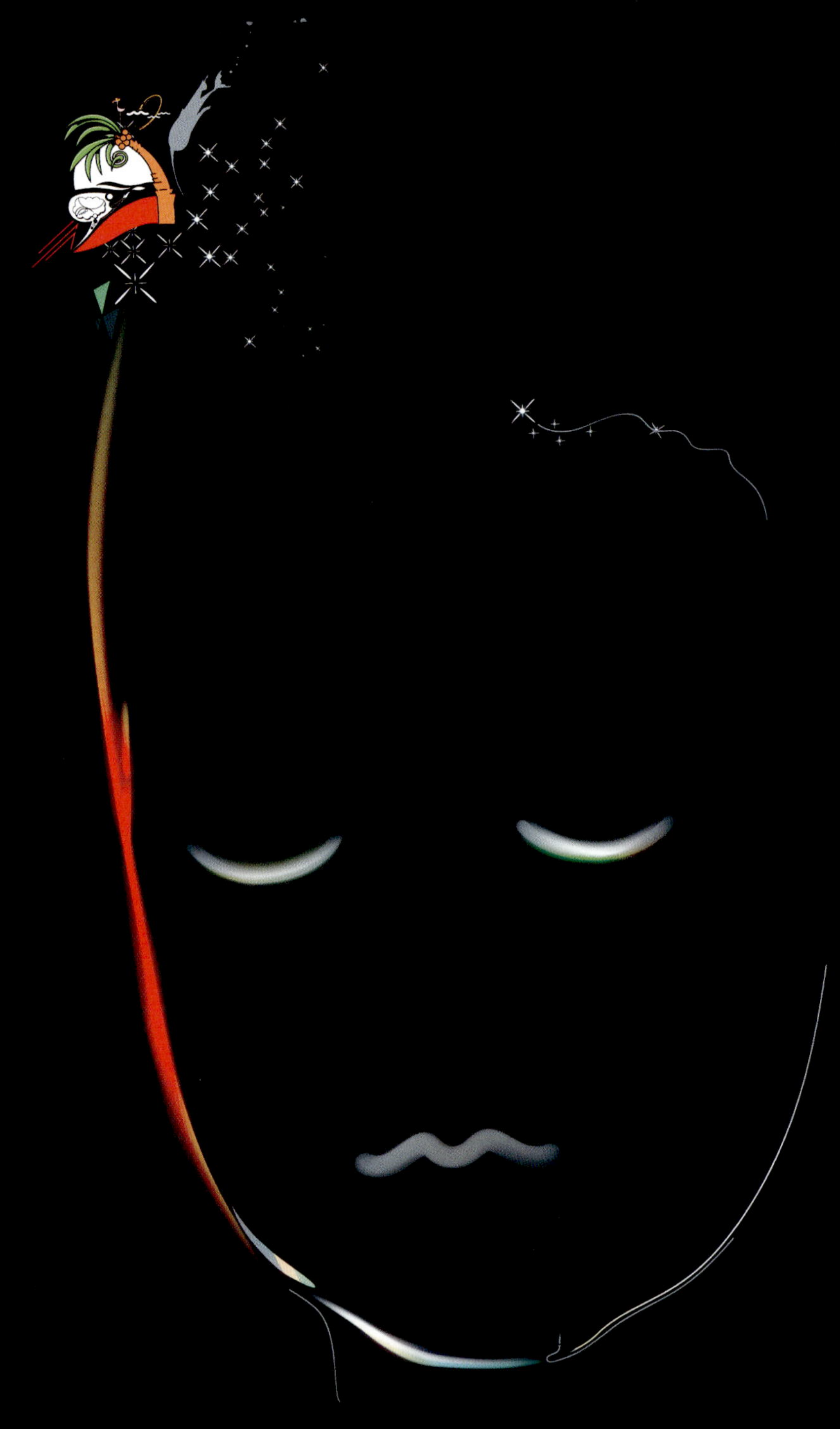

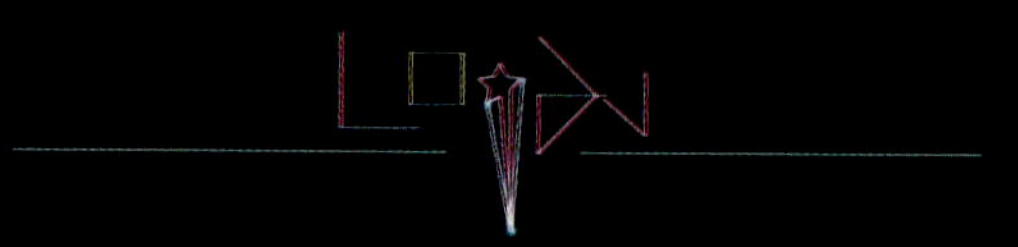

Alexei Tylevich_Logan

By Fons Scheidon

What I think is great about Logan's work, is that there's a directorial approach throughout, both in the live action and graphics driven work, as well as the print design. There's a strong conceptual motivation to the basis of each project that results in a convincing diversity of work. It doesn't look like they purposely try to do something different each time, I think it's just the result of having an open approach to whatever a project requires. I strongly relate to that. Their work is clearly referential to elements of popular (or less popular) culture, showing an apparent awareness of the origin of their sources. But the output is simply refreshing.

Alexei Tylevich is a Los Angeles-based director / designer / artist. He is a co-founder, with Ben Conrad, of Logan, a multidisciplinary creative studio. Projects range from live-action direction and production of music videos and tv commercials, to broadcast design and animation, to environmental, fashion and print design. Alexei and Ben co-direct tv spots and music videos using the name Logan as their directorial pseudonym. Projects include tv and print campaigns for Apple; music videos for Madonna, Money Mark, Ken Ishii, Felix Da Housecat and Jurassic5; projects for Volkswagen, Konami, DKNY, Target, Motorola, VH1, Current TV, among others.

Alexei's work has been recognized over the years in numerous publications and exhibitions, including: *Eye, Creative Review, Boards, +81, Idea, GASBook, RES, Wired* (which named him one of "20 people bringing 21-st century Hollywood to life"), *I.D.* magazine (where he was recognized as one of it's Top 40 designers), and by RESfest, onedotzero, American Center for Design, Broadcast Designers Association, SIGGRAPH and Arts Electronica, among others.

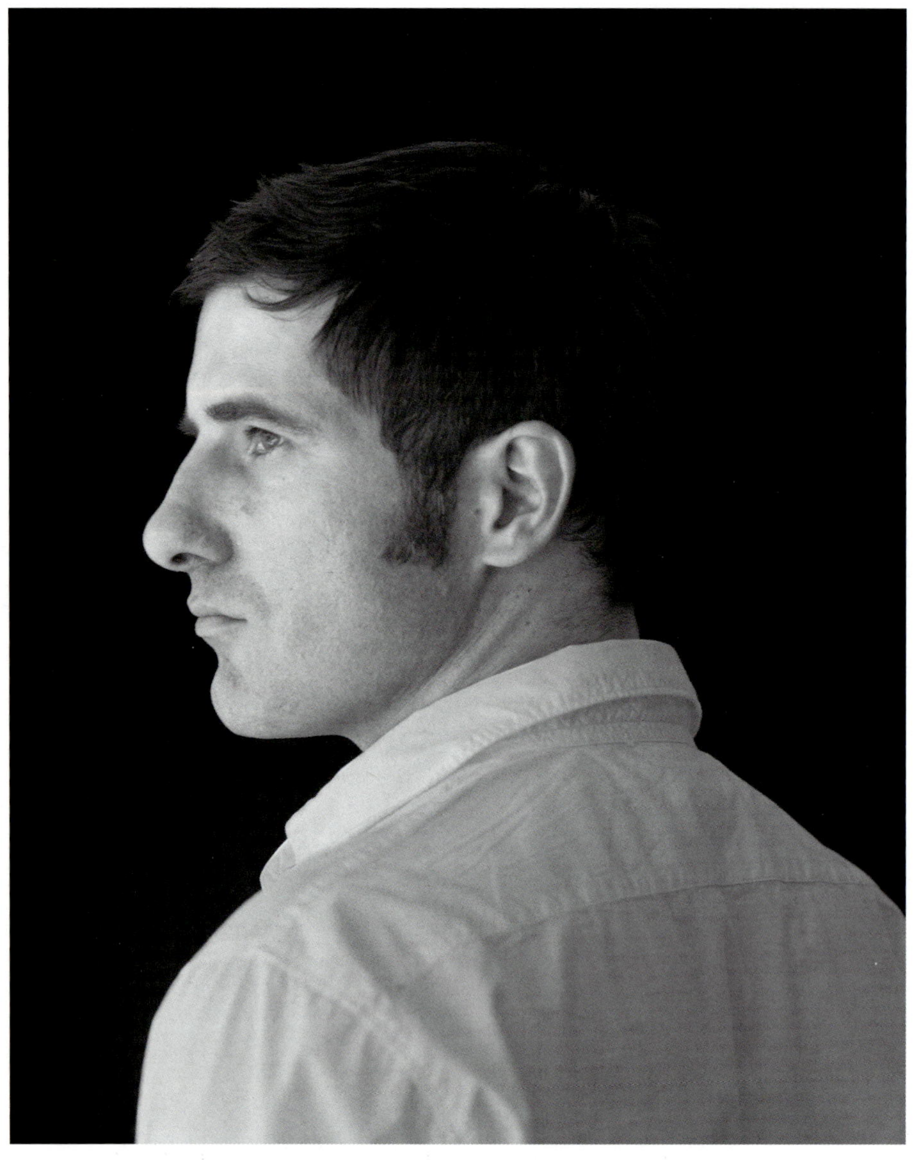

Gregory Gilbert-Lodge /
By Shirana Shahbazi

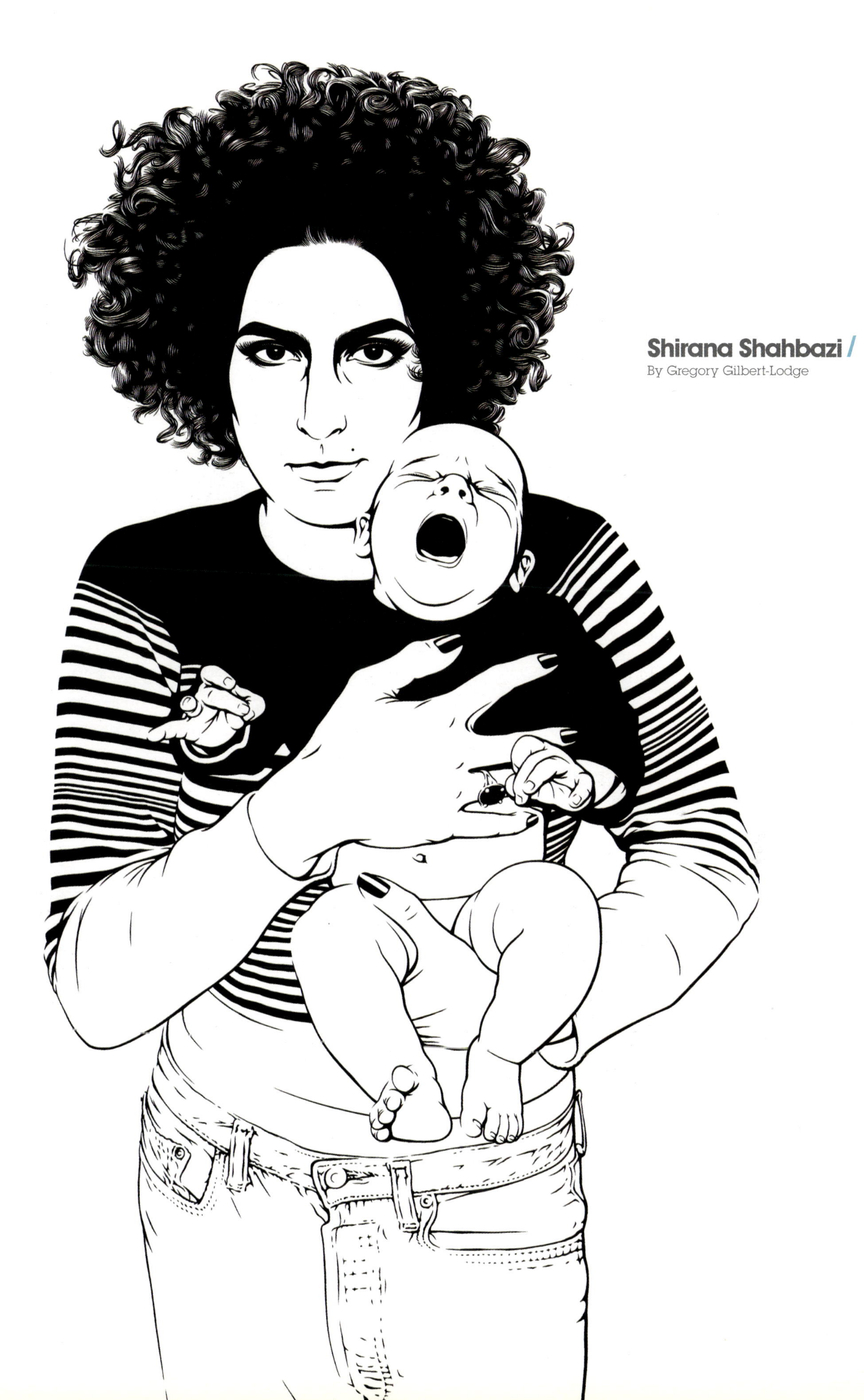

Shirana Shahbazi /
By Gregory Gilbert-Lodge

Maureen Gubia /
By Julia Sonmi

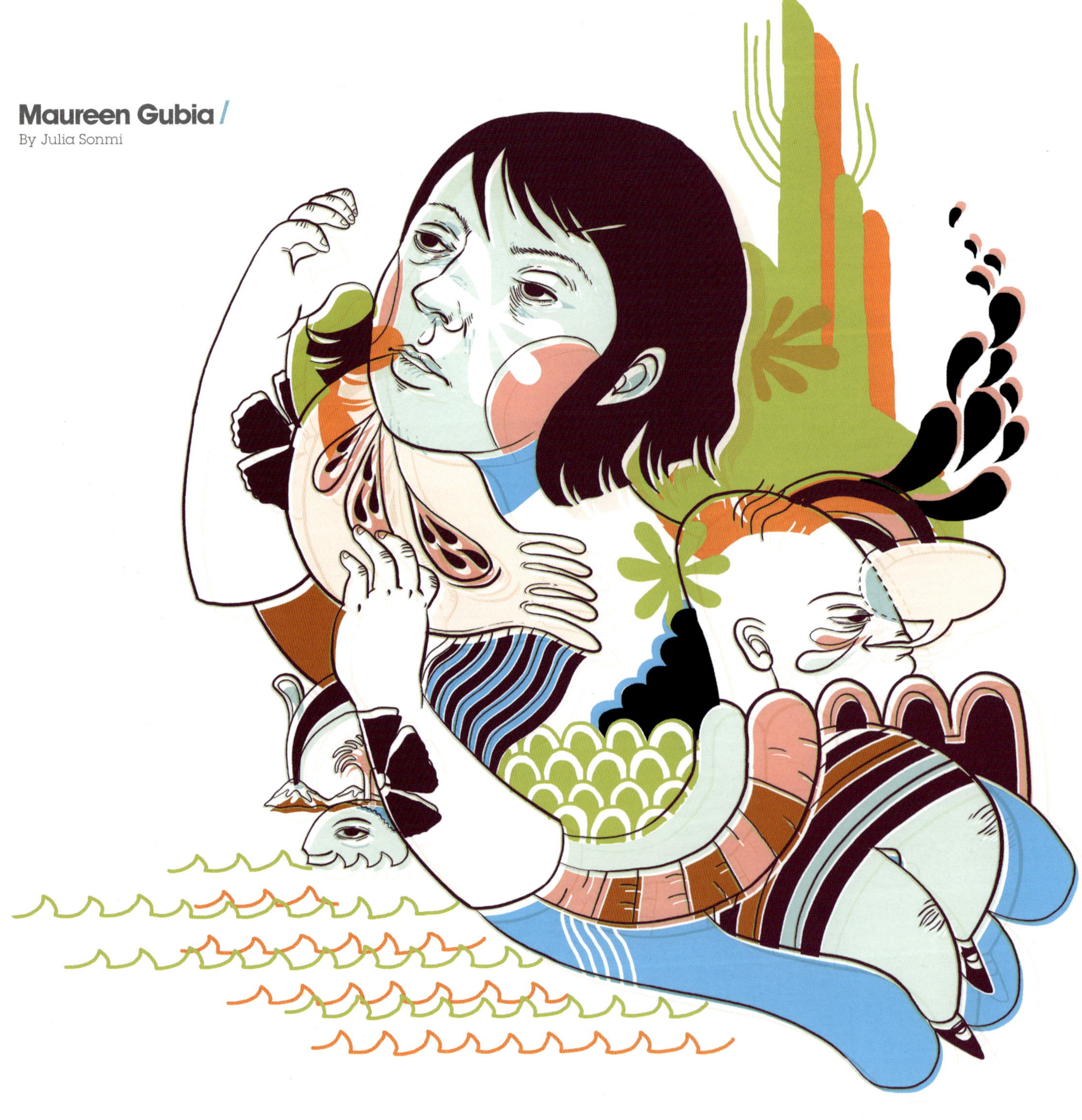

Julia Sonmi /
By Maureen Gubia

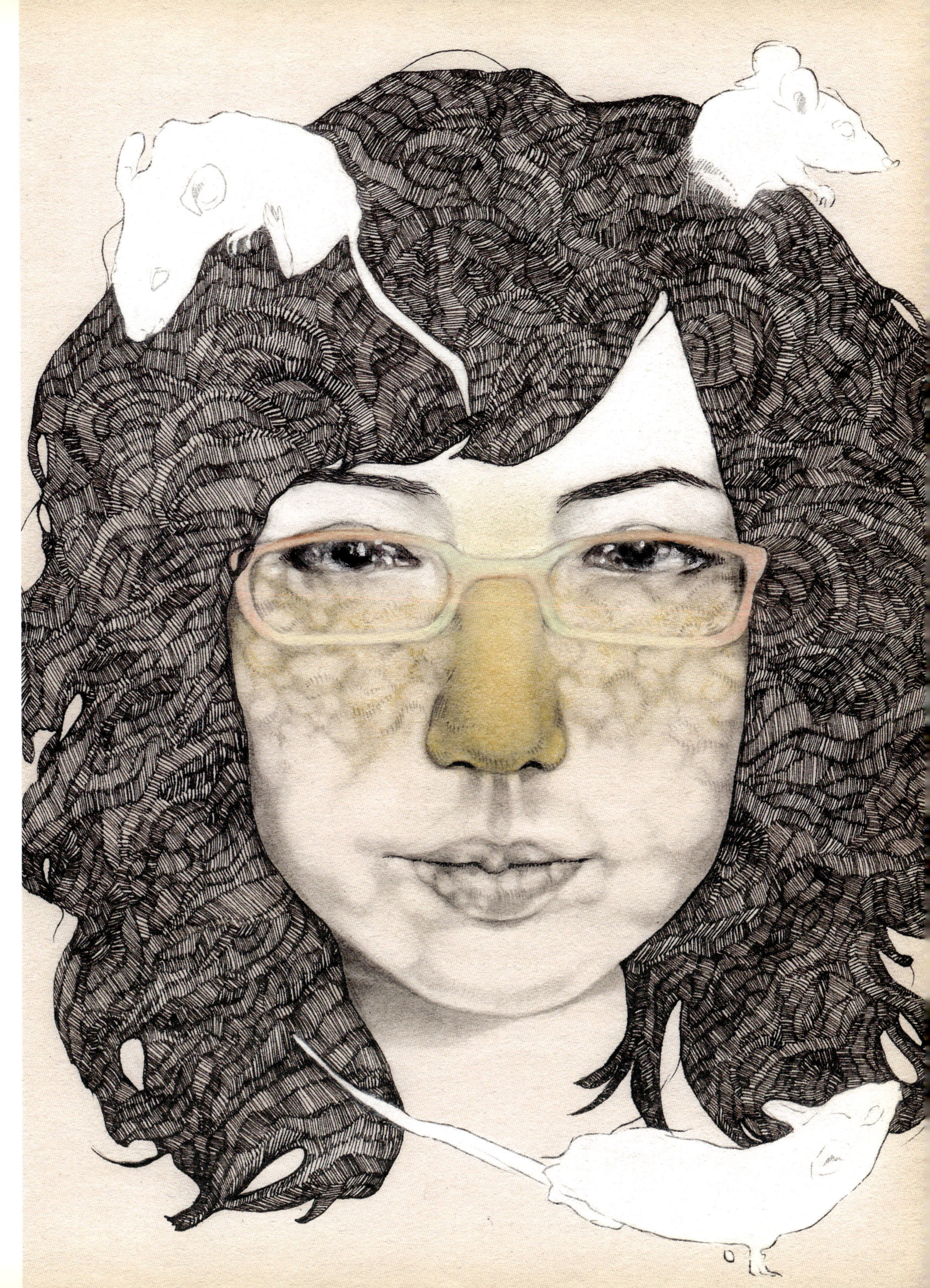

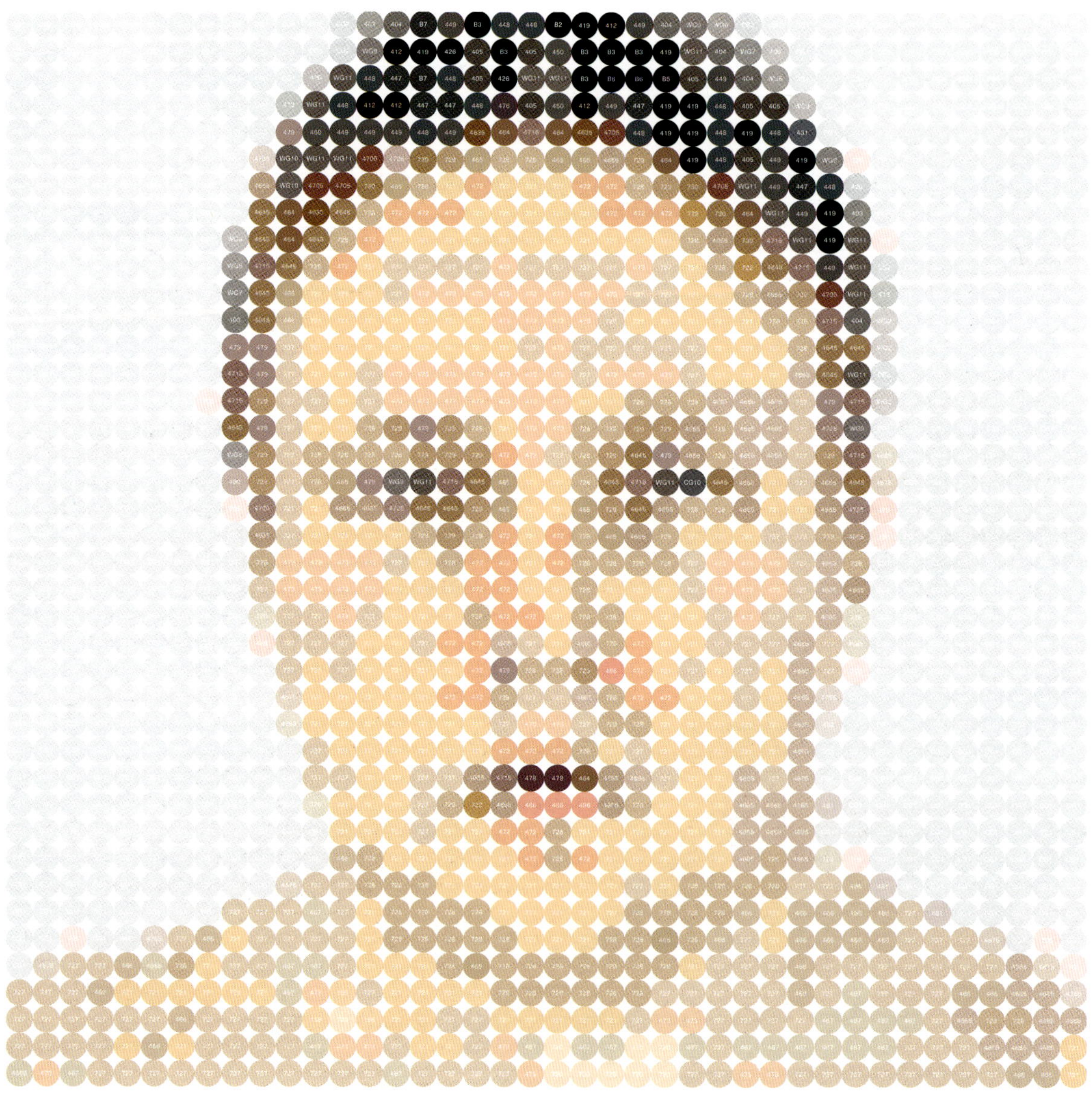

Rankin /

By Mark Blamire

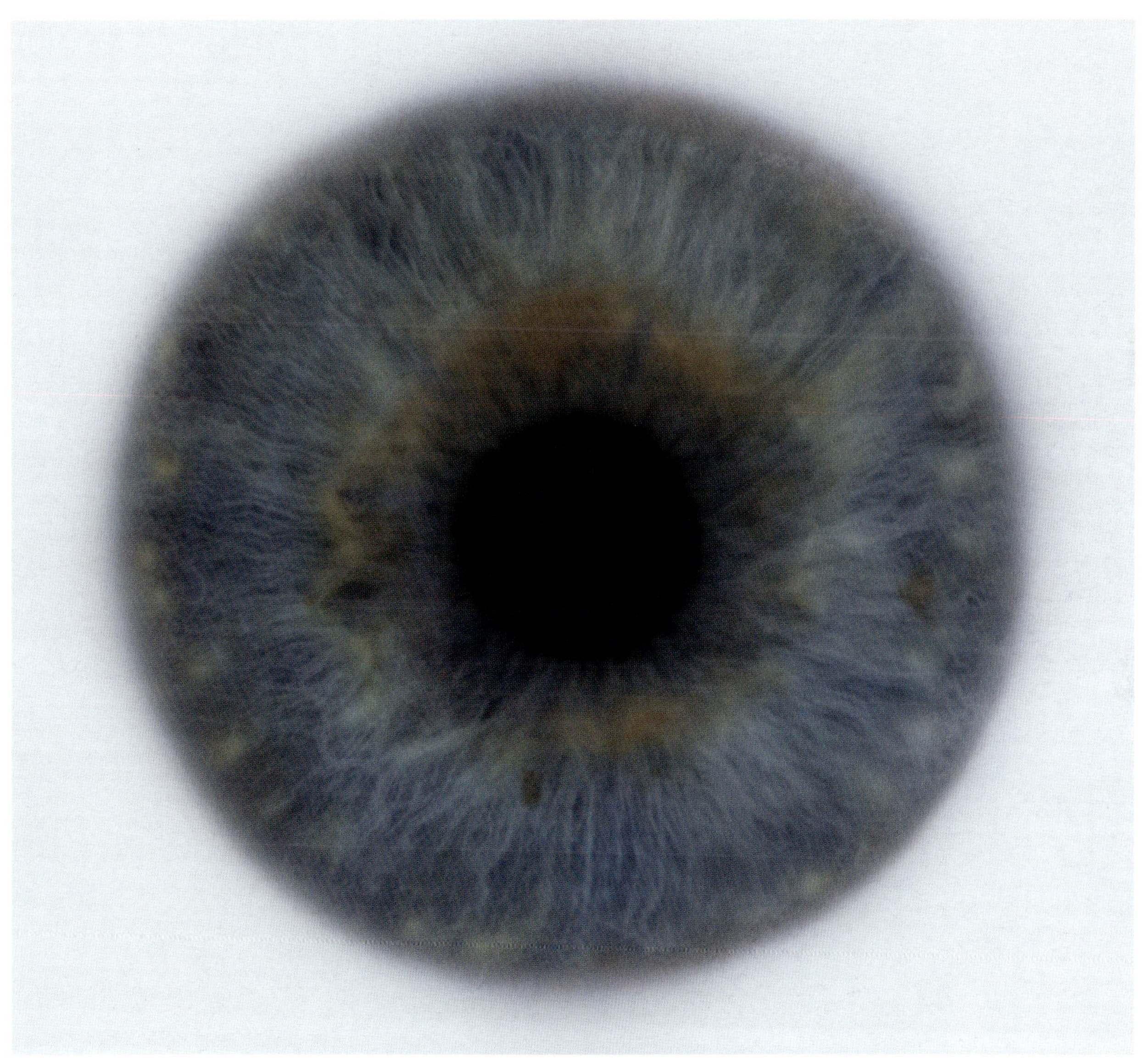

Mark Blamire /

By Rankin

David Foldvari /

By Andy Potts

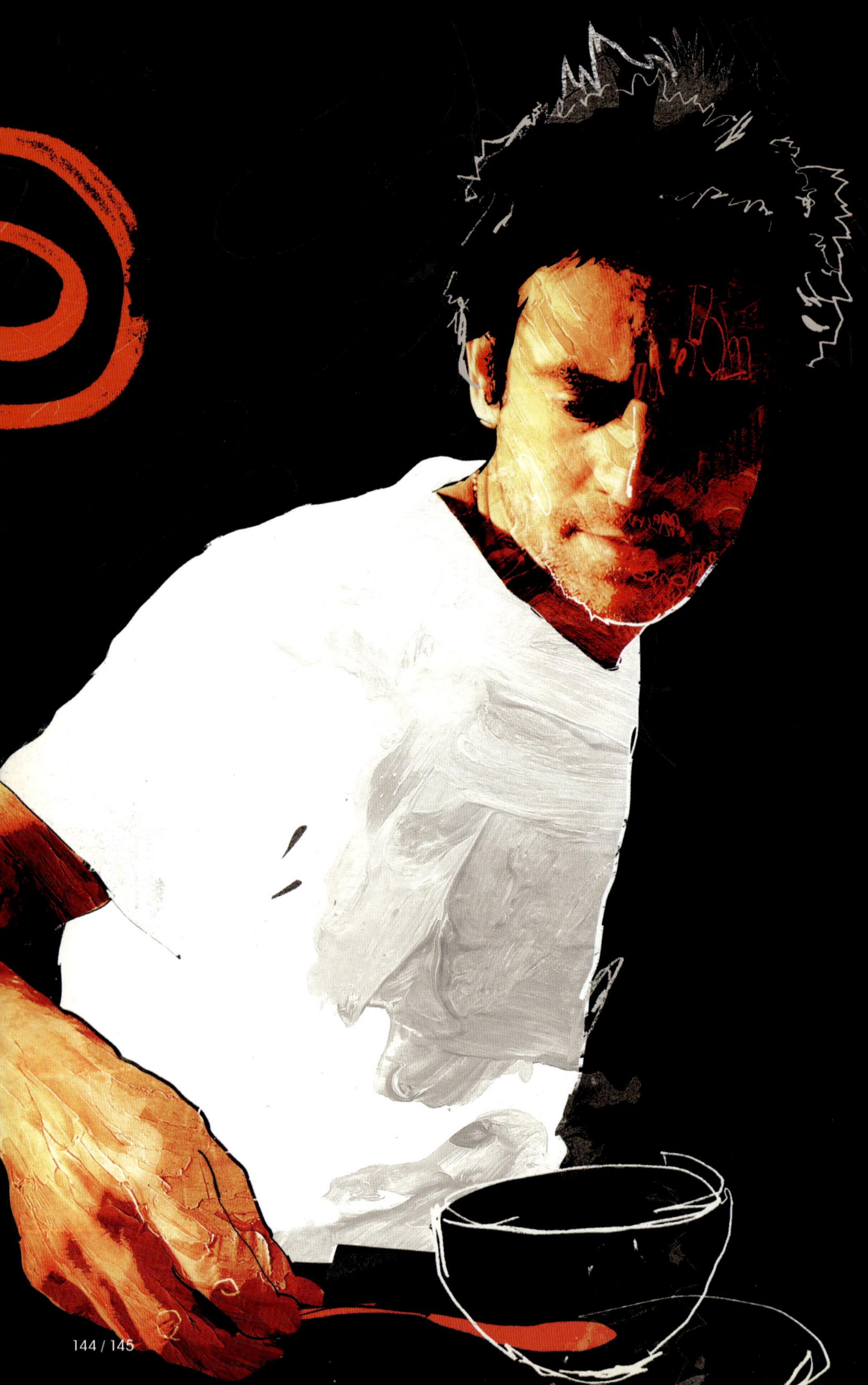

Andy Potts /

By David Foldvari

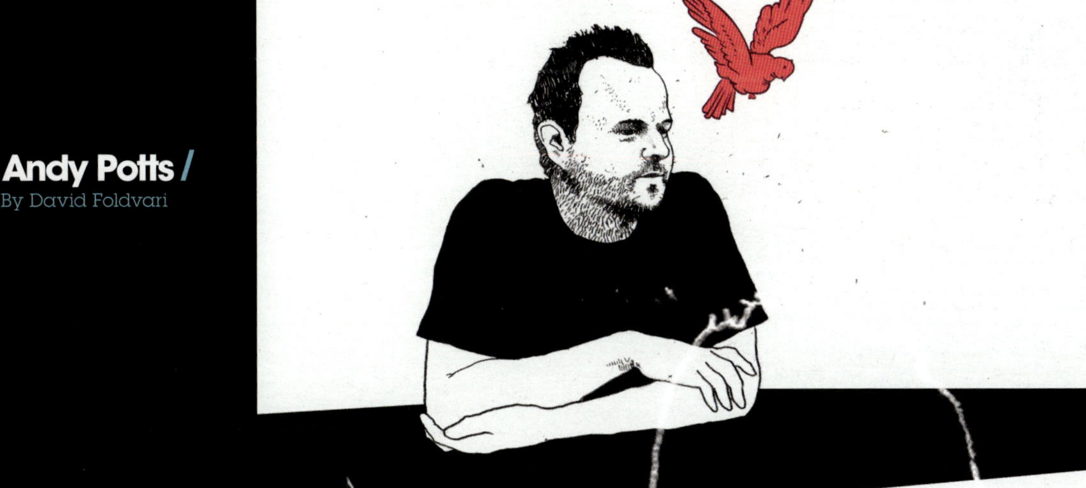

Fl@33

By Antoine+Manuel

Agathe and Tomi invited us this year to make button badges for their internet label Stereohype.com. They re-contacted us to be part of the TwoFaced project. Just have a look at their Butterfly sculpture made of colour pencils.

FL@33 is a multi-lingual and multi-specialised studio for visual communication based in London. Founders Agathe Jacquillat [French from Paris; Academy Julian, ESAG] and Tomi Vollauschek [Austrian, originally from Frankfurt; FH Darmstadt] met on the Royal College of Art's [RCA] postgraduate Communication Art and Design course in 1999 and set up their company in Notting Hill after graduating in July 2001. The studio is working across all media in the areas Concept Generation, Print, Screenbased Work [Broadcast, Motion Graphics, Interface Design, Websites], Exhibition Design and Publishing. FL@33s' mission is to create a professional, vibrant, fresh and artistic body of work while keeping a balance between commissioned and self-initiated projects and publications.

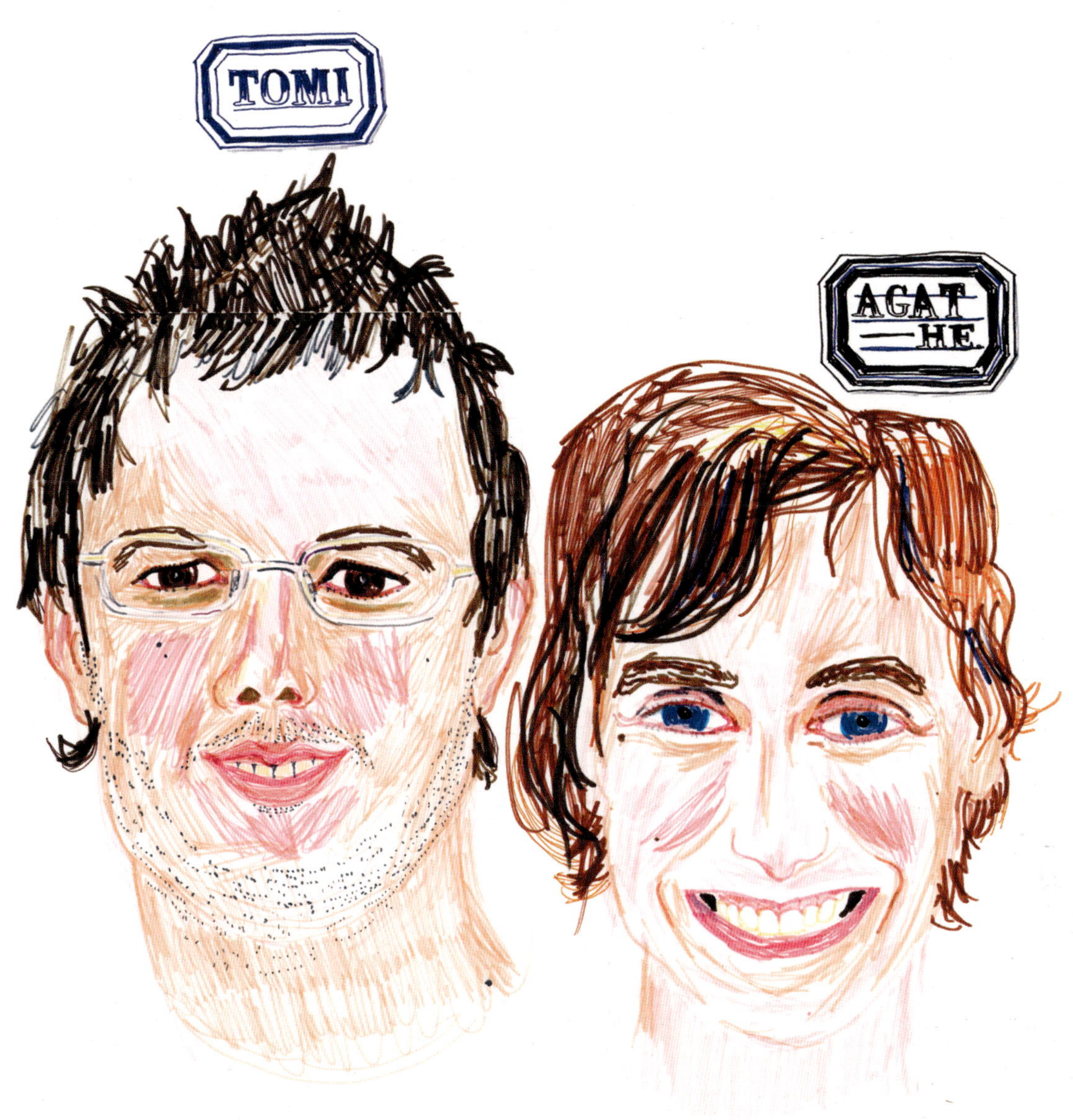

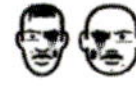

antoinetmanuel
for twofaced
2006

Antoine +Manuel

By FL@33

Antoine Audiau and Manuel Warosz met in art school in Paris. They quickly decided to work together under the name Antoine +Manuel. Since the begining they combined hand drawing and computer illustration with their own typography and photography. They work for fashion (Christian Lacroix), home (Habitat, Galeries Lafayette), publishing houses (Larousse, Gallimard), contemporary dance, theatre and art.

We first saw Antoine+Manuel's work in 2005 when their monograph was published at the same time as ours, as part of the design & designer (d&d) series by french Pyramyd Editions ('d&d 032 Antoine+Manuel' and 'd&d 033 FL@33'). Their theatrical style immediately fascinated us, especially the stunning body of work they have created for Christian Lacroix, since 2002, which probably makes every graphic designer and aesthete drool all over the place. Since then we have had the pleasure of collaborating with them for our stereohype.com design initiative B.I.O.

Antoine and Manuel are usually wearing theatrical make-up when portraits of the two are shown in the press. We therefore tried to respect this wish and kept our visual relatively abstract.

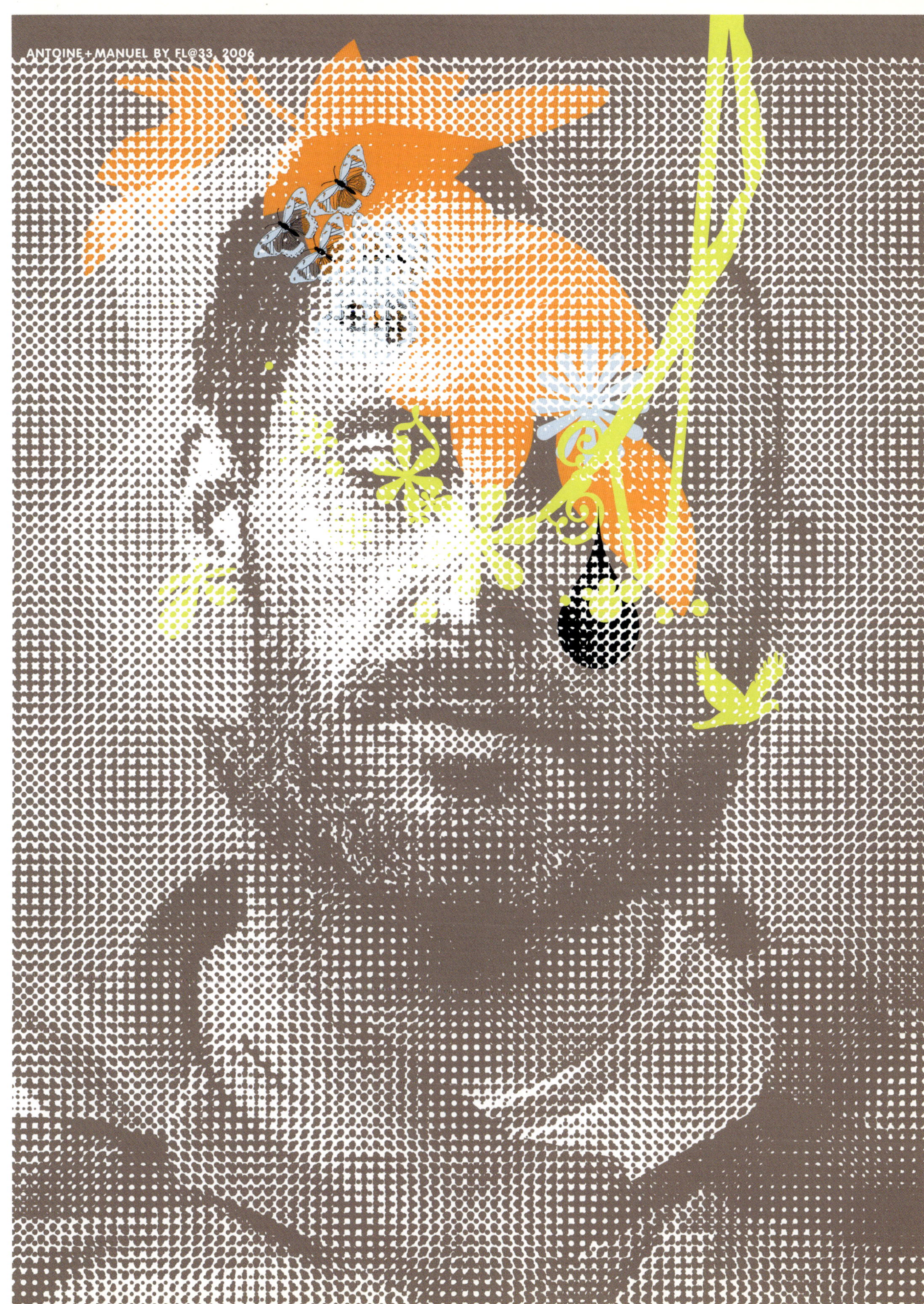
ANTOINE+MANUEL BY FL@33, 2006

Tom Muller

By WeWorkForThem

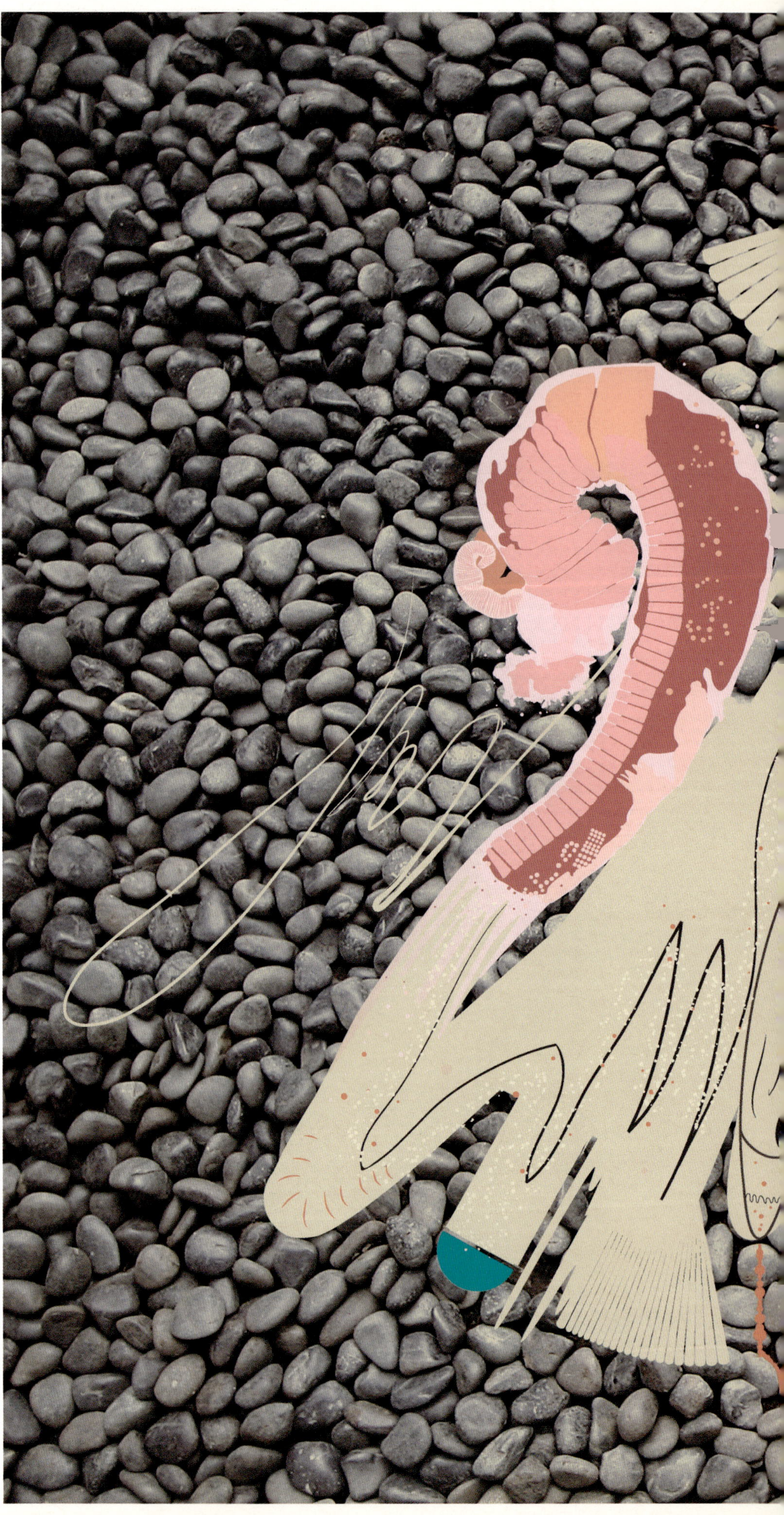

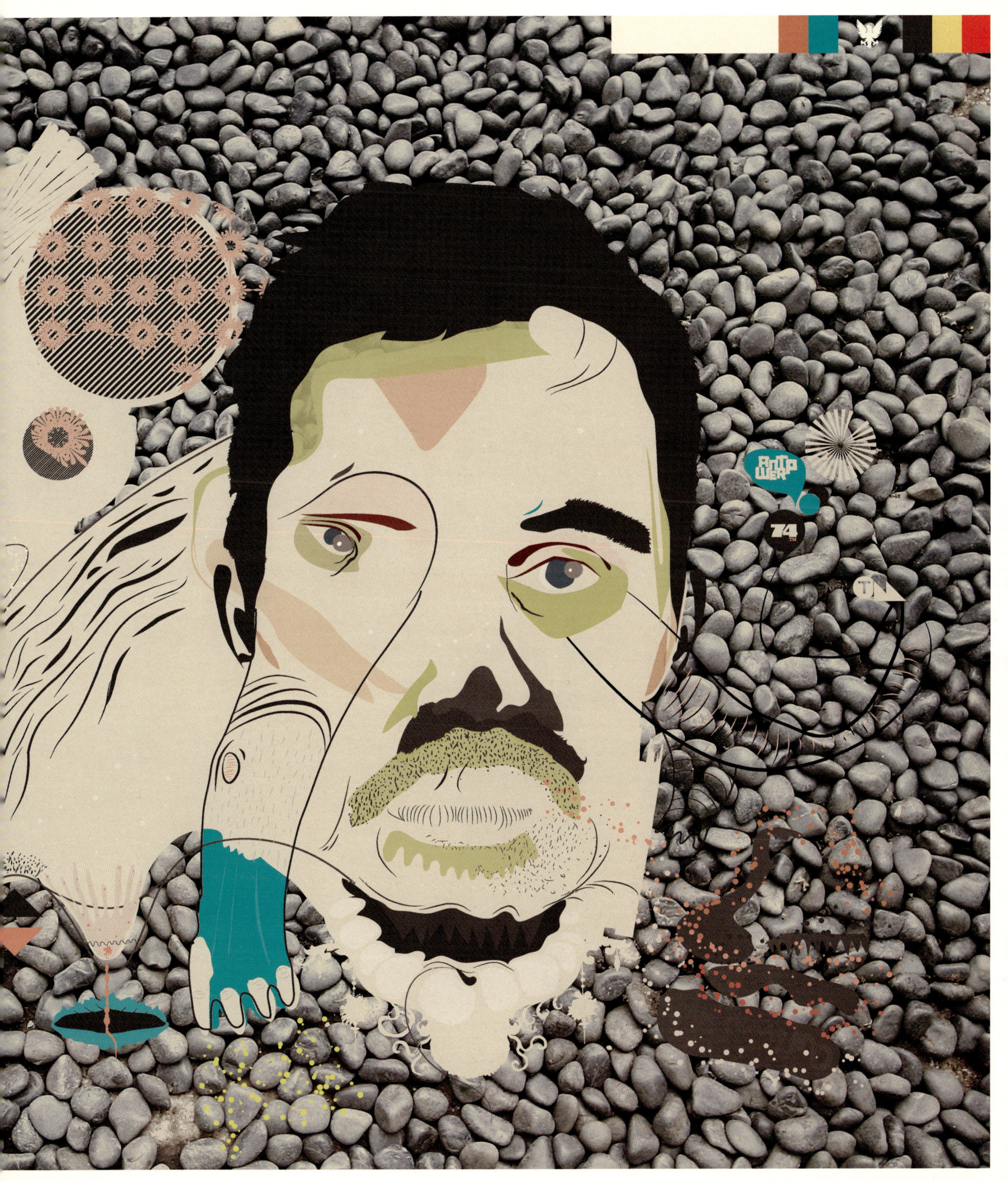
ANTWERP
74
TM
TN

> W/YWFT_Cina
source: IMG_8535.jpg
300KB
SPHERICAL PROJECTION
IMAGE IN/FORMATION:

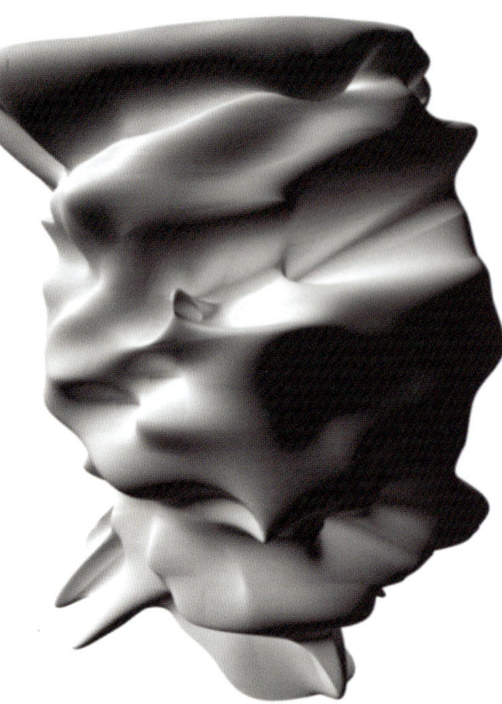

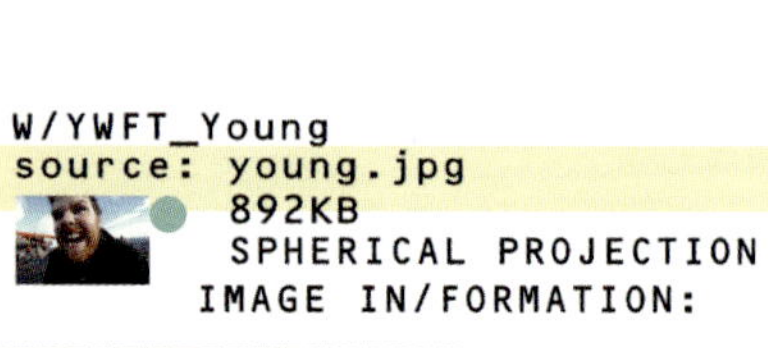

> W/YWFT_Young
source: young.jpg
892KB
SPHERICAL PROJECTION
IMAGE IN/FORMATION:

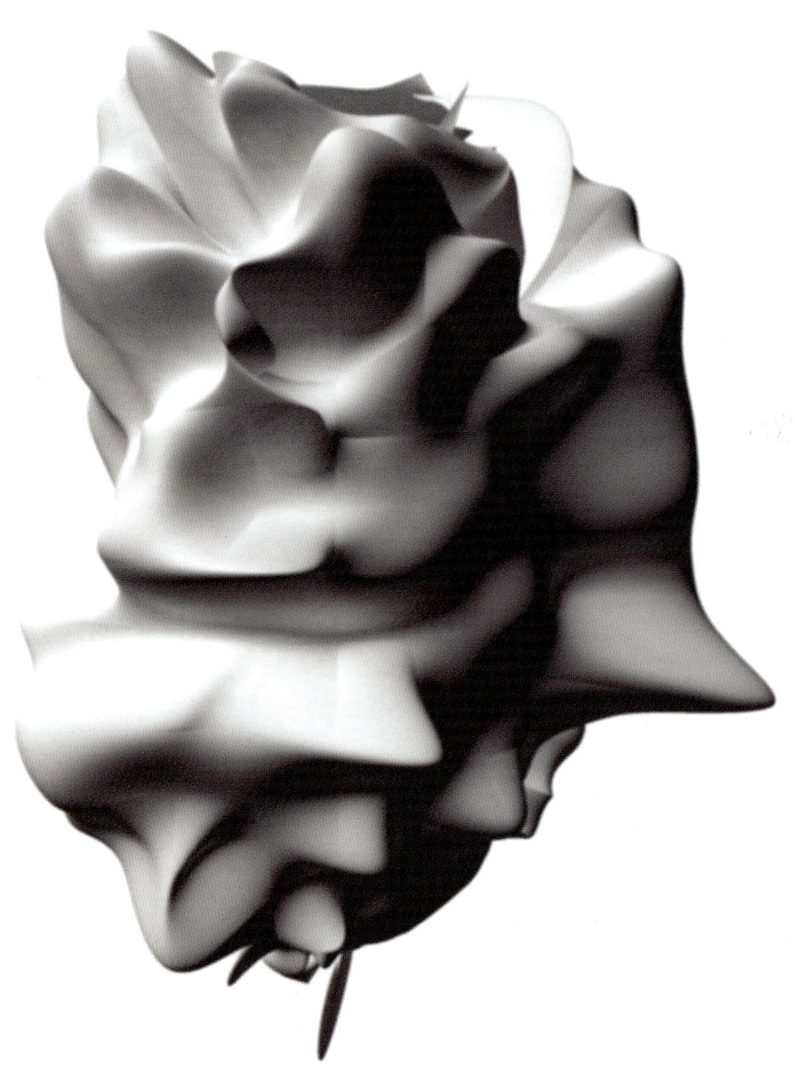

WeWork ForThem

By Tom Muller

My first thought when I got paired up with the two Michaels from You/WeWorkForThem, I knew I wasn't going to do straight forward portraits of them. They have always profiled themselves by their forward thinking and expressive approach to design and art, which balances between a freedom of expression and an almost methodical, informed practice of design and that was what I wanted to portray.

I played around with a couple of ideas, each time catching myself trying to come up with an overly complex solution for a simple problem; And then I started thinking: what makes a portrait a portrait? Do you have to recognise the person? Portraits are always a tricky thing to do. You usually want to have either a good resemblance of your subject, or evoke some kind of emotion through it. This usually leads to more abstract approaches where you'd forgo the literal image for a more free approach, trying to visualise what your subject represents. I wanted to represent Y/WWFT as an idea, rather than two faces.

The end result is quite simple: I took the photos they supplied and ran them through a 3D program, interpreting the data of the image to create a 3-dimensional object. That object, although completely abstract in shape and form, is a truthful representation of them, and therefore an accurate portrait, although not in the traditional sense of the word.

WeWorkForThem is the creative duo of Michael Cina and Michael Young. Since their uniting as a single identity, they have gone on to create endless amounts of work in all scopes of the creative arena. WeWorkForThem's unique approach is why their work has been sought after by a diverse group of companies, art galleries, architects, musicians and also for their live performances. The work they have created over the years reflects knowledge of post WW2 modernist theory with modern day technology and abstraction.

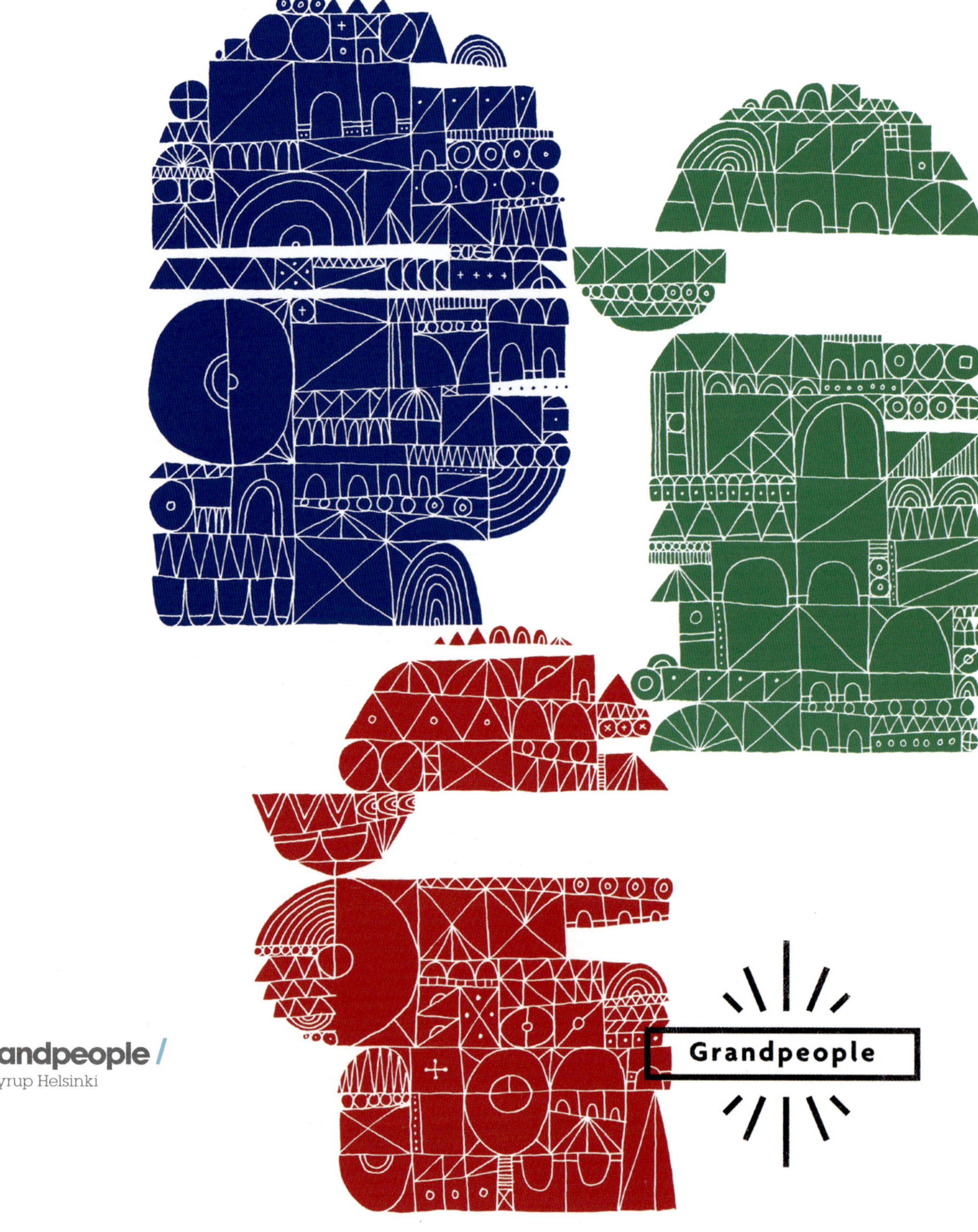

Grandpeople /

By Syrup Helsinki

Syrup Helsinki /

By Grandpeople

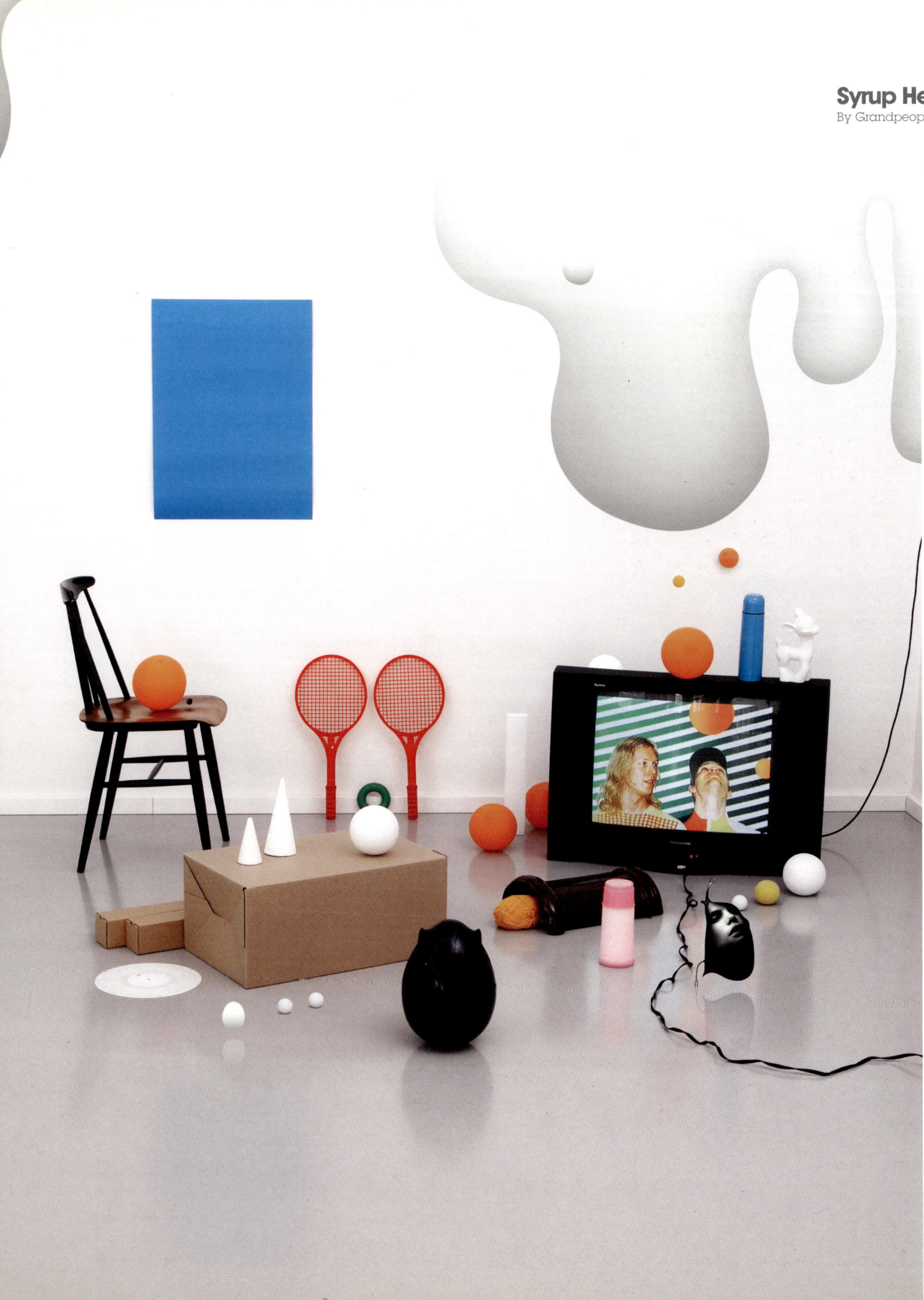

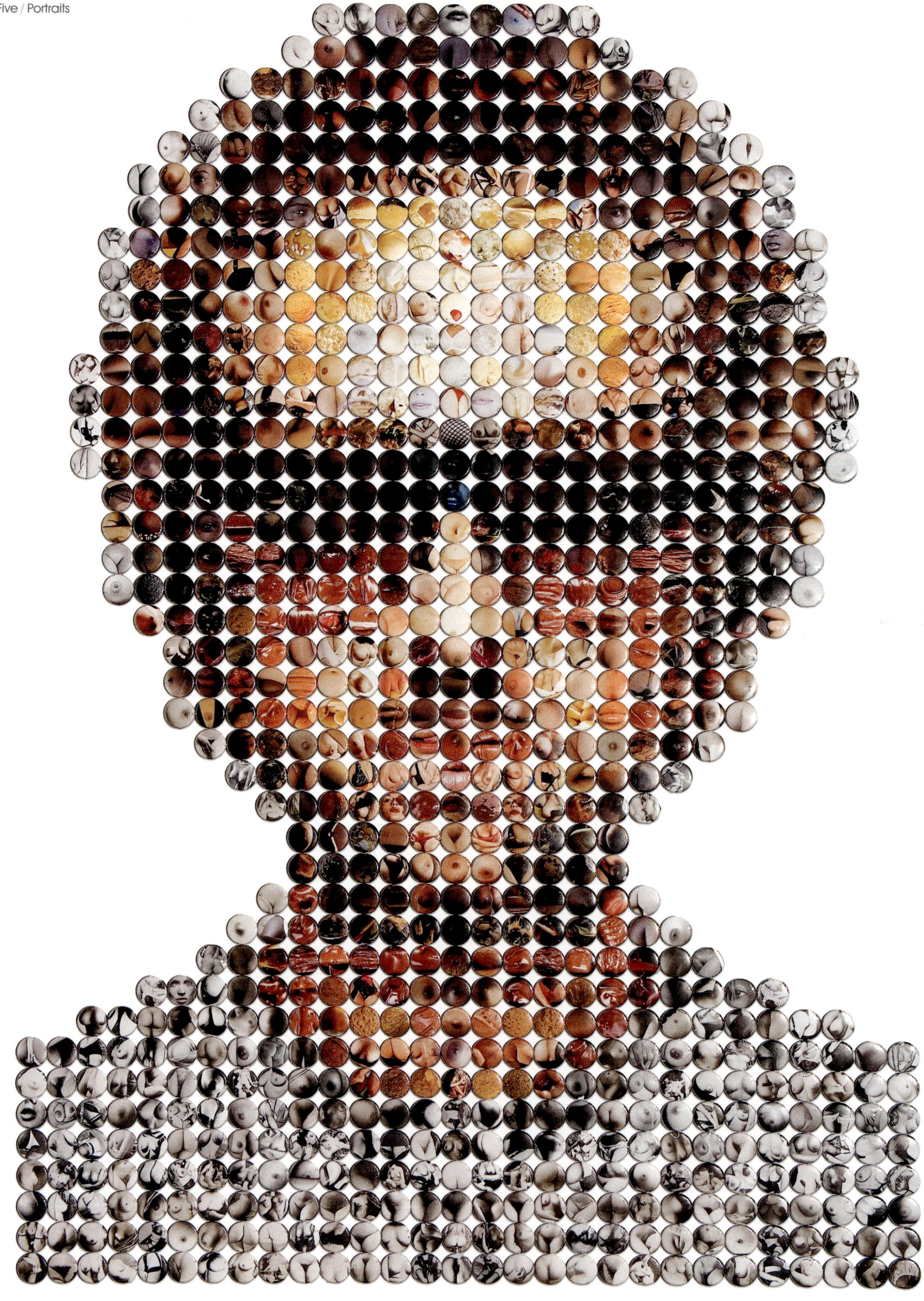

Trevor Jackson

By Ian Wright

Ian Wright

By Trevor Jackson

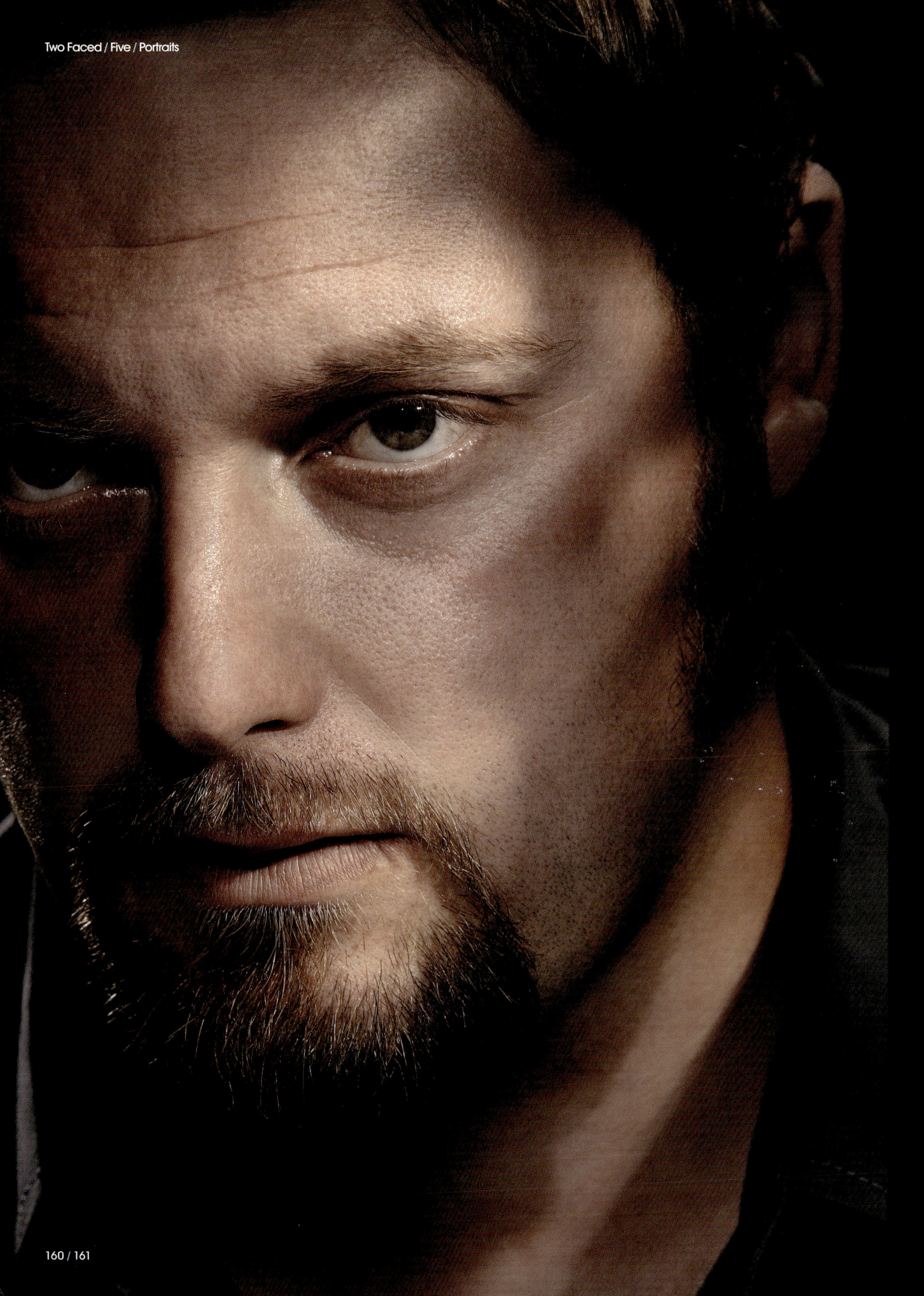

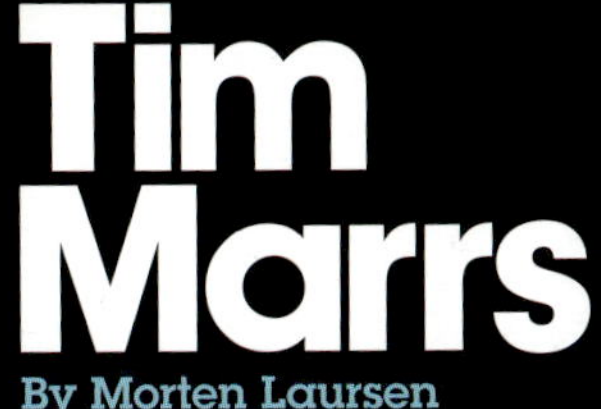

Tim Marrs

By Morten Laursen

I didn't think I knew Tim's work until we were paired for this project. But as soon as I saw his website I realised I had seen and admired his work many times before, he's a cool geezer with a strong consistent style. One of the things I really like about his work is his ability to do stuff that is both busy and simple, realistic and abstract at the same time. Respect.

With an illustration career spanning over 10 years, Marrs is a graduate of Humberside University and Central St.Martins, one has seen his work evolve, develop and inspire. Producing a frenzied mix of drawings, photography, screen printing and Photoshop techniques. His work sports a hand made and dynamic look, but yet considered.

Marrs's broad and flexible style has also attracted a wide variety of commissions in Advertising, Editorial, Publishing and Design with worldwide clients including Nike: Brand Jordan, Asics nyc marathon, Reebok, Kswiss, Ogilvy and Mather, Geffen records, Publicis & Hal Rine, and Orion publishing to name but a few. His technique is one of the most influential styles in modern illustration and is now starting to get the recognition it deserves.

" I always got excited about textures, marks, skuzz, even when I was painting back in the day. I guess the mac has helped bring a balance and ease to the making process and a flexibility, if I want to scan stuff from my sketch books I can, equally from a screen printed texture or photocopy. I like to think I produce images that look like I've enjoyed the process and got excited about making 'em, that people dig "

Morten Laursen

By Tim Marrs

date at London bridge and spent a few minutes scanning the area, who could be the photographer? You guessed it, the guy with the black shades, pointy shoes, semi mohican and skin tight black jeans. Anyway, the date went very well – joke! Morten's work impressed me along with his easy going and typically friendly Danish attitude. This guy takes some amazing shots including lots of beautiful ladies wearing little more than their smile, but all done with an eye for colour, shadow and balance... very moody and sexy! So in making the portrait I visited his studio, off the very hectic Old Street area of London and came away thinking in all of this regeneration, hectic inner city living, he produces these often very sensitive relaxed shots, a challenging balance to capture in an image.

In the end the piece was influenced by a record sleeve he showed me in his studio, an early punk band, half tone imagery and very bold. So in essence this image is a homage to this and alongside capturing Morten's boldness in work and in fashion, and "make sure you have my pointy shoes in the illustration, Tim"

Born in Copenhagen. Grew up in a small Tuscan village. Studied journalism in Denmark, while working as a press photographer. Moved to Milan, to assist in fashion and advertising. Returned to Copenhagen two years later, to set up his own photographic studio. Based in London since 1999. His clients include *Arena*, *The Face*, *Dansk*, *Grazia*, *Exit*, *Phamous69*, *Cover*, *CAR*, *Café*, *Smag*, *Euroman*, *BIG-magazine*, Vertu, Jaguar, Audi, Sony, BMG. EMI, Polydor, Paul Smith, Full Circle, Levis, Esso, Lacroix, Harvey Nichols, Hugo Boss, Falke, Coca Cola, Drambuie, and many more.

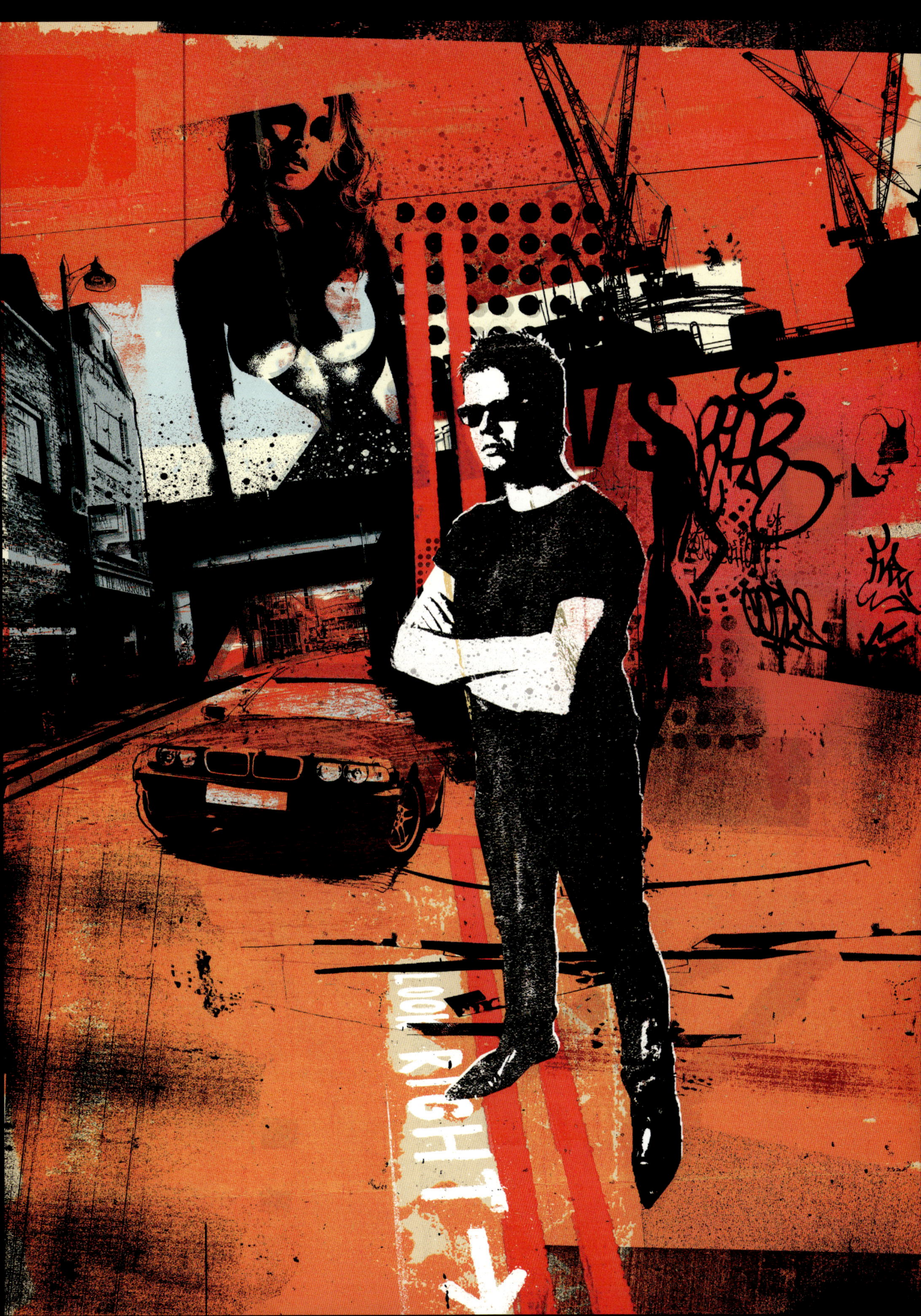
VS
RIGHT

Kinsey /

By Ben Tour

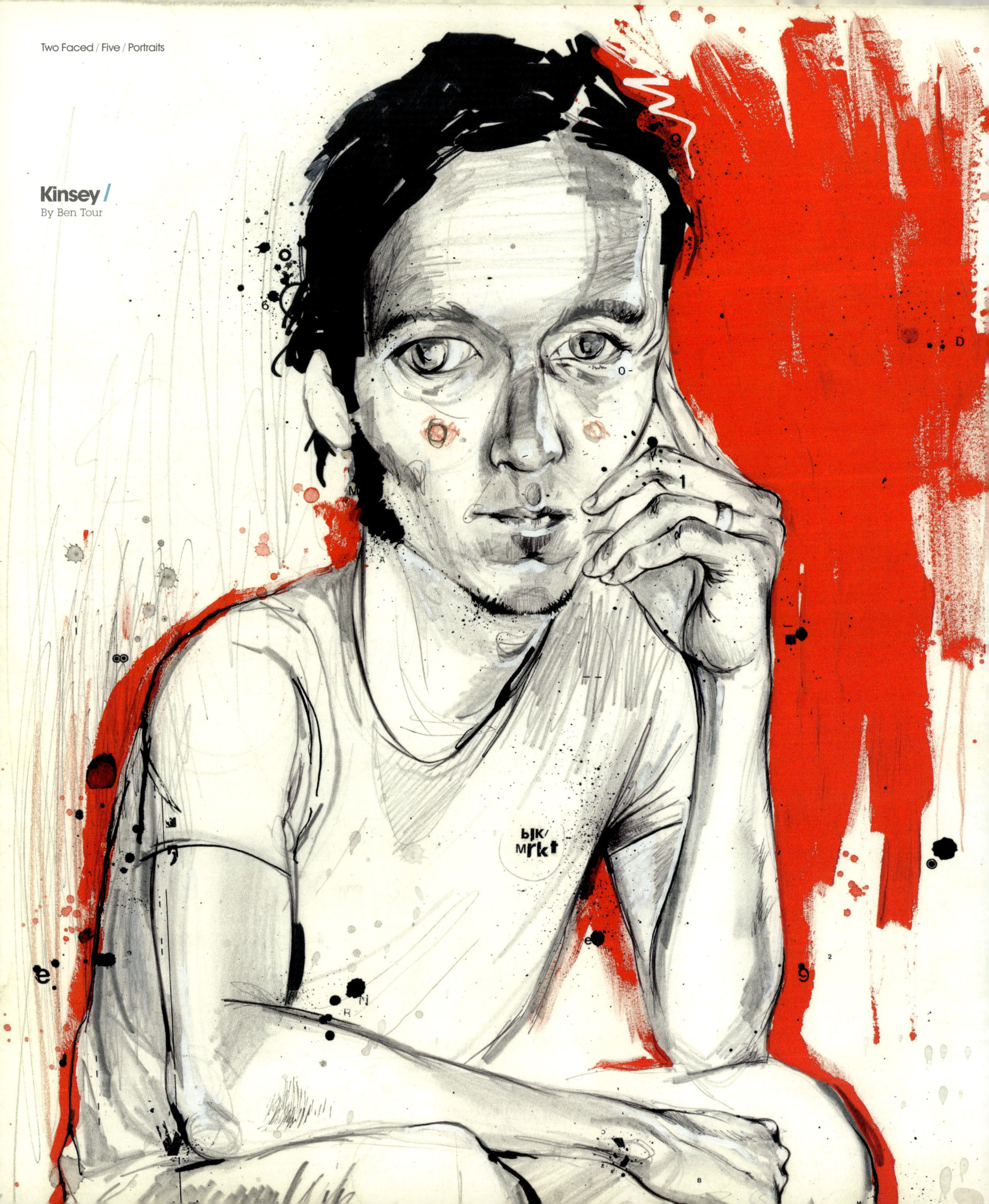

Ben Tour /

By Kinsey

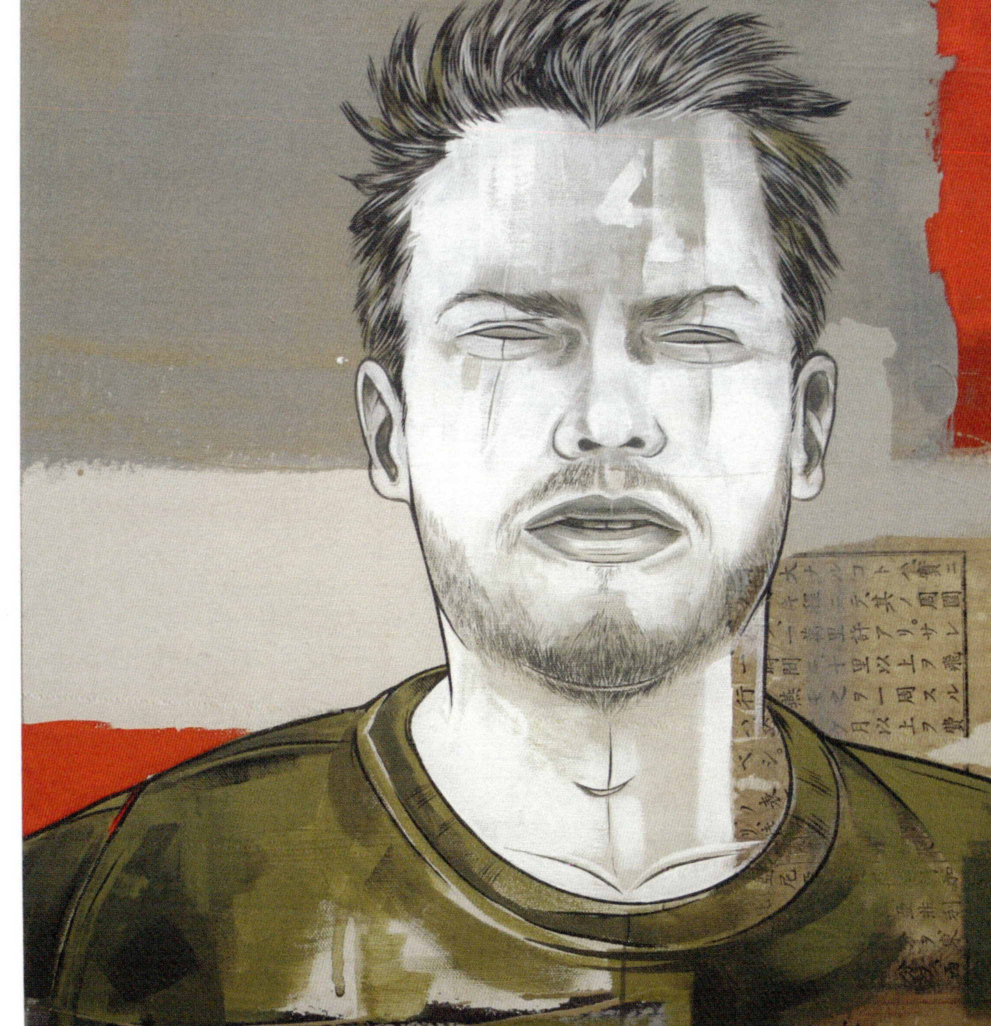

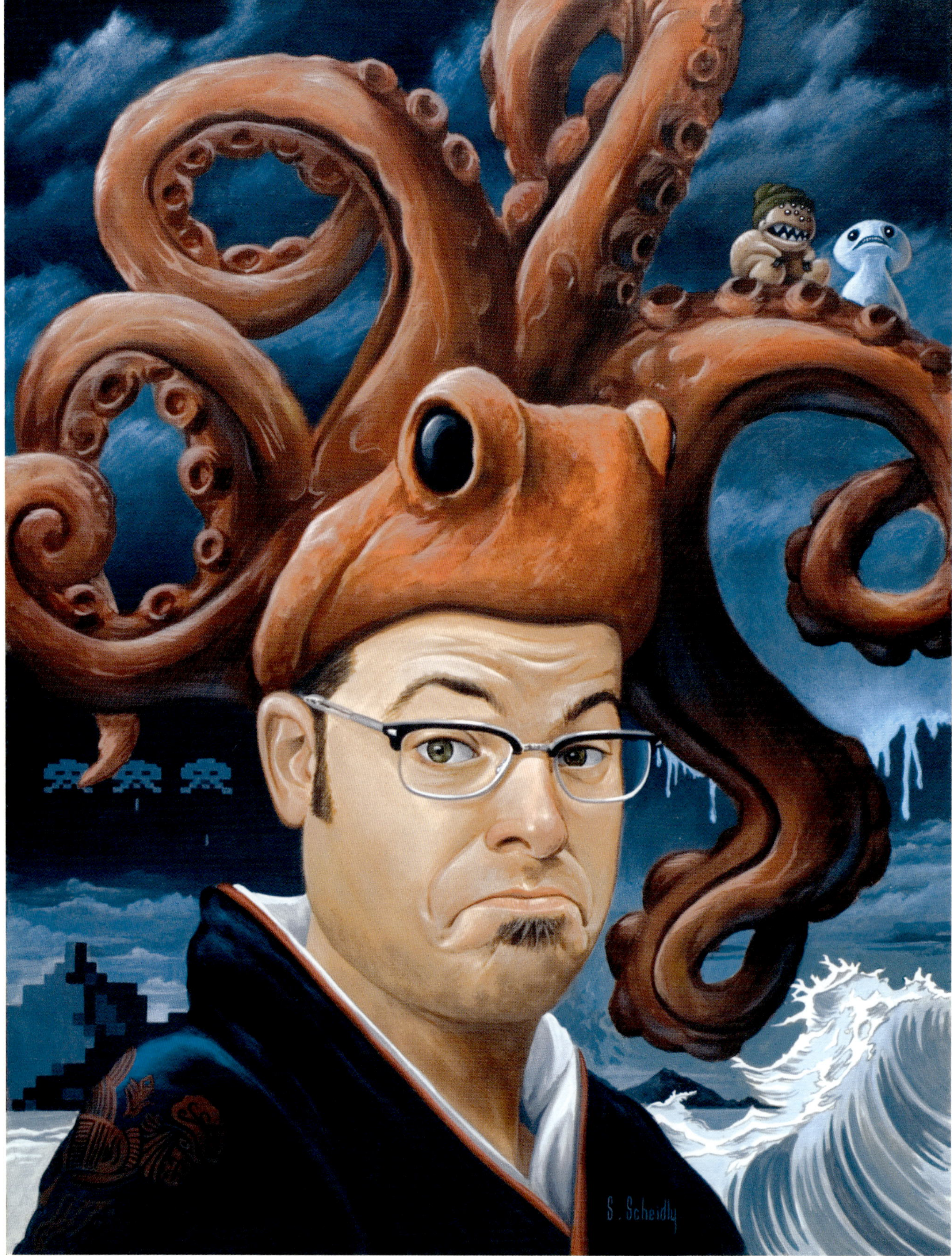
S. Scheidly

Nathan Fox

By Scott Scheidly

My painting of Nathan is just a repositioning of 10 packs of crayons. It is a story conveyed with the rearranging of colours. A tale of a man who grew up on LEGOs and Atari just as I had. A man who dreams of Japan as do I. A man who wears octopi on his head. Well, I've never worn octopi on my head but did once play with a dead bloated dog by the river for a day. That's almost the same, right? I'm really not sure about what I'm writing, about Nathan, or about art in general. I'm just rearranging colours in the smoking mirror as I wait to arrive at a colourful and joyful insanity. The truth will set you confused.

Nathan Fox currently lives and works in Milwaukee, WI. He received his MFA in 'Illustration as Visual Essay' from the School of Visual Arts in 2002 and has been freelancing ever since. Dabbling in comics whenever possible, Nathan's works span the gamut of narrative forms from gallery-hung work to printed matter.

Scott Scheidly

By Nathan Fox

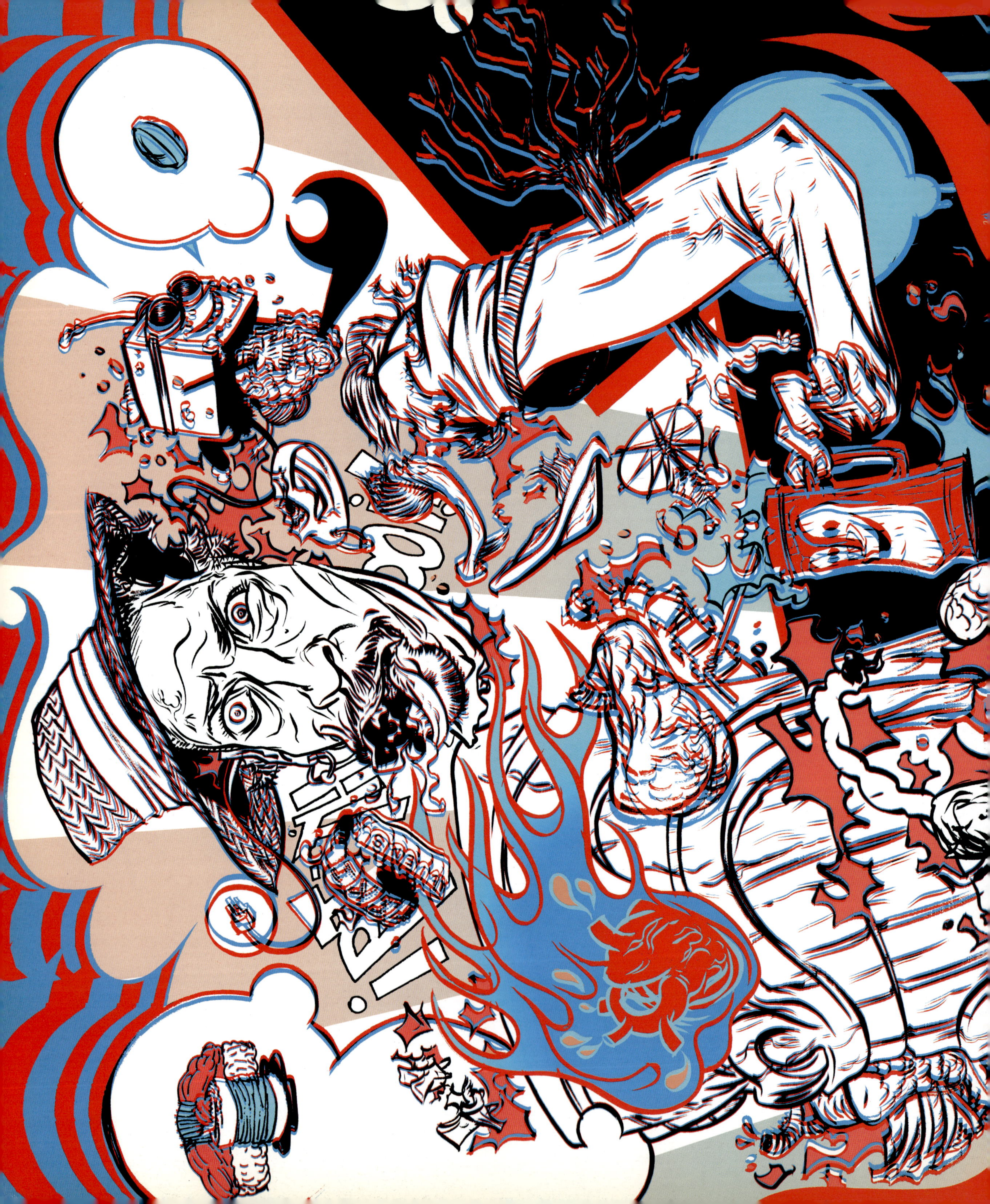

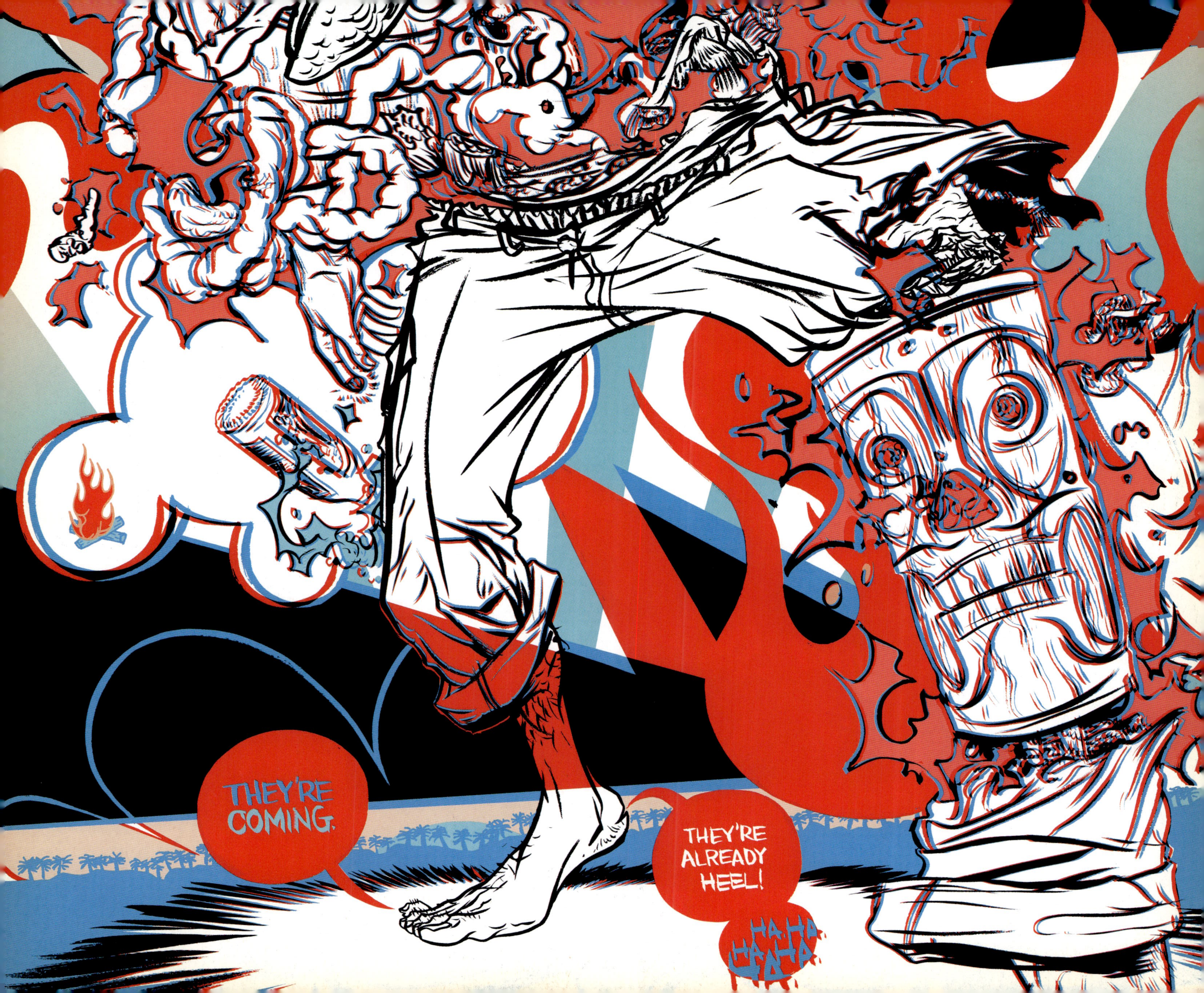
THEY'RE COMING.
THEY'RE ALREADY HEEL!
HA HA
HA HA

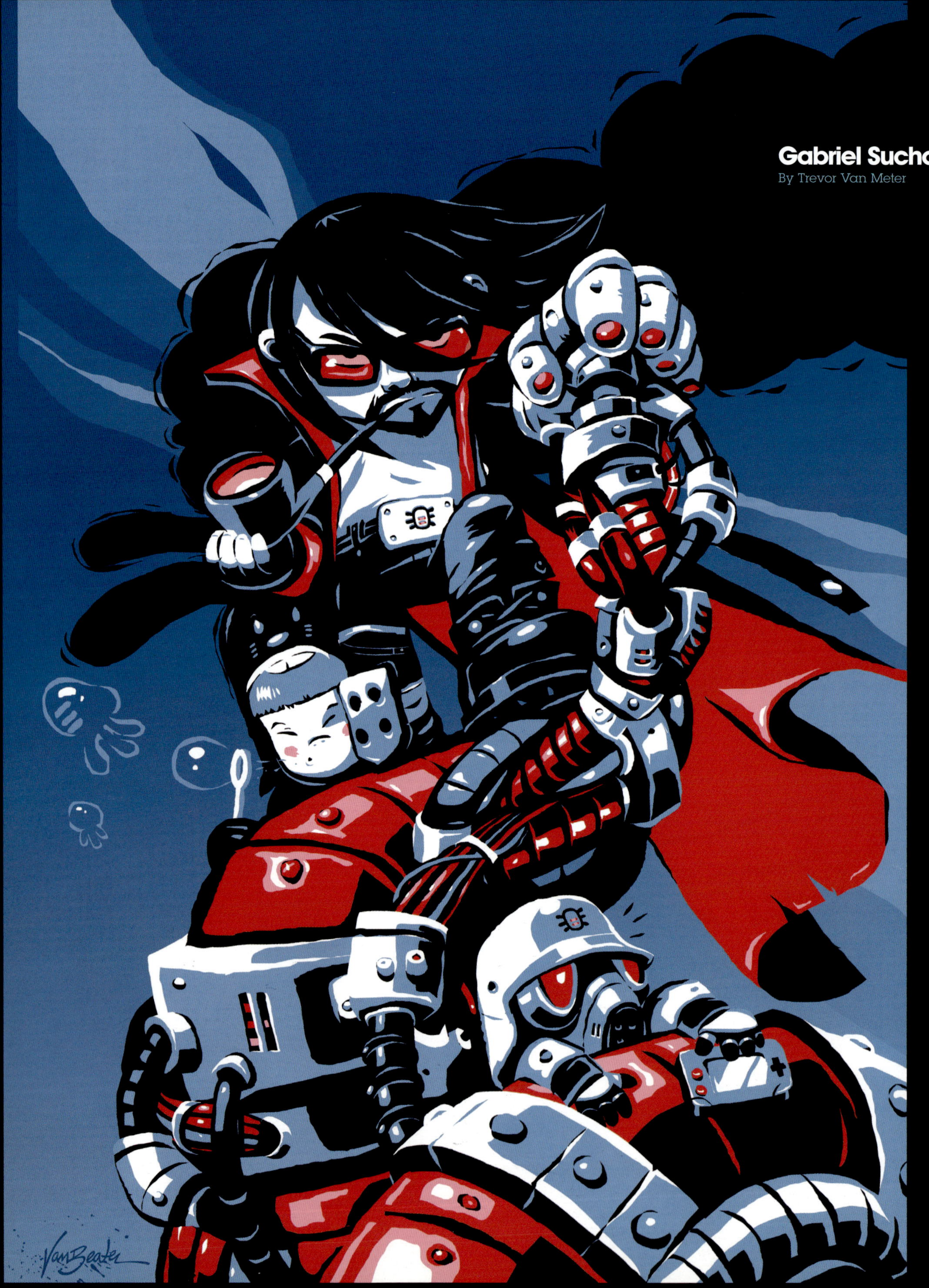

Gabriel Suchowolski /

By Trevor Van Meter

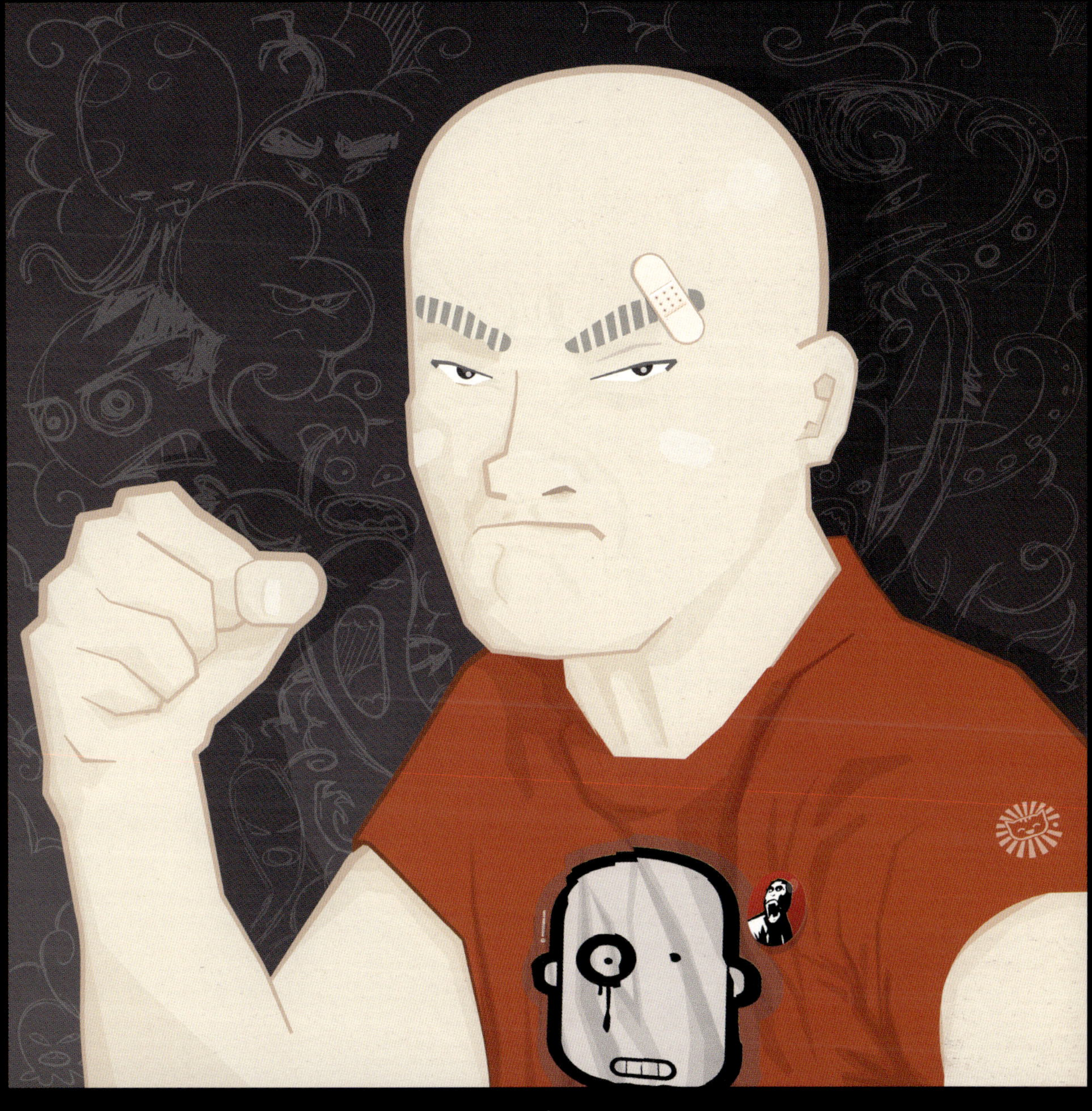

Trevor Van Meter /

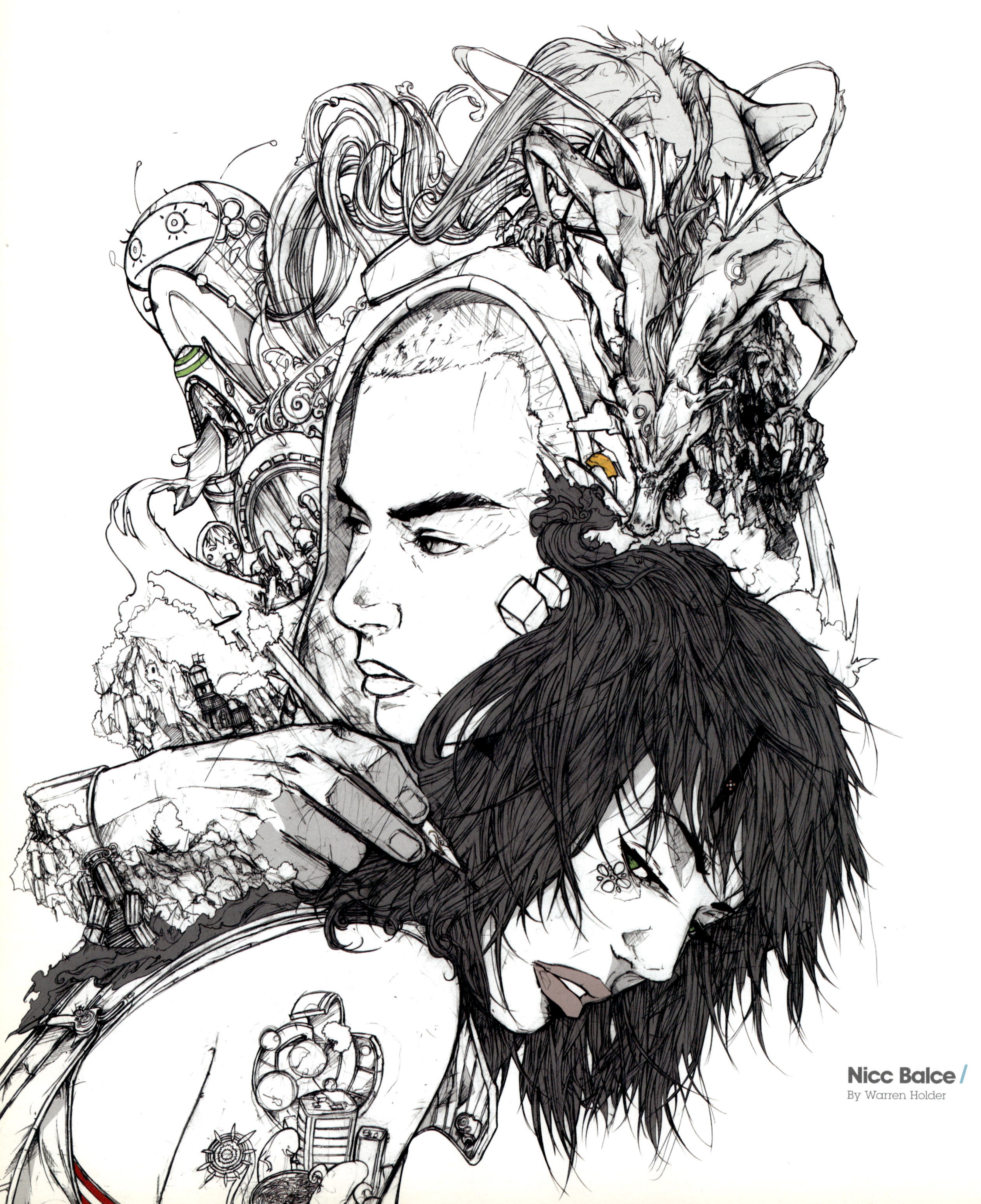

Nicc Balce /

By Warren Holder

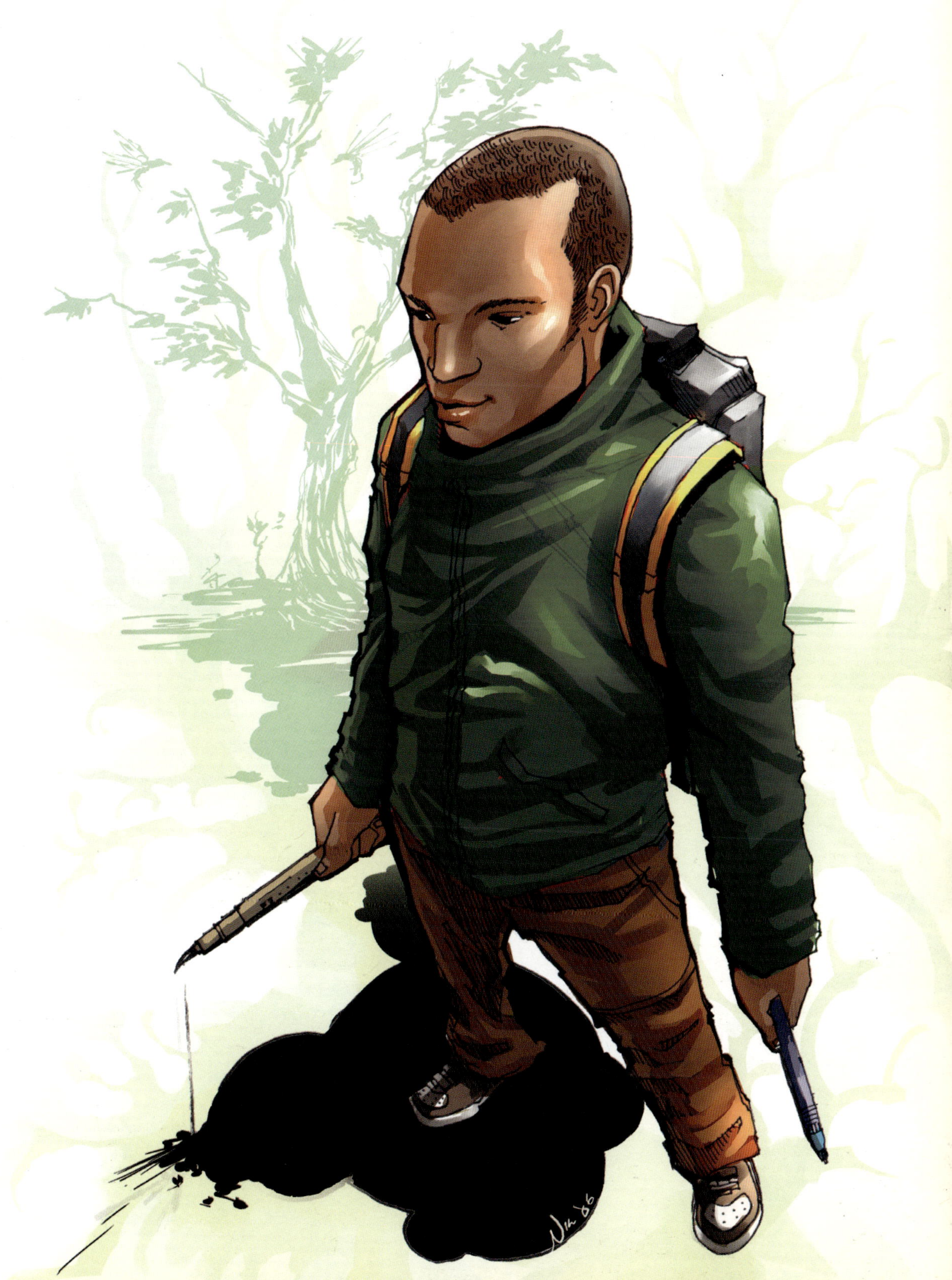

Warren Holder /

By Nicc Balce

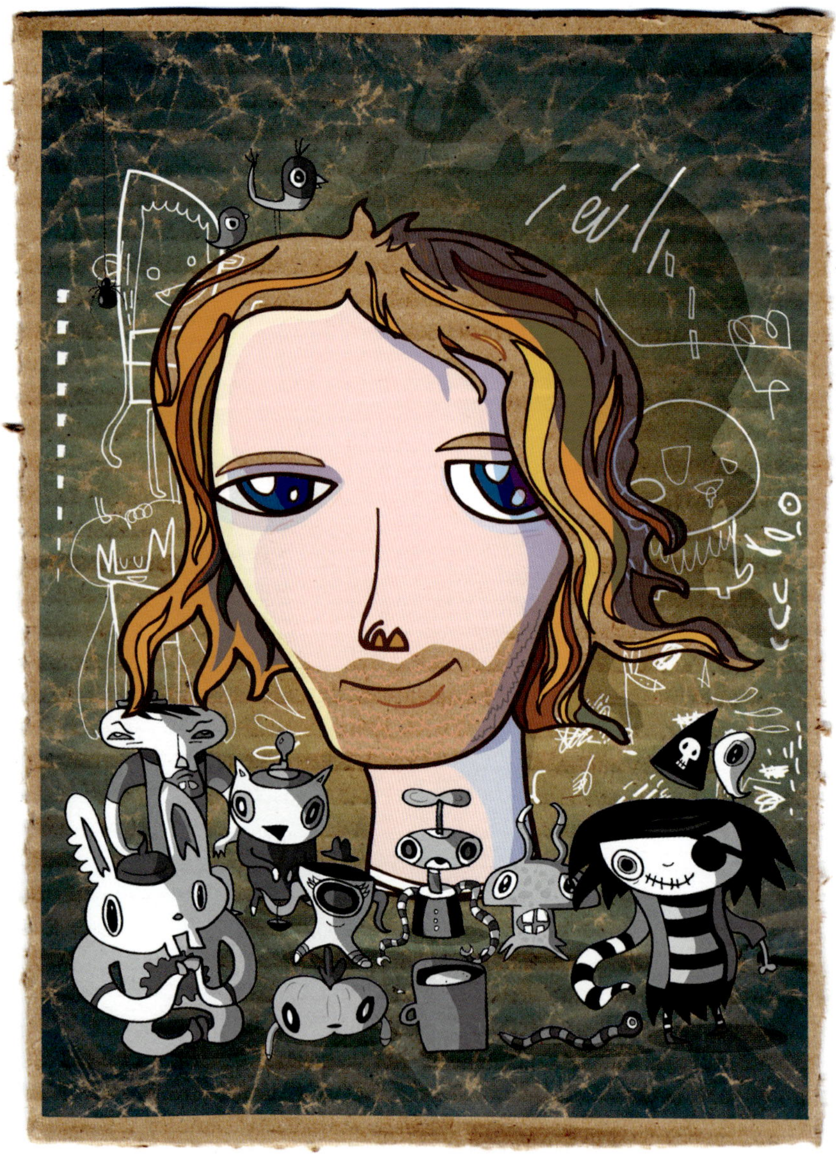

Nathan Jurevicius_Scarygirl /
By John Burgerman

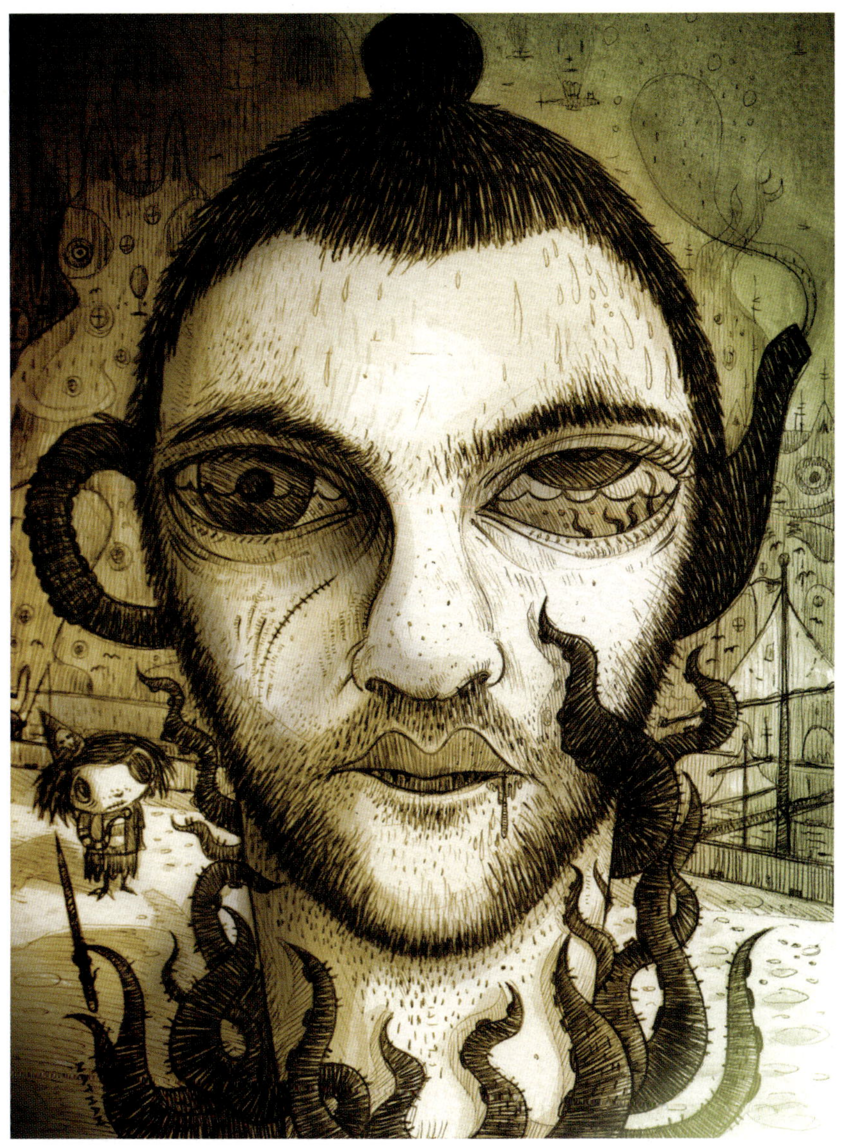

Jon Burgerman /
By Nathan Jurevicius_Scarygirl

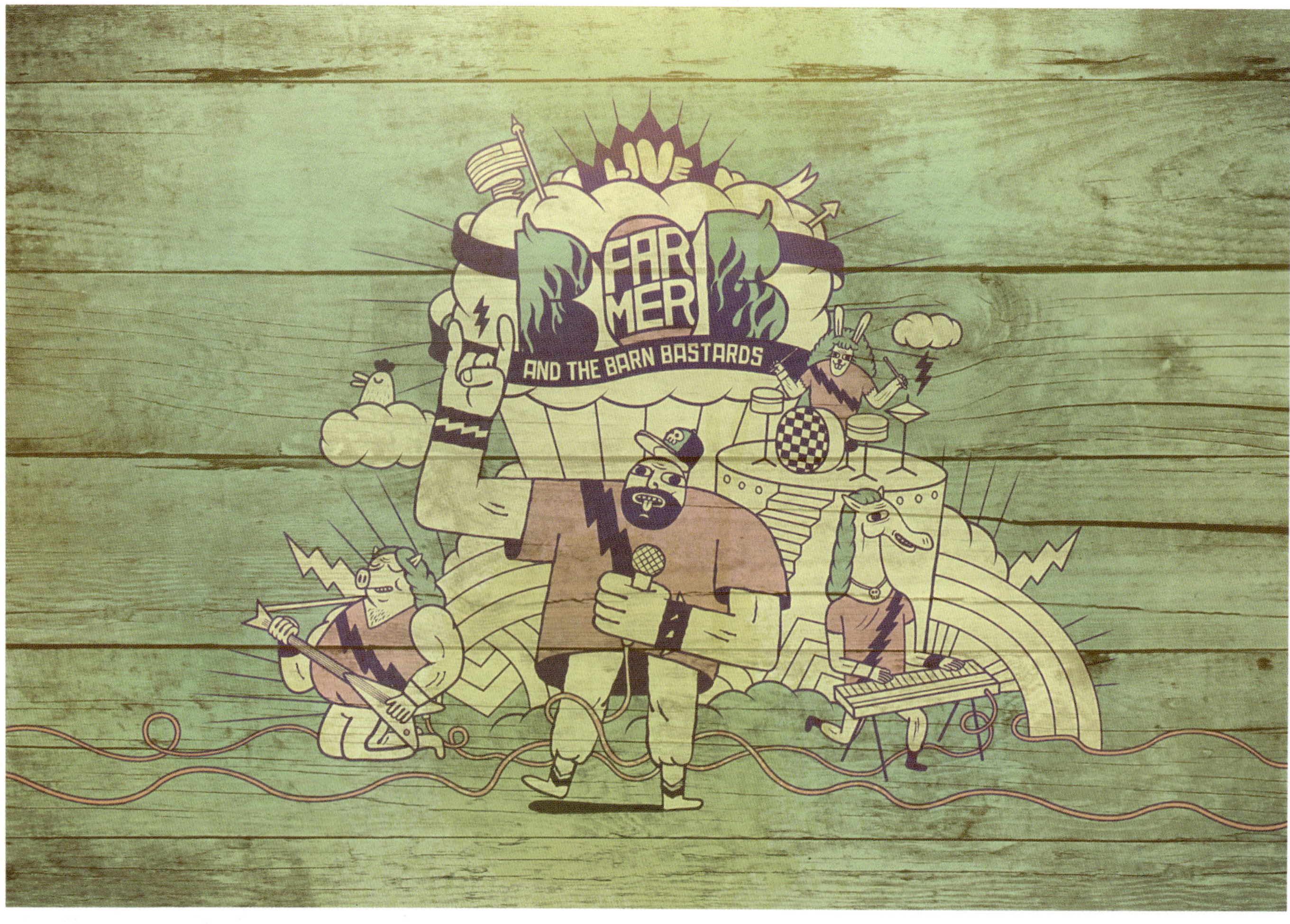

Farmerbob /
By Mauro Gatti

Mauro Gatti /
By Farmerbob

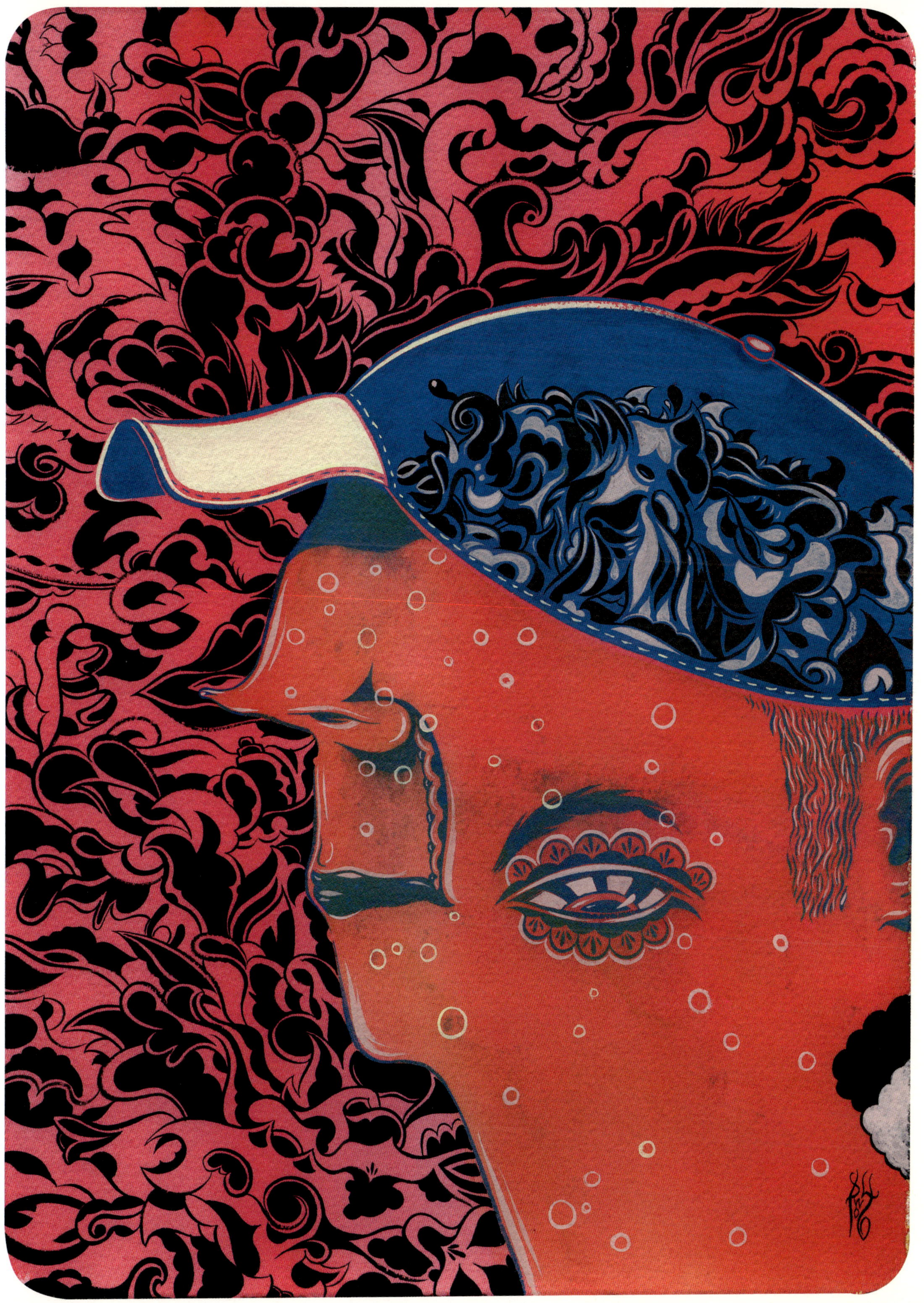

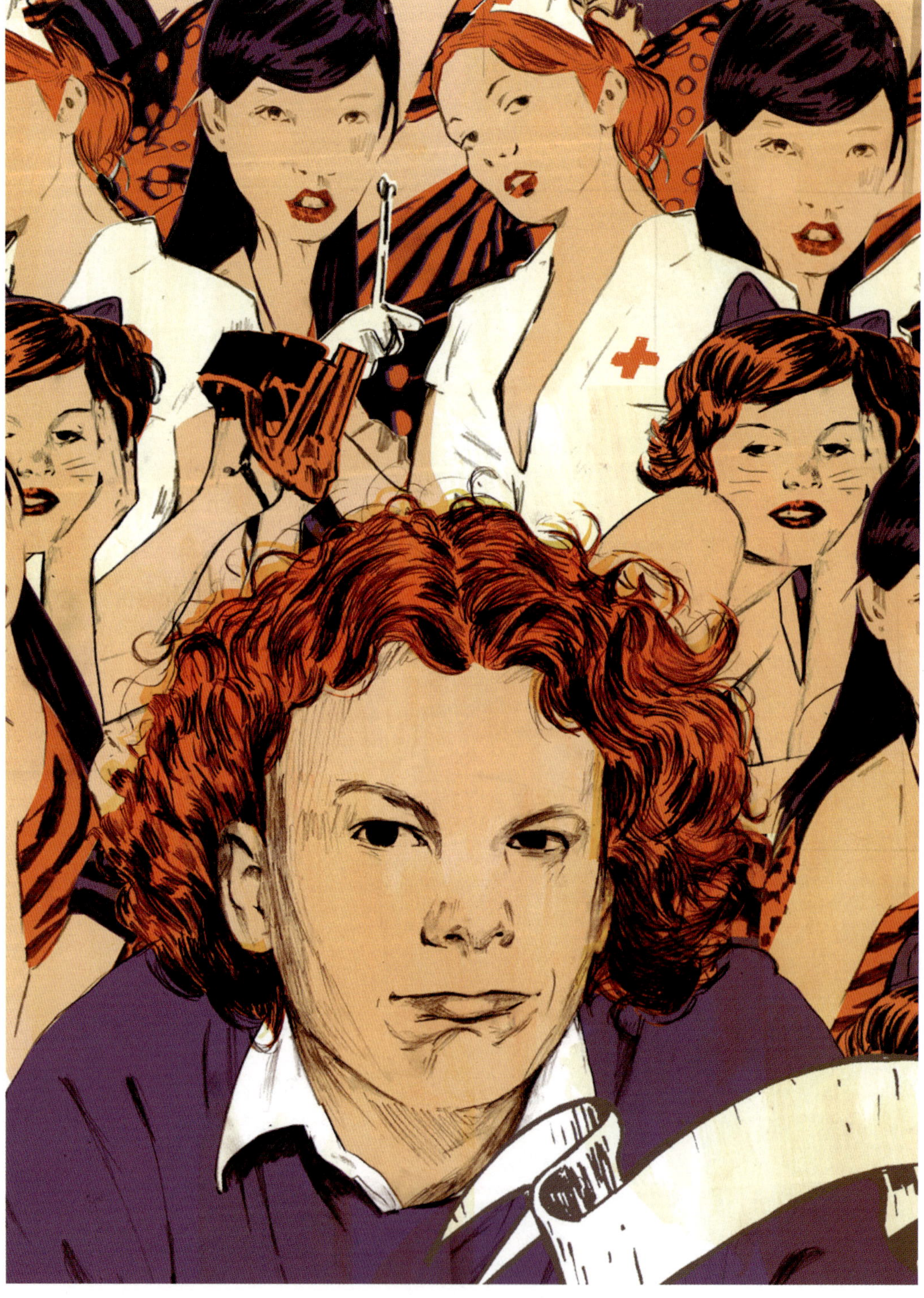

Stuntkid

By Rachel Domm

Stuntkid / Jason Levesque's paintings are a modern follow-up to the Gil Everyn and Vargas girls and are a beautifully executed homage to the rise of the alternative/indie pin-up girl. Levesque's girls are wholesome, charming and unaware while still retaining edginess through the style and tone of their ensembles and Levesque's execution. It is not a world of excess and overly glamorized women but an environment of playful healthy sexuality. His smooth colours and application of paint and texture are as fresh and confident as the girls he paints.

Stuntkid / Jason Levesque is a self-taught illustrator living in Norfolk Virginia. His texture-rich portraits focus on the many facets of the female personality. Sometimes bold, sexy, nonchalant, and always beautiful. Among his works you'll also find illustrations depicting his many creations ranging from vicious toothy bunny monsters to alluring lady octopuses.

Levesque's work can be found at www.stuntkid.com. You'll find several experiments to play with in a special "toybox" section. You'll also find links to the various outlets where you can purchase his work including his recently published book of illustrations *girls are pretty*.

Rachel Domm

By Stuntkid

Rachel Domm is an incredible talent living in Brooklyn New York. Her distinctive style has earned her an impressive client list. There is no doubt that she'll continue to expand her abilities and increase her exposure. I was lucky enough to be paired up with Miss Rachel and thoroughly enjoyed working with her on this project. She's a lovely girl and a lovely artist.

Rachel Domm is totally obsessed with her to-do list. Constantly adding and crossing off new and old projects, assignments, ideas and collaborations. Born and bred in the deep south, she quickly departed from the slow and steady pace of southern living to move to Brooklyn, NY where she received her BFA from the Pratt Institute. Continuing to live and work in Brooklyn, she has contributed to publications domestically and internationally and has exhibited in New York and LA.

Working in a variety of mediums and formats, she is feverishly working to create a new body of work that includes illustrations, prints, books, T-shirts, and various other ephemera.

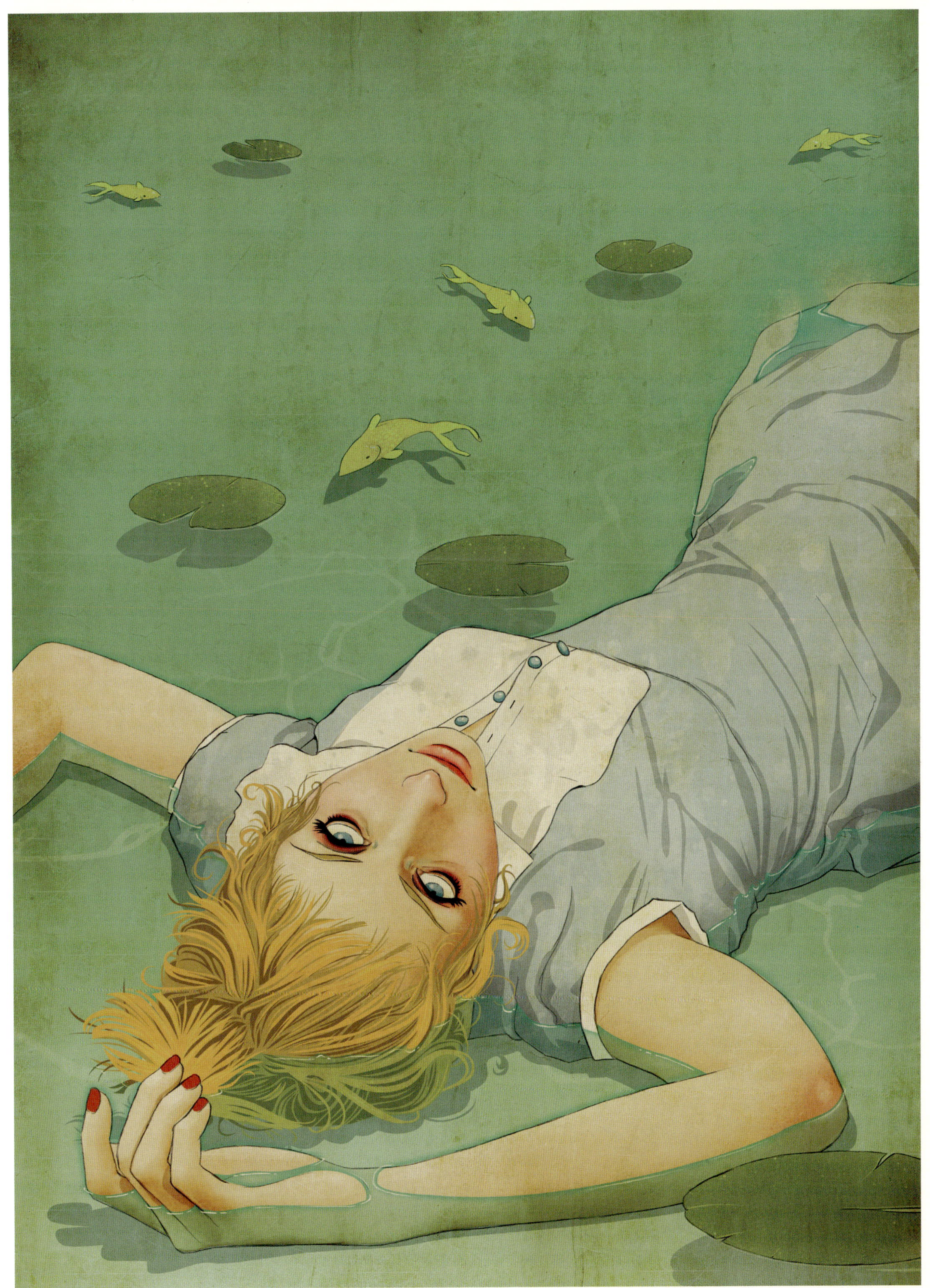

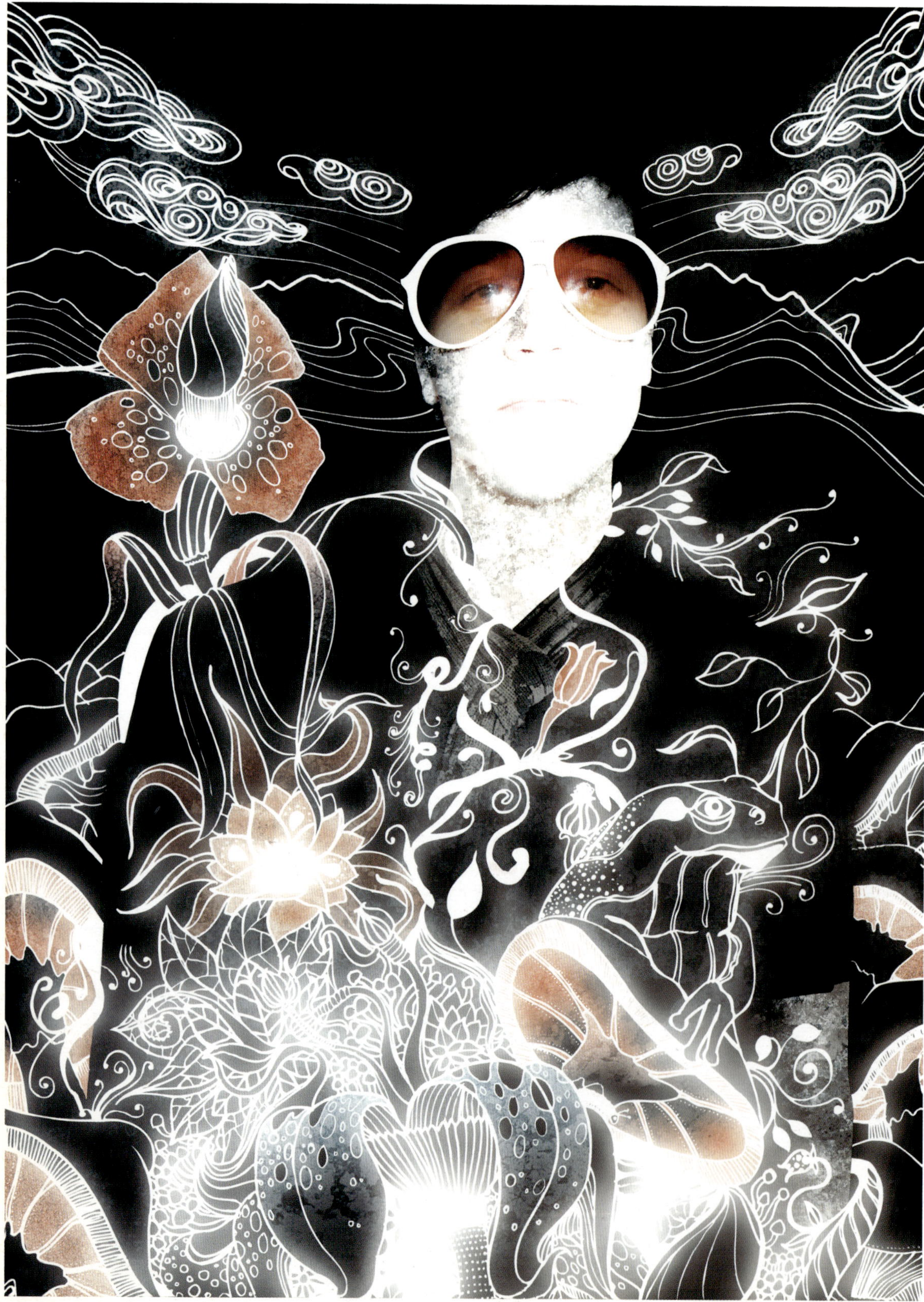

Darren Firth

By McFaul

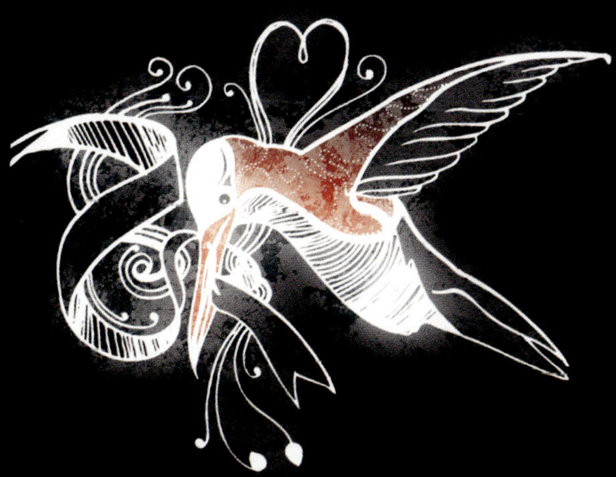

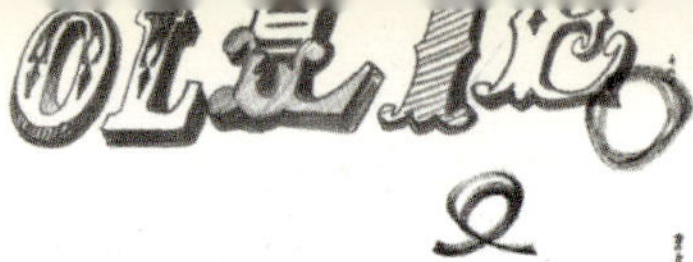

McFaul
By Darren Firth

BLACK CONVOY

YUC

UNSTOPP

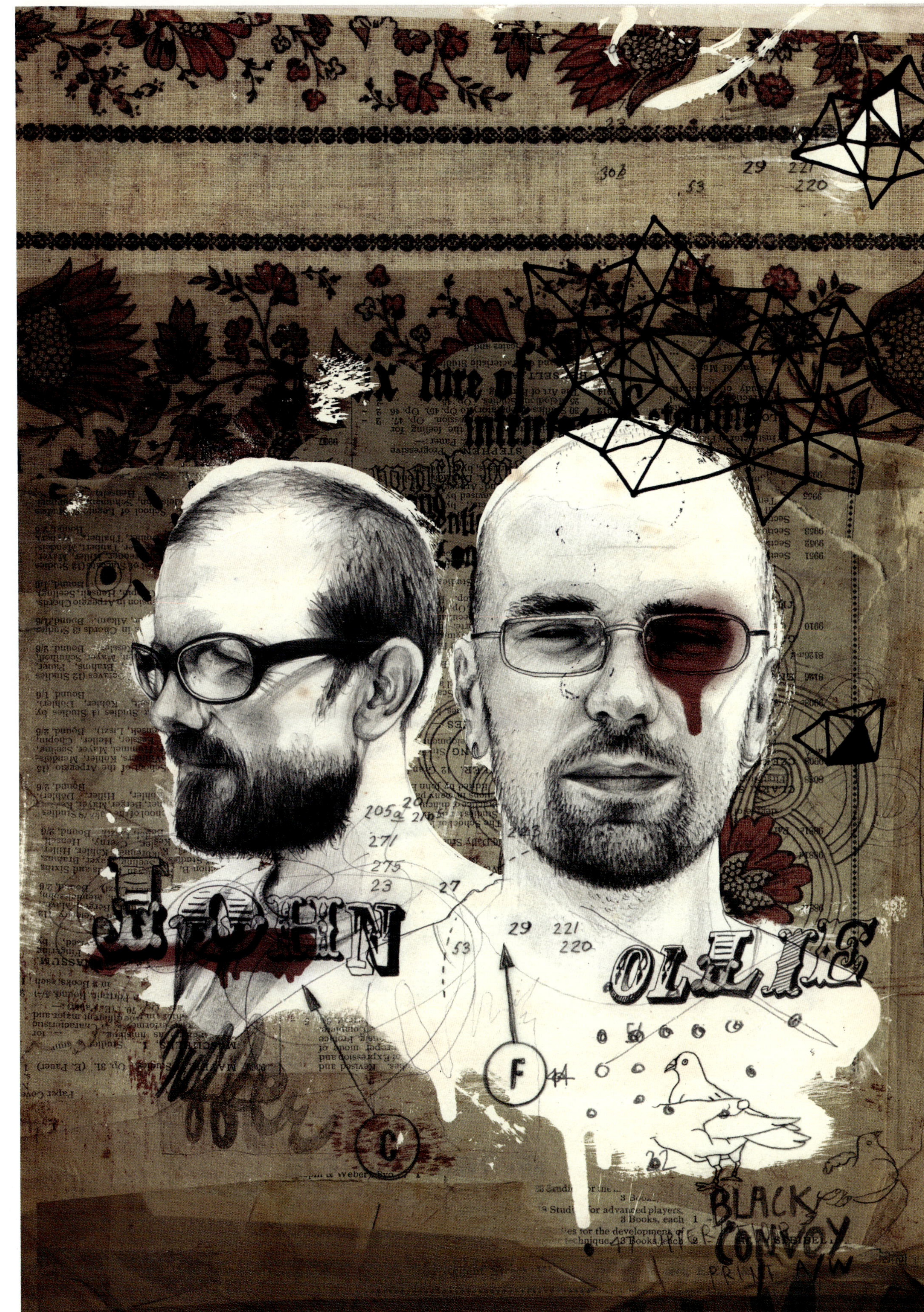

OLLIE
BLACK CONVOY

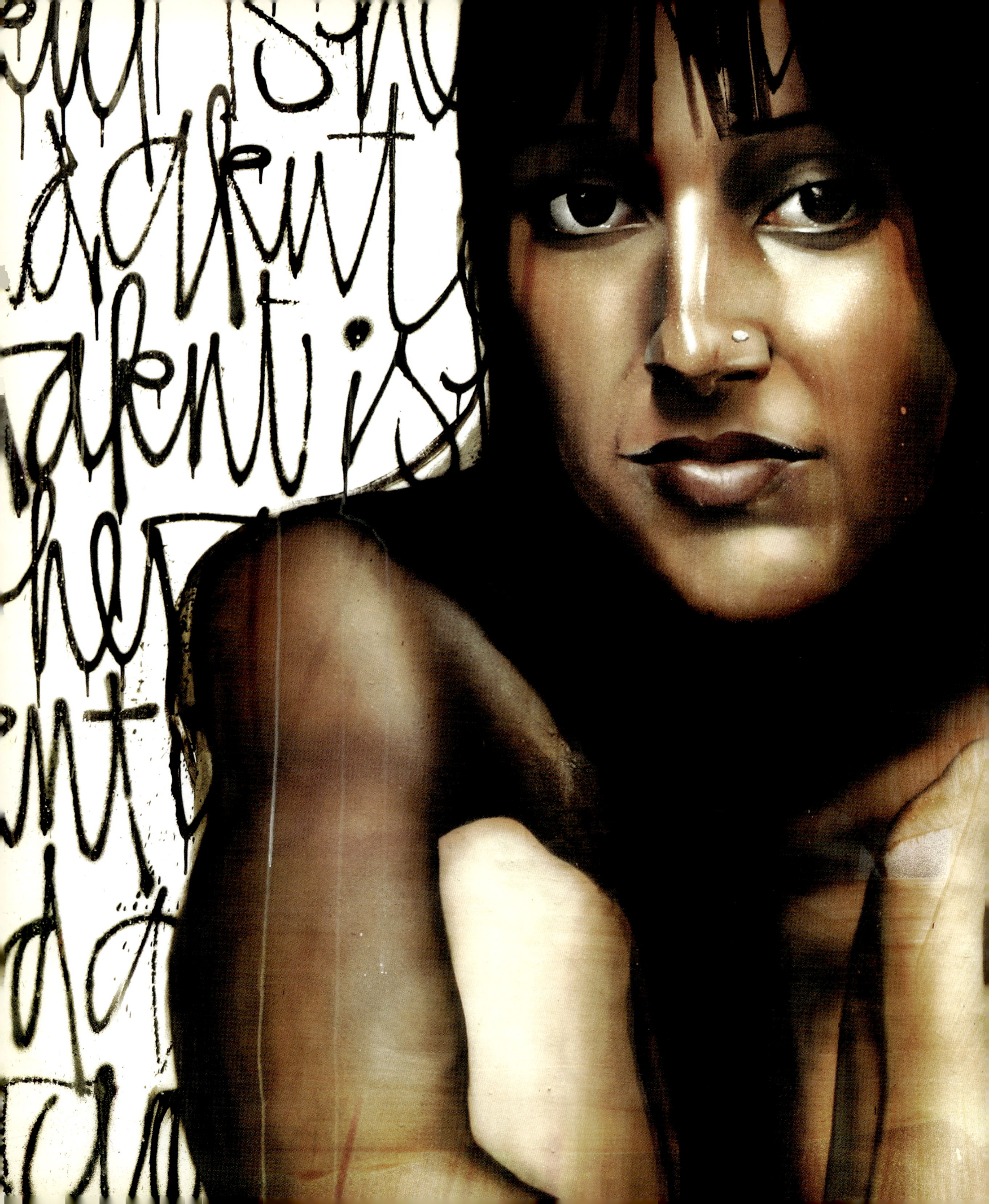

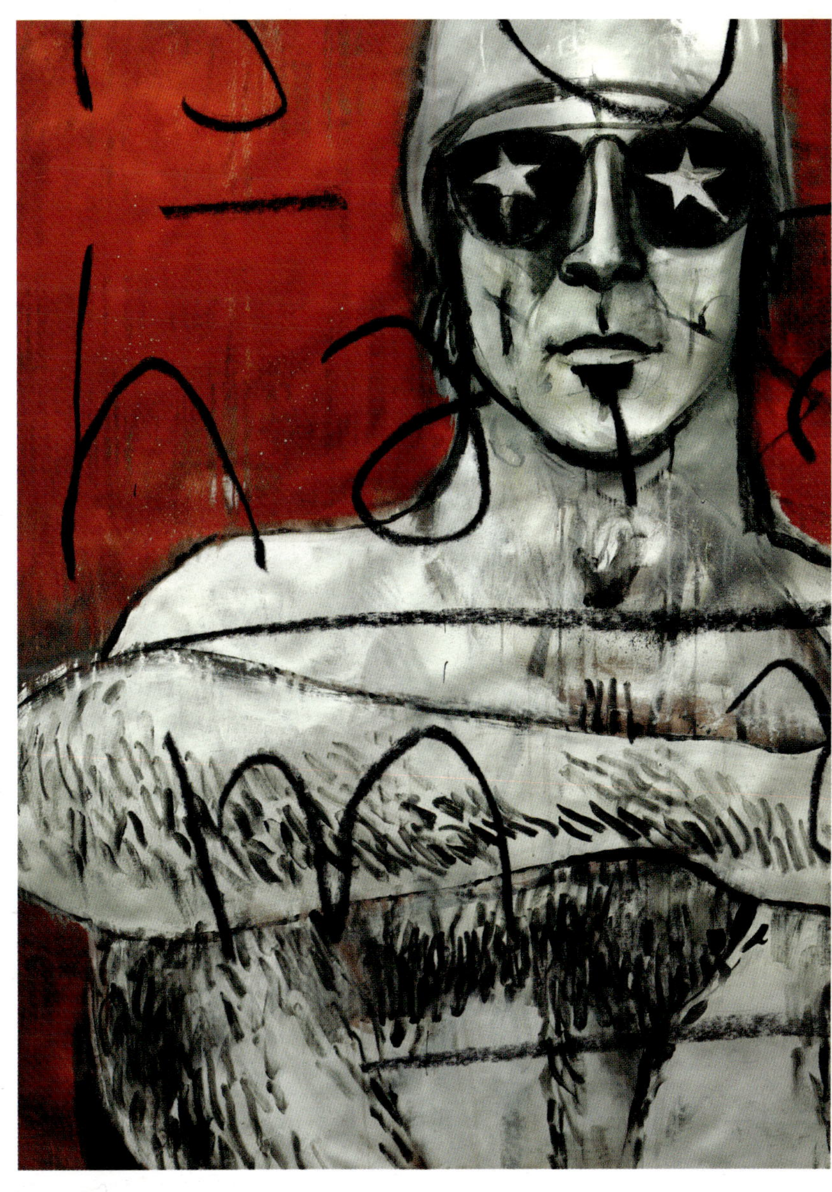

Hera /
By Akut

Akut /
By Hera

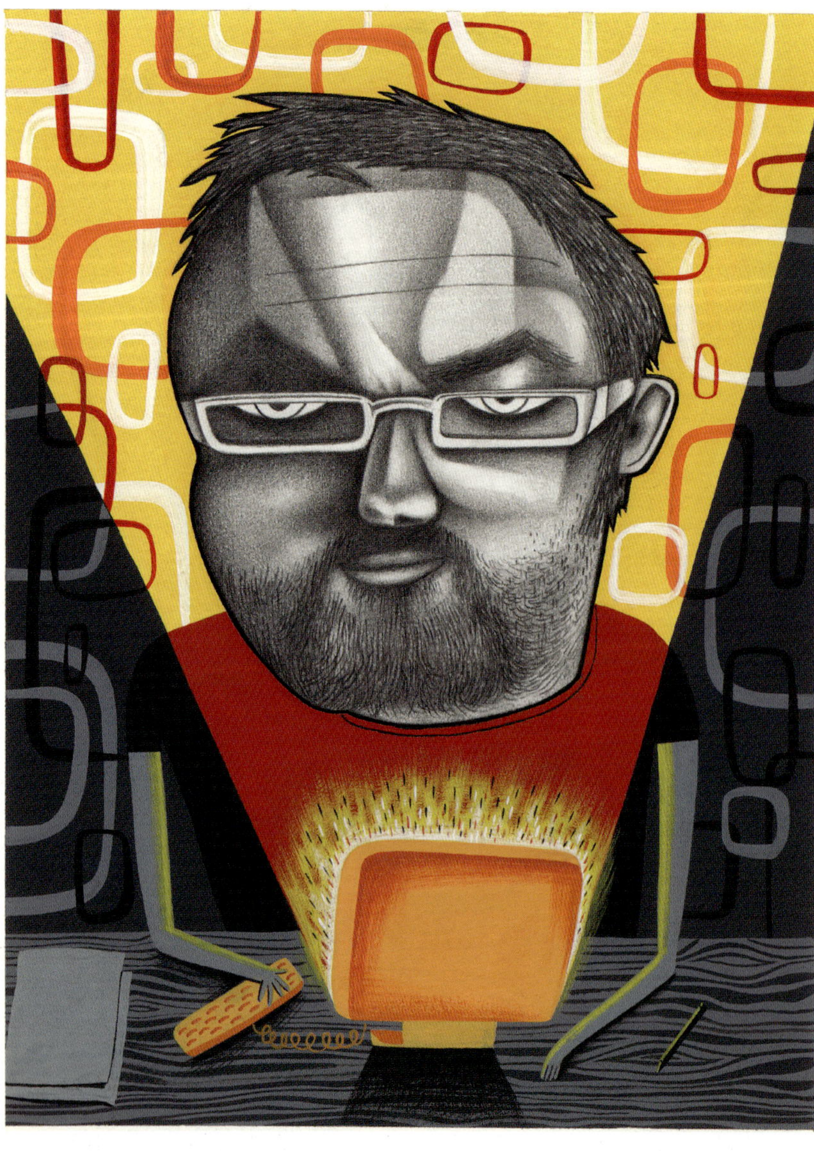

Jason Arber /
By Chris Pyle

Chris Pyle /
By Jason Arber

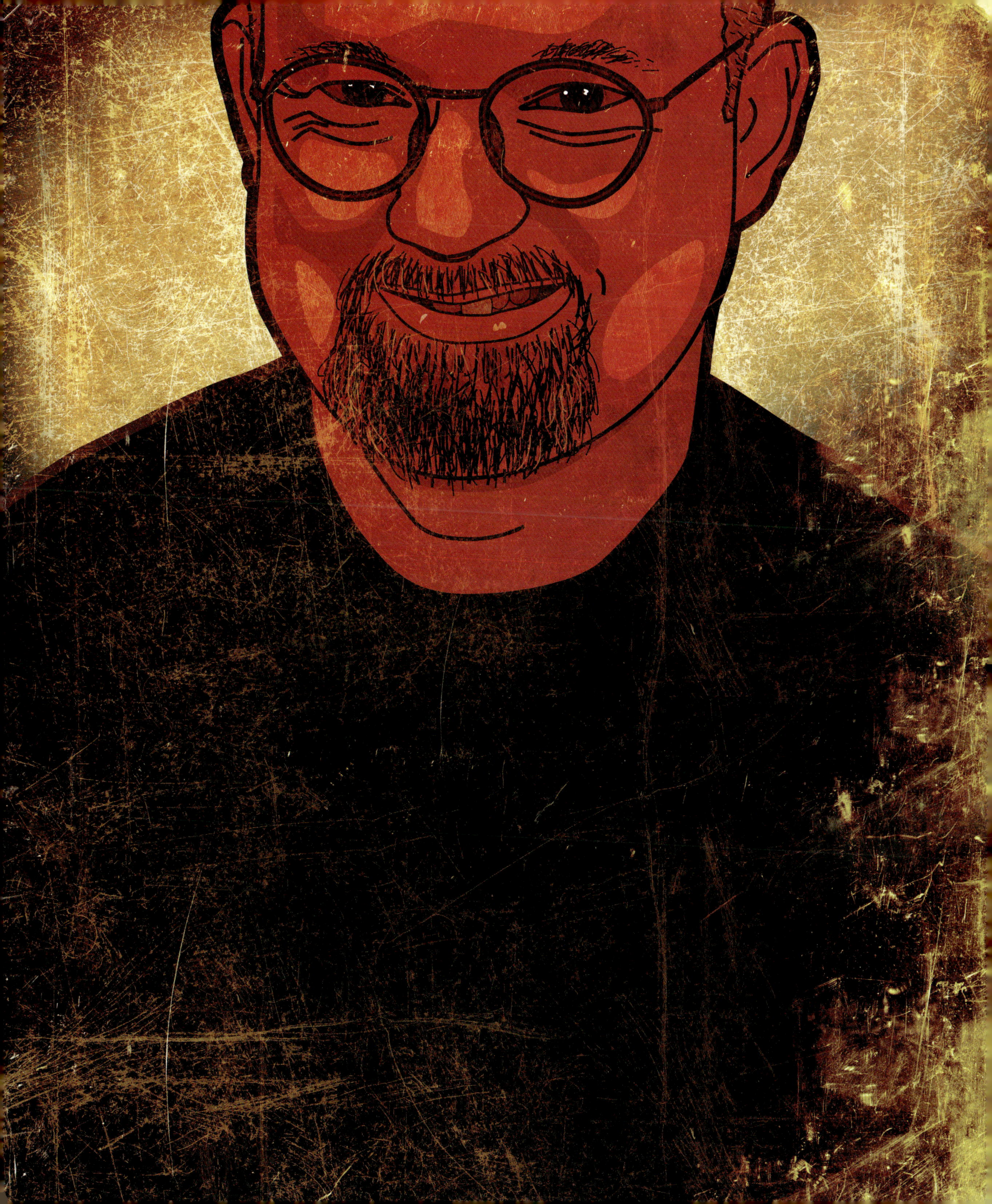

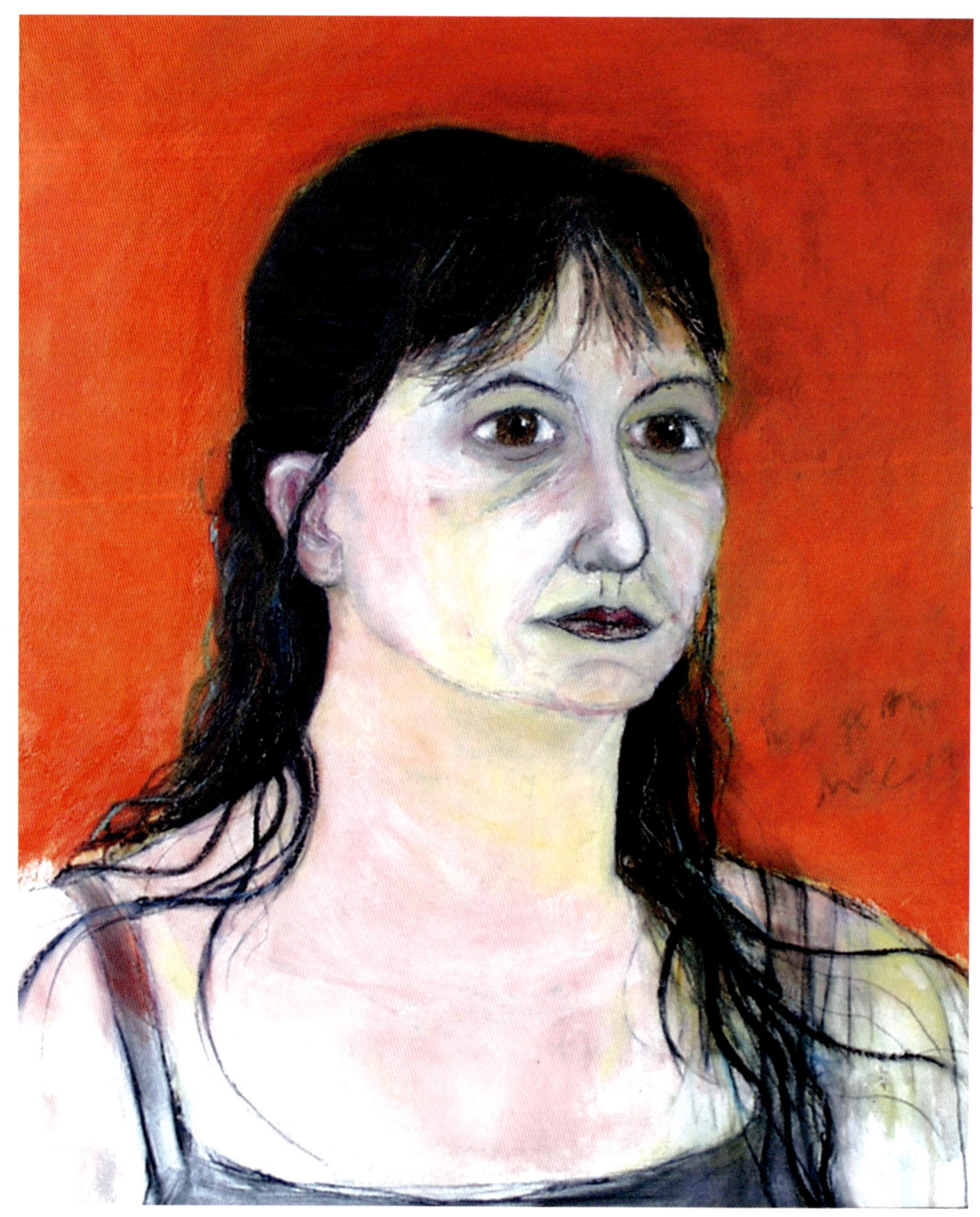

Josie McCoy /
By John Gray

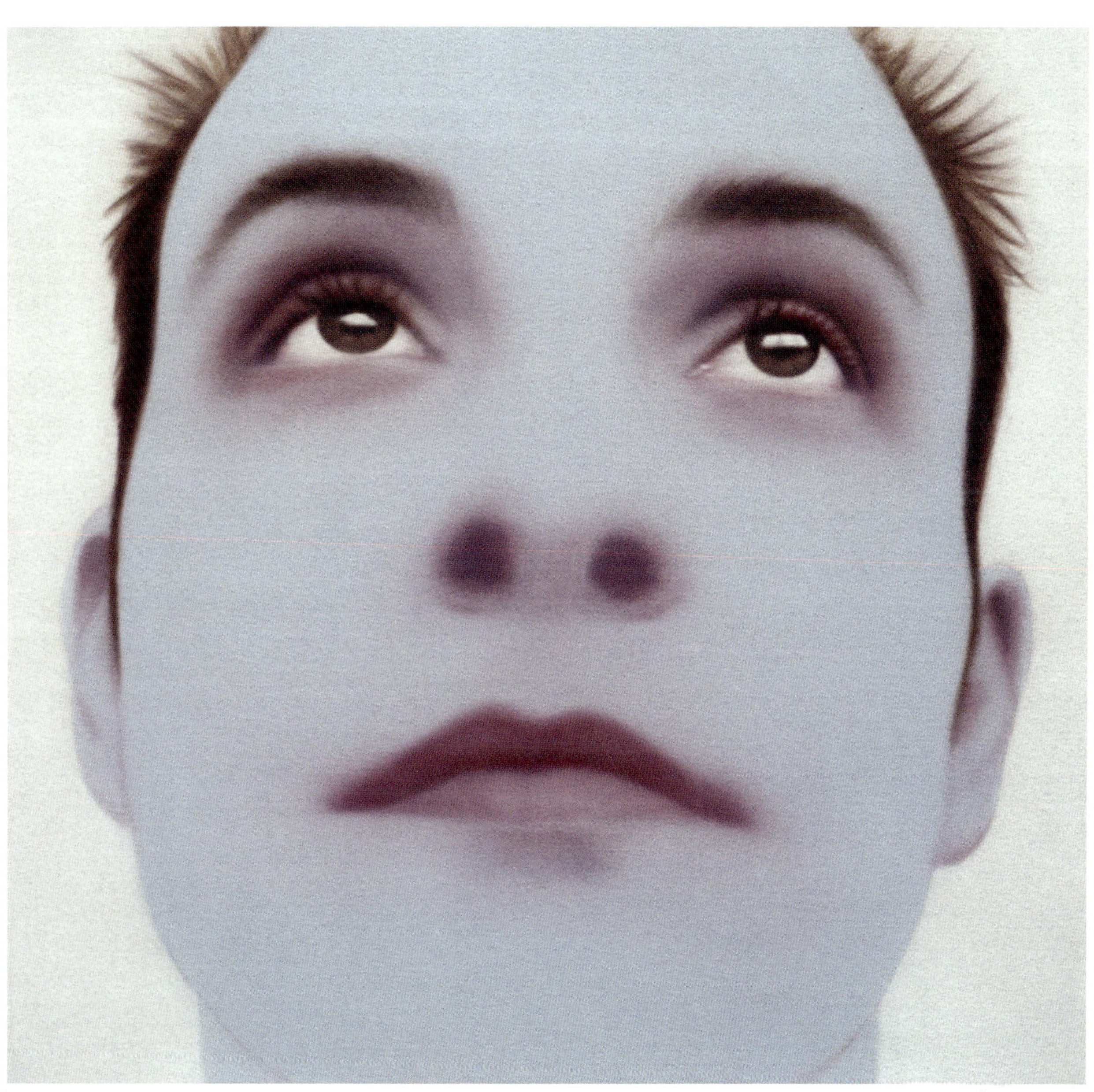

John Gray /

By Josie McCoy

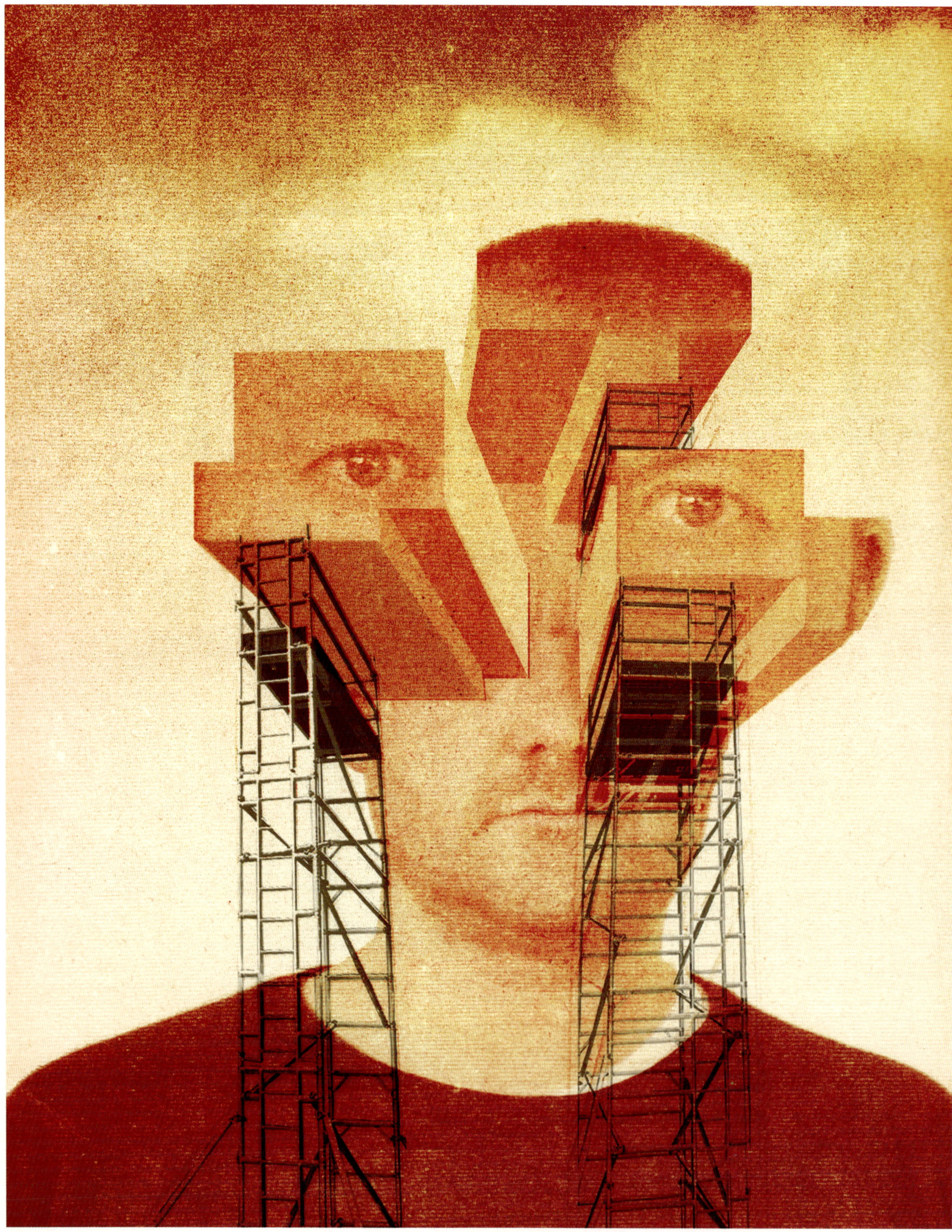

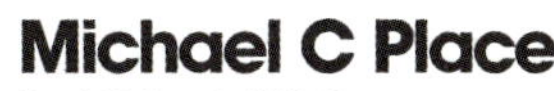

Michael C Place

By Michael Gillette

Michael Gillette

By Michael C Place

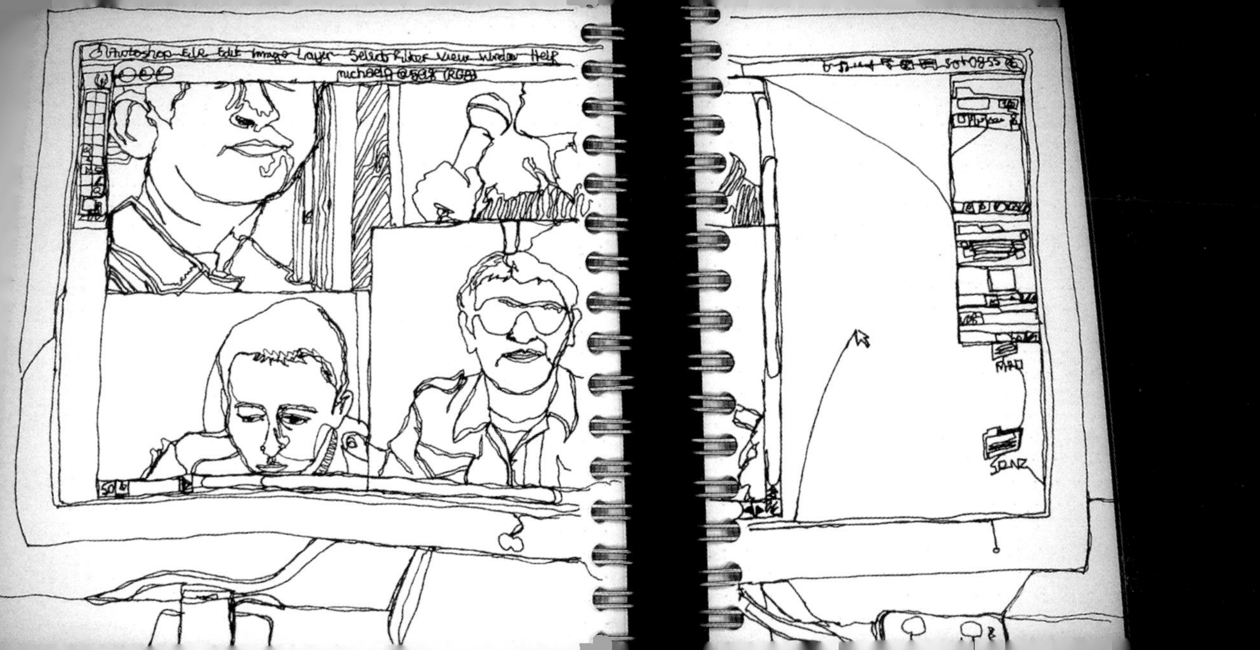

Nathan Gale

By Marion Deuchars

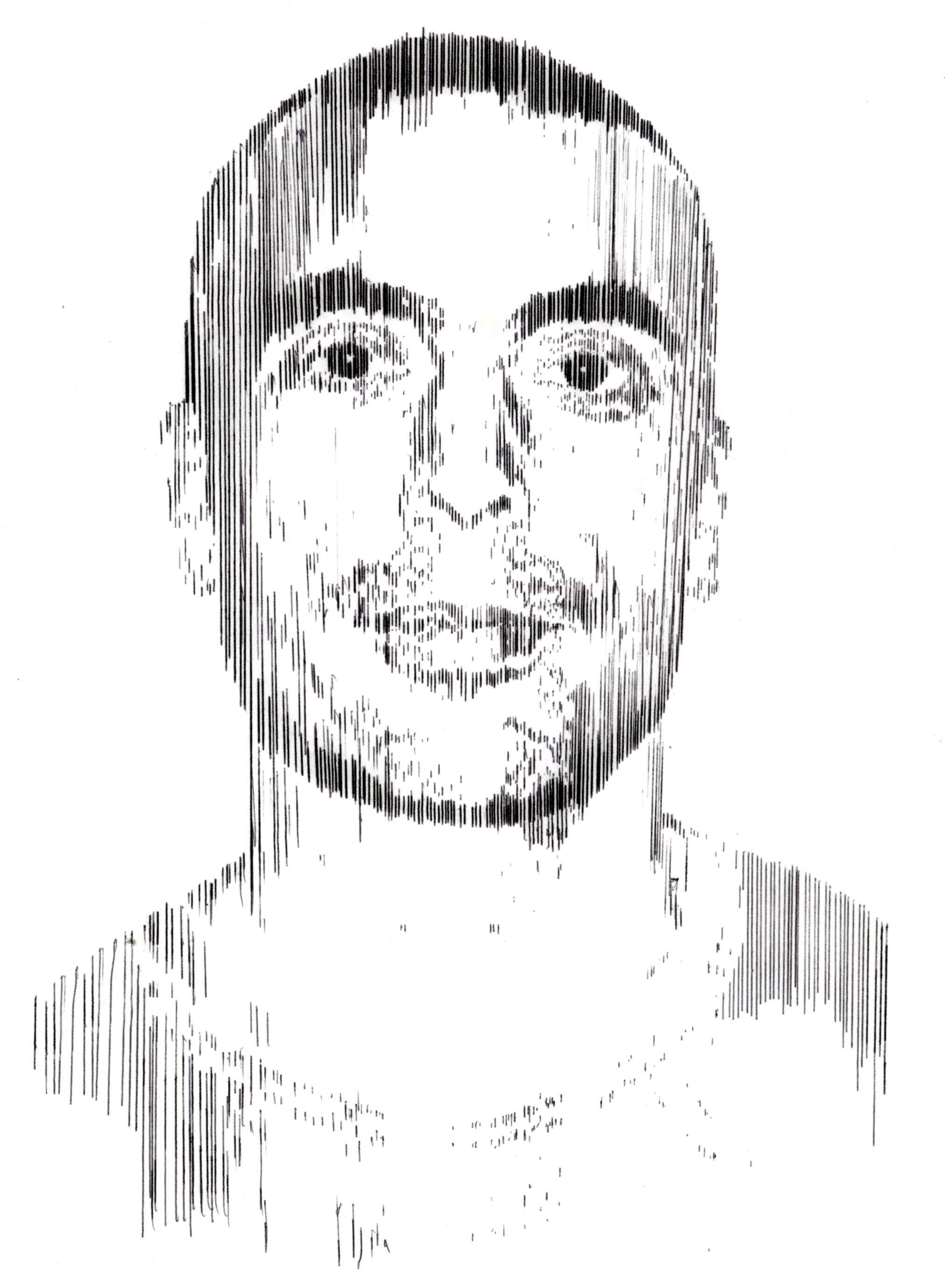

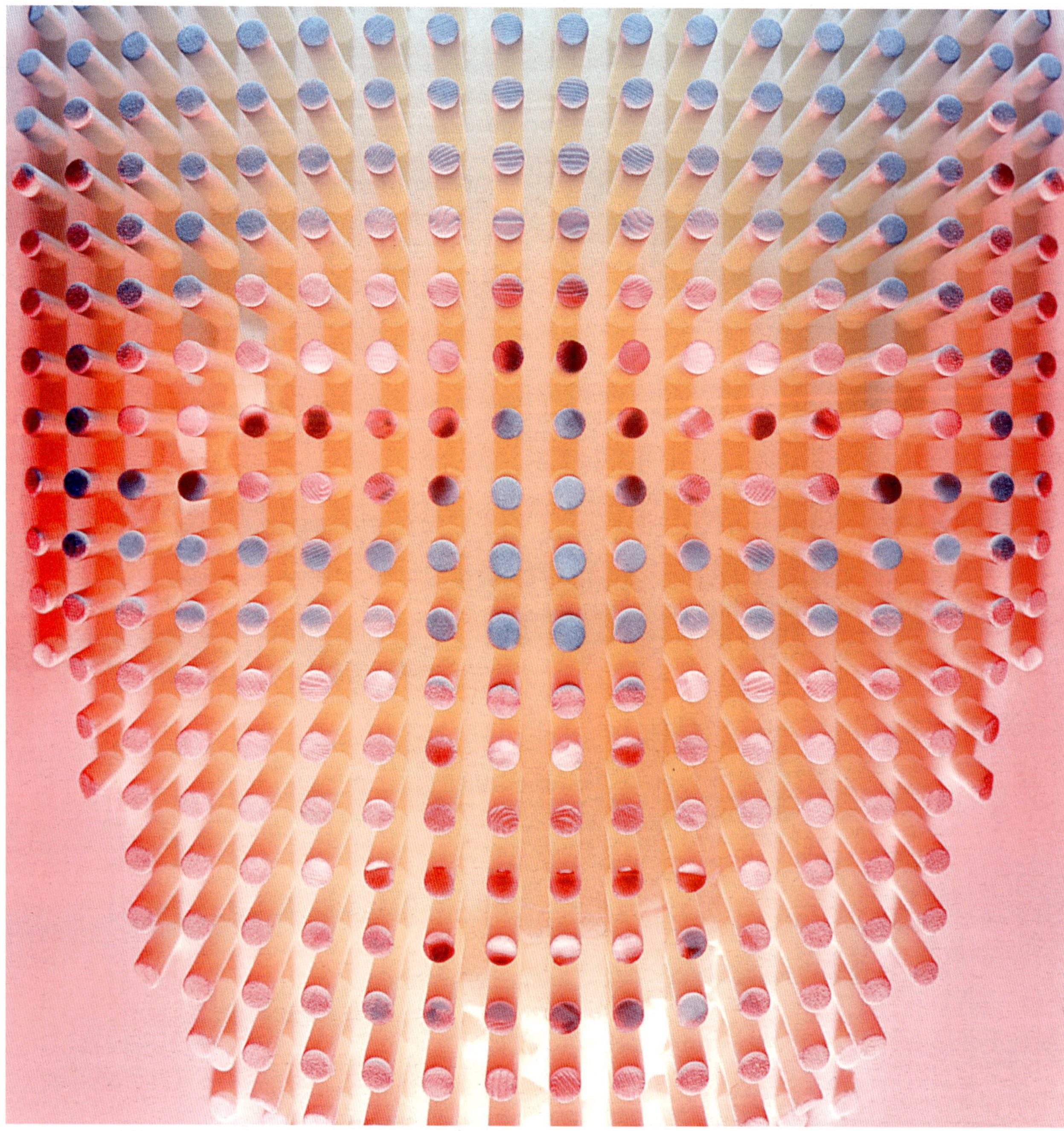

Produced in the rapid prototyping lab at Metropolitan Works, London Metropolitan University.

Original 3D modelling by Matthew Ratcliffe.

Photography by Jenny Van Sommers

Marion Deuchars

By Nathan Gale

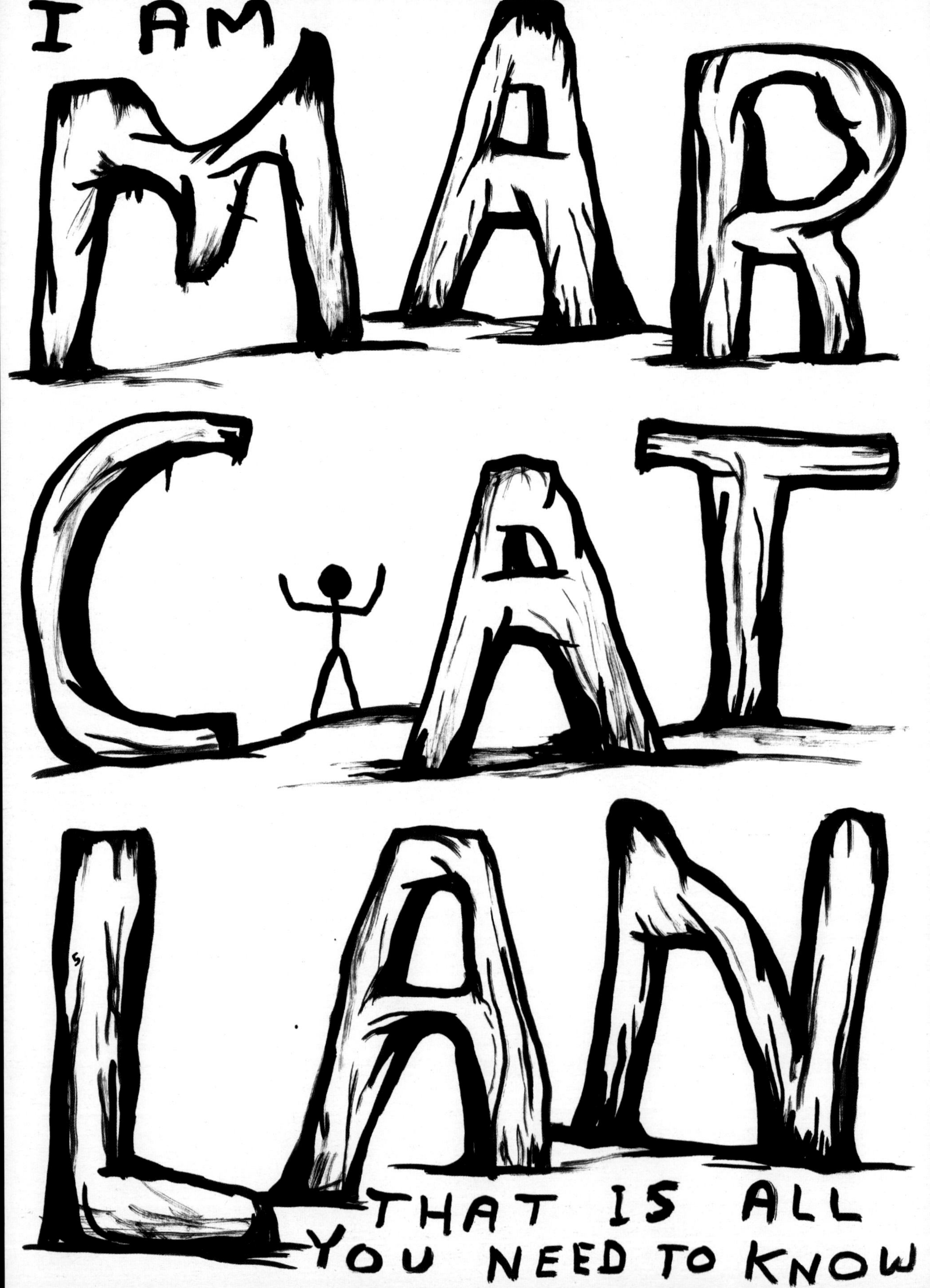
I AM
MAR
CAT
LAN
THAT IS ALL
YOU NEED TO KNOW

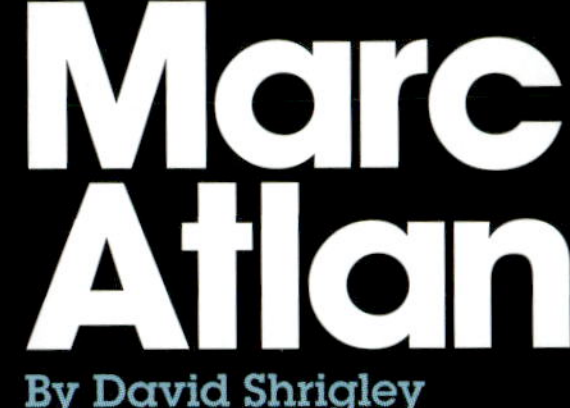

Marc Atlan

By David Shrigley

I think Marc is a very talented artist. I saw his work in magazines before I knew anything about him. The art that he makes looks very different to mine and often serves a different purpose. I find it quite exotic. The images Marc makes tell you everything you need to know. Saying exactly what you mean is a difficult thing to do. This is what really impresses me. Looking at them is like being poked in the eye.

Marc Atlan was born in the suburbs of Paris, France in 1967, studied industrial design for way too long at the end of the 80s, and lives now in Venice, California. He designs perfume packagings, art directs ad campaigns, illustrates T-shirts, takes photographs, builds installations and window displays, collaborates with fine artists and messes with everything printed. Equally likes greasy junk food and outrageously expensive restaurants. Has flirted with Tom Ford, Rei Kawakubo, Oliver Stone, Andrée Putman, Philippe Starck, Helmut Lang and James Perse but loves only his wife and two kids. Doesn't like name dropping or star fuckers.

David Shrigley

By Marc Atlan

David Shrigley was born in Macclesfield, England in 1968. He studied Fine Art at Glasgow School of Art from 1988 to 1991, He has exhibited widely in Europe and North America and his illustrations have appeared in newspapers and magazines such as *Esquire* (Japan), *Donna* (Italy), *Frieze* (UK), *The Gaurdian* (UK), *Maisonneuve* (Canada) *Du* (Switzerland). He has produced animated pop promos for artists such as Blur and Bonnie Prince Billy and is also the author of numerous books of drawings details of which can be found at redstonepress.co.uk, He now lives and works in Glasgow and is represented by the Stephen Friedman Gallery, London.

The first time I heard the name David Shrigley was when I attended the opening of his exhibition at the Yvon Lambert gallery in Paris in 1998. I remember not being extremely attracted to his drawings, and was not far from thinking that the guy was a bit of a fraud. It took me a couple of years, with the evolution of my own personality and tastes, as well as additional "double takes" on his work, to start to really enjoy the brutality, the silliness and the pathos of his art. Almost 10 years later, as proof that only fools don't change their minds, I am now one of David's biggest supporters. He makes me laugh, wince, cringe and sometimes cry at the same time, which is not that pleasant, but I deeply thank him anyway for the experience. One of the other reasons why I appreciate his work so much is because it makes me feel that it is somewhat OK to be fucked-up.

For the assignment of creating his portrait, I decided to reproduce and cut out a photo of a bewildered David and embed it in a crystal paperweight. It seemed appropriate to dismember this giant who, himself, draws monsters or the occasional squirrel severing or eating each others' heads. The anecdotal remark, "it's freezing in here", borrowed from a side text on one of his drawings, imposed itself as the perfect unconcerned and ridiculous comment of someone who has just lost his head (which then improbably ended up frozen in an ice-cube trophy).

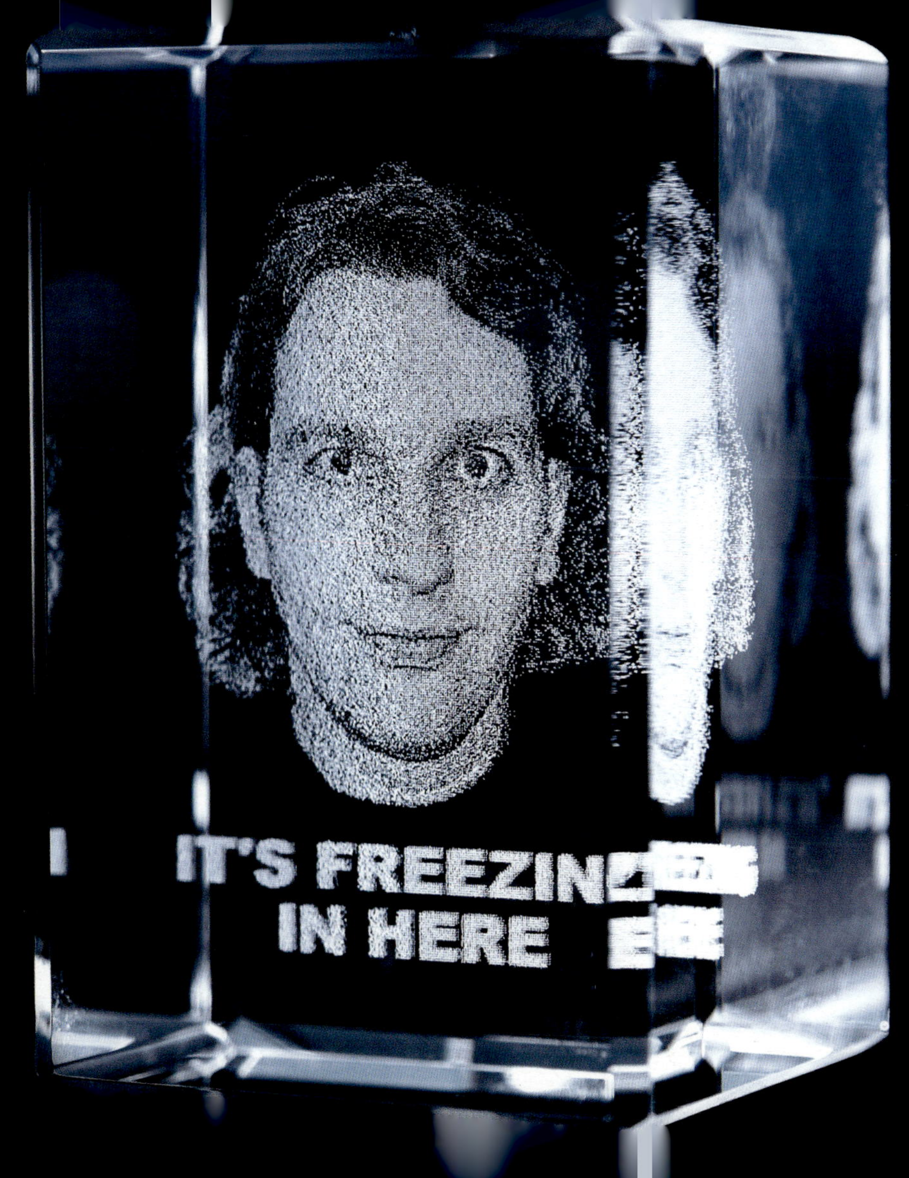
IT'S FREEZING
IN HERE

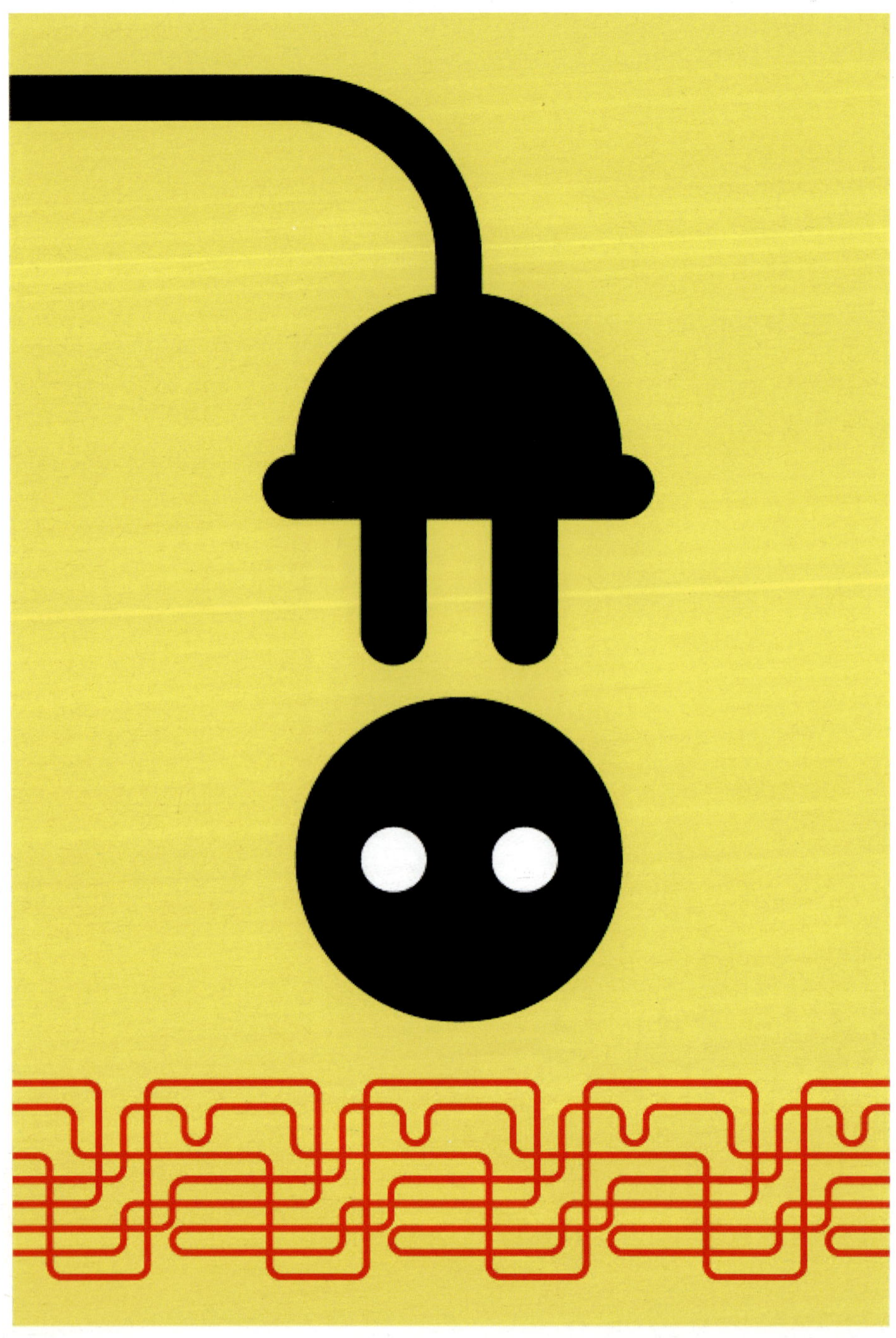

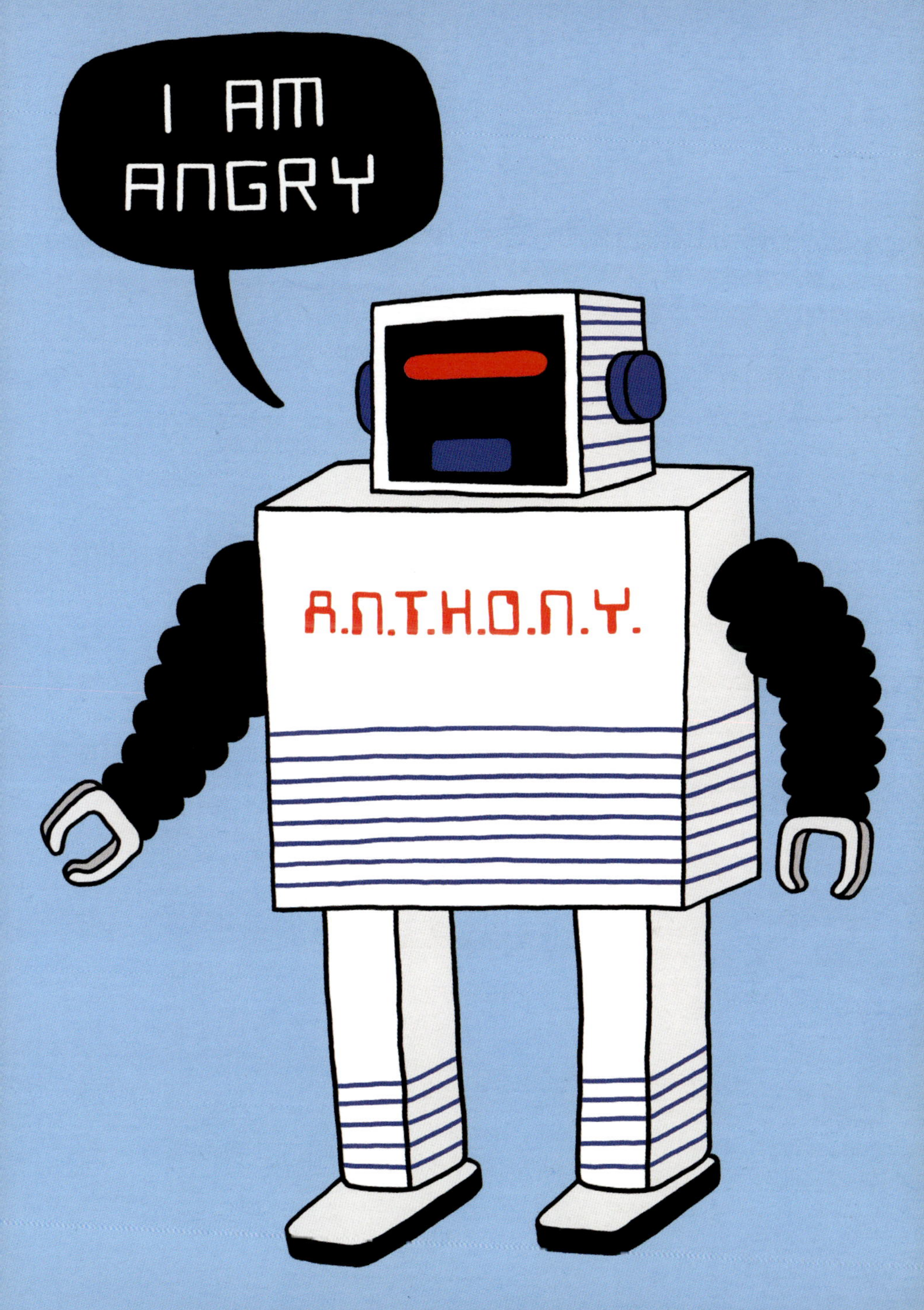
I AM ANGRY
A.N.T.H.O.N.Y.

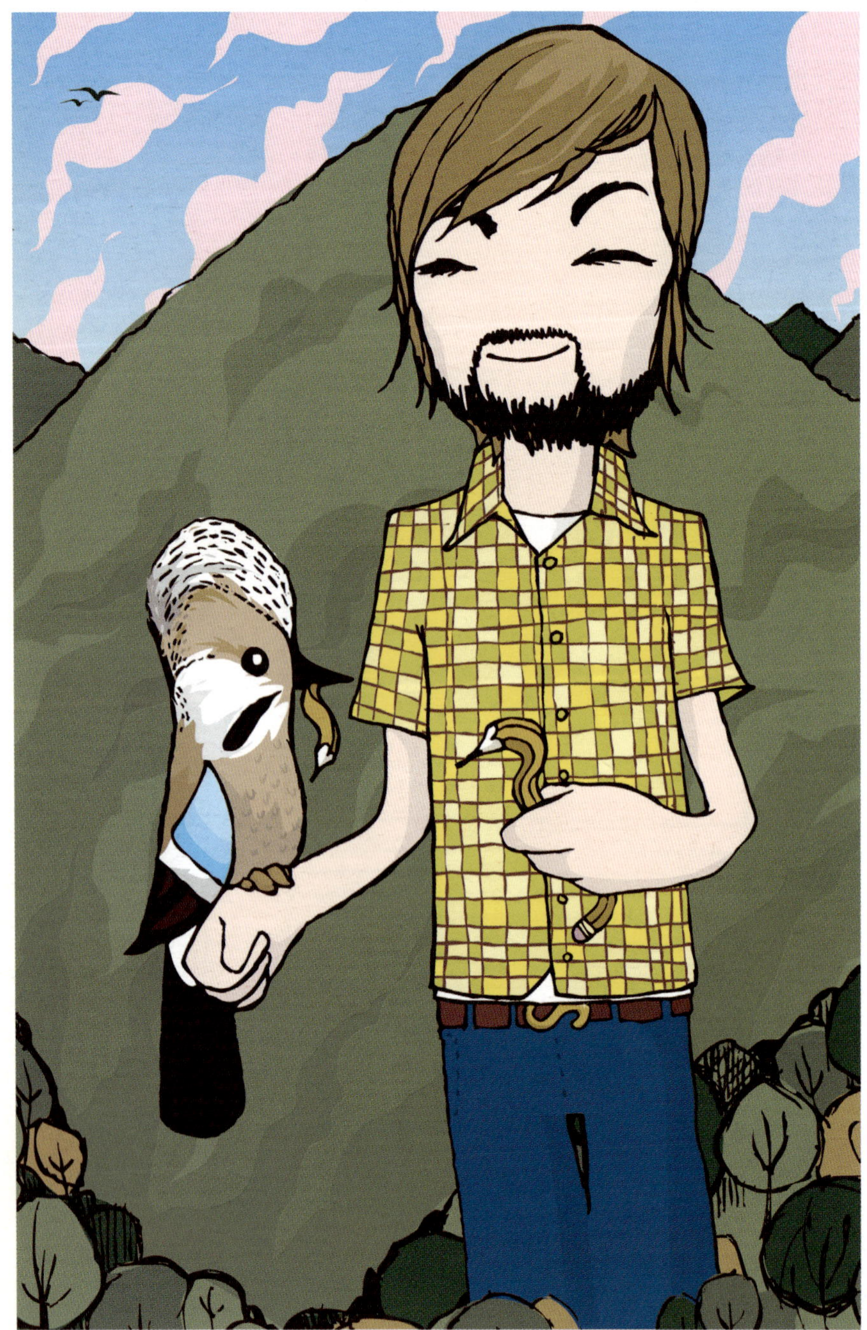

Neil McFarland /
By Matt Sewell

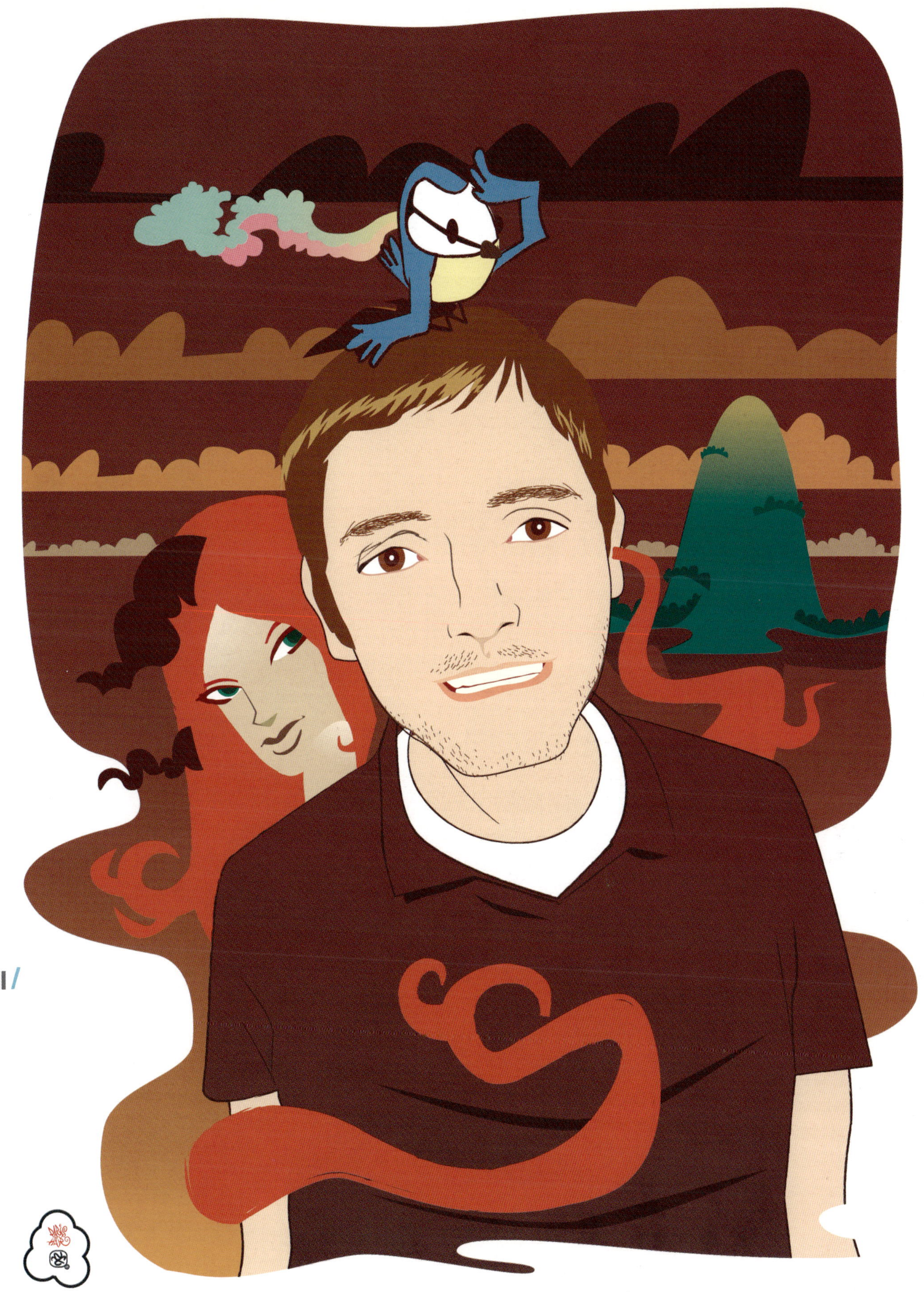

Matt Sewell /

By Neil McFarland

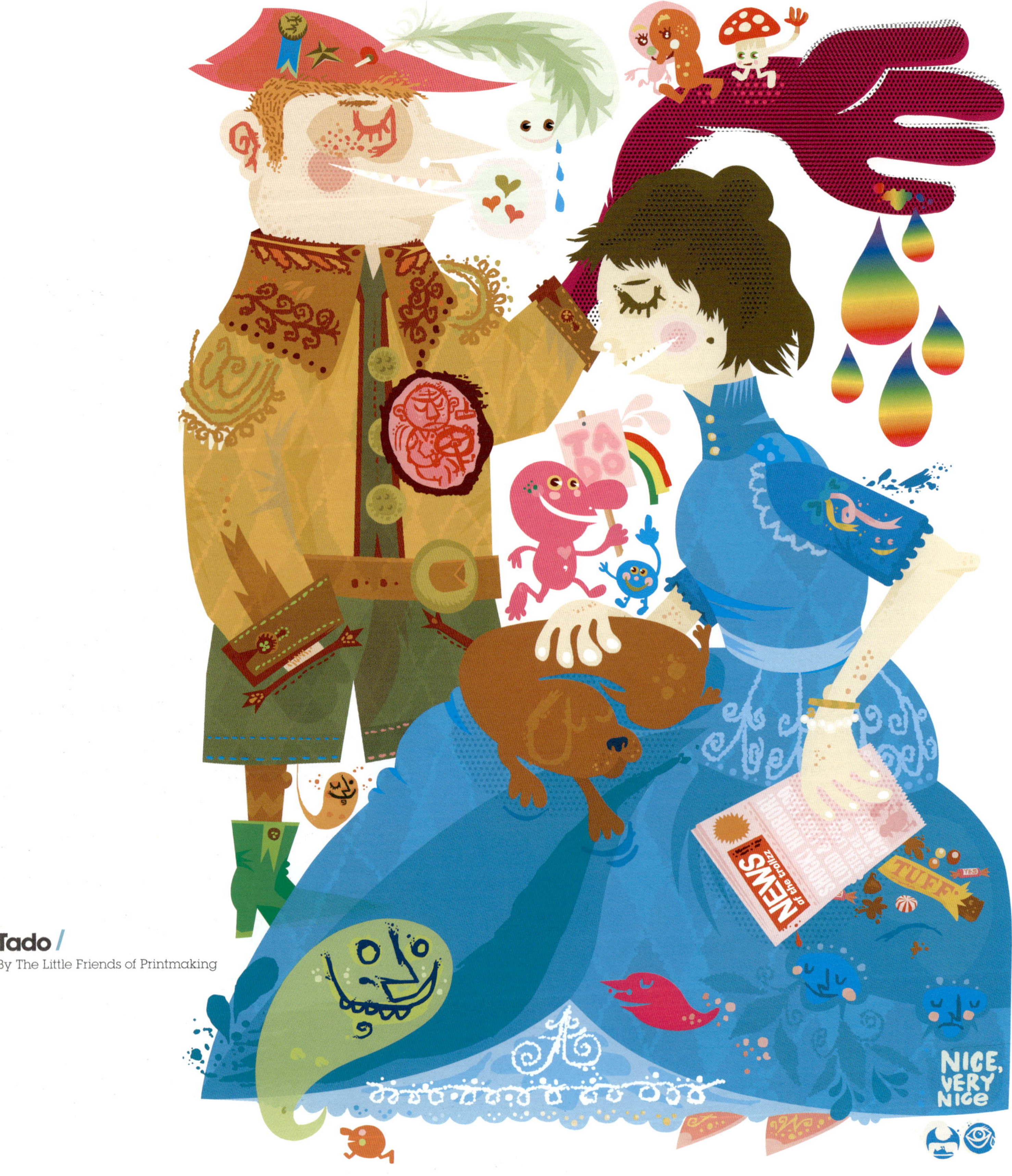

Tado /
By The Little Friends of Printmaking

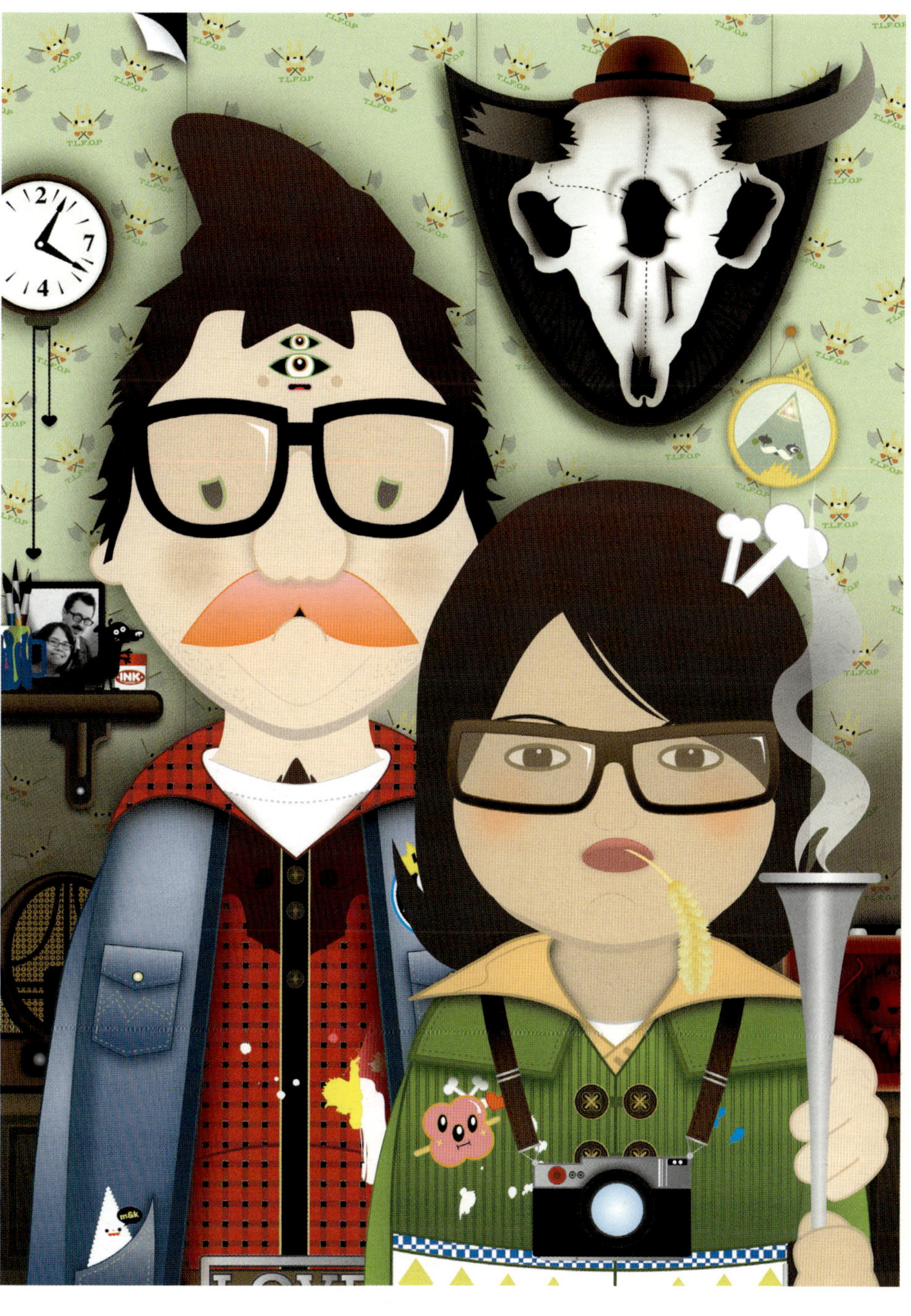

The Little Friends of Printmaking /
By Tado

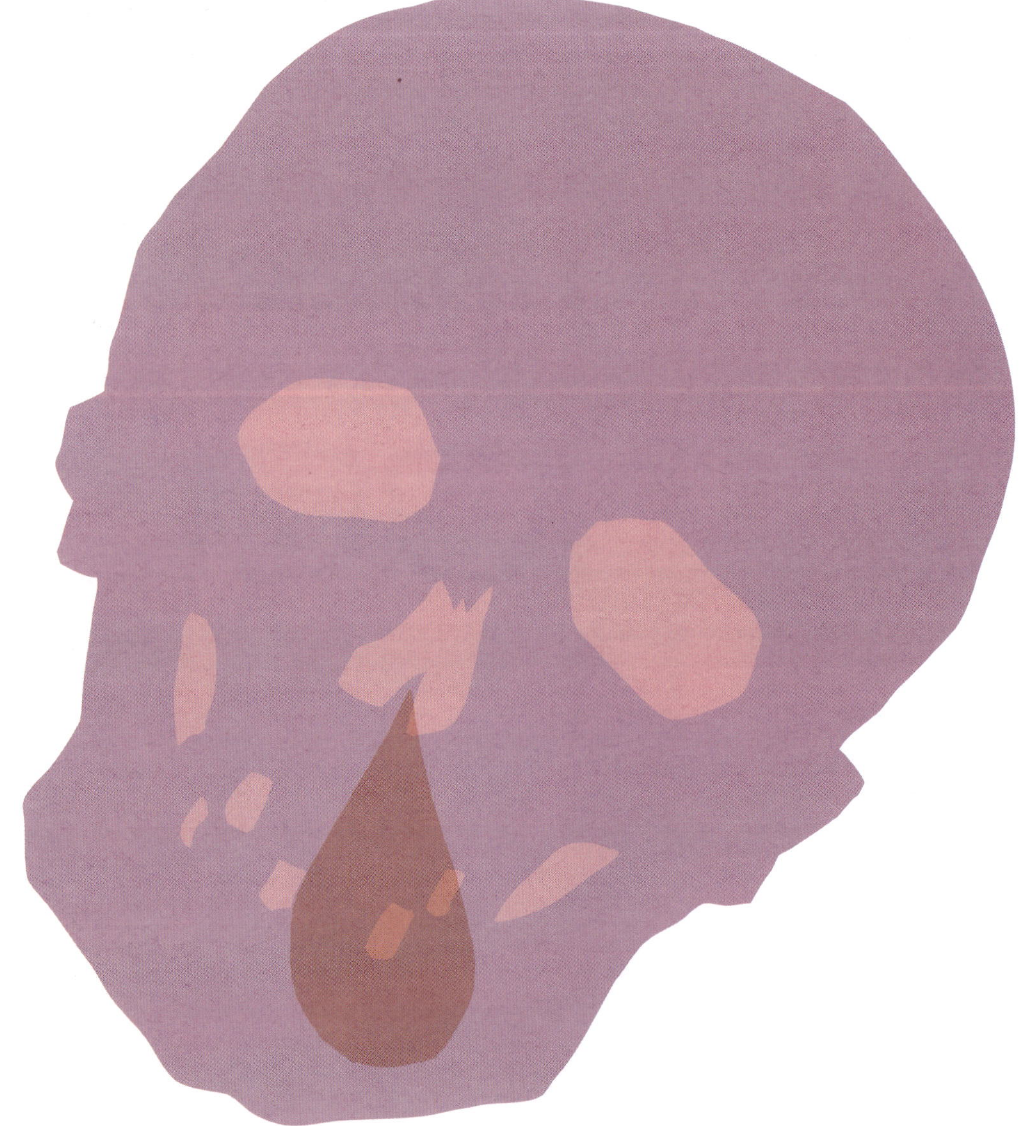

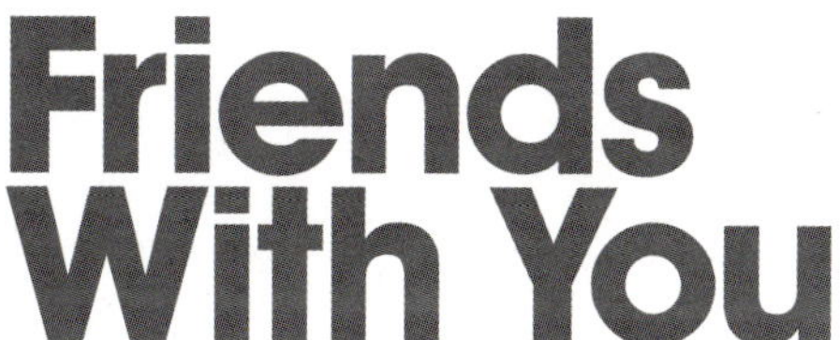

Friends With You

By Harmen Liemburg

Friends With You's presentation at the 2004 Pictoplasma conference in Berlin blew my mind! I love their outrageously crazy and cute world. A unique mixture of magic, darkness and positive thinking gives their work a special position in the world of 'designer toys'. Shoe_Baca, a brownish furry being with detachable kidneys (that looks a bit like it's makers Sam and Tury) is my absolute favourite!

Friends are extracted from an unimaginably small microcosm. They are microbes that have been enlarged one billion times their original size. They live in your breath and under the part of your brain used for wishing. Lieutenant Captain Lee Karl discovered a world very much like ours. The only difference being that ours is made up of plants, animals, and humans, and this sub-amoebic world contains an unexplored realm of living organisms. The few strains of organisms that survived the enlargemnet process have been carefully studied and tested. And we have concluded that these new "Friends," have actual life enhancing skills. The friends have magic powers never before seen, and are improving lives one person at a time. Share your wishes and desires with your new friends and watch as everything you ever dreamed of becomes a reality! Welcome friends into your heart and home and start living better TODAY!

The following submission is a collaboration between Harmen Liemburg & Friends With You.

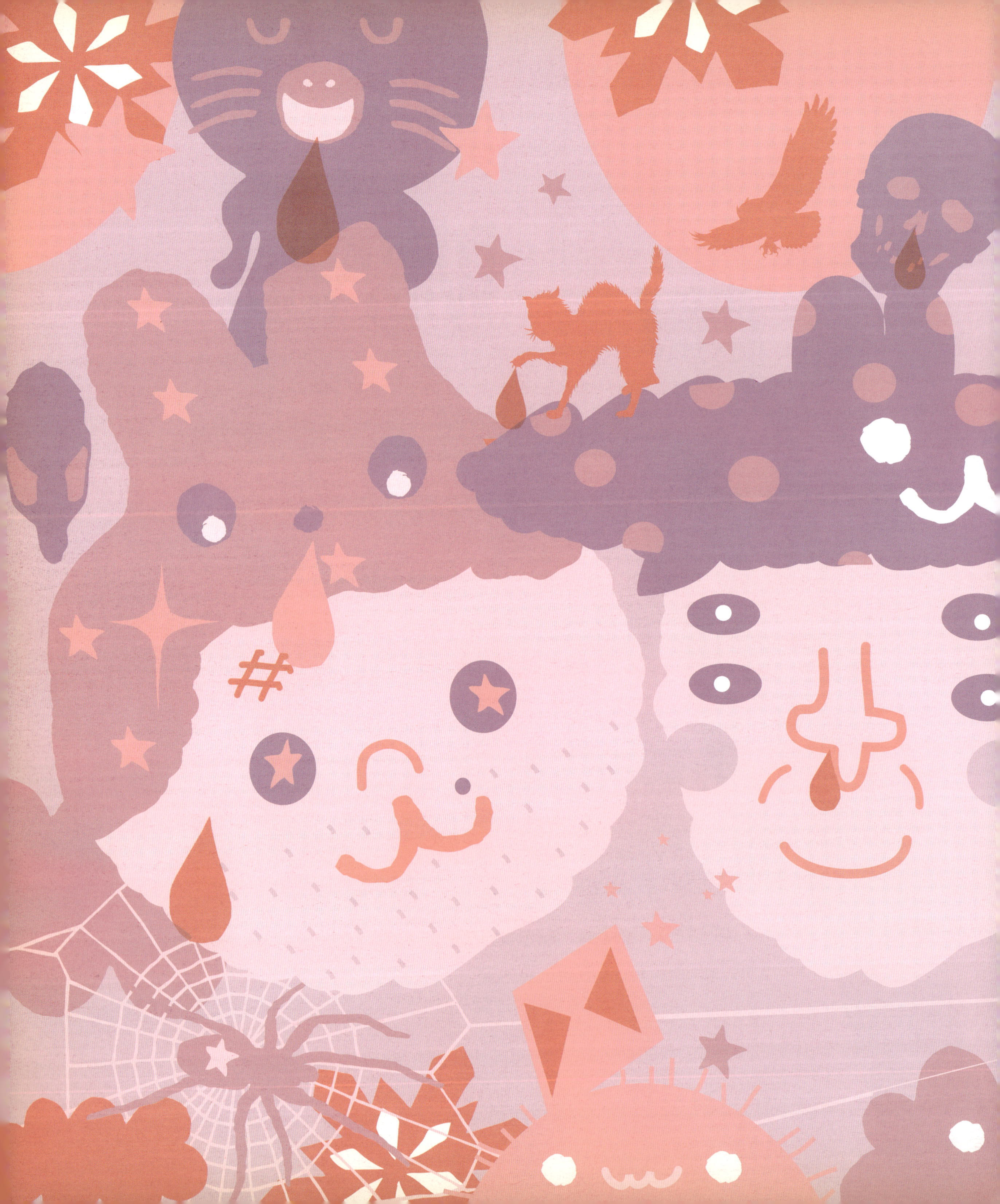

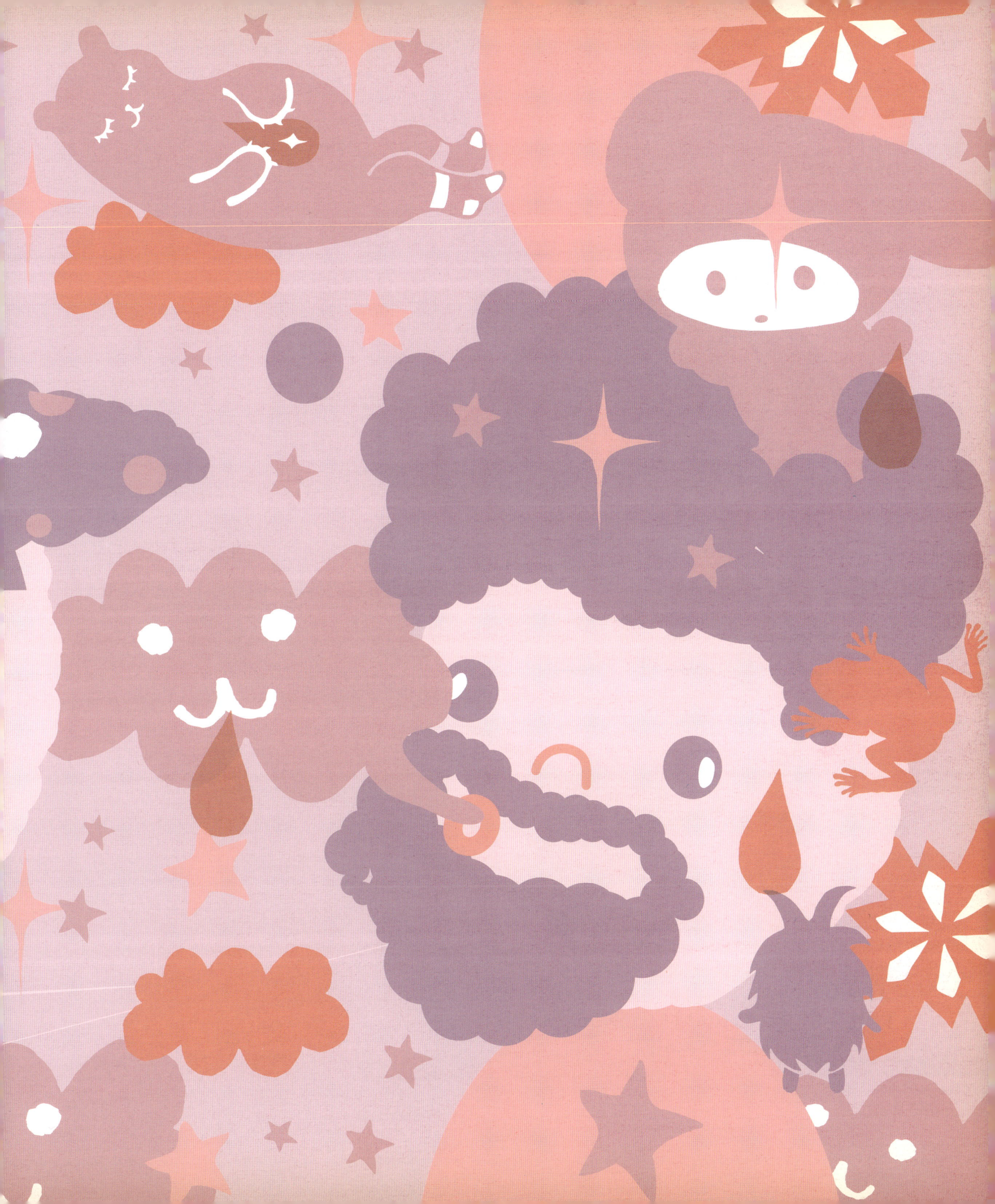

Hellobard /

By The Boy Fitz Hammond

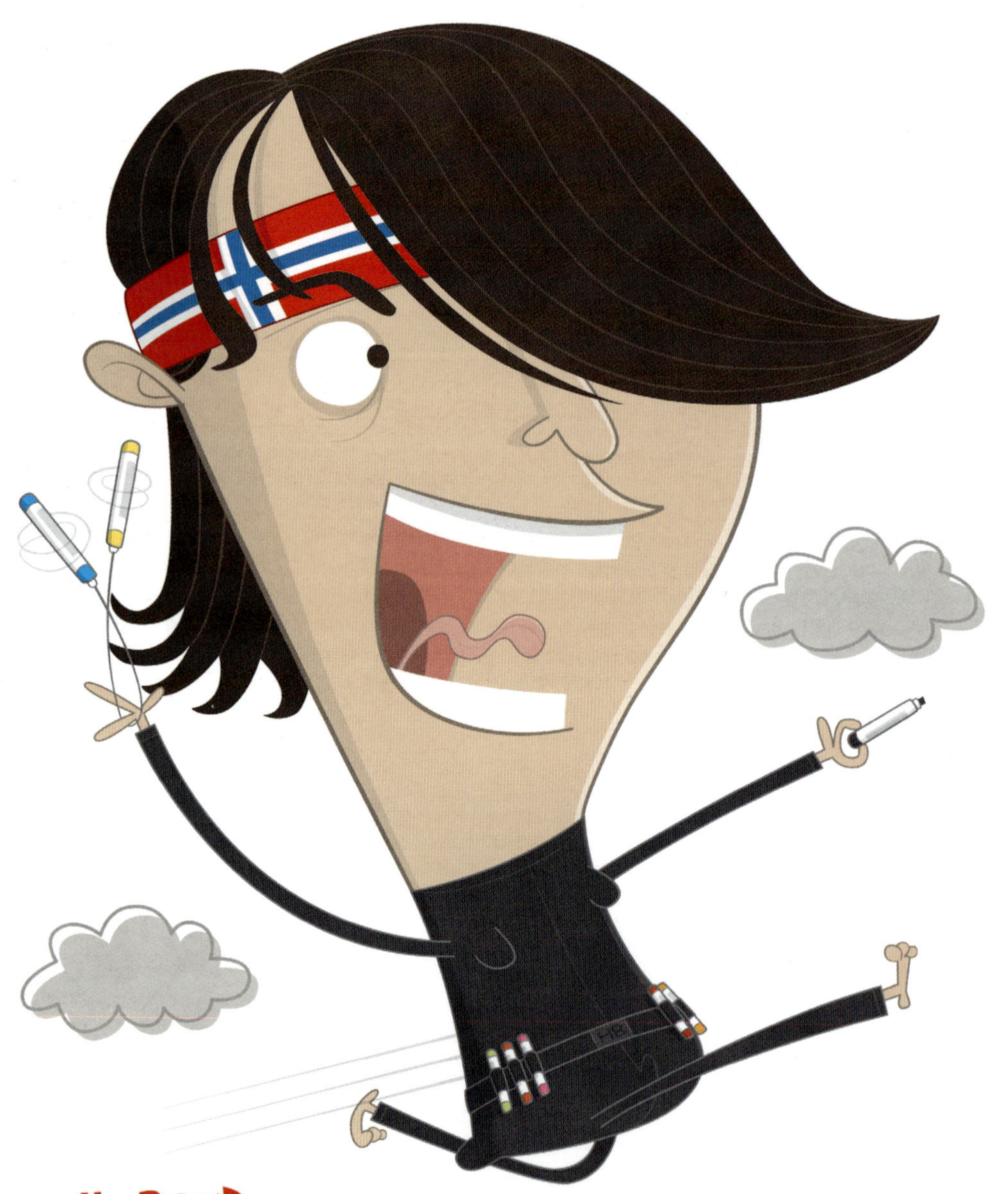

The Boy Fitz Hammond /

By Hellobard

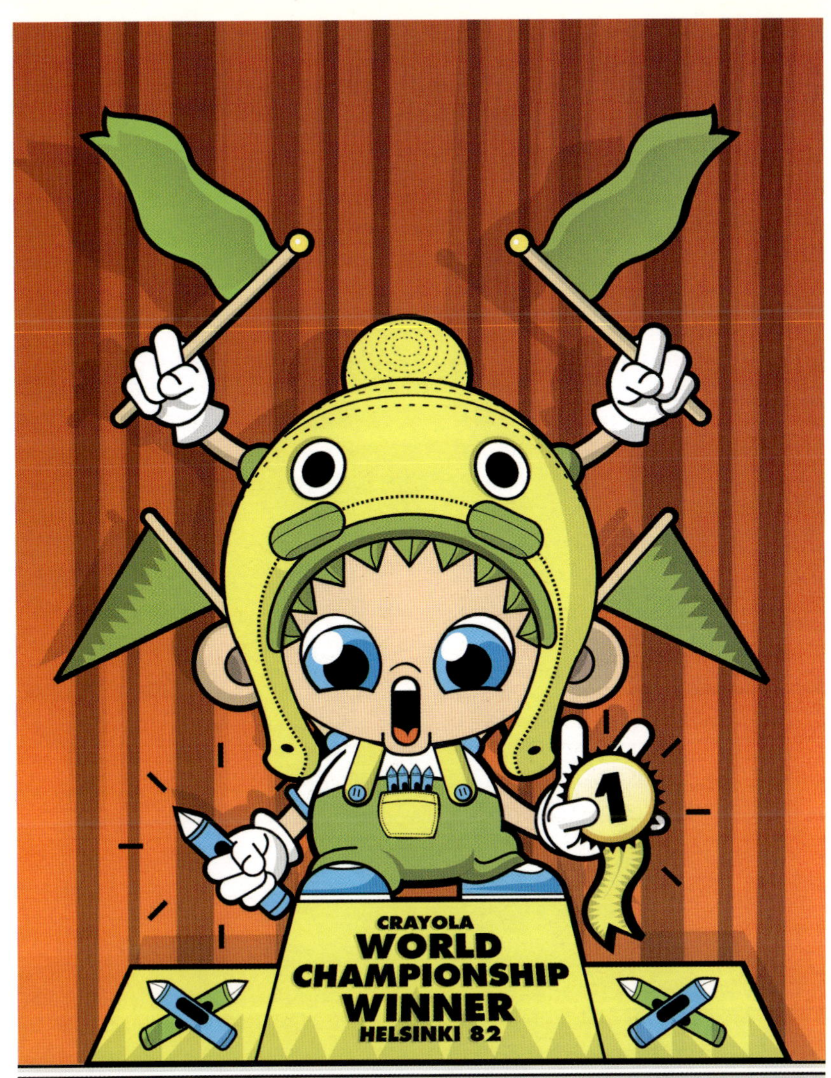

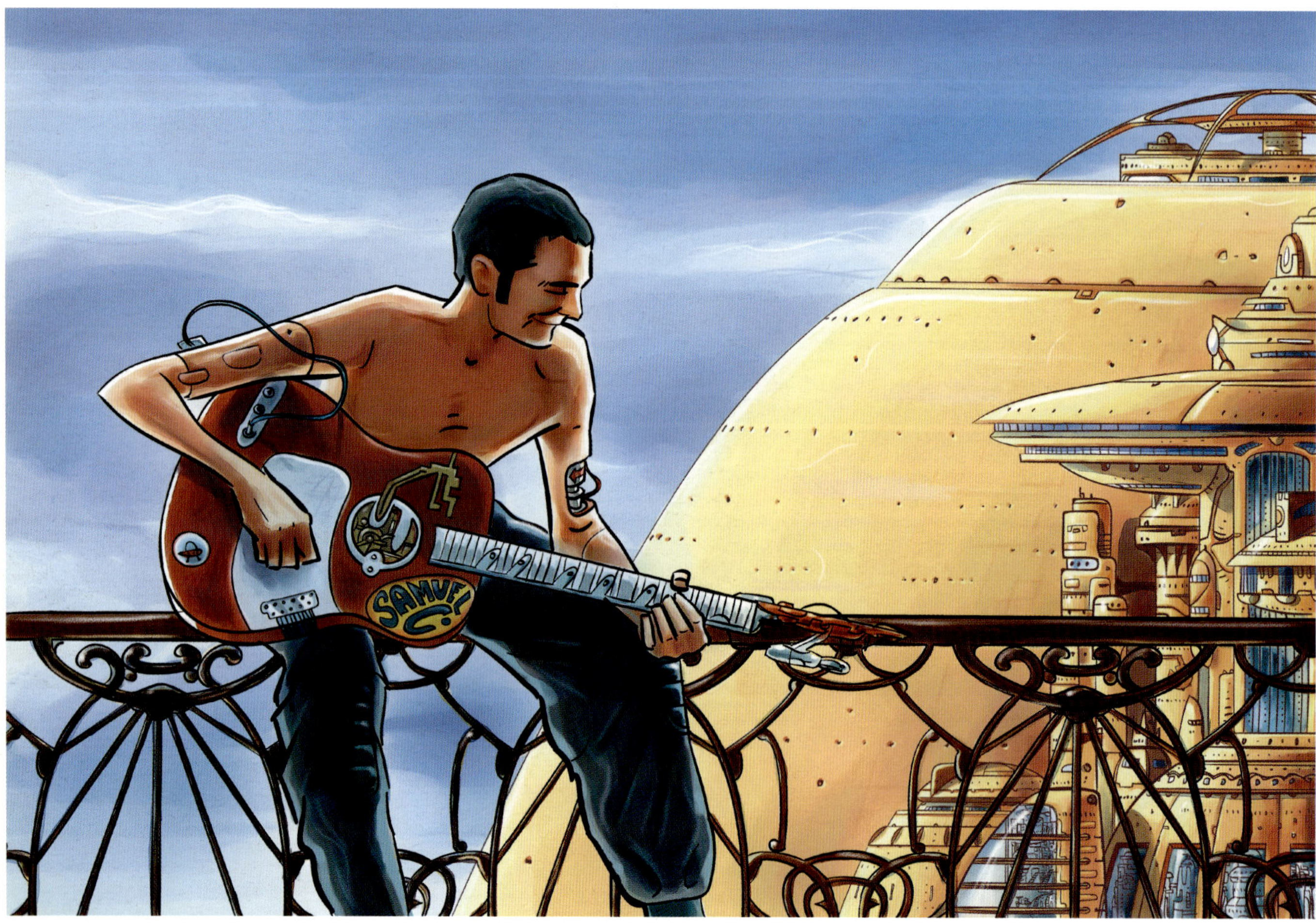

Jean Duprez /
By Samuel Cochetel

Samuel Cochetel /
By Jean Duprez

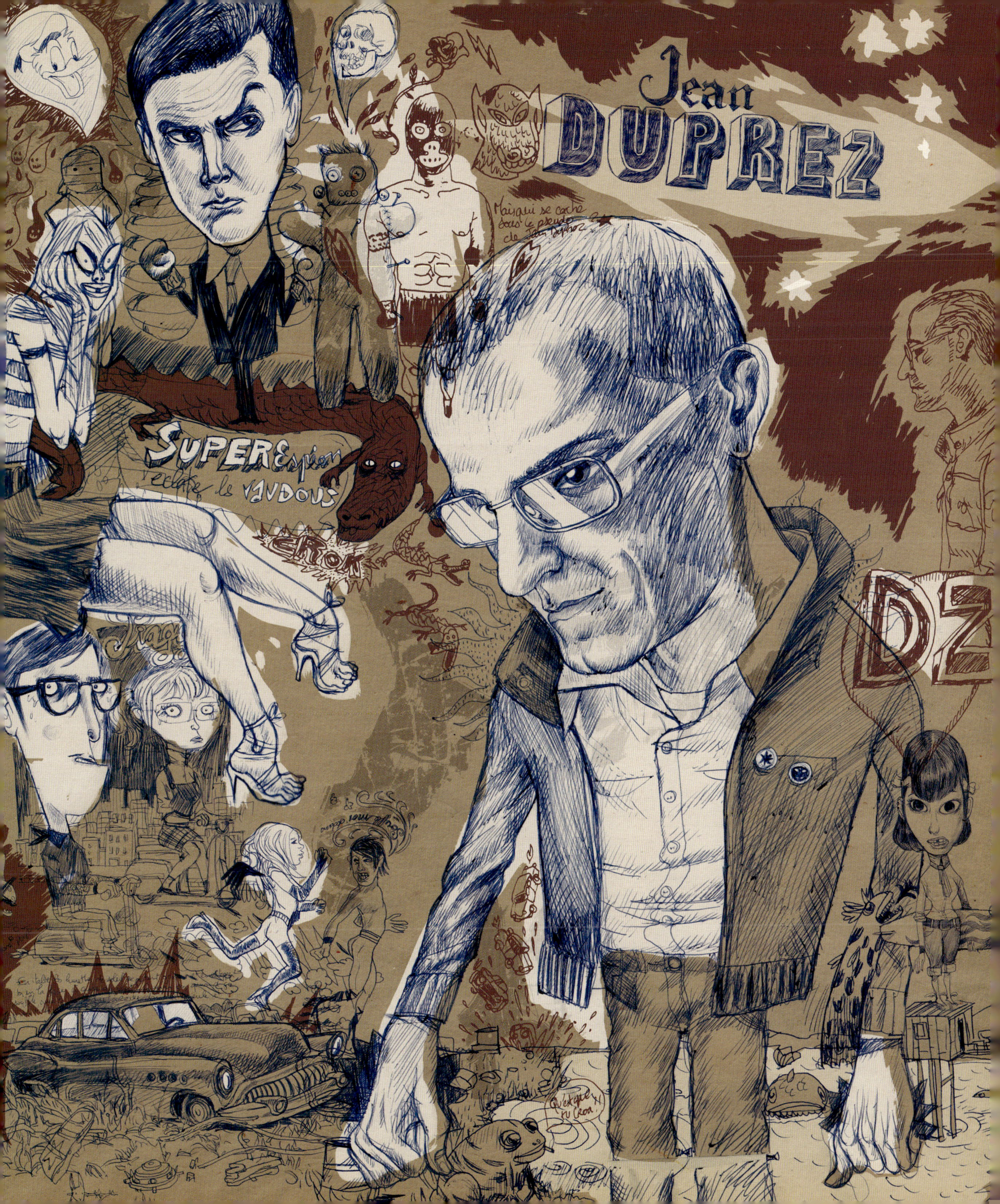

Jean
DUPREZ
SUPER Espion
eclate le vaudous
CROA
DZ

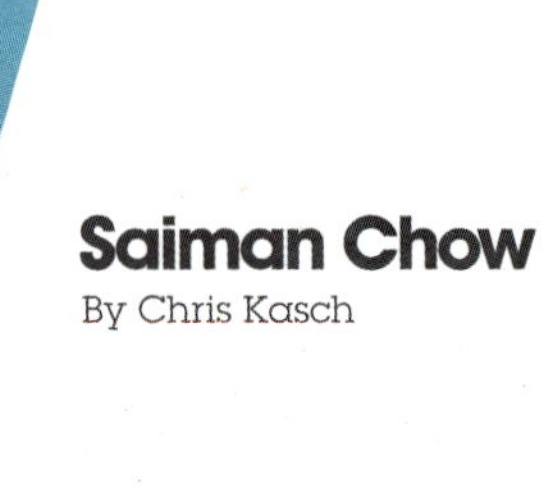

Saiman Chow

By Chris Kasch

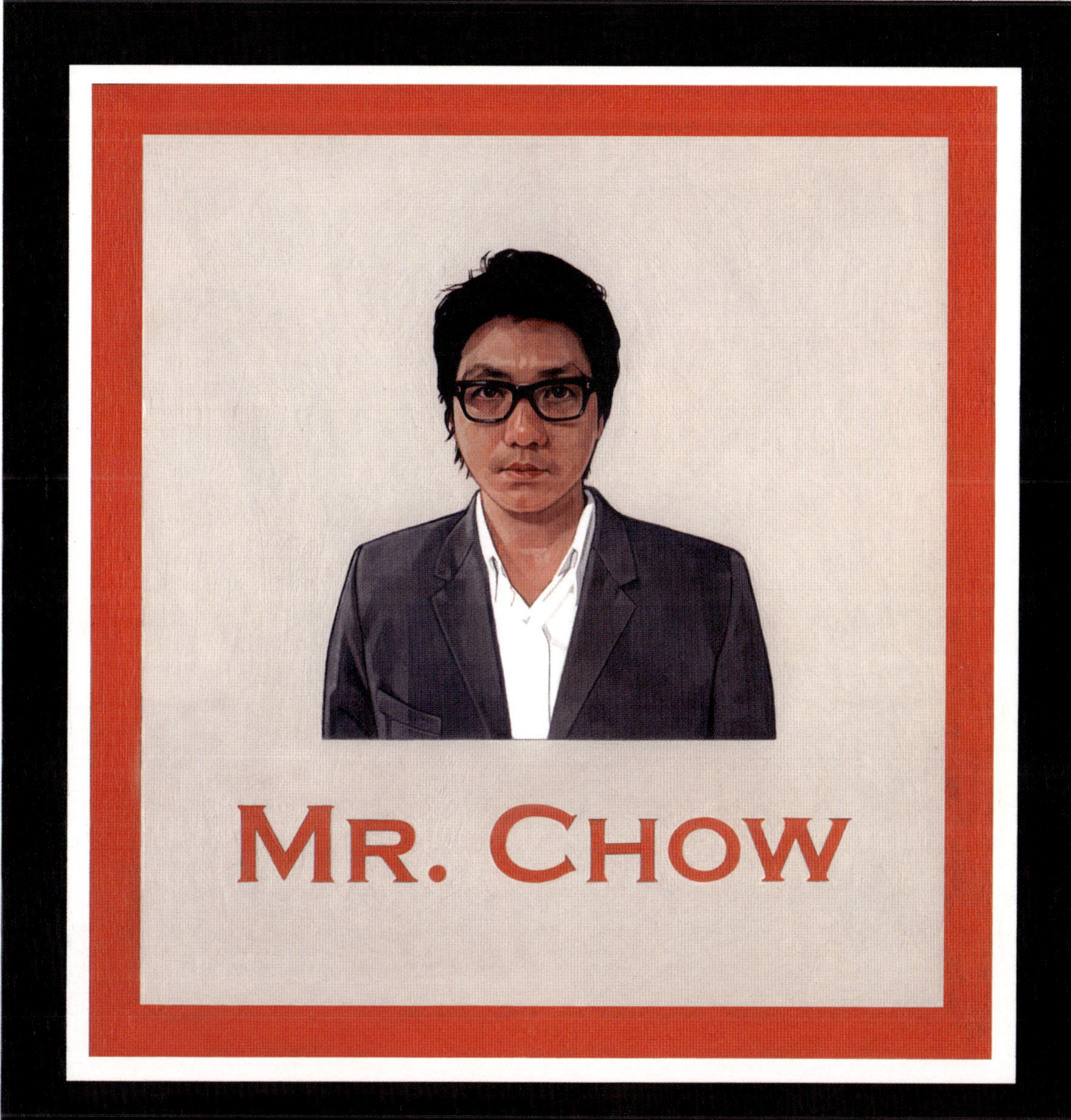
MR. CHOW

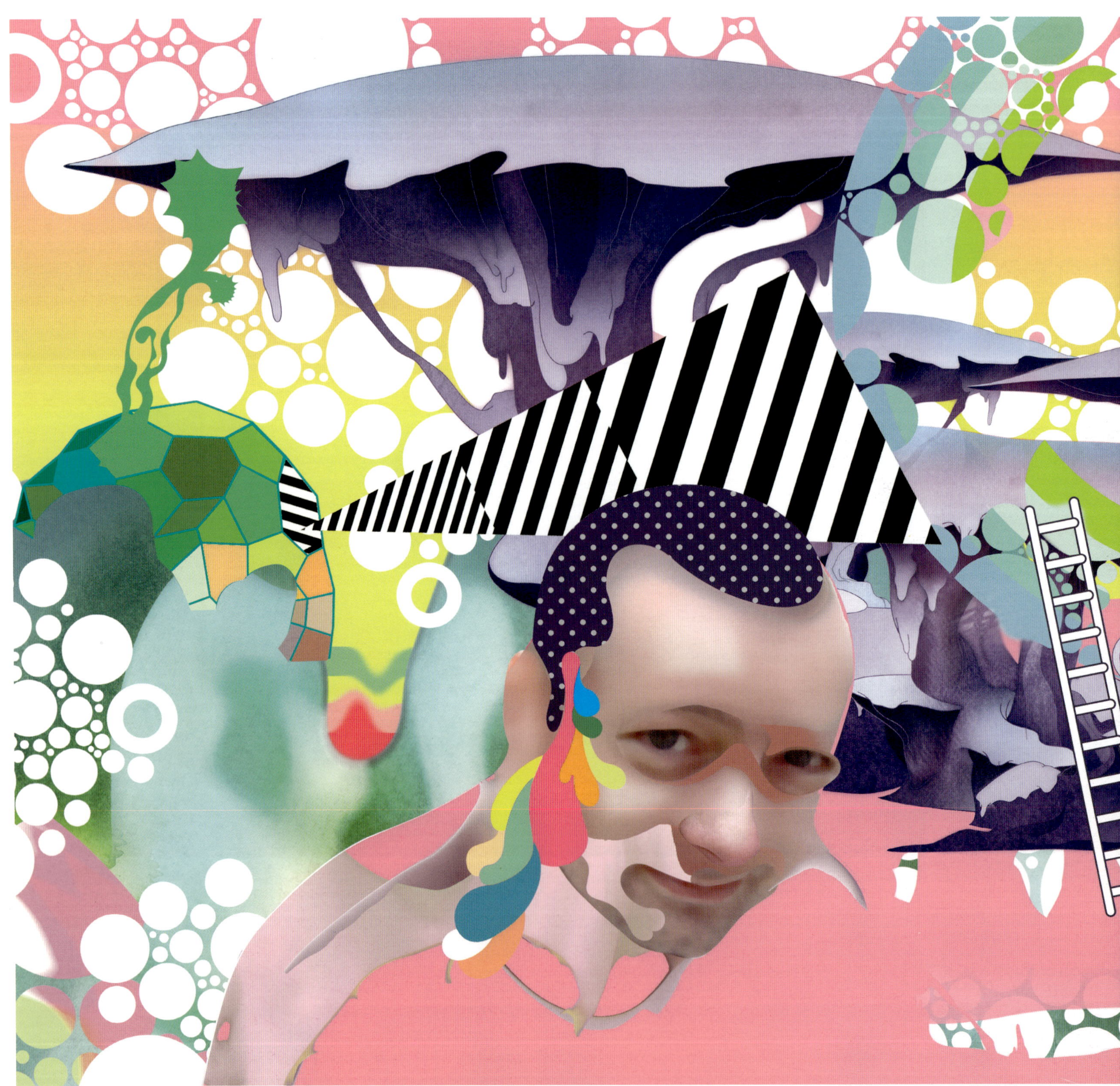

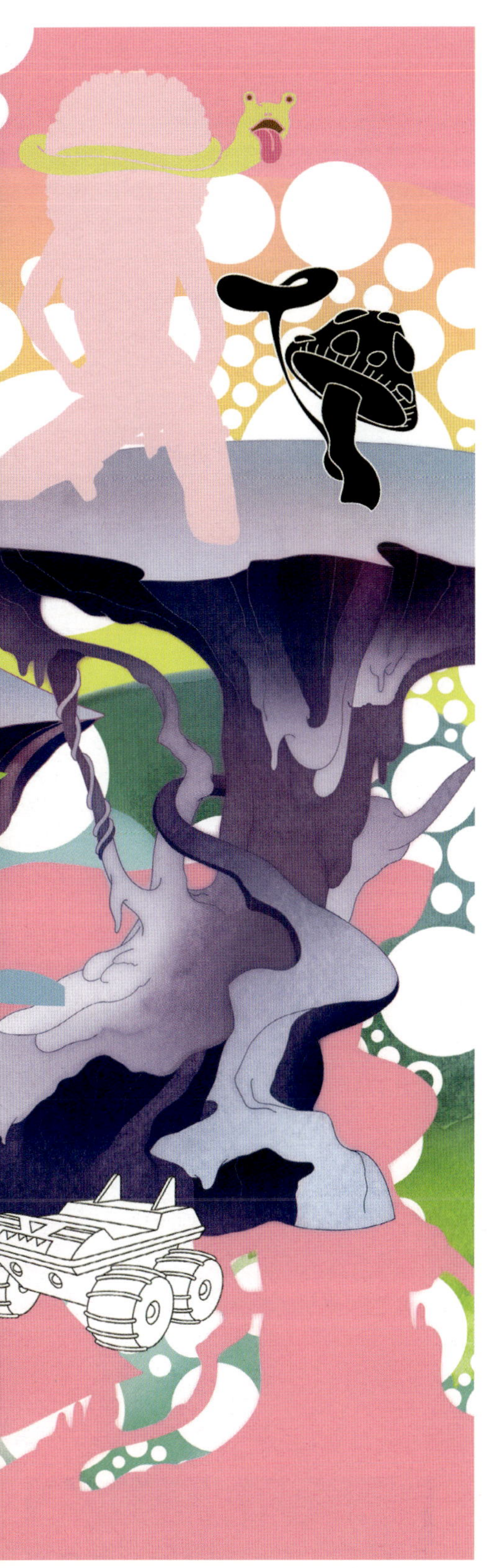

Chris Kasch

By Saiman Chow

David Stewart

By Joshua Davis

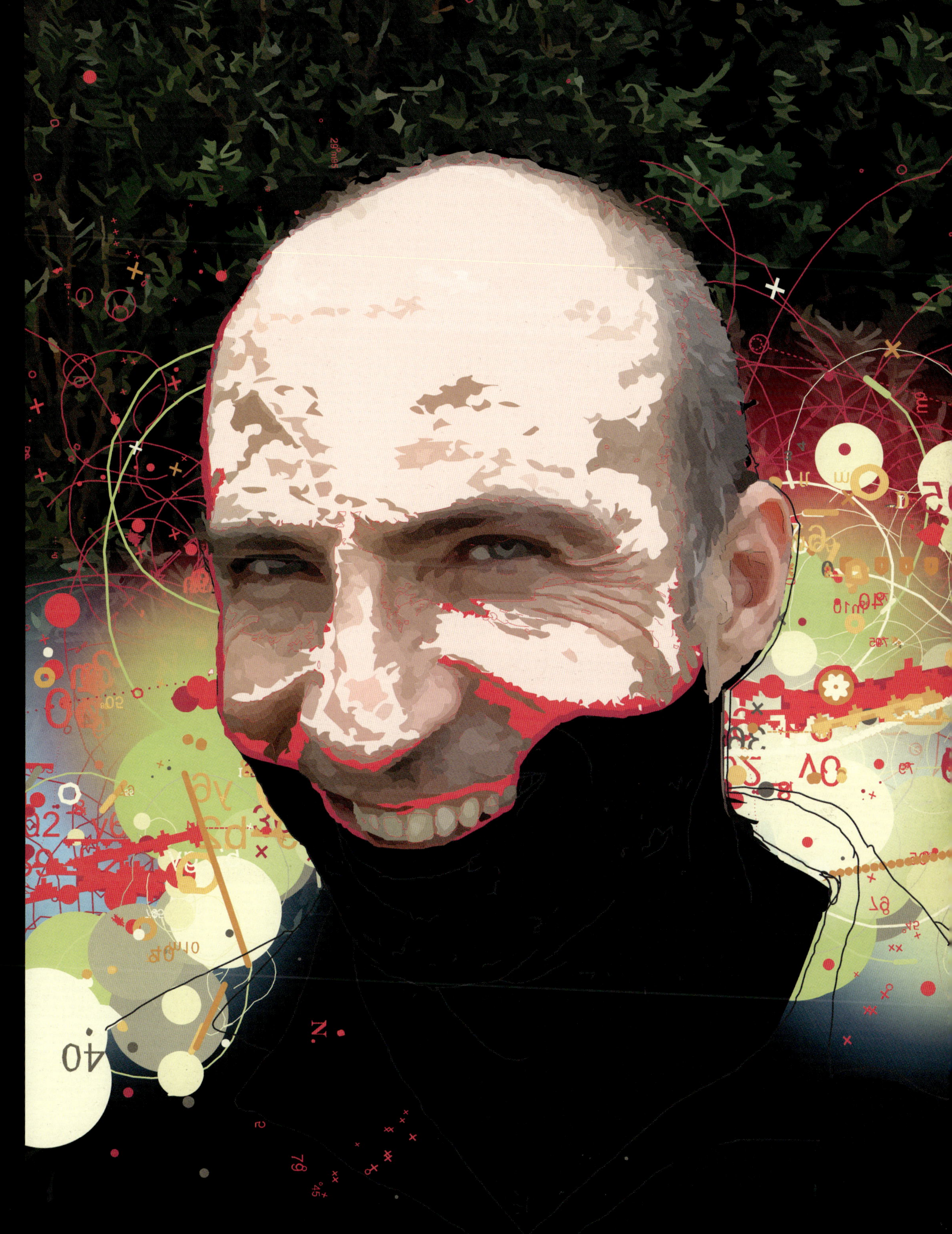

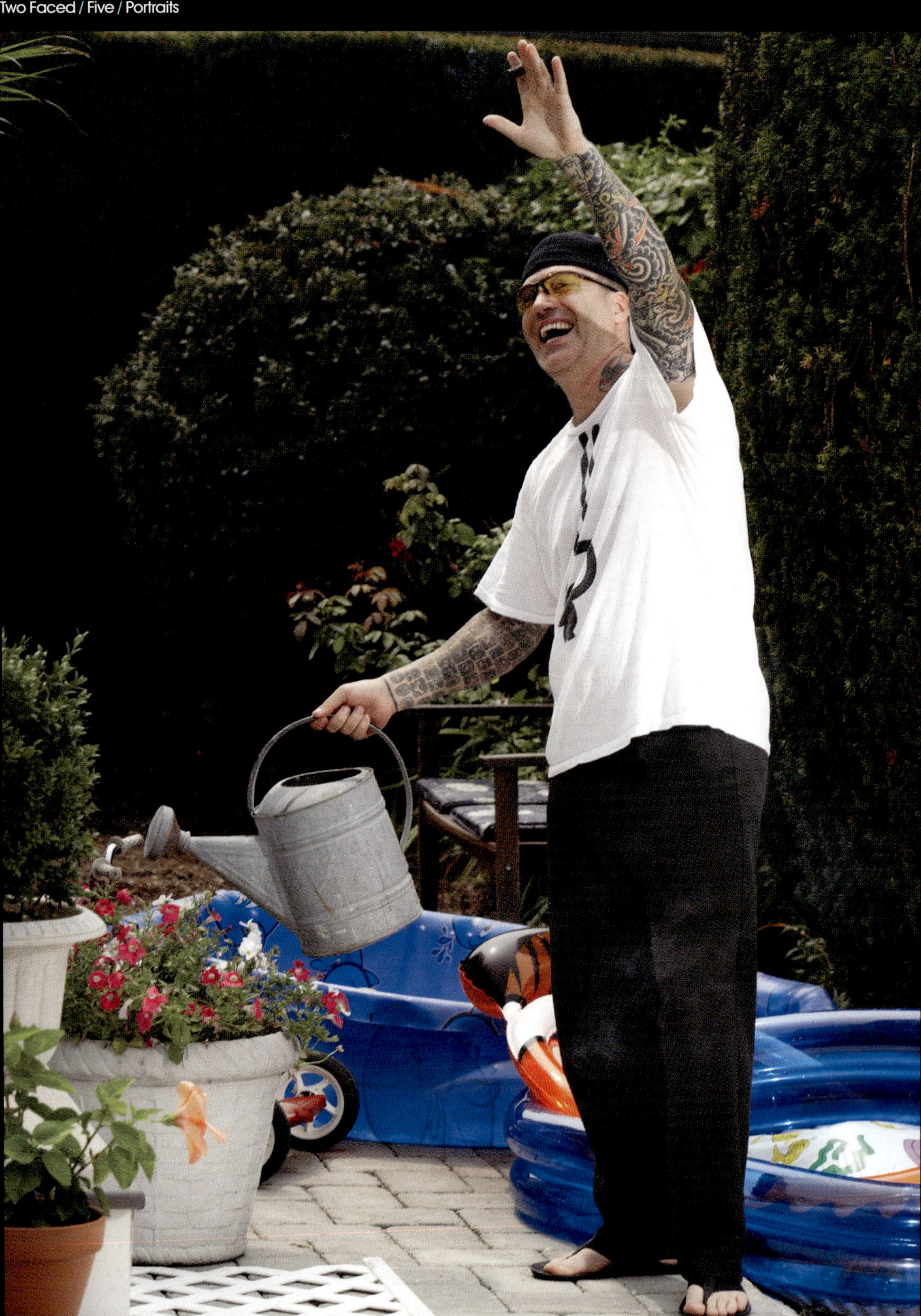

Joshua Davis

By David Stewart

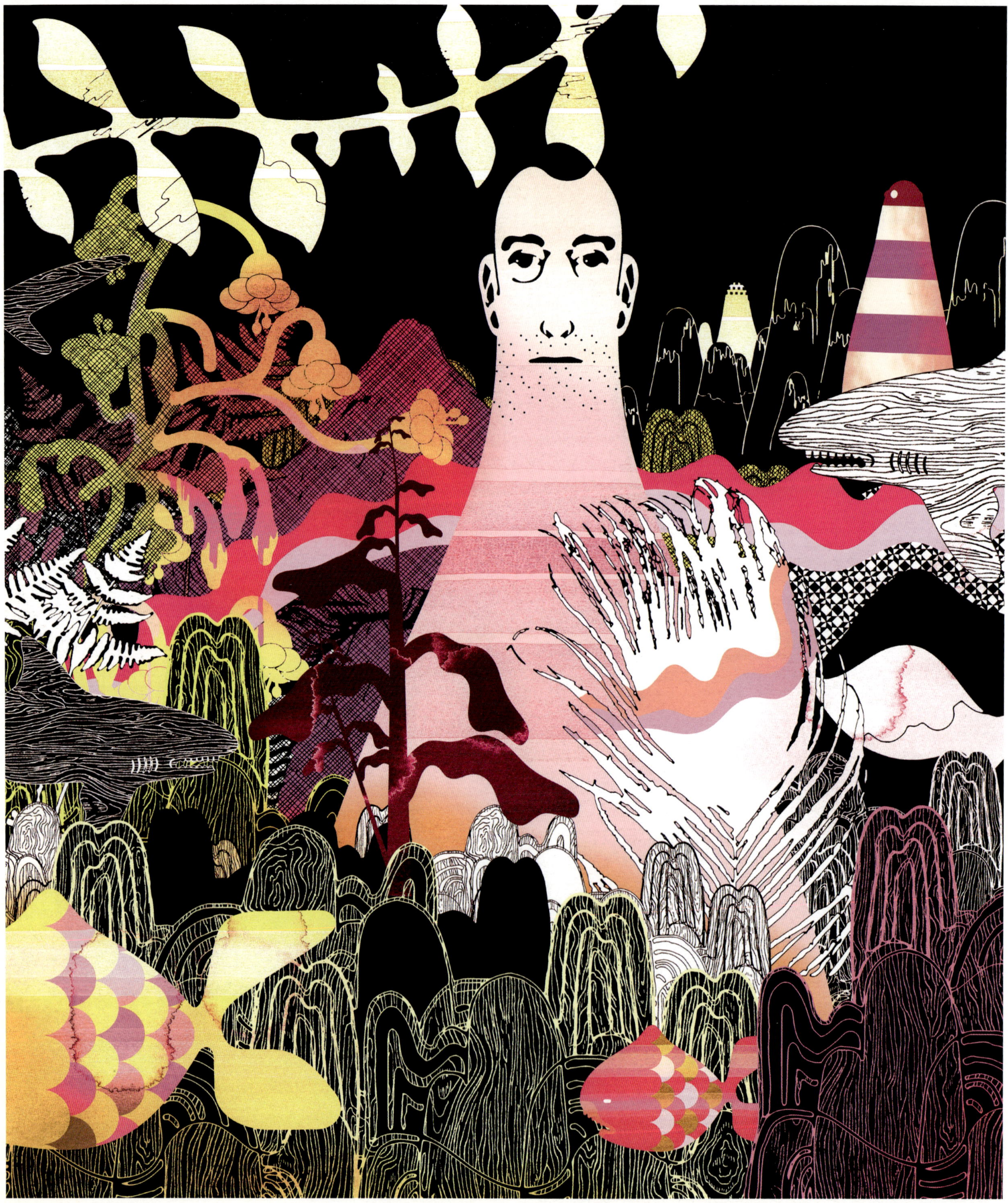

Toby Neilan /

By Kustaa Saksi

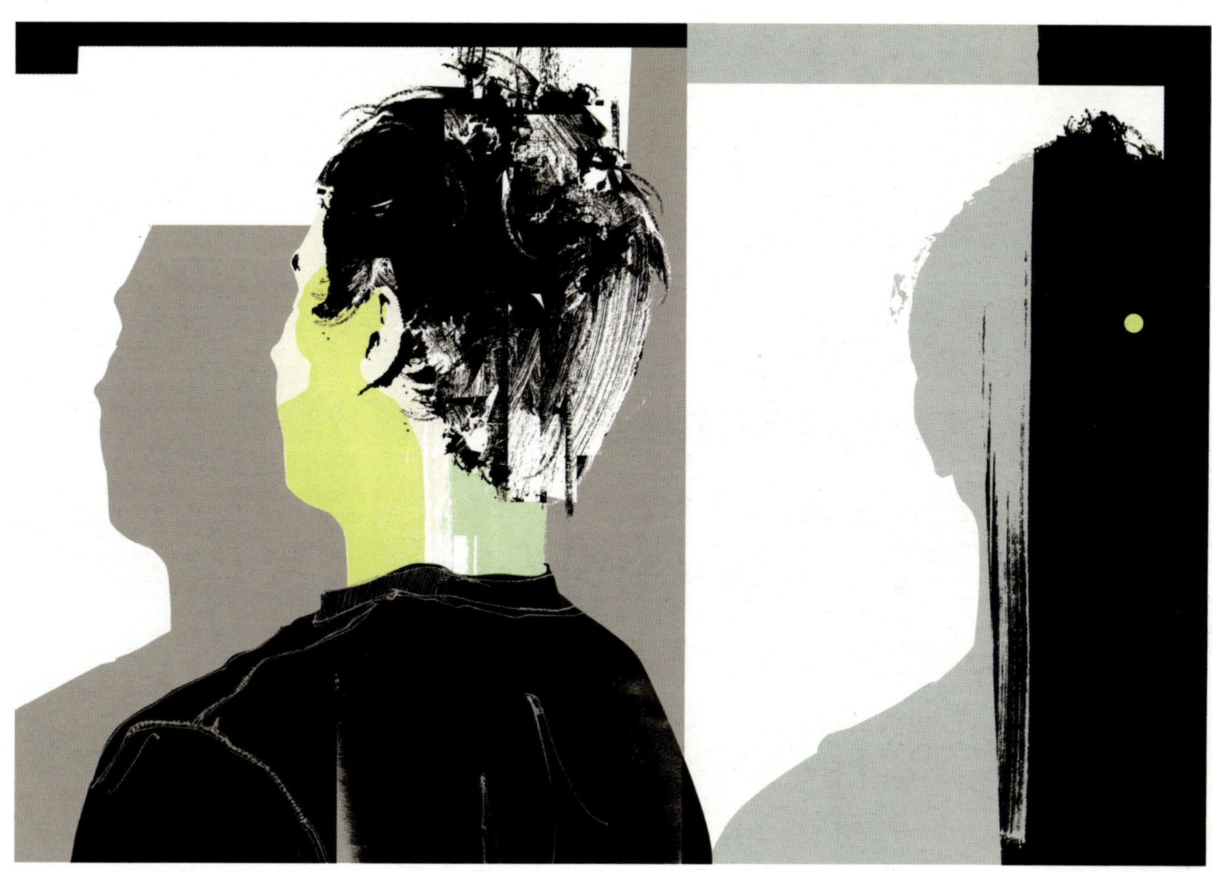

Kustaa Saksi /

By Toby Neilan

Dustin Hostetler_Upso /

By Hope Gangloff

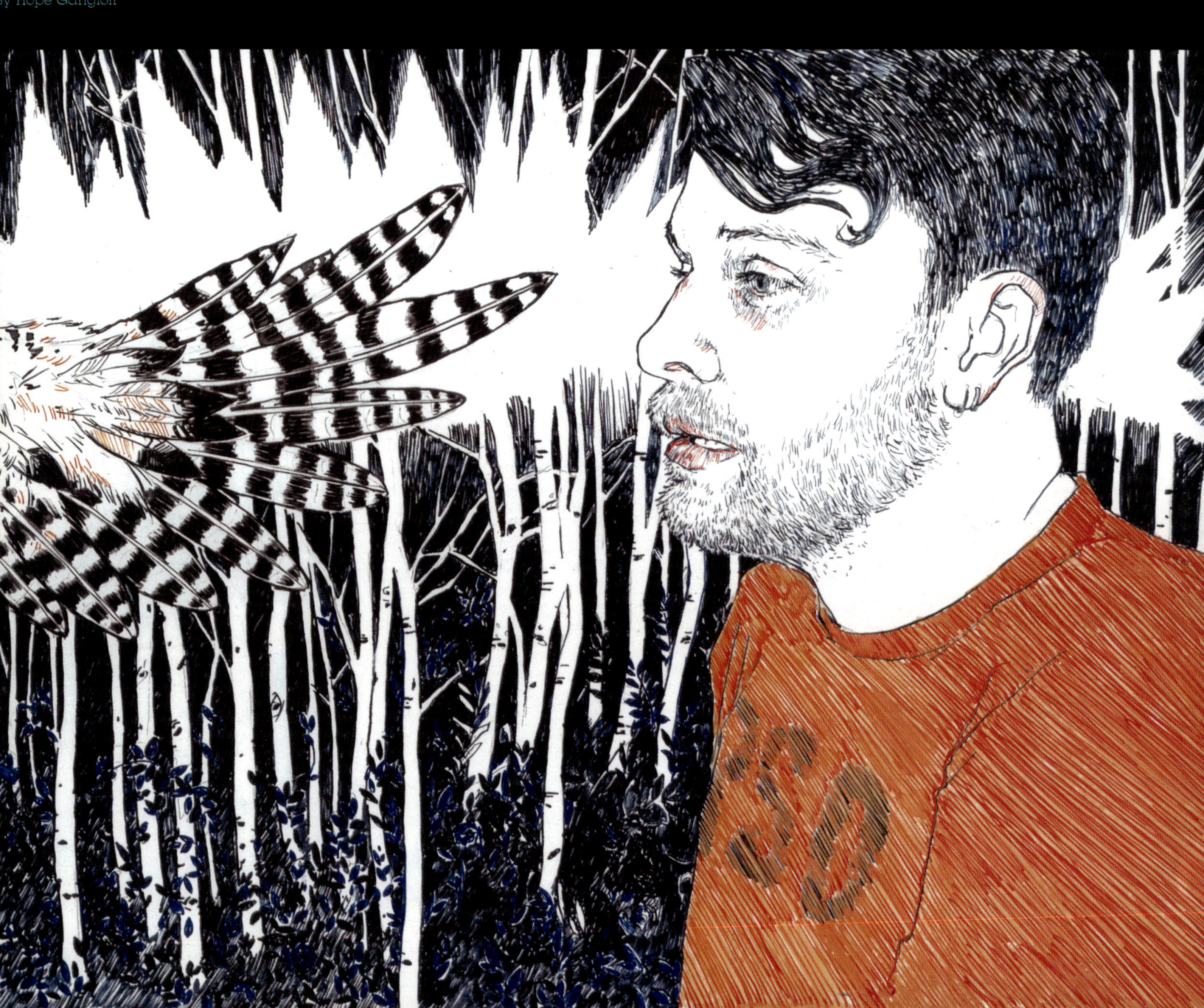

Hope Gangloff/

By Dustin Hostetler_Upso

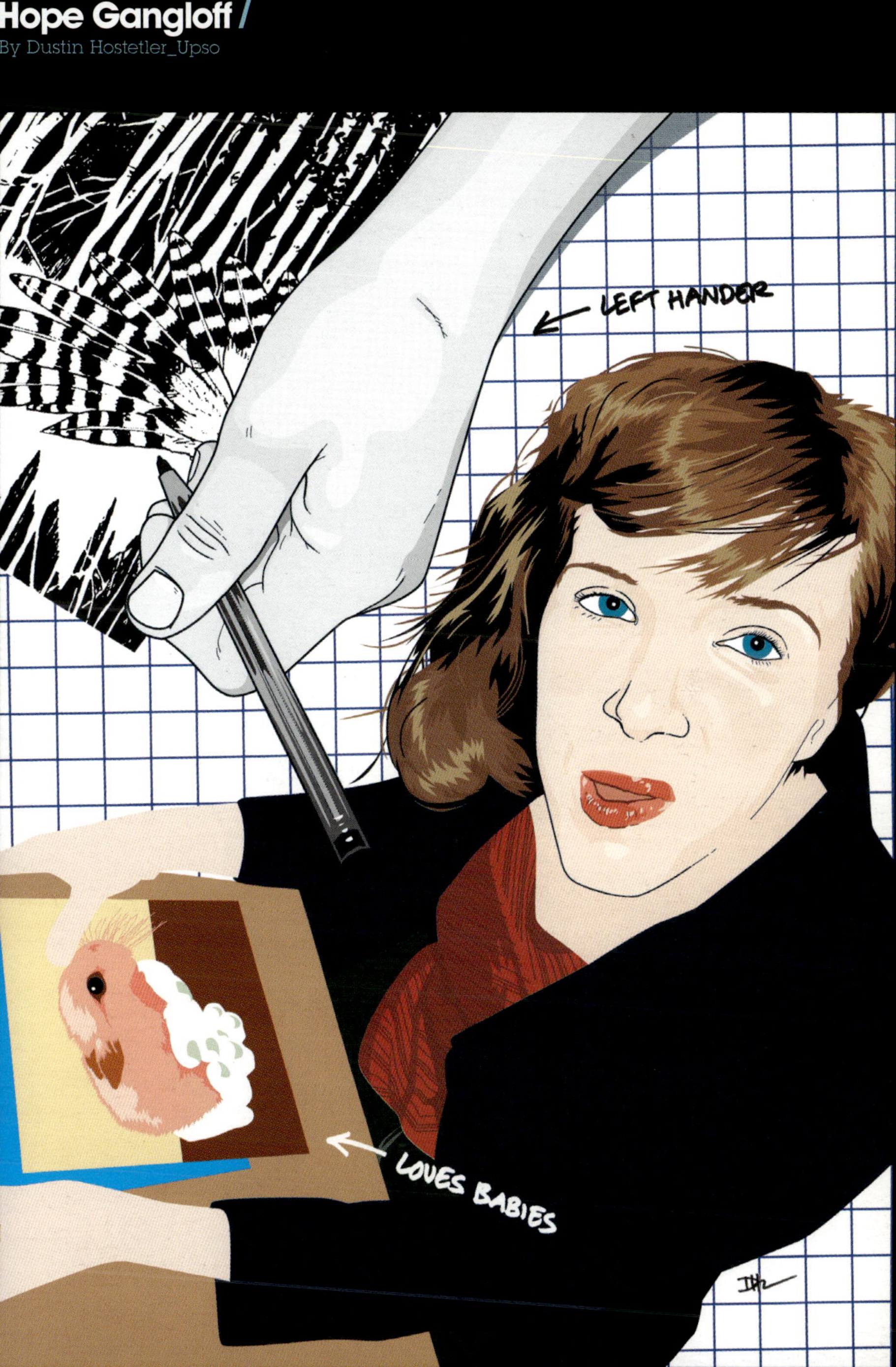

Matt Owens /

By 123Klan

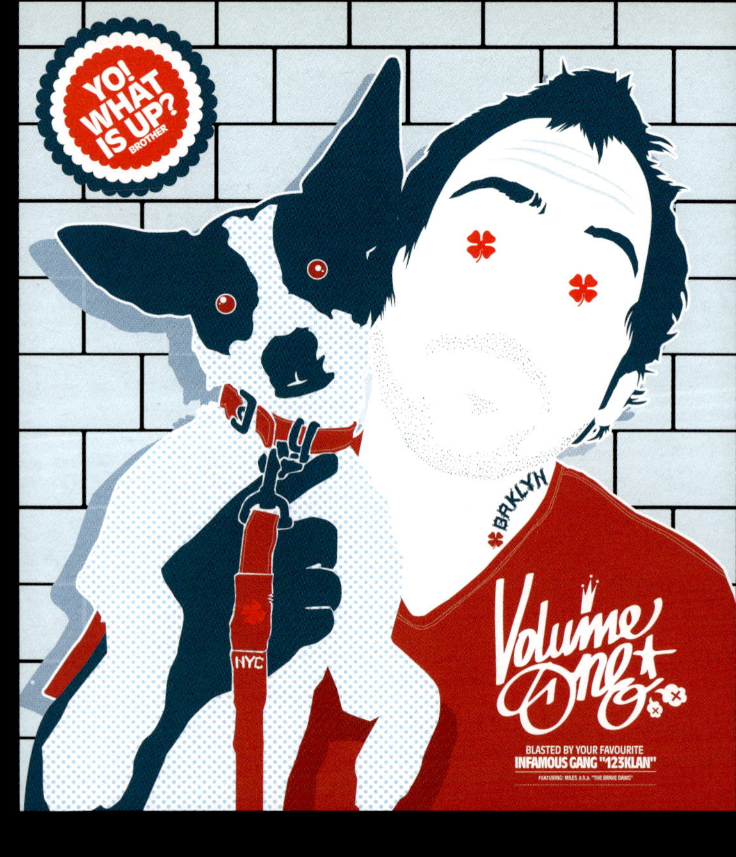

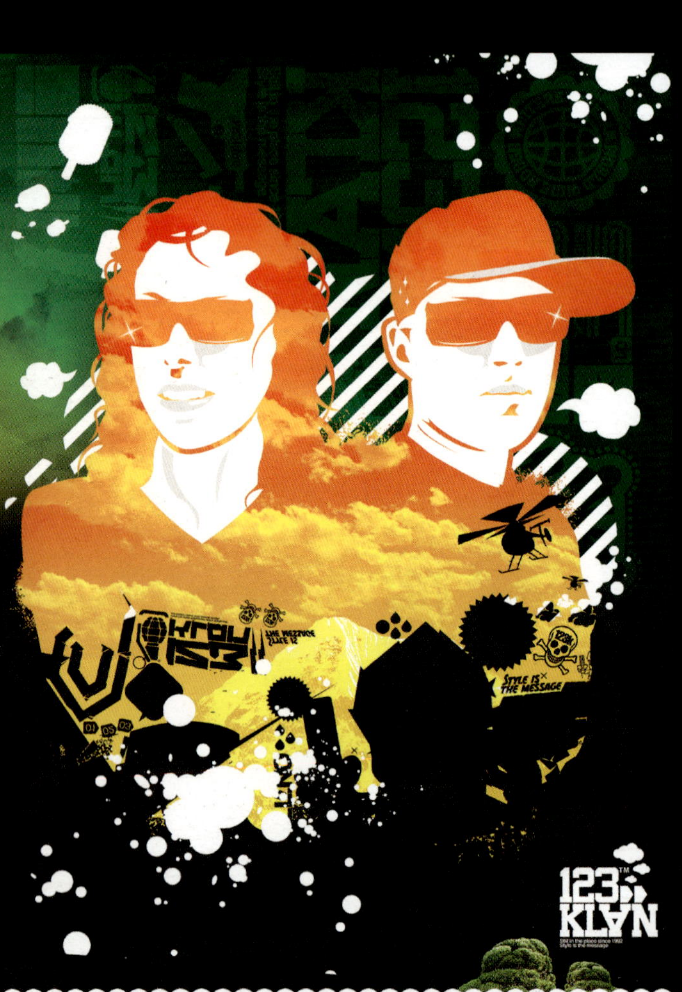

123Klan /

By Matt Owens

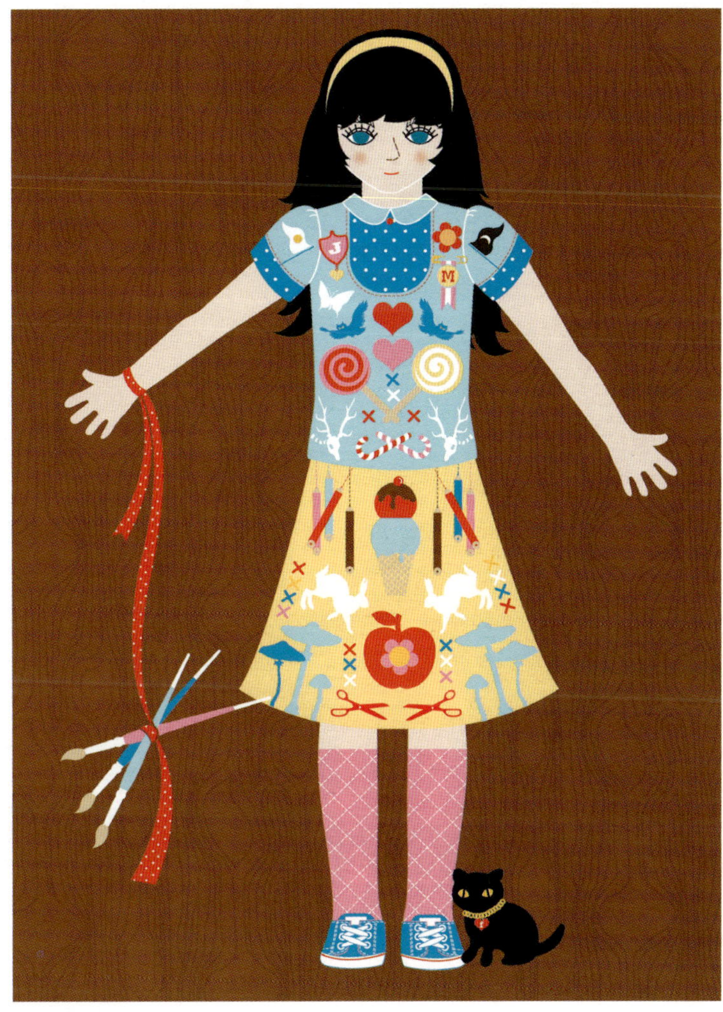

Fawn Gehweiler /
By Beci Orpin

Beci Orpin /
By Fawn Gehweiler

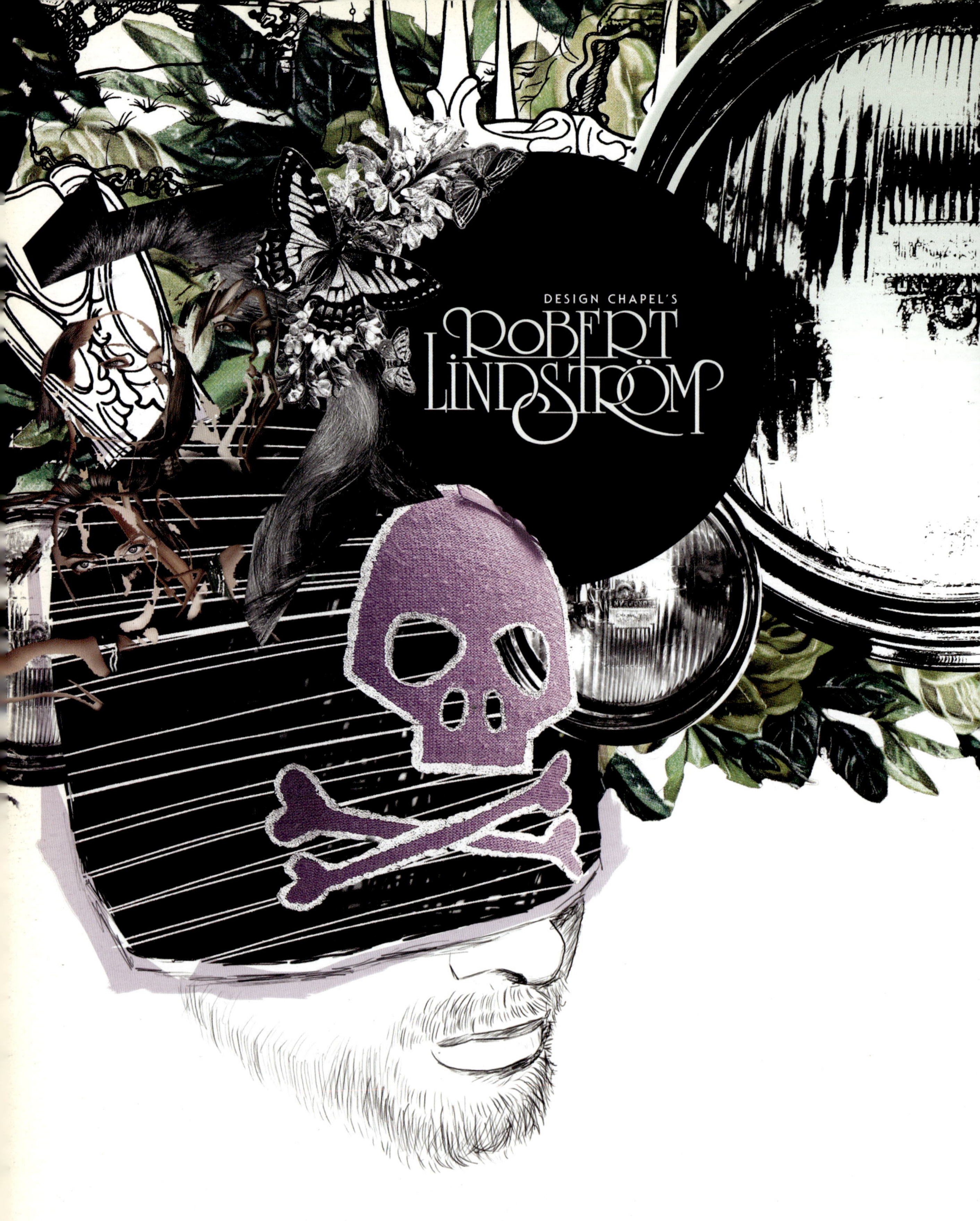

Robert Lindstrom /

By Vasava

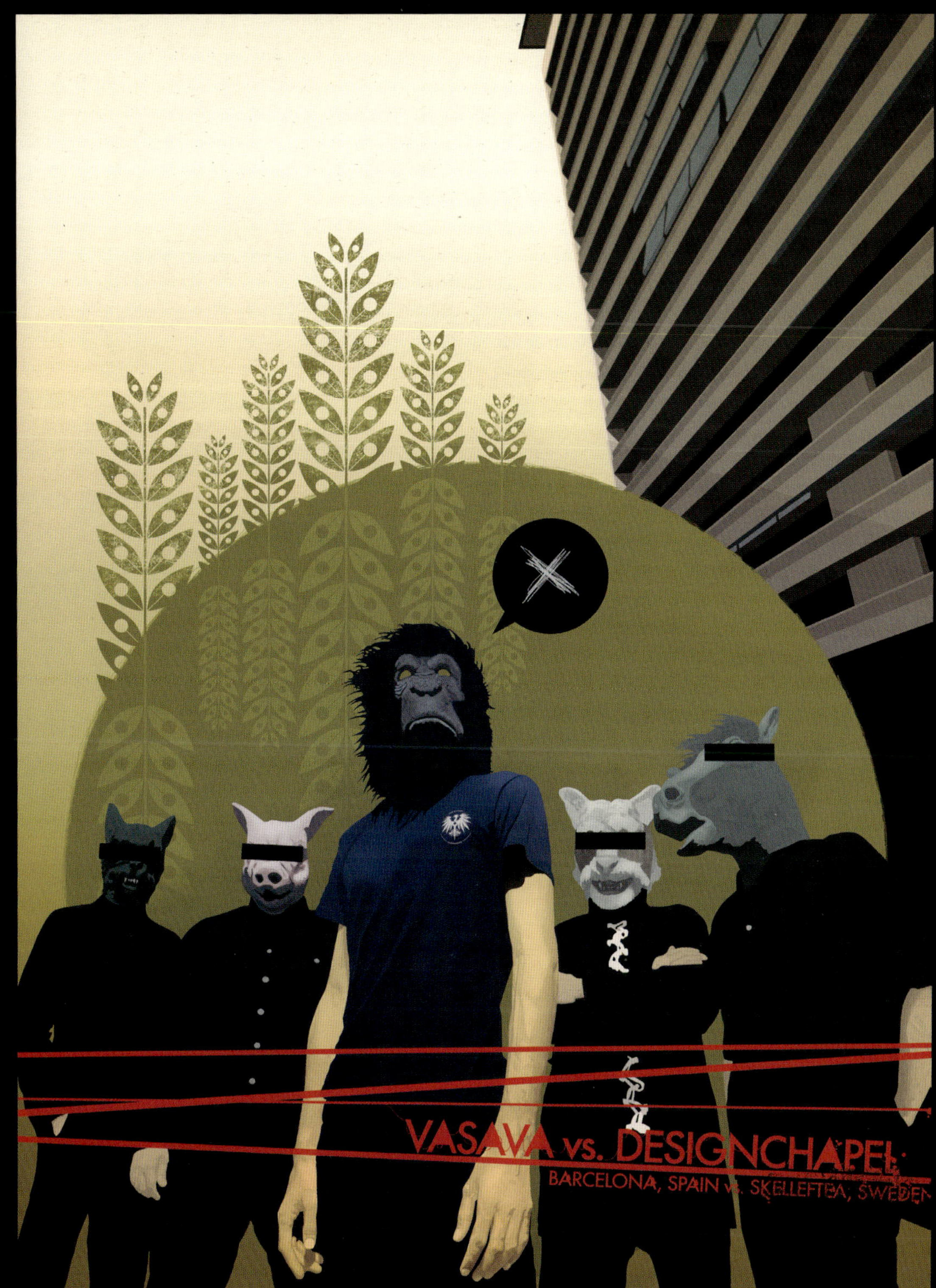

Vasava /

By Robert Lindstrom

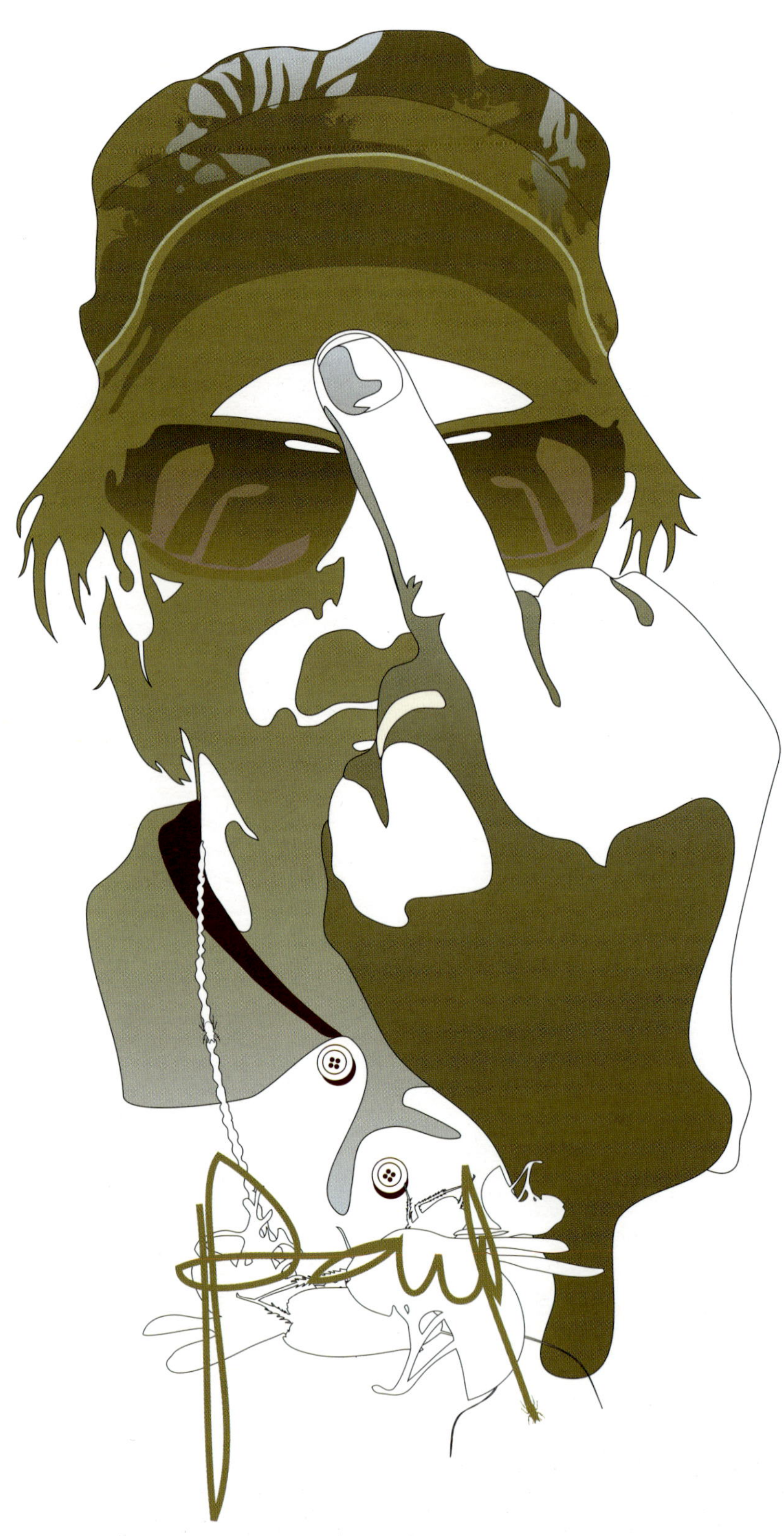

Paul Insect /
By Adam Pointer

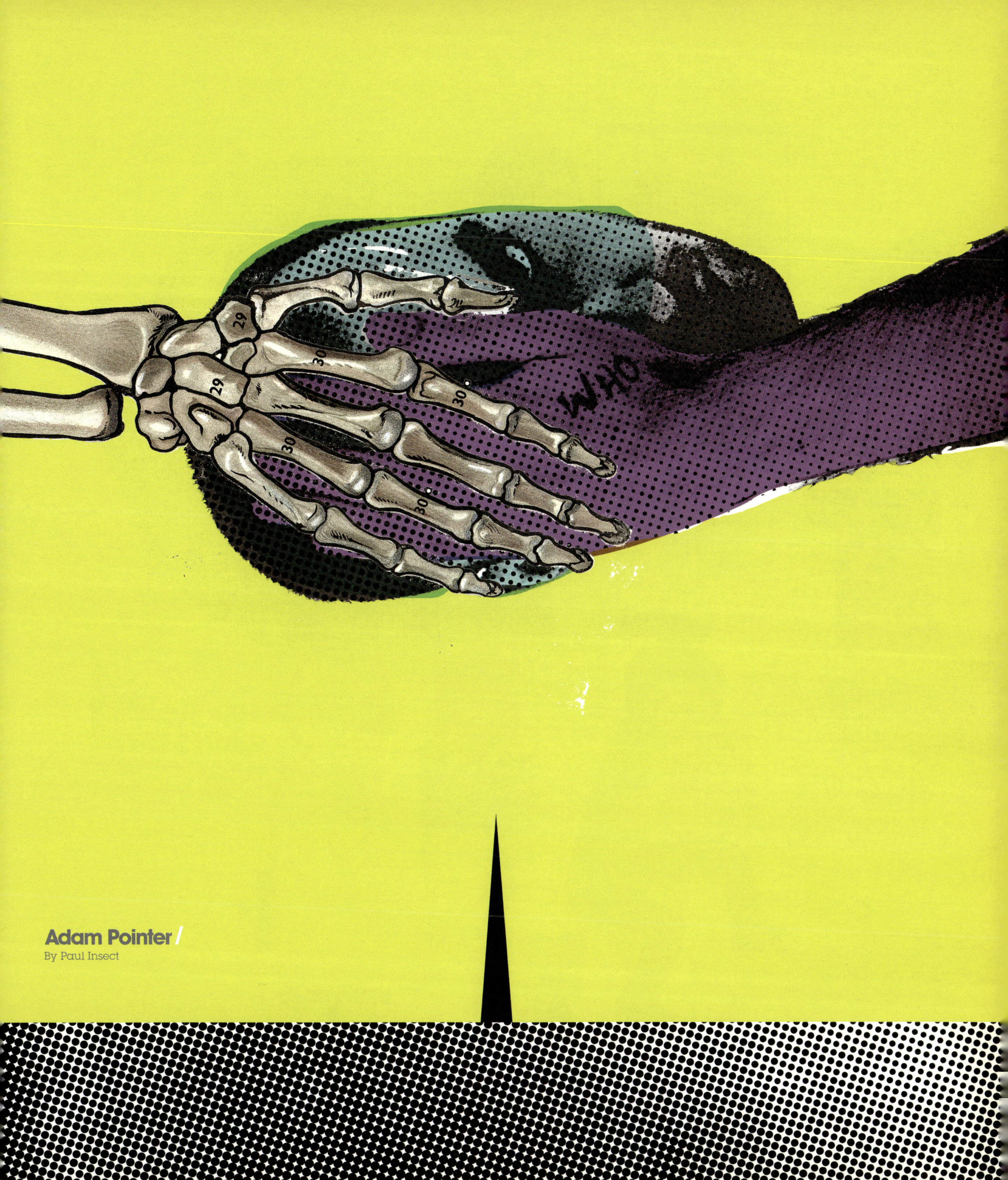

Adam Pointer /

By Paul Insect

Jeremyville /
By Geoff McFetridge

Geoff McFetridge /
By Jeremyville

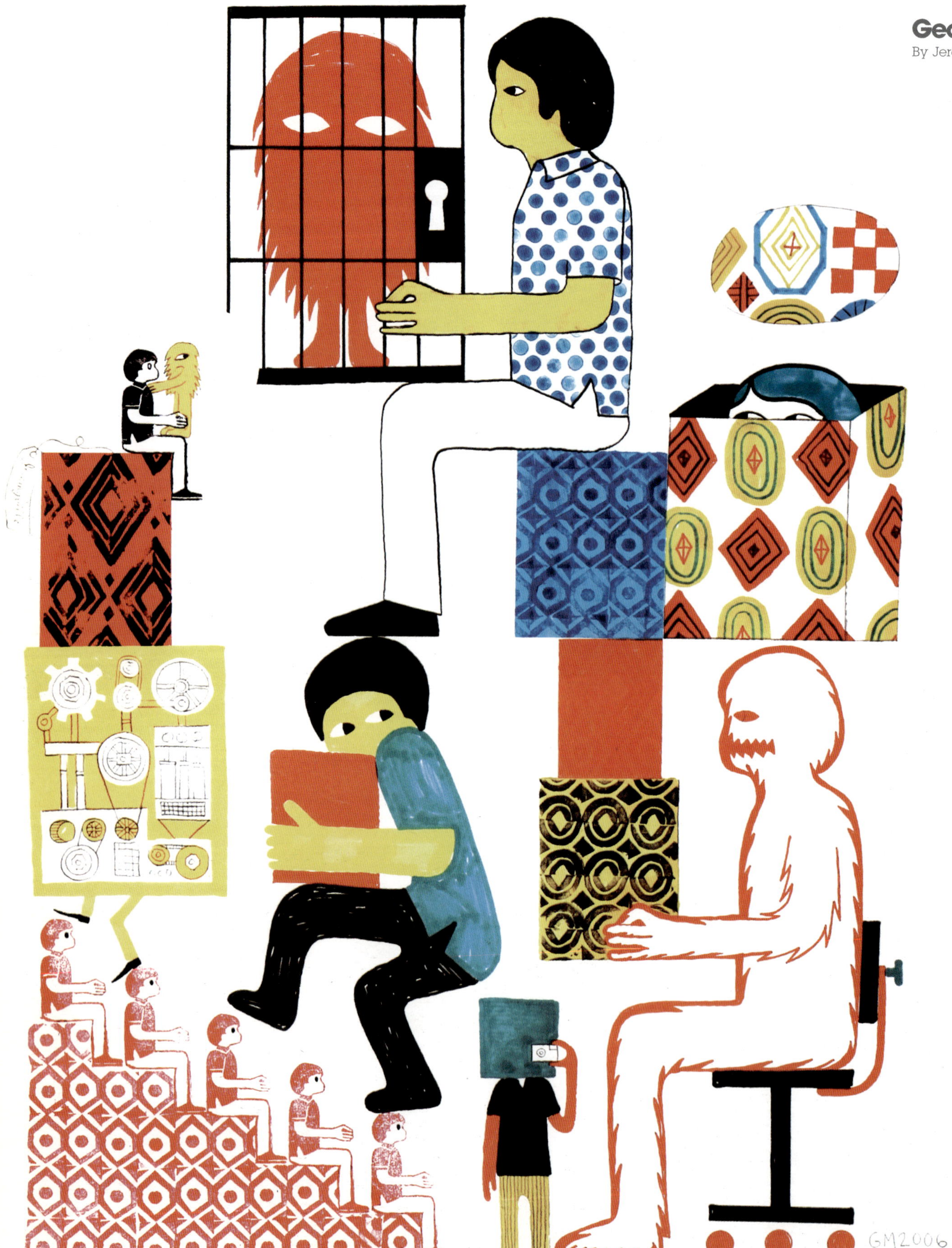

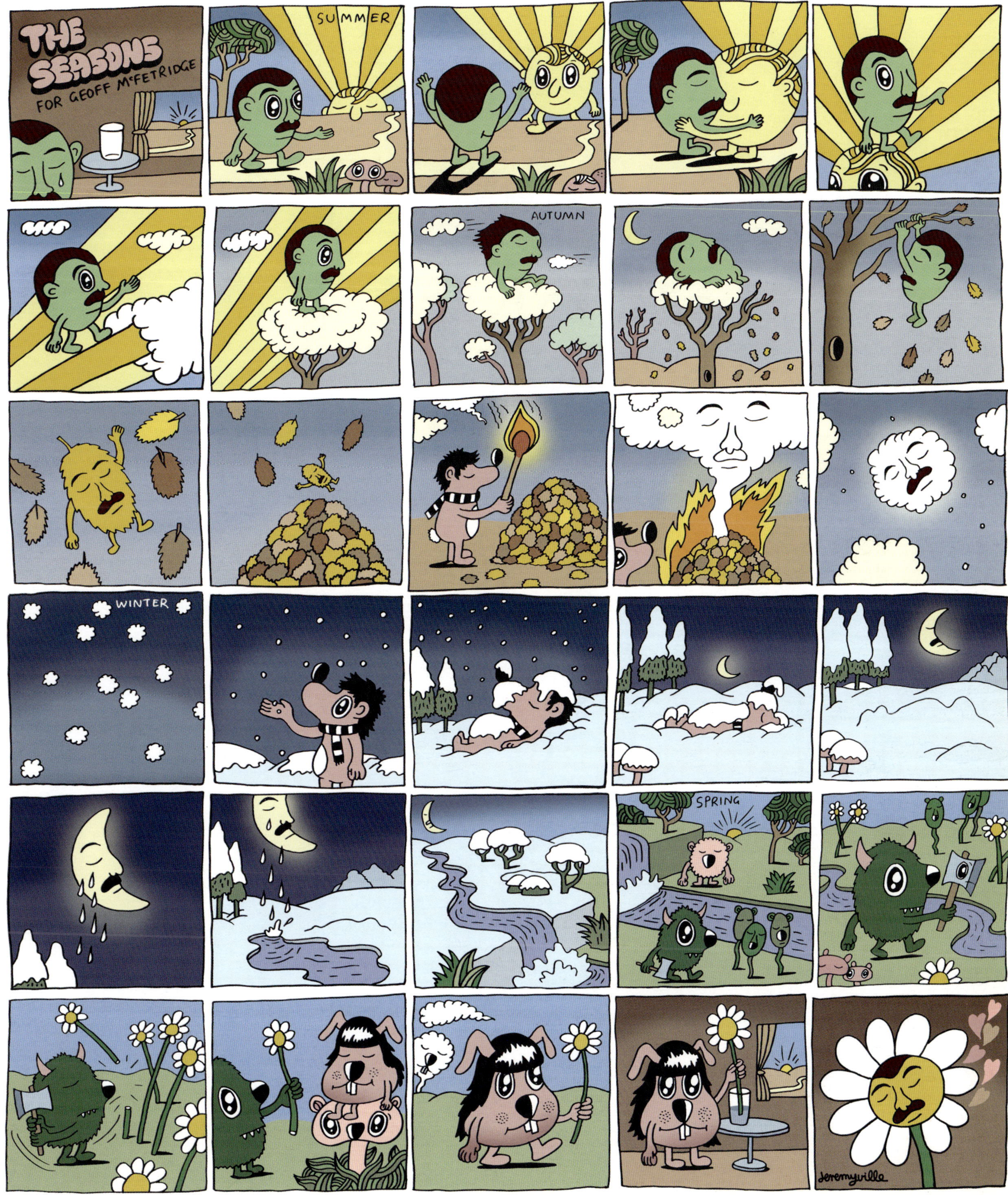
THE SEASONS
FOR GEOFF McFETRIDGE
SUMMER
AUTUMN
WINTER
SPRING
jeremyville

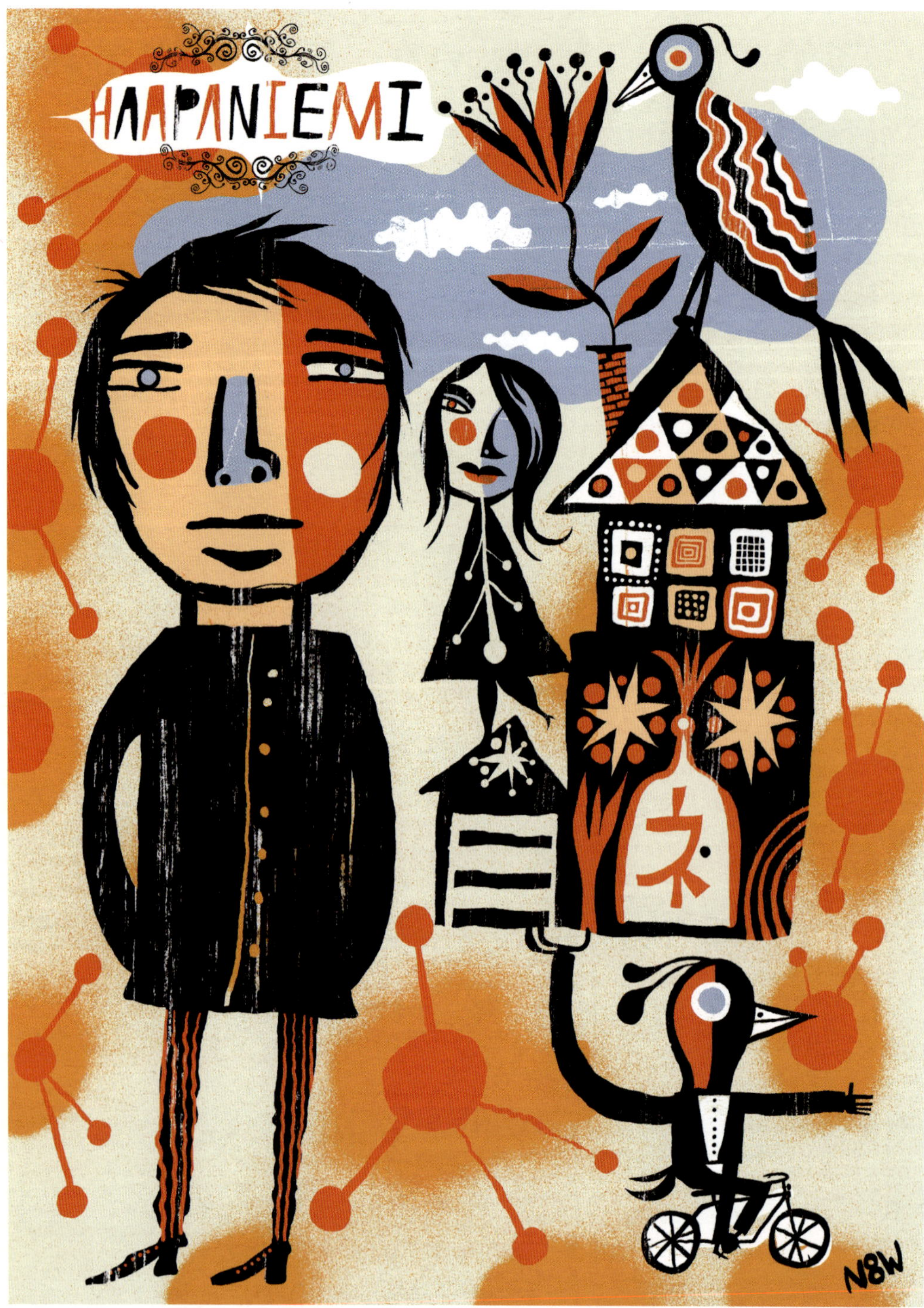

Klaus Haapaniemi /
By Nate Williams

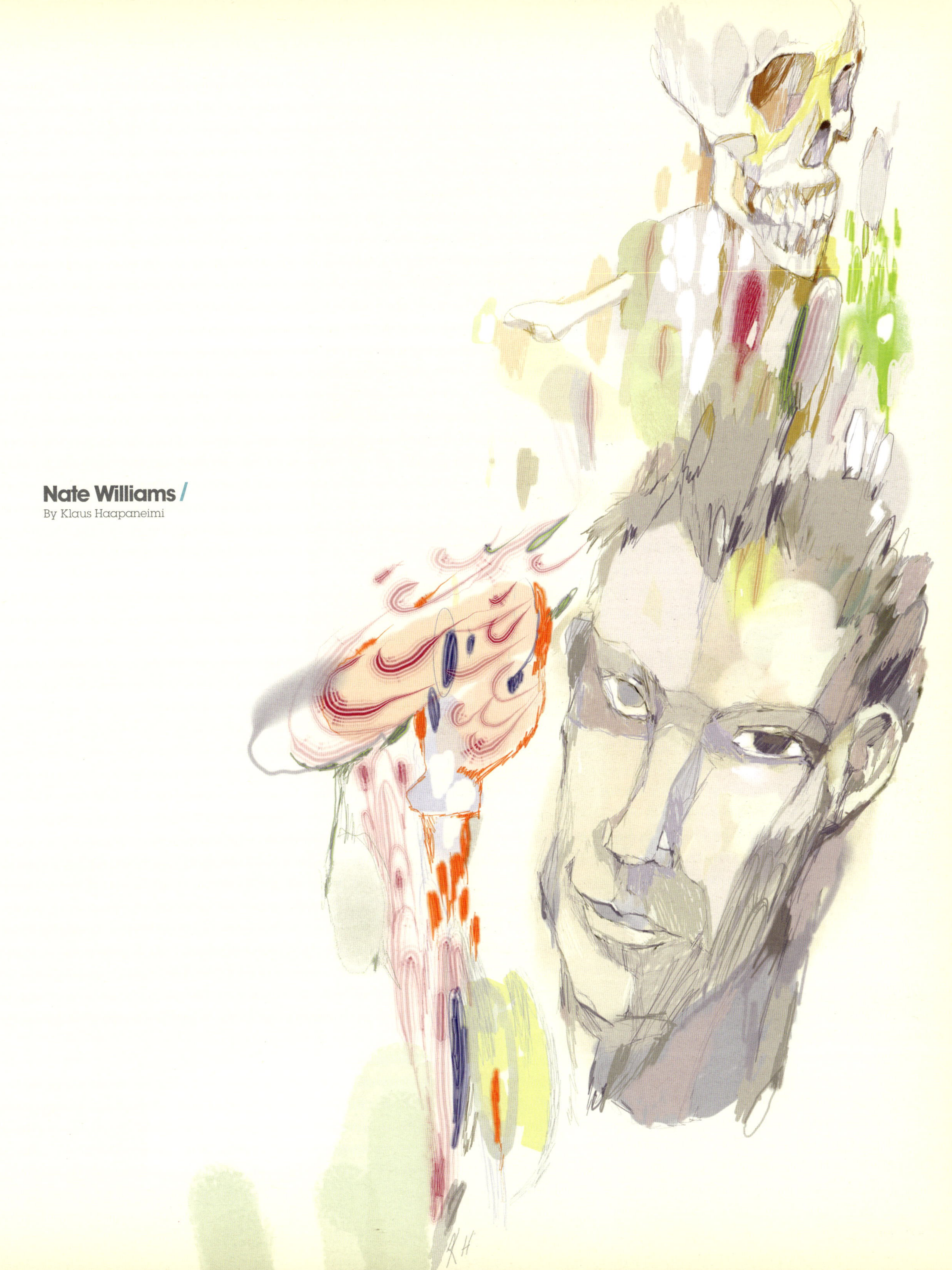

Nate Williams /

By Klaus Haapaneimi

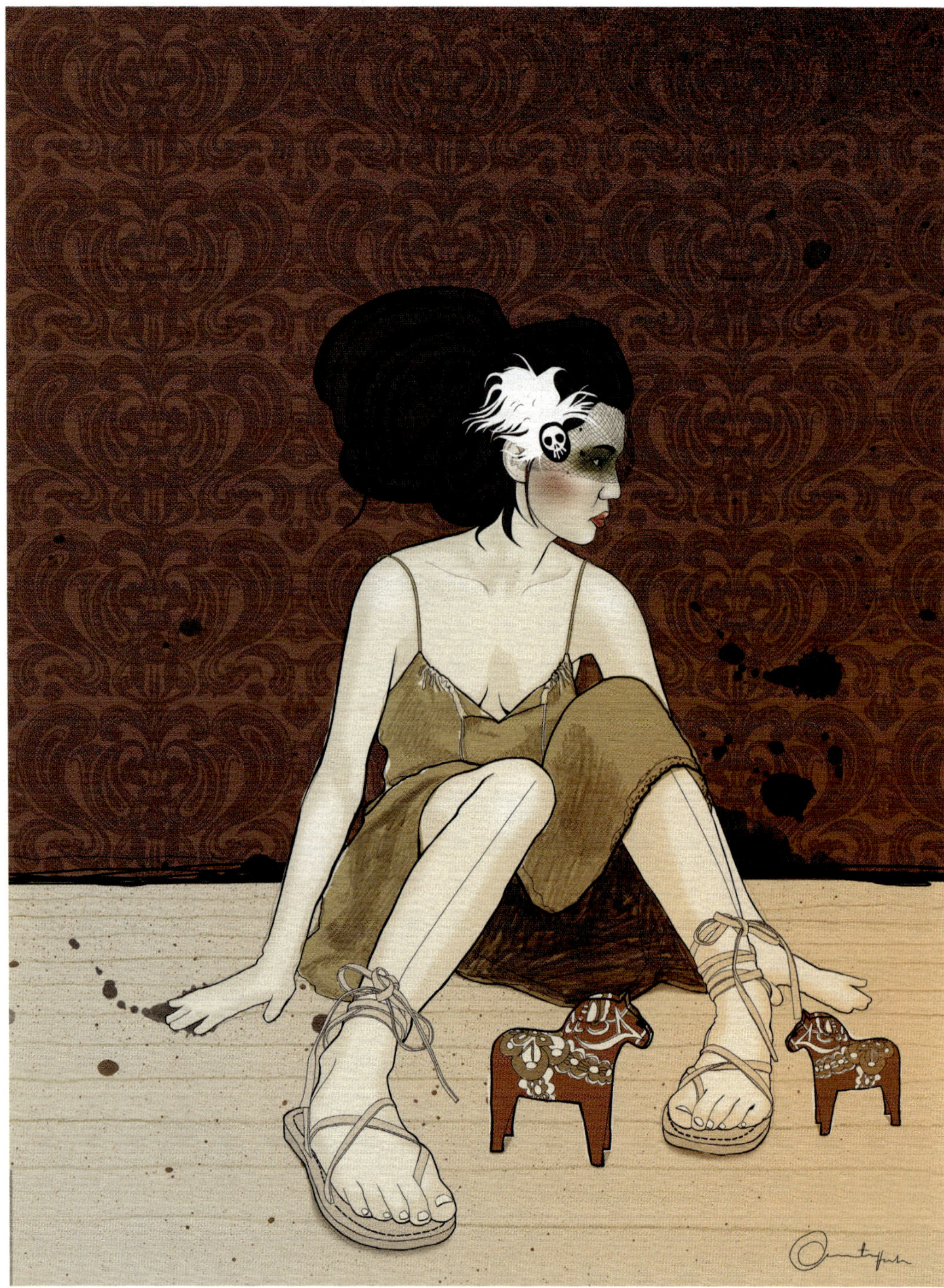

Autumn Whitehurst /
By Charlotta Havh

Charlotta Havh /
By Autumn Whitehurst

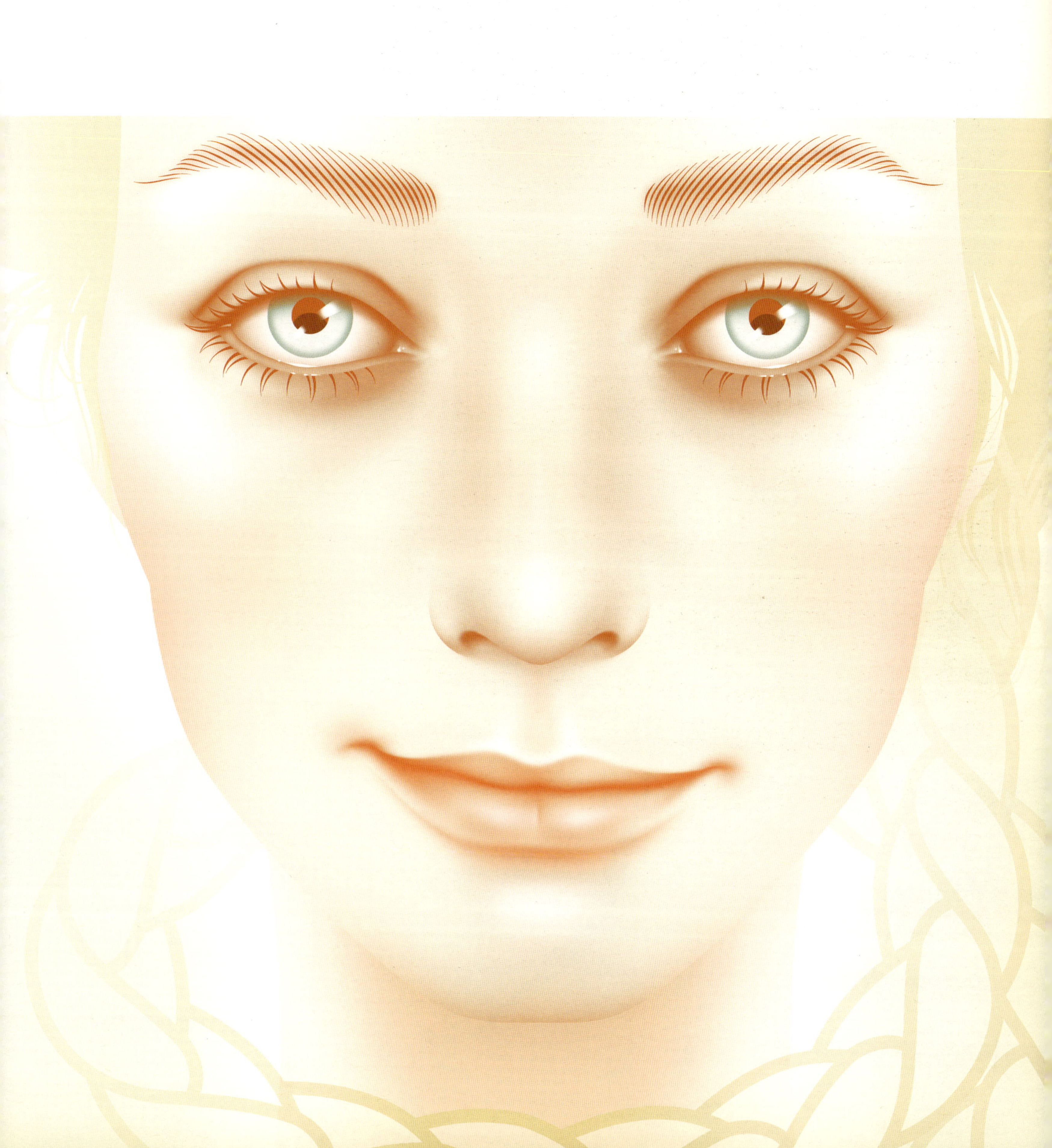

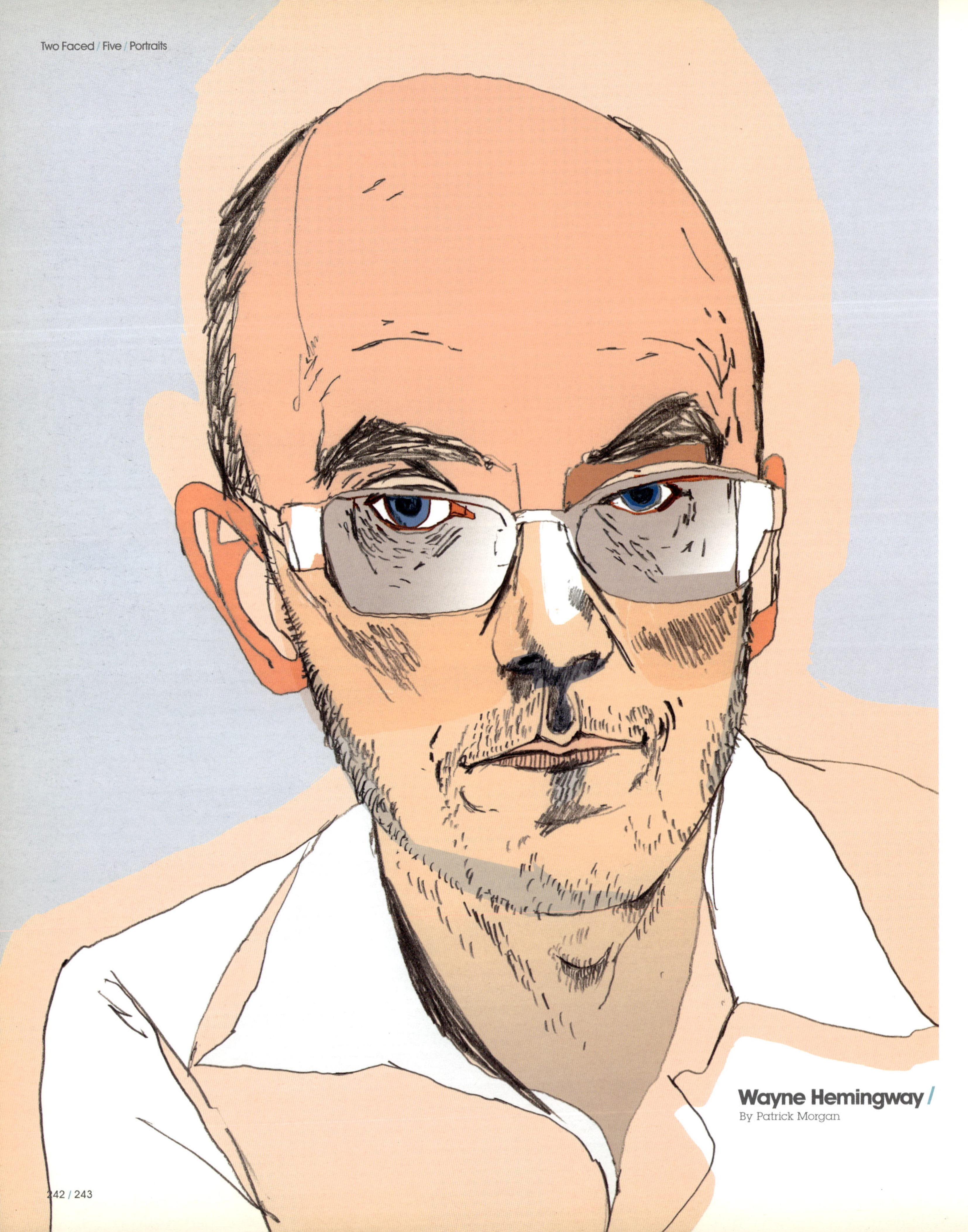

Wayne Hemingway /
By Patrick Morgan

Patrick Morgan /

By Wayne Hemingway

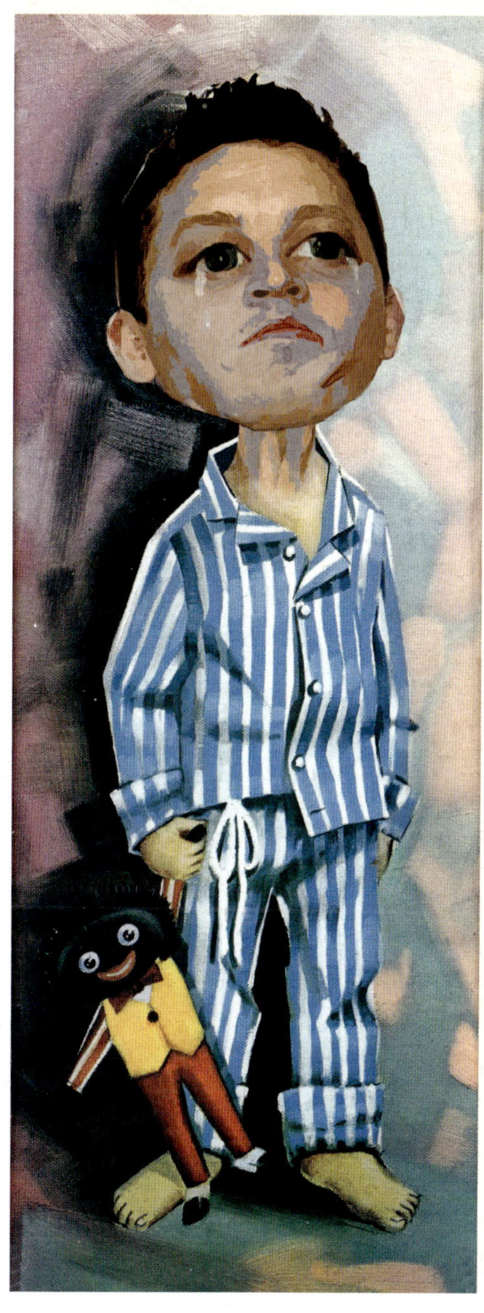

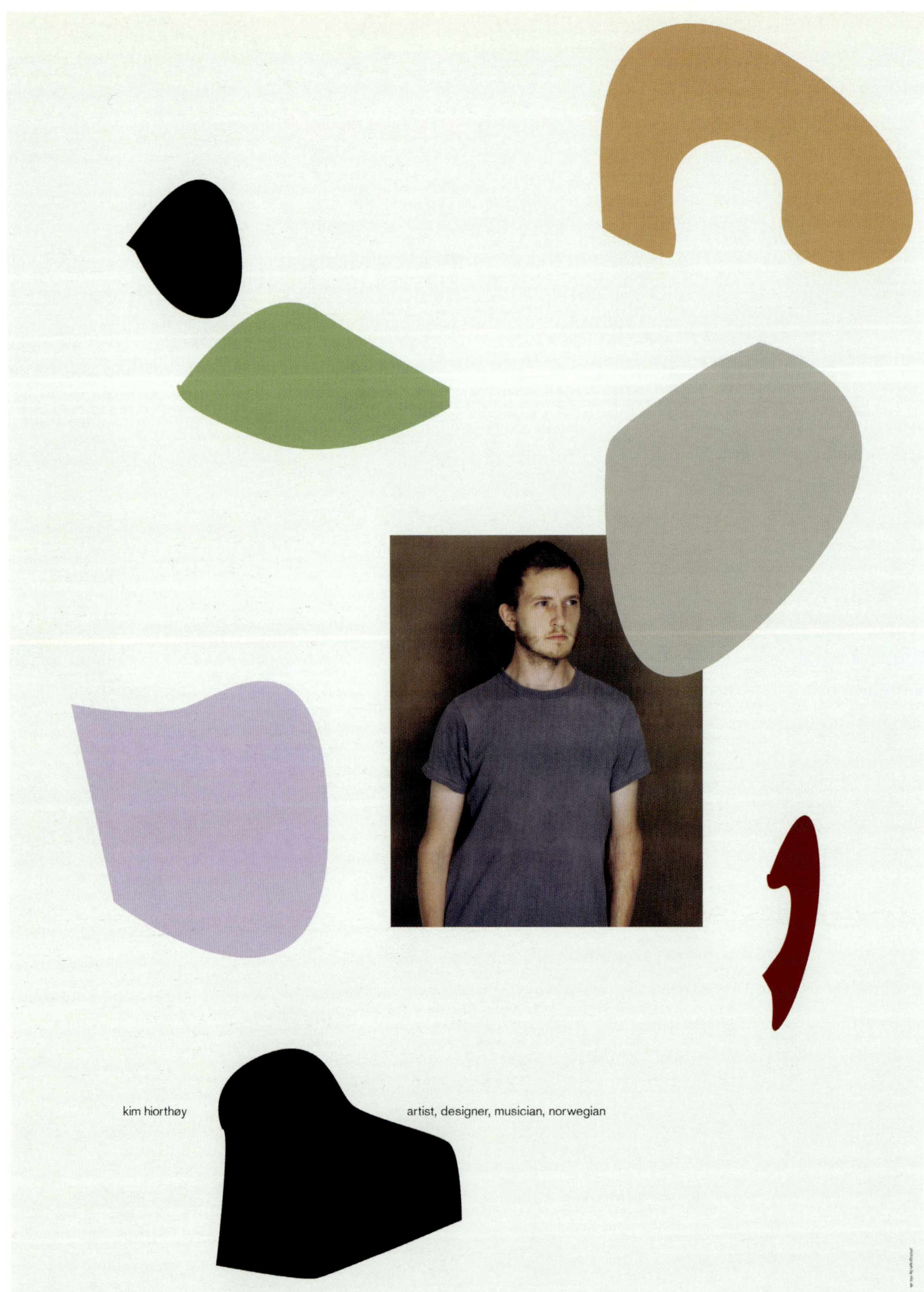

Kim Hiorthoy /

By Adrian Shaughnessey

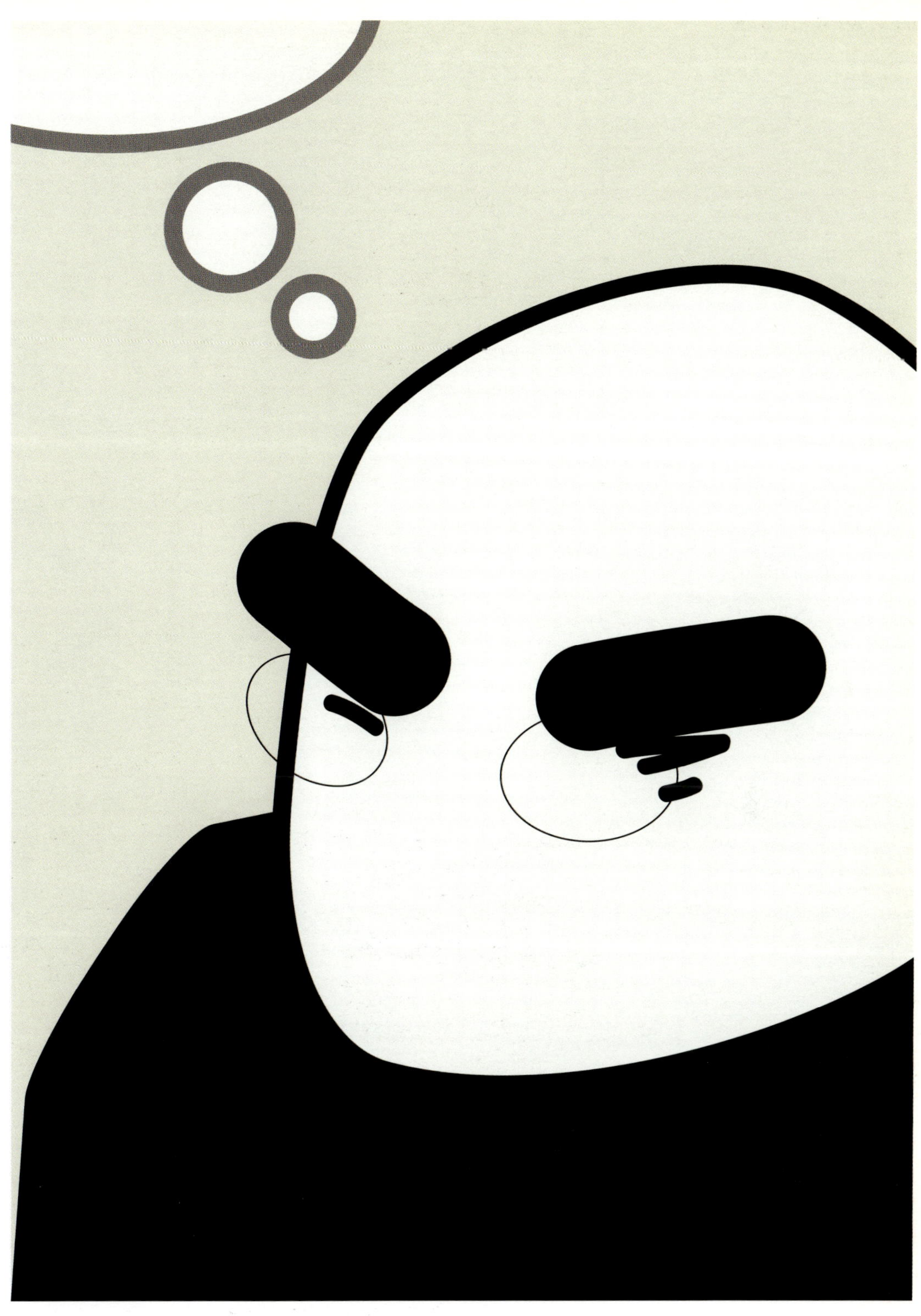

Adrian Shaughnessy /

By Kim Hiorthoy

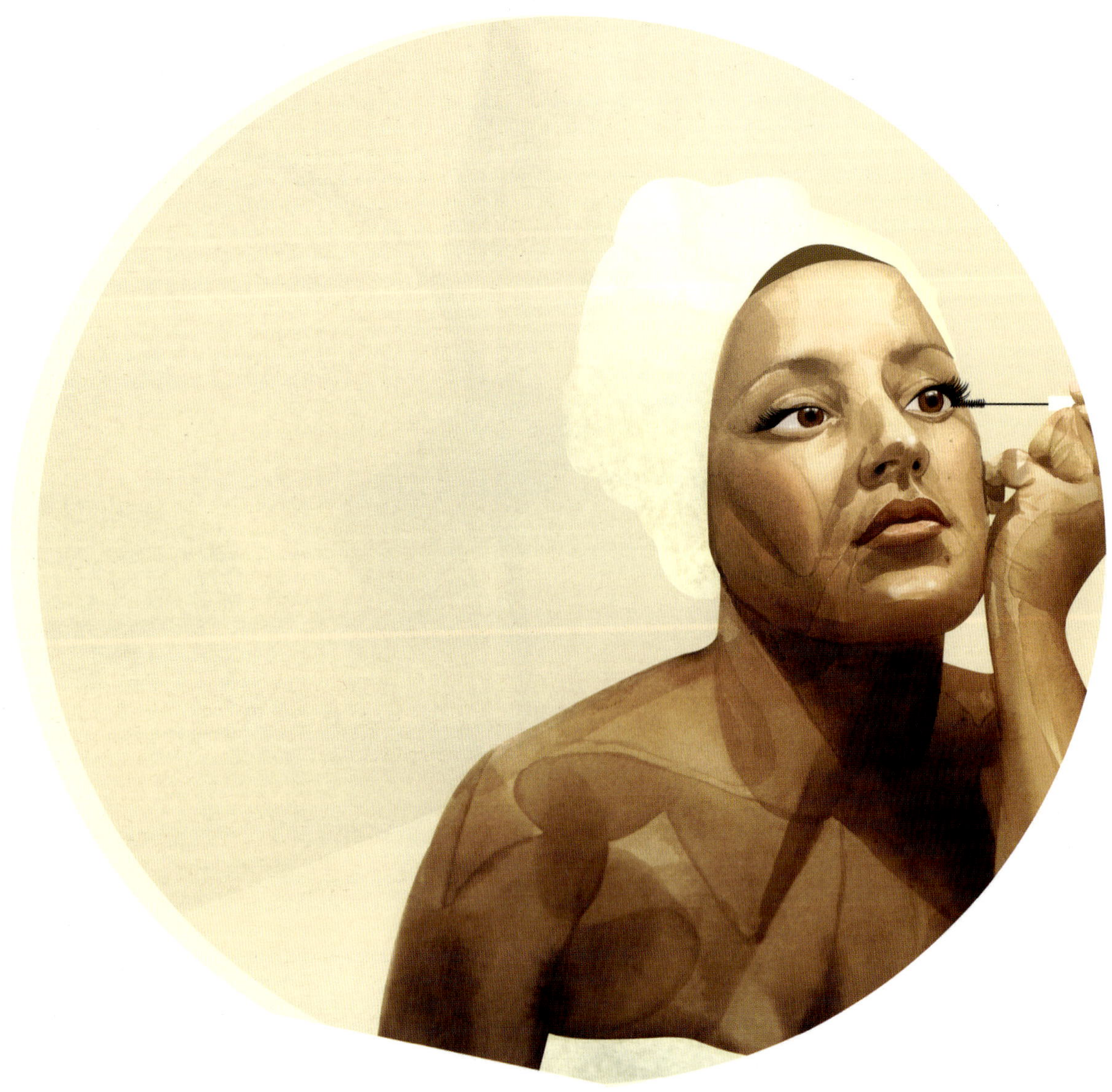

Anna Fowler /
By Hellovon

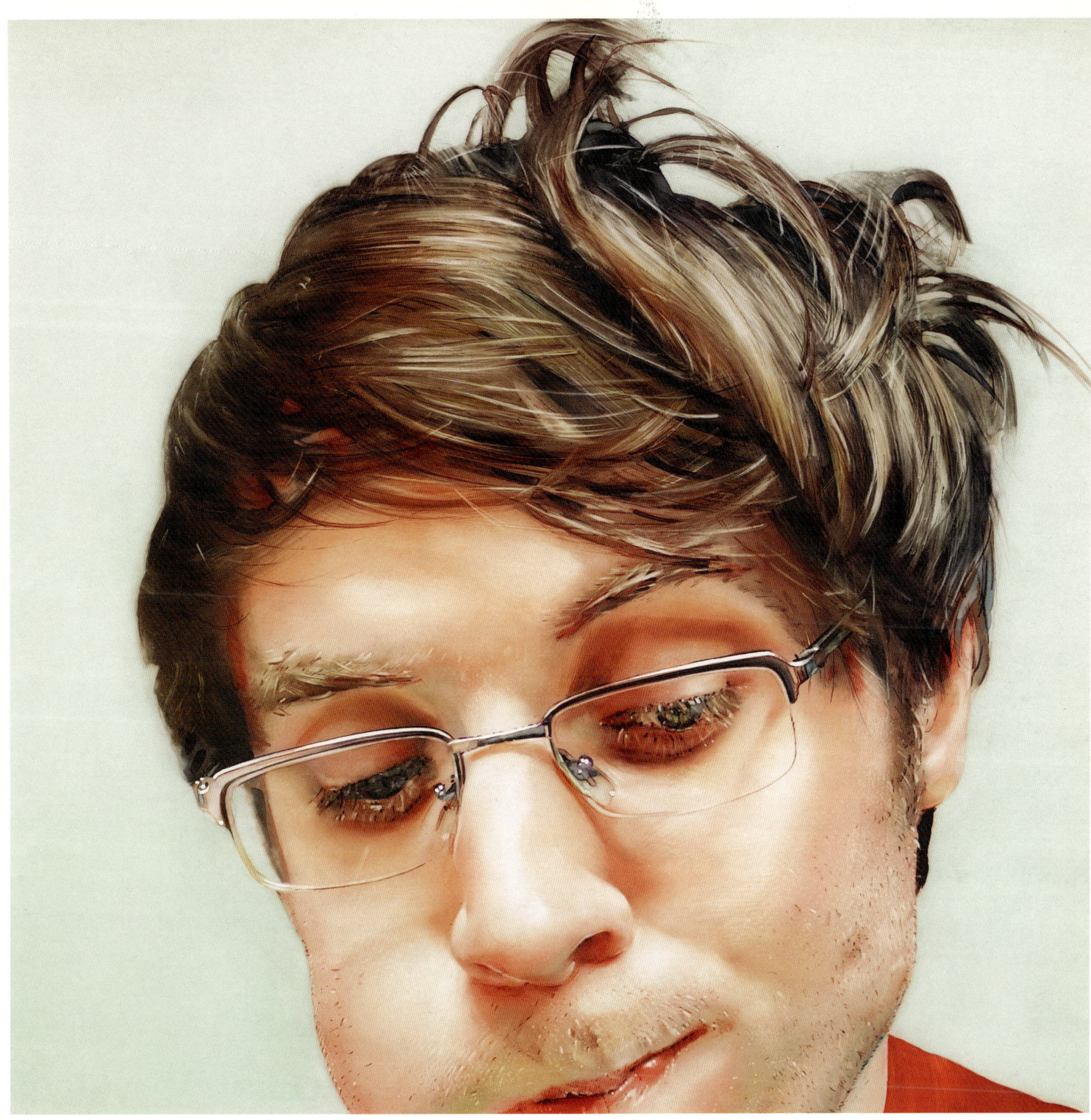

Hellovon /

By Anna Fowler

Paul Davis

By Jonathan Ellery

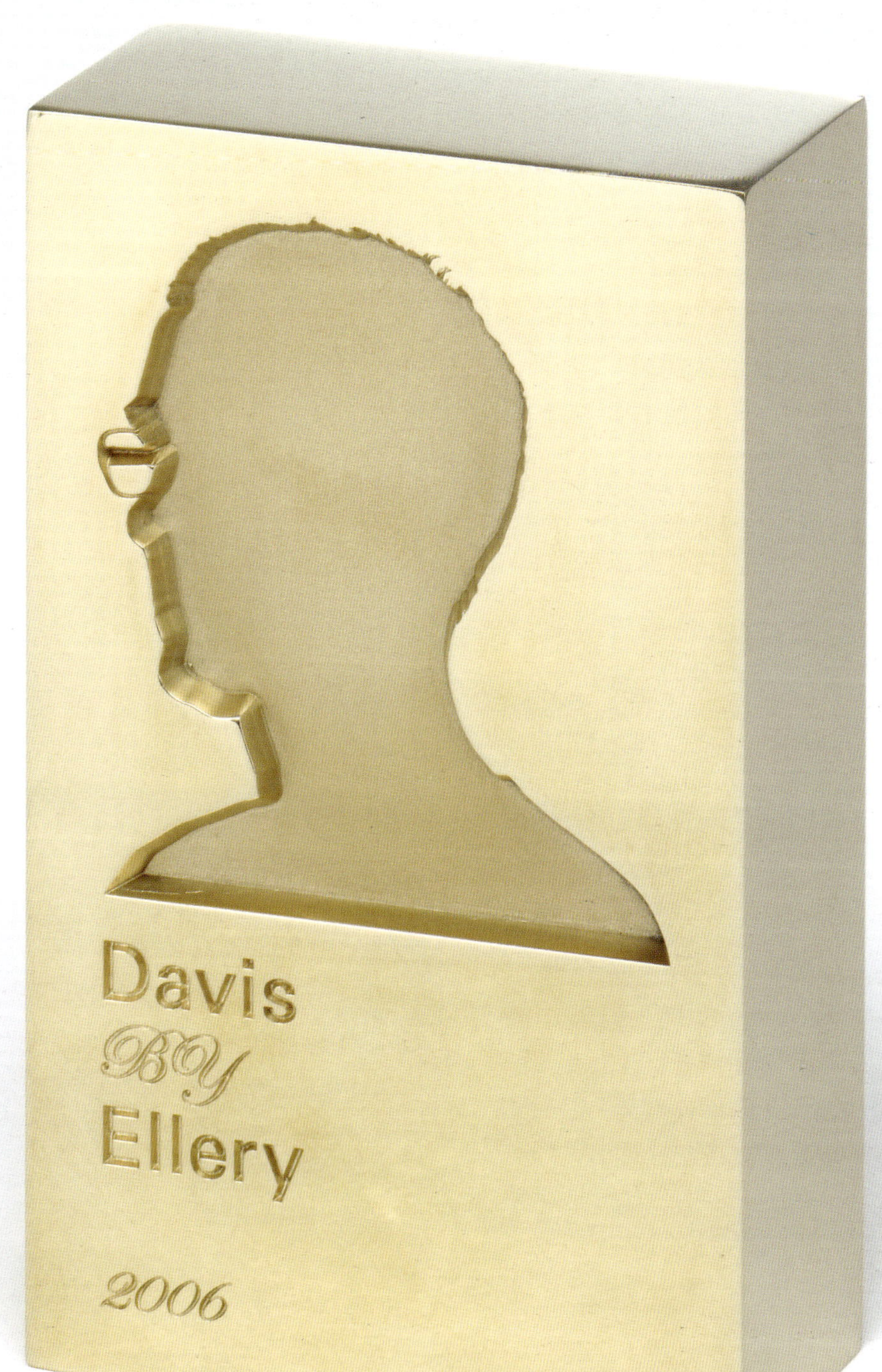
Davis
BY
Ellery
2006

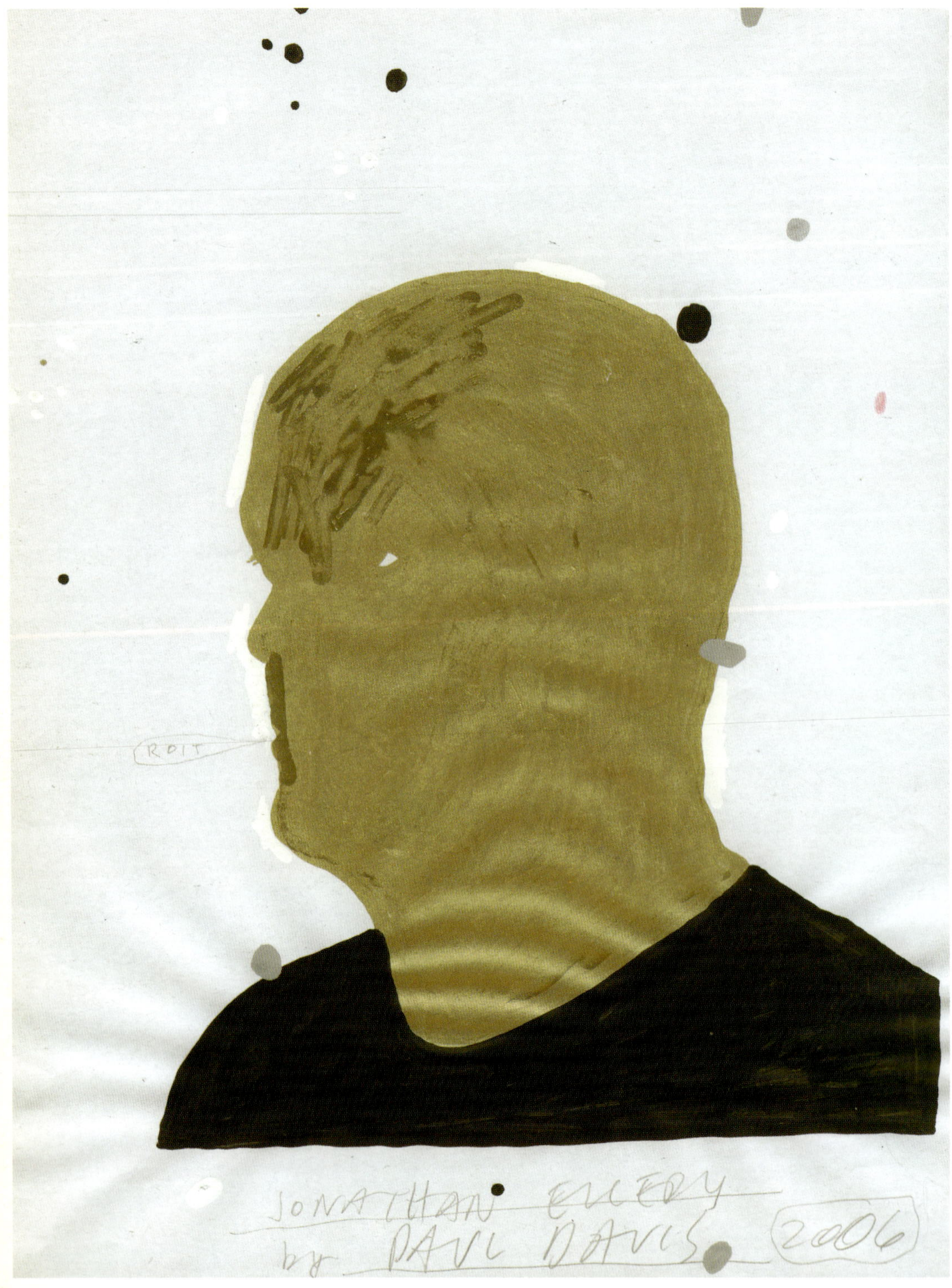
JONATHAN ELLERY
by PAUL DAVIS
2006

Jonathan Ellery

By Paul Davis

Maya Hayuk /

By Armsrock

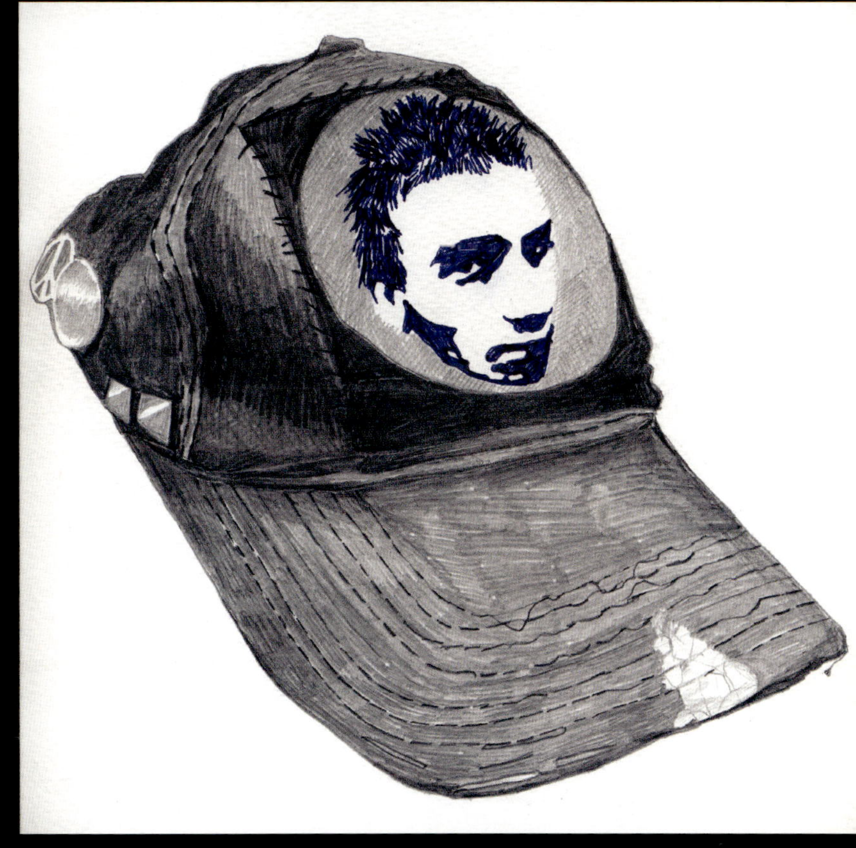

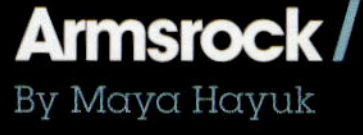

Armsrock /
By Maya Hayuk

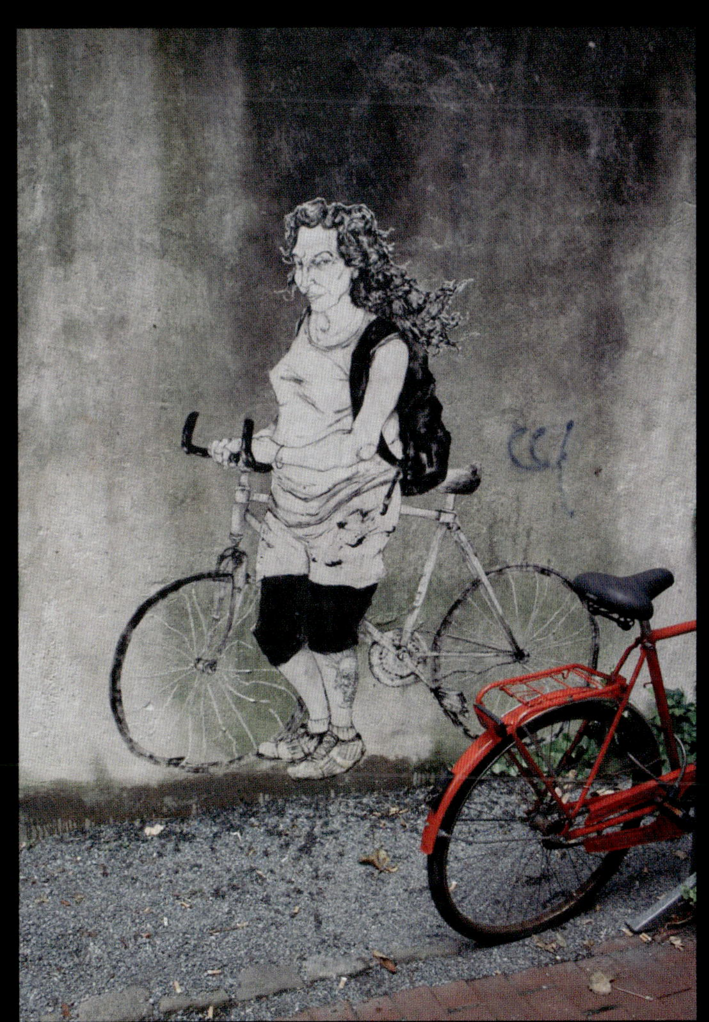

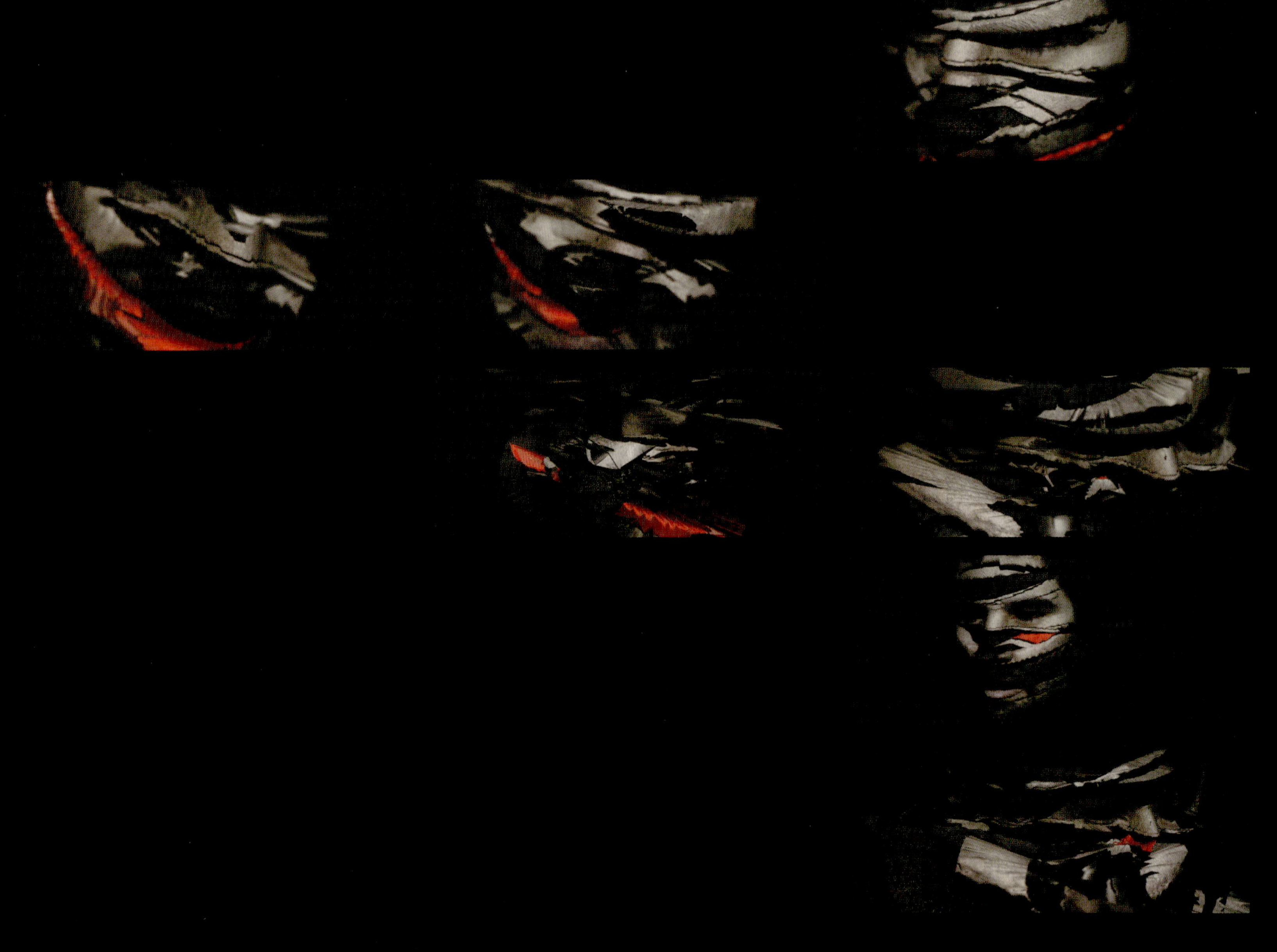

Jesse Seppi_Tronic /

By Joost Korngold

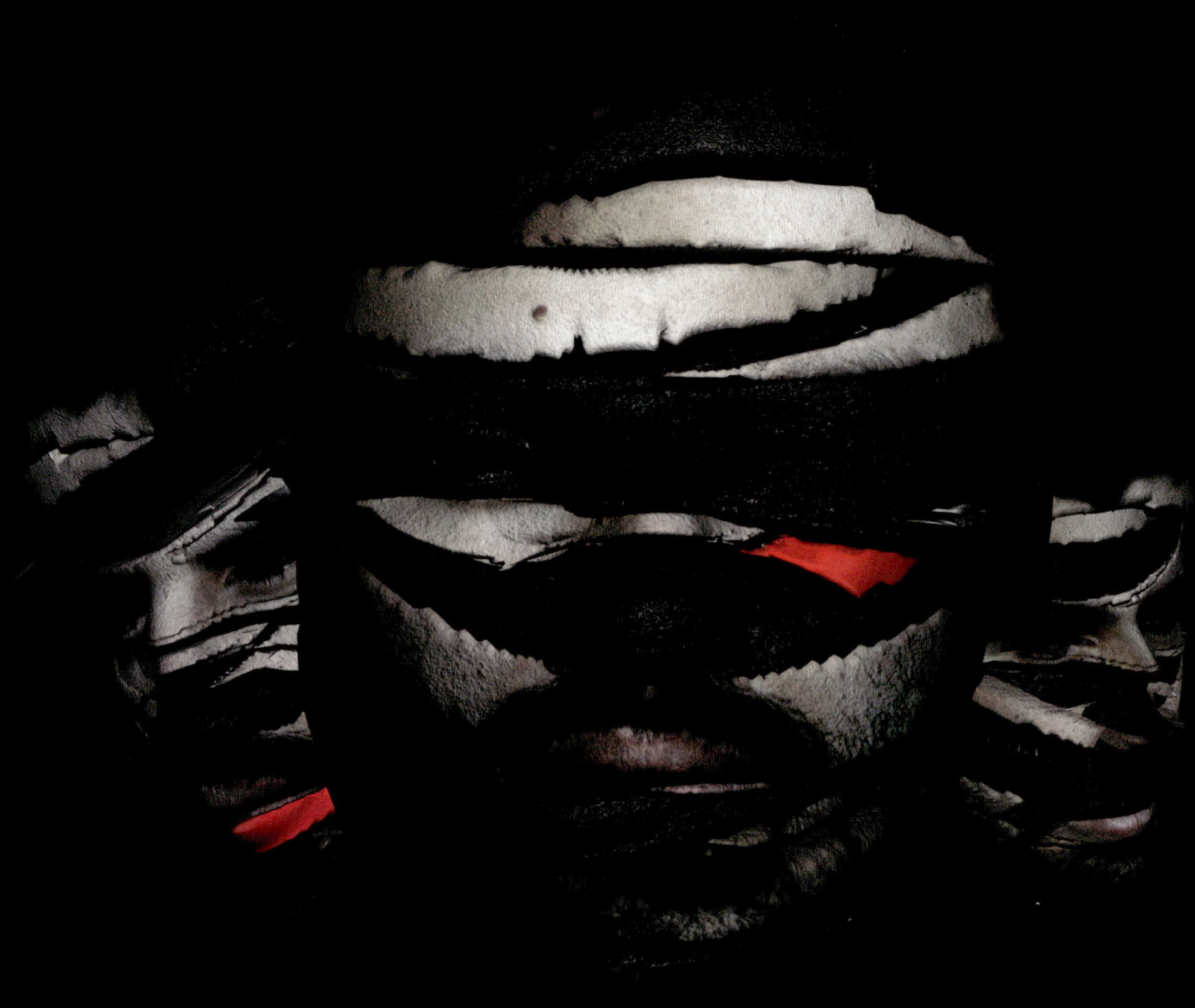

Jesse Seppi_Tronic /
By Joost Korngold

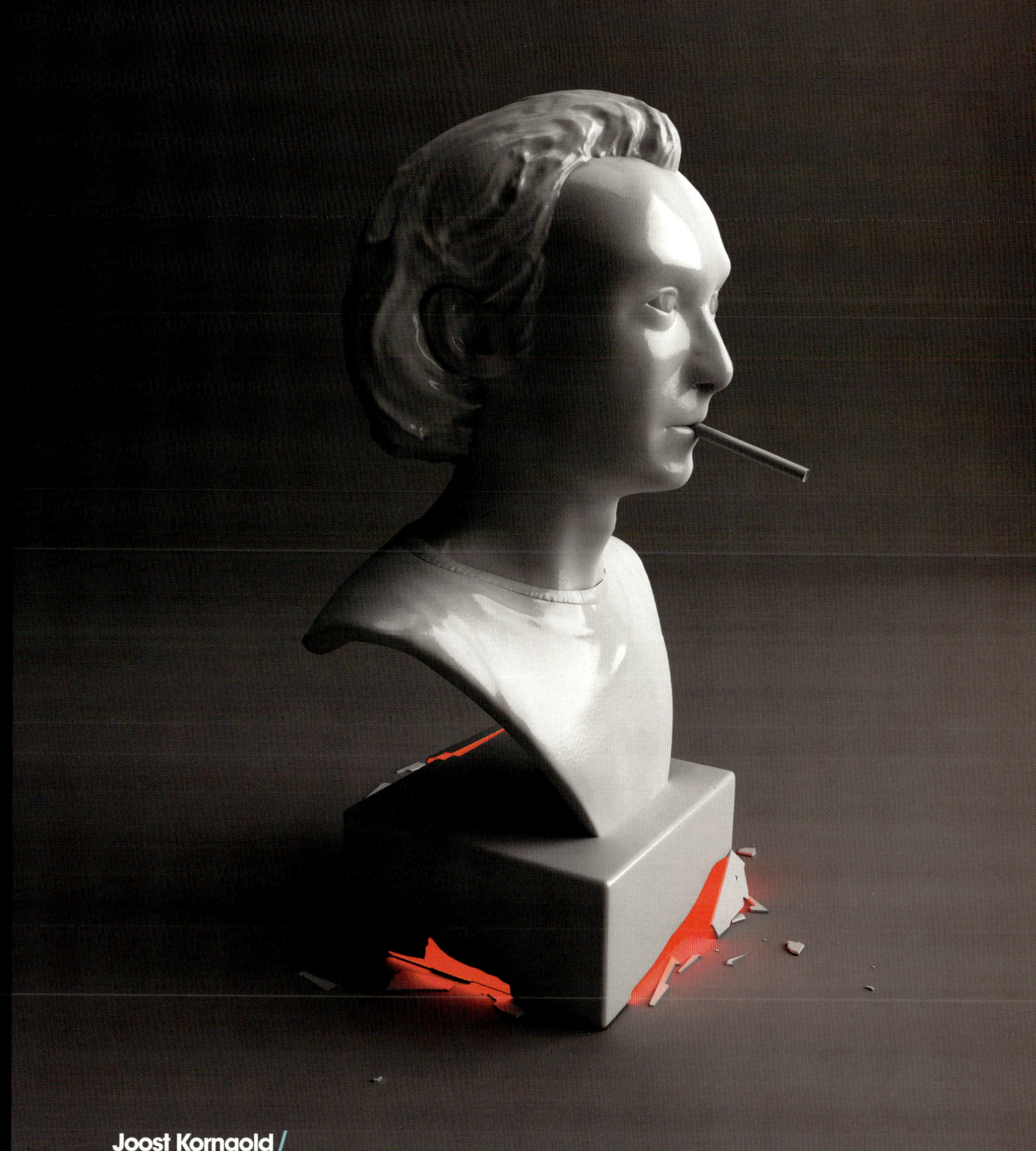

Joost Korngold /
By Jesse Seppi _Tronic

Hillman Curtis

By Timothy Saccenti

Hillman Curtis is a designer and filmmaker, whose company hillmancurtis, inc. has designed sites for Yahoo!, Adobe, Aquent, the American Institute of Graphic Design, Paramount and Fox Searchlight Pictures among others. His film work includes the documentary series "Artist Series", as well as two short feature films. His commercial film work includes shorts for Rolling Stone, Adobe and BMW. His three books on design and film have sold close to 200 thousand copies and have been translated into 14 languages. He splits his time between San Francisco and New York City.

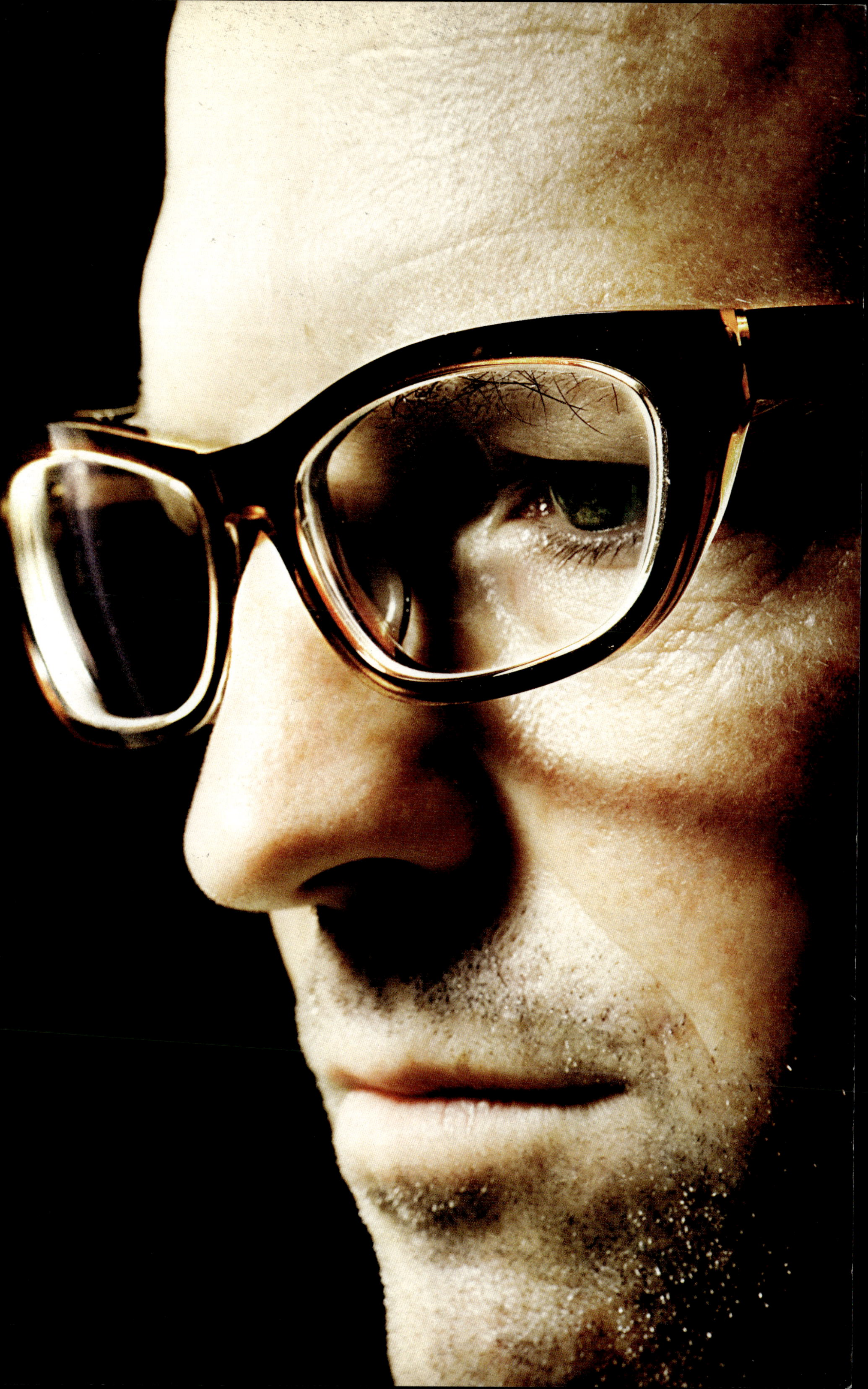

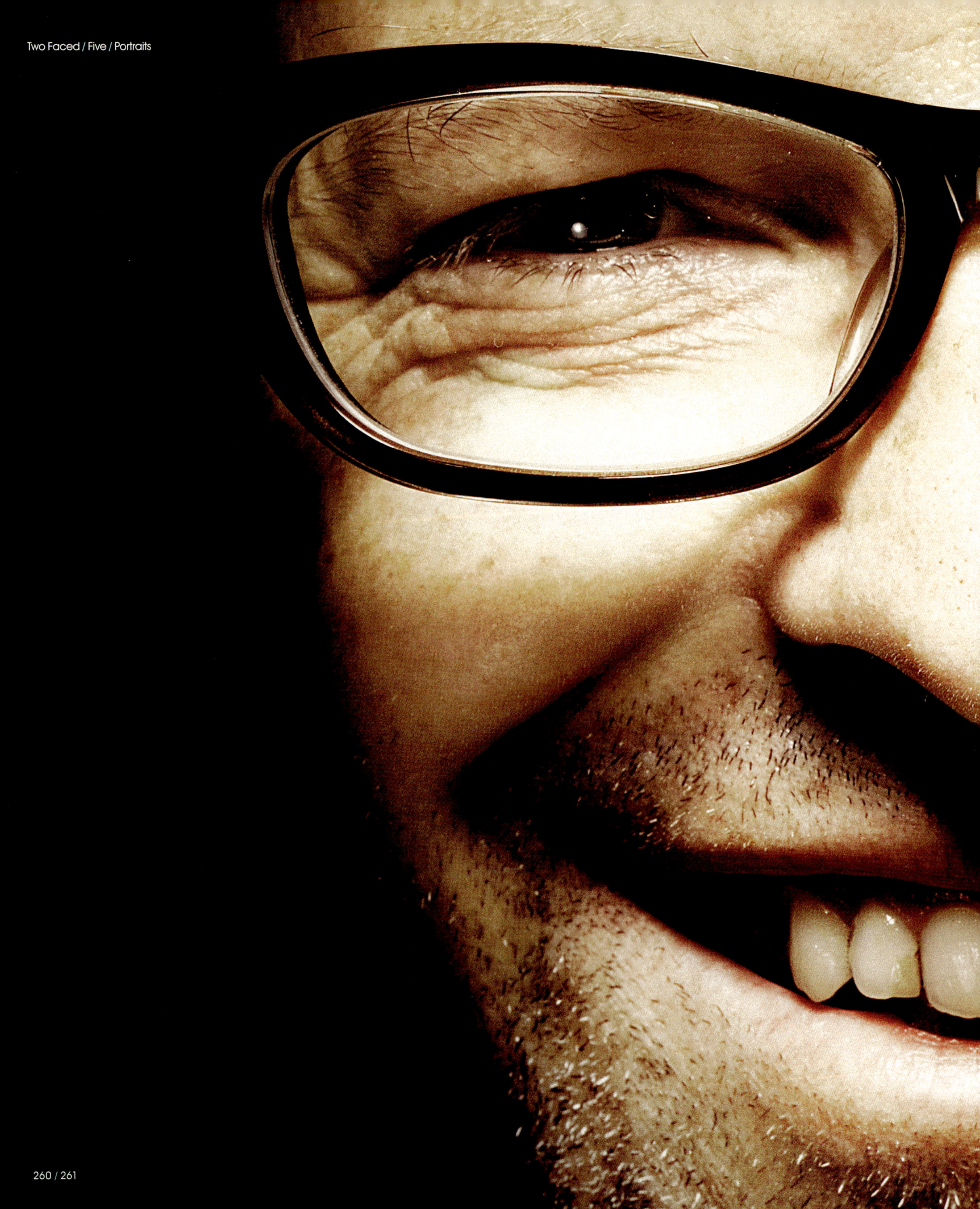

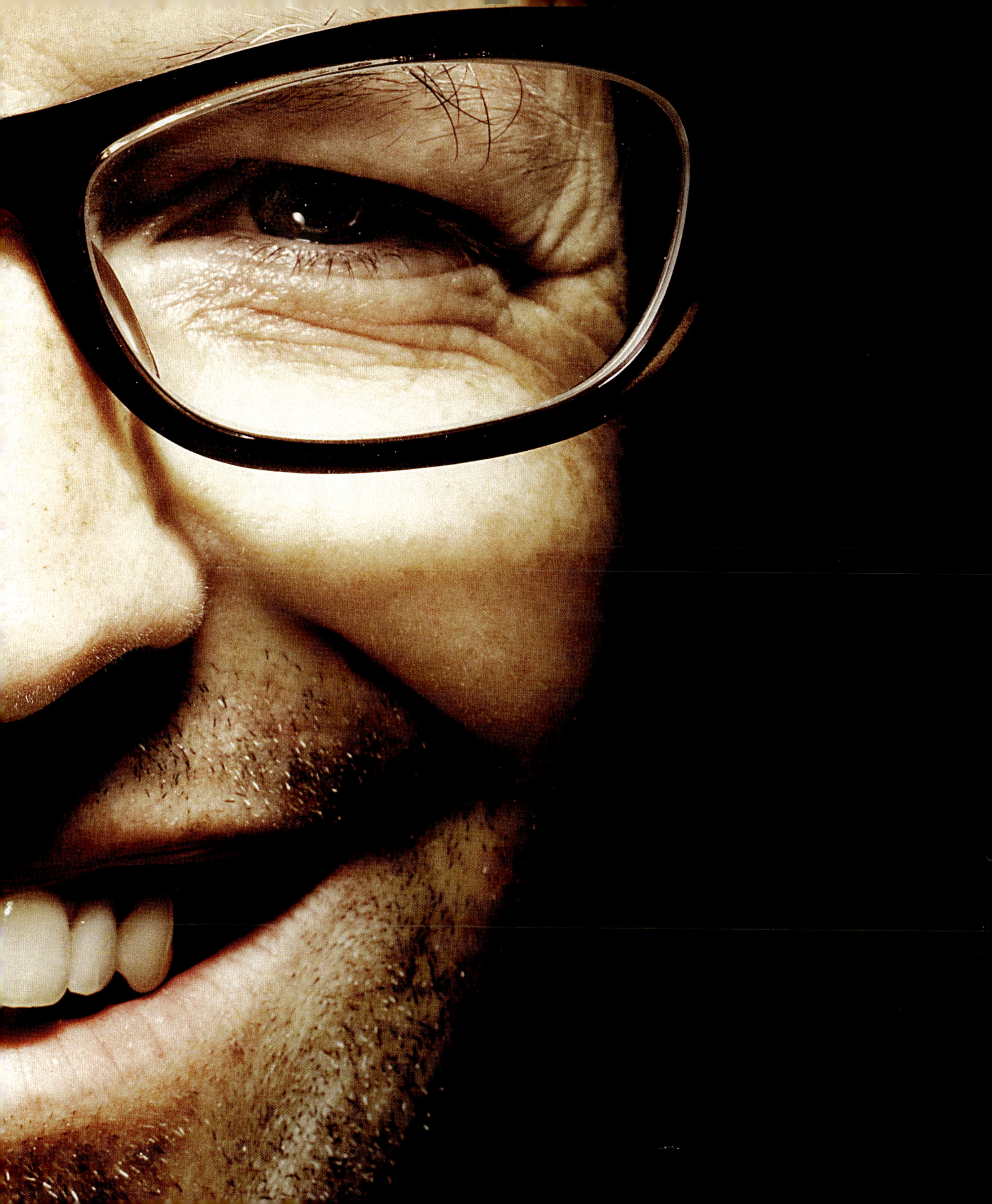

_ PHOTO SHOOT
START DATE
_ 04.08.06
END DATE
_ 04.08.06
/ DURATION,
TWO HOURS

_Equipment

Canon 1 DS Mark II Digital Camera.
Canon 100mm Macro "L" series Lens.
Canon 14mm "L" series Lens.
Canon 24-70mm "L" series Lens.

Profoto Pro 7-a 2400 Watt generator.
3 Profoto 900709 Fan cooled heads.
1 Pro-7 ringflash.
1 pro-7 magnum reflector with Grid.
4 2-gigabyte Scandisk memory Cards.
Firewire Card reader.

4 foot white seamless.
4 foot black velvet.

Mamiya 7II 6x7 cm with 65mm lens.
kodak 160 NC portra film.

_Software

Adobe Photoshop CS2.
Transmit 3.5.4.

_Capture

Approx. 8.4 gigabytes raw tiff files.

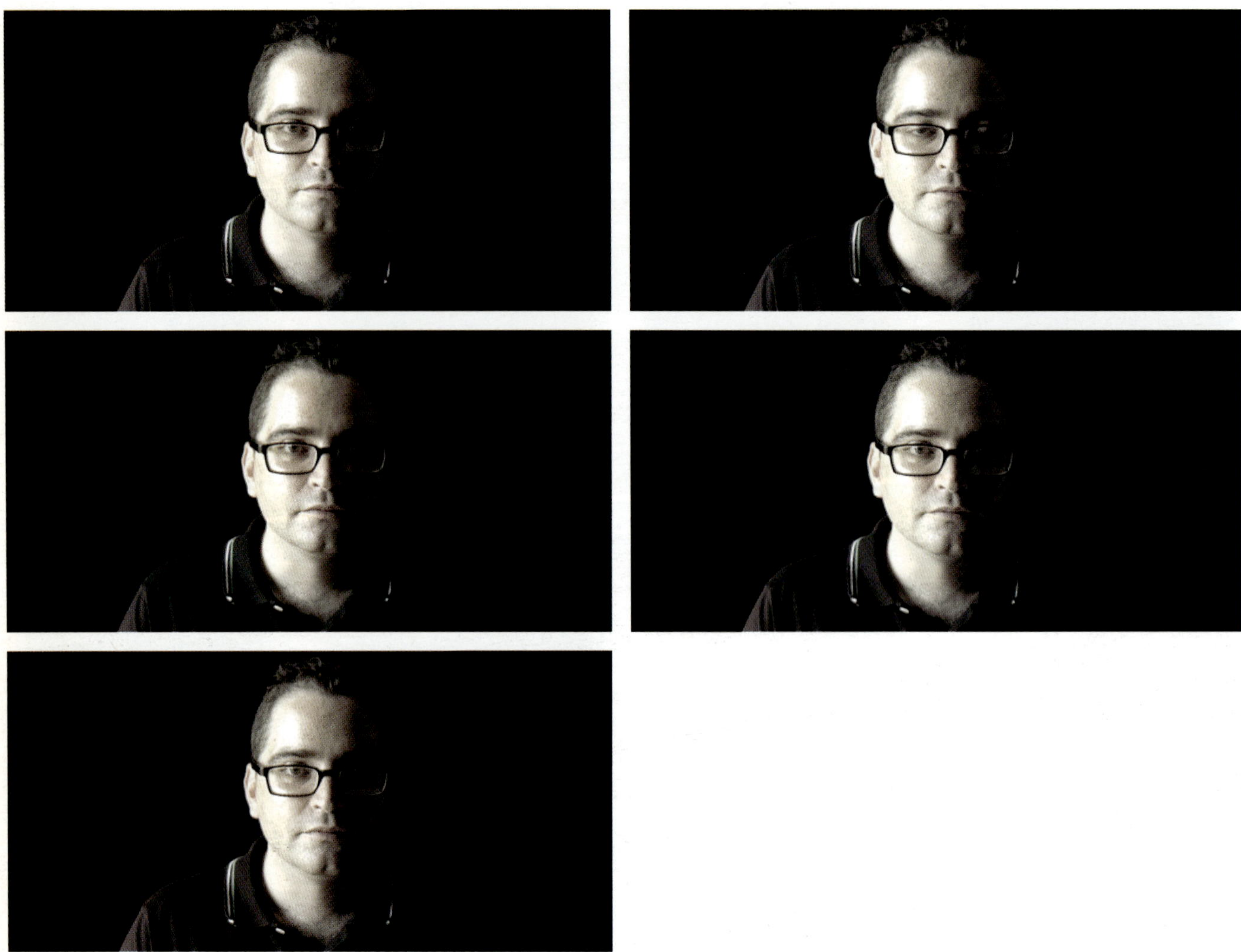

Timothy Saccenti

By Hillman Curtis

I was excited to be paired up with Timothy on this project. I loved the way he treated light in his work. He seemed to have a fixation with auras, which I liked and my favourite of his portraits were beautifully radiant. The shoot itself was a pleasure. We came to his apartment down in Chinatown and I very much appreciated Timothy's style of shooting. I had brought along my five year old, Jasper, with me and Timothy was kind enough to share his robot collection with him.

I have been taking video portraits for a few years now, influenced by the portraiture work of Avedon and Thomas Ruff, so my plan was to shoot Timothy straight on, with as little distraction as possible for 30 seconds or so and hopefully get a compelling shot; maybe I'd get lucky and catch a light shift or a couple of blinks or a facial twitch, or just deep breathing where you barely see the person's body moving rhythmically. I submitted the video for online and grabbed a still for the book. I shot on high definition so the picture quality was pretty good. I experimented a bit with the photo, trying to mimic the work of Sam Taylor Wood in one comp, where the portrait occupied the majority of the frame and a strip of images - in this case of Timothy and his assistant, lay right below it. Then I also submitted a straight portrait – no bells, no whistles. I'm not sure which one made it into the book – which you're looking at now.

Timothy Saccenti has been taking photographs since the age of 16. His first batch of photos, experiments in the darkroom with light, were strong enough to earn him admittance to the School of Visual Arts. After moving to New York City in the mid 90s he had the opportunity to work with many great artists and travel the world learning his technique, being featured in art shows and magazines along the way. In late 2001 Timothy Saccenti Photography officially began with an idea of creating sophisticated, cutting edge, thoroughly modern portraits. Acclaimed underground art magazine *REFILL* said recently "His crisp, colour saturated compositions are marked by stark simplicity that's unnervingly real, his meticulous, minimalist style has proven to be uncannily effective." With a combination of sets, art direction, and lighting he creates a unique universe for each of his subjects. Recently his work has spread from portraits to fashion, still life, and moving images.

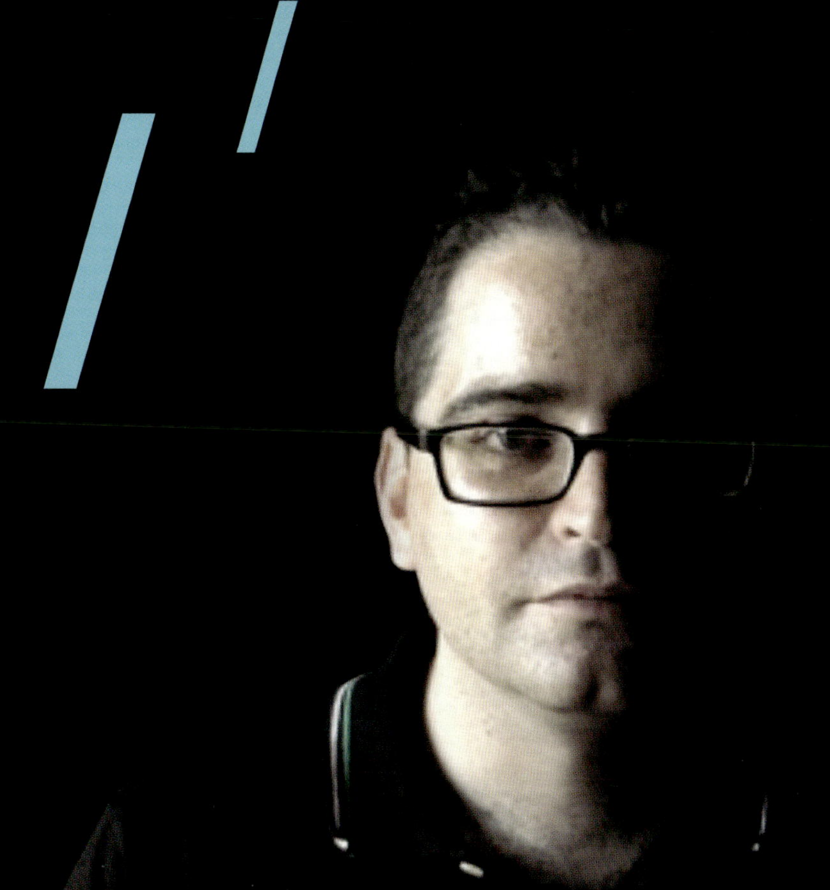

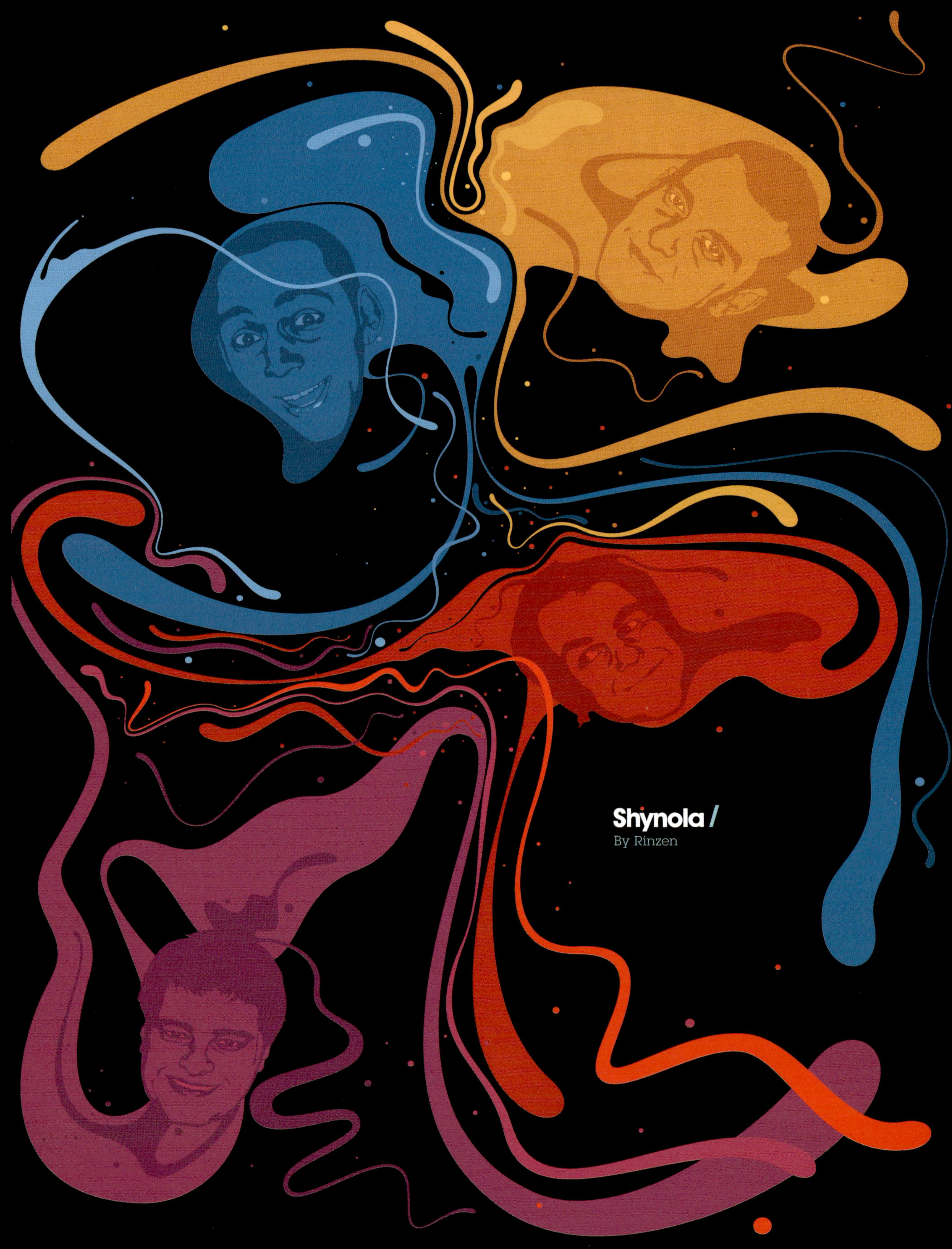

Shynola /
By Rinzen

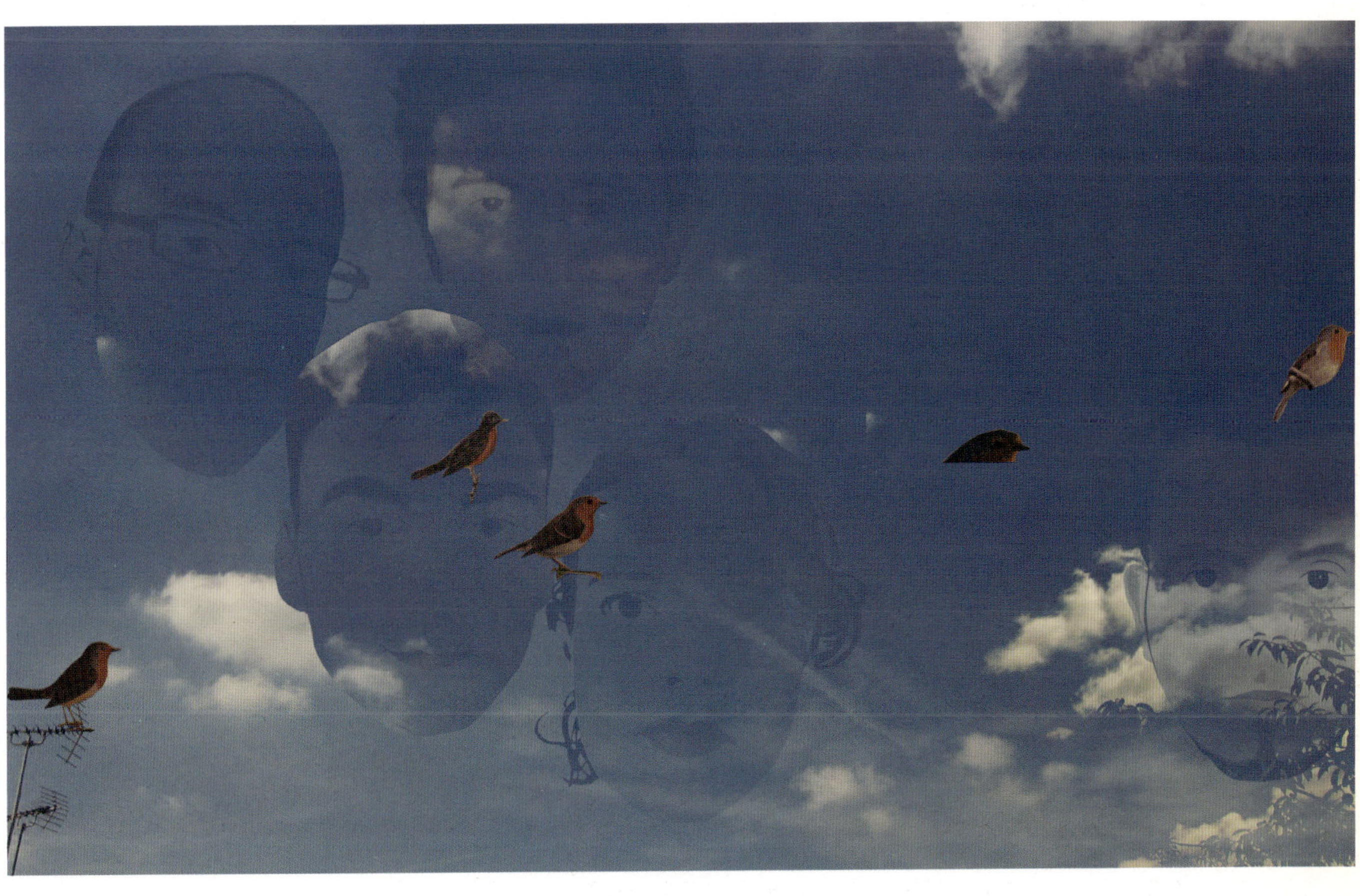

Rinzen /

By Shynola

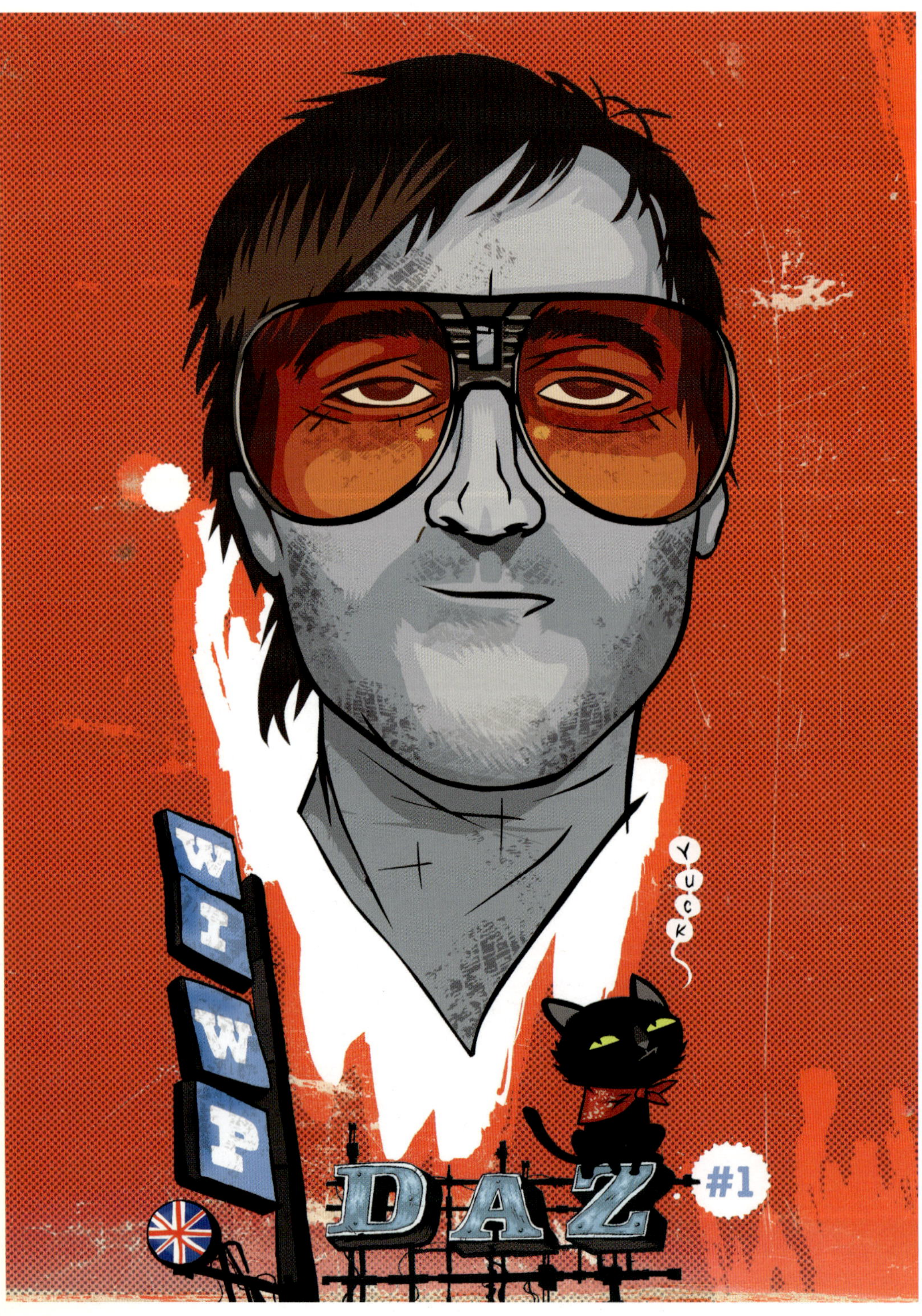

Darren Firth /
By Yuck

Yuck /
By Darren Firth

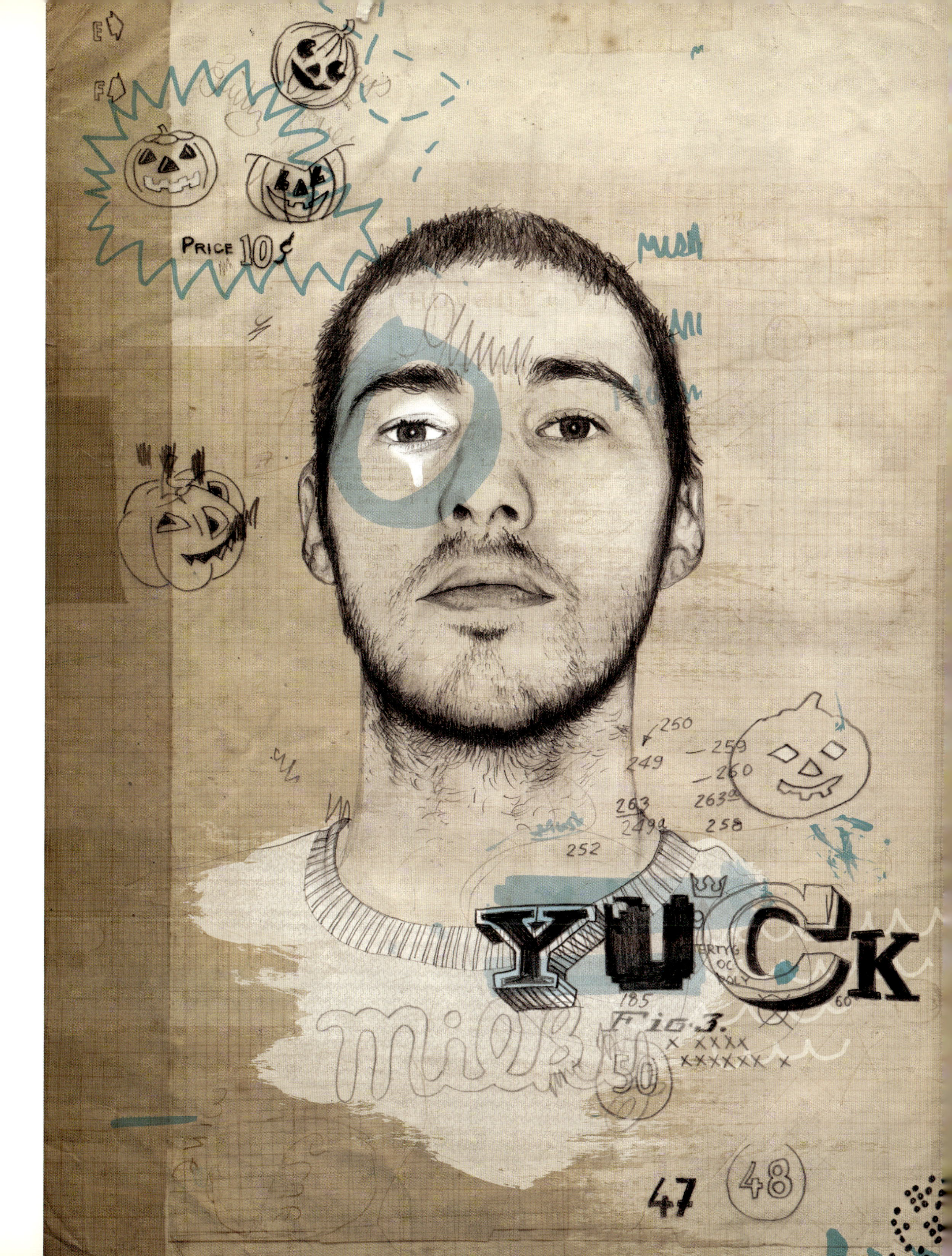
PRICE 10¢
250
249
259
260
263
263
249
258
252
YUCK
185
Fig.3.
50
47
48

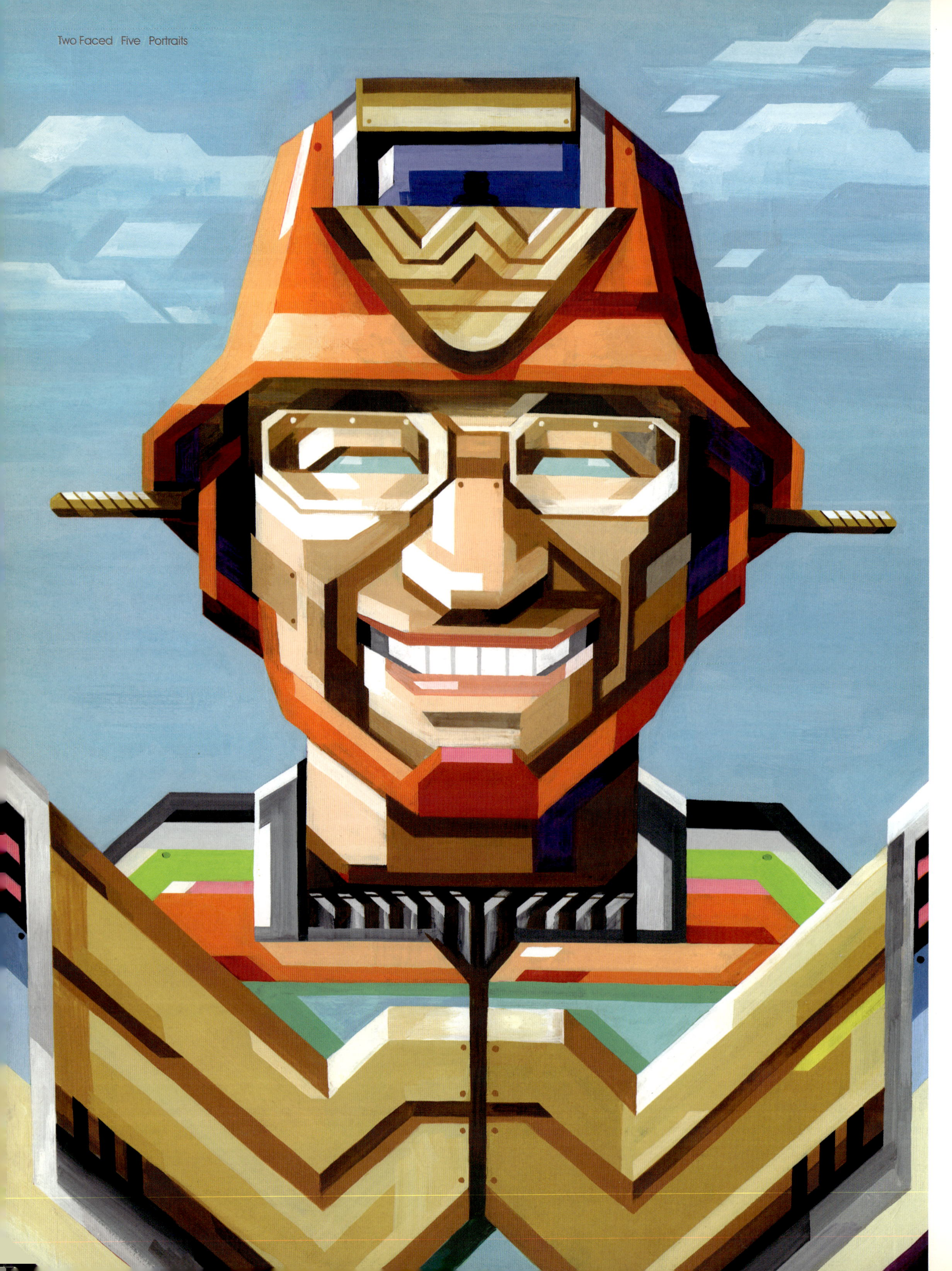

Wilfred Wood /

By Shibuya

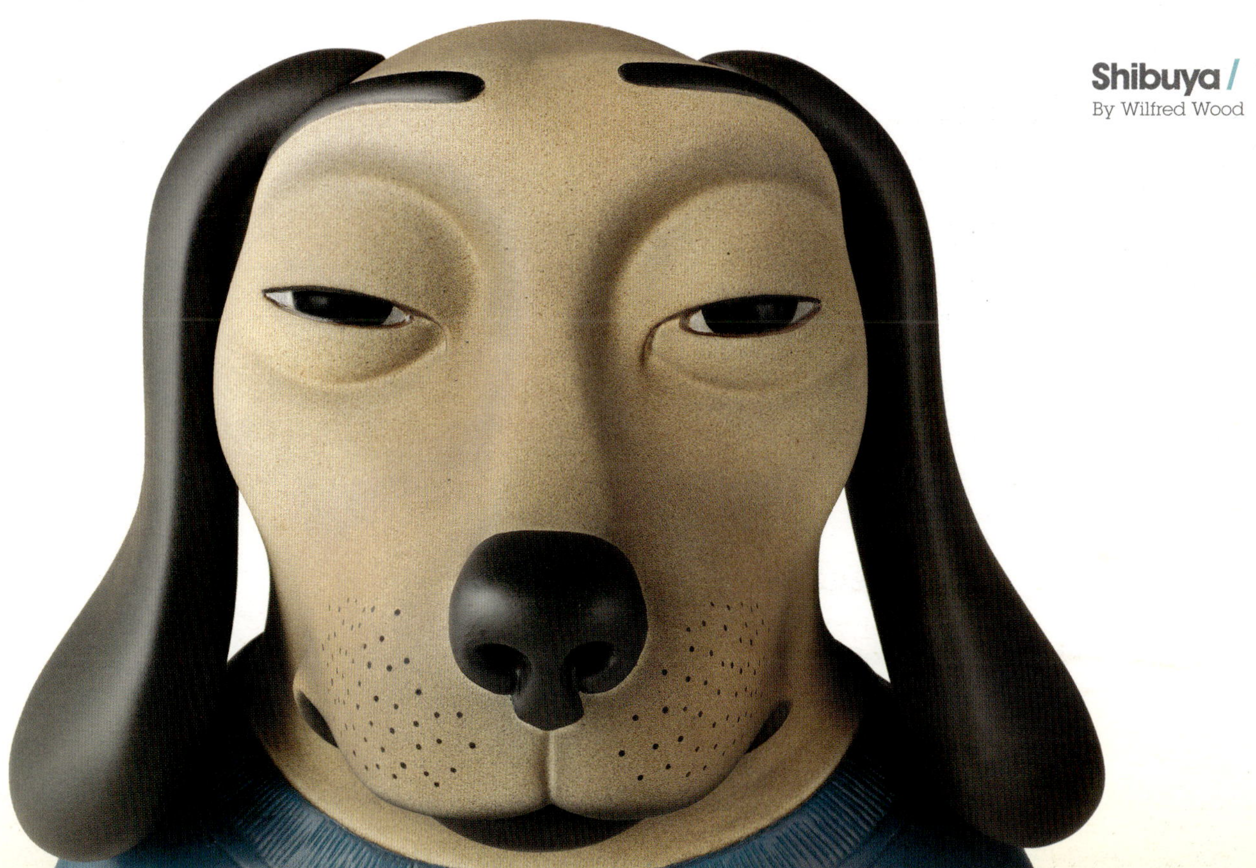

Shibuya /

By Wilfred Wood

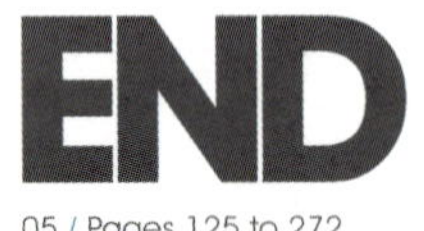

05 / Pages 125 to 272

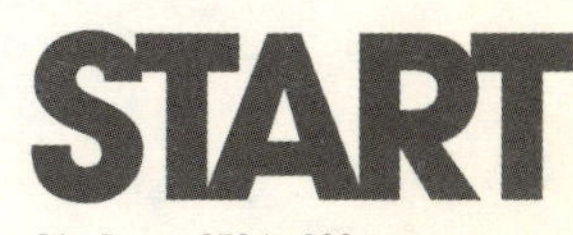
START
06 / Pages 273 to 288

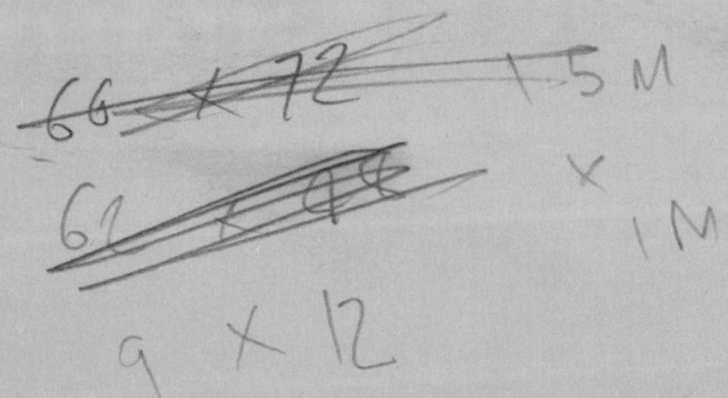
66 x 72
1.5 M
61 x 48
x
1 M
9 x 12

SIX / SKETCHBOOK

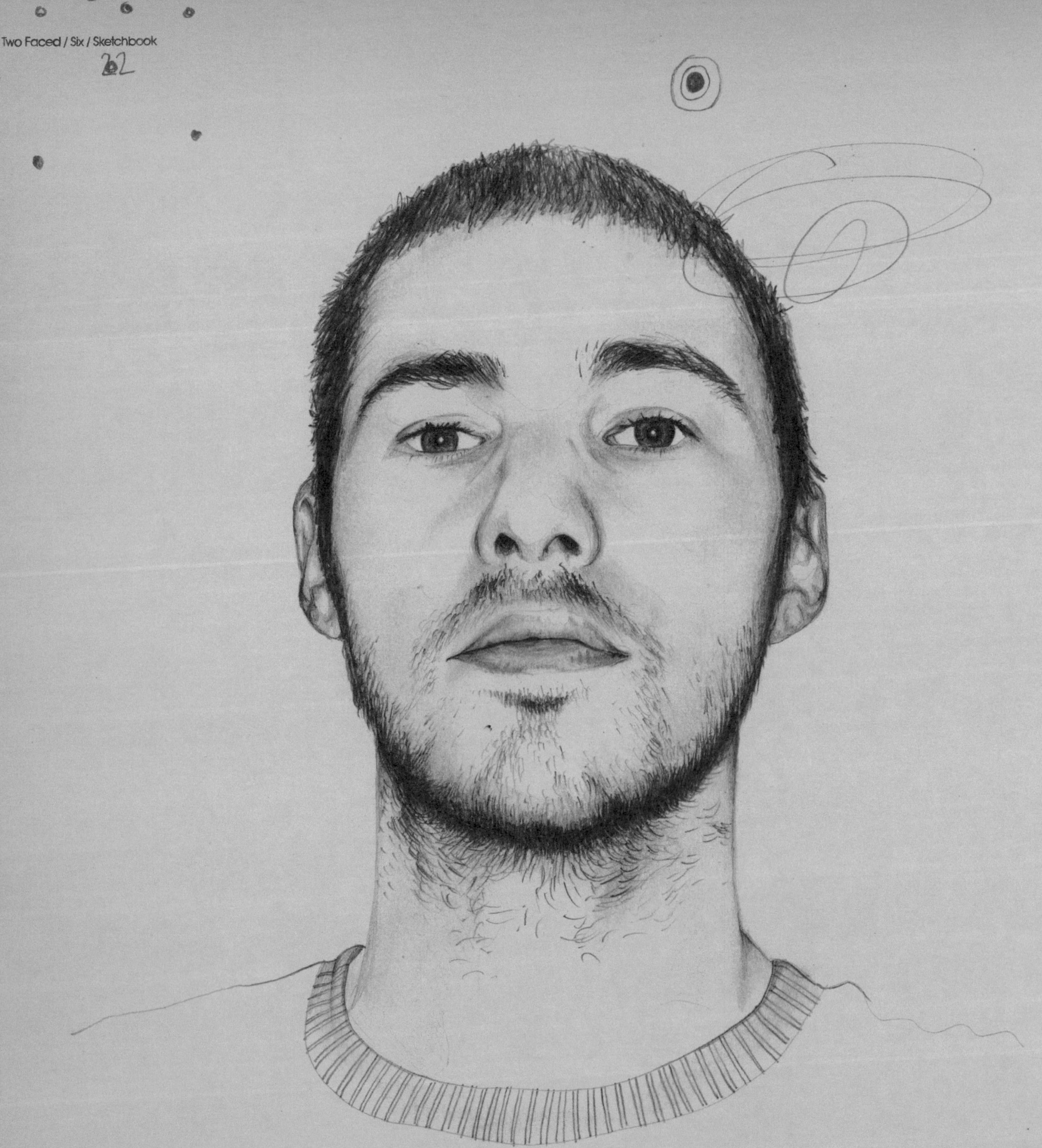

Darren Firth /

Original sketches and typography for both his submissions.

47 UPPER FLOOR
PRINT A/W

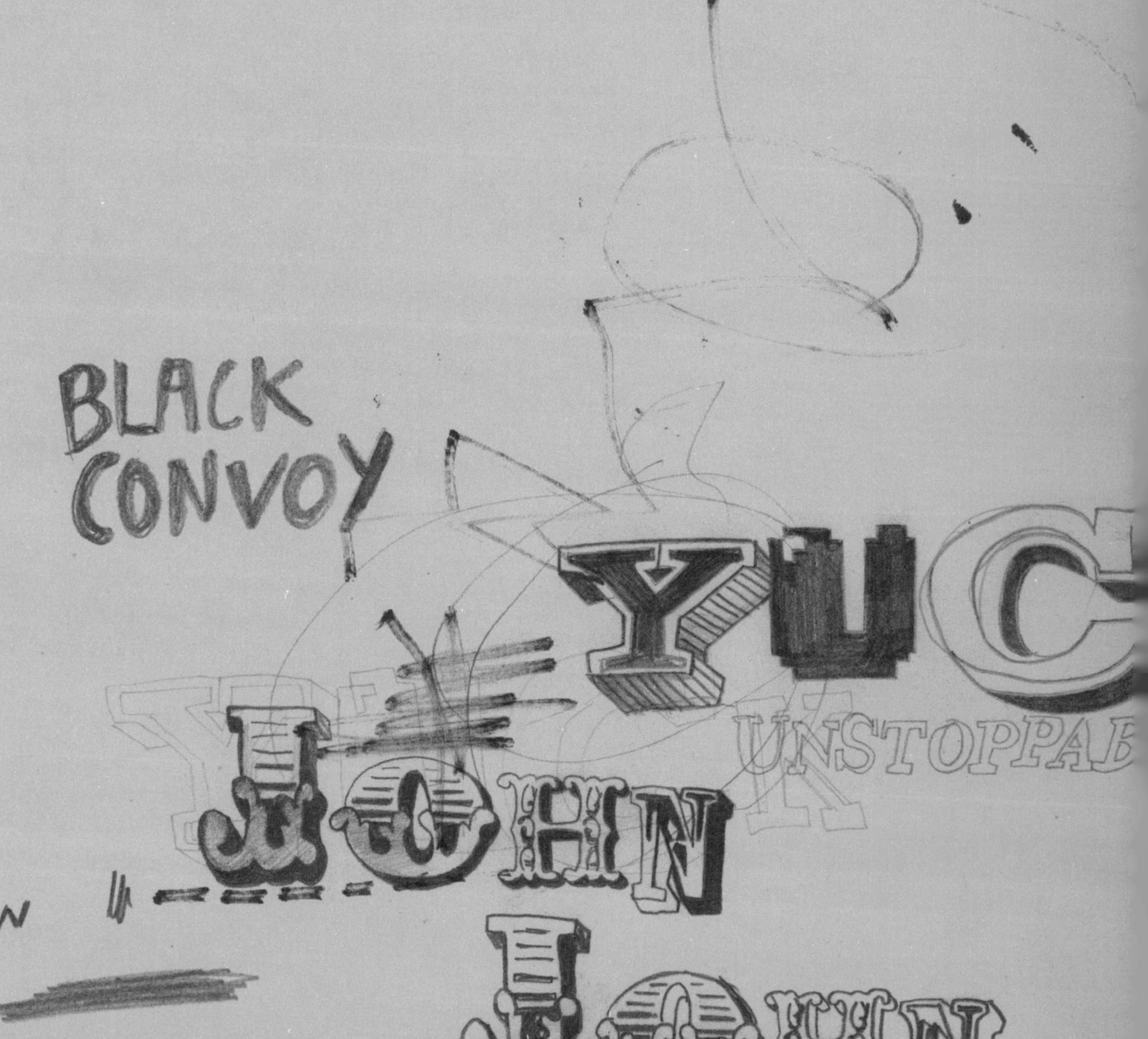

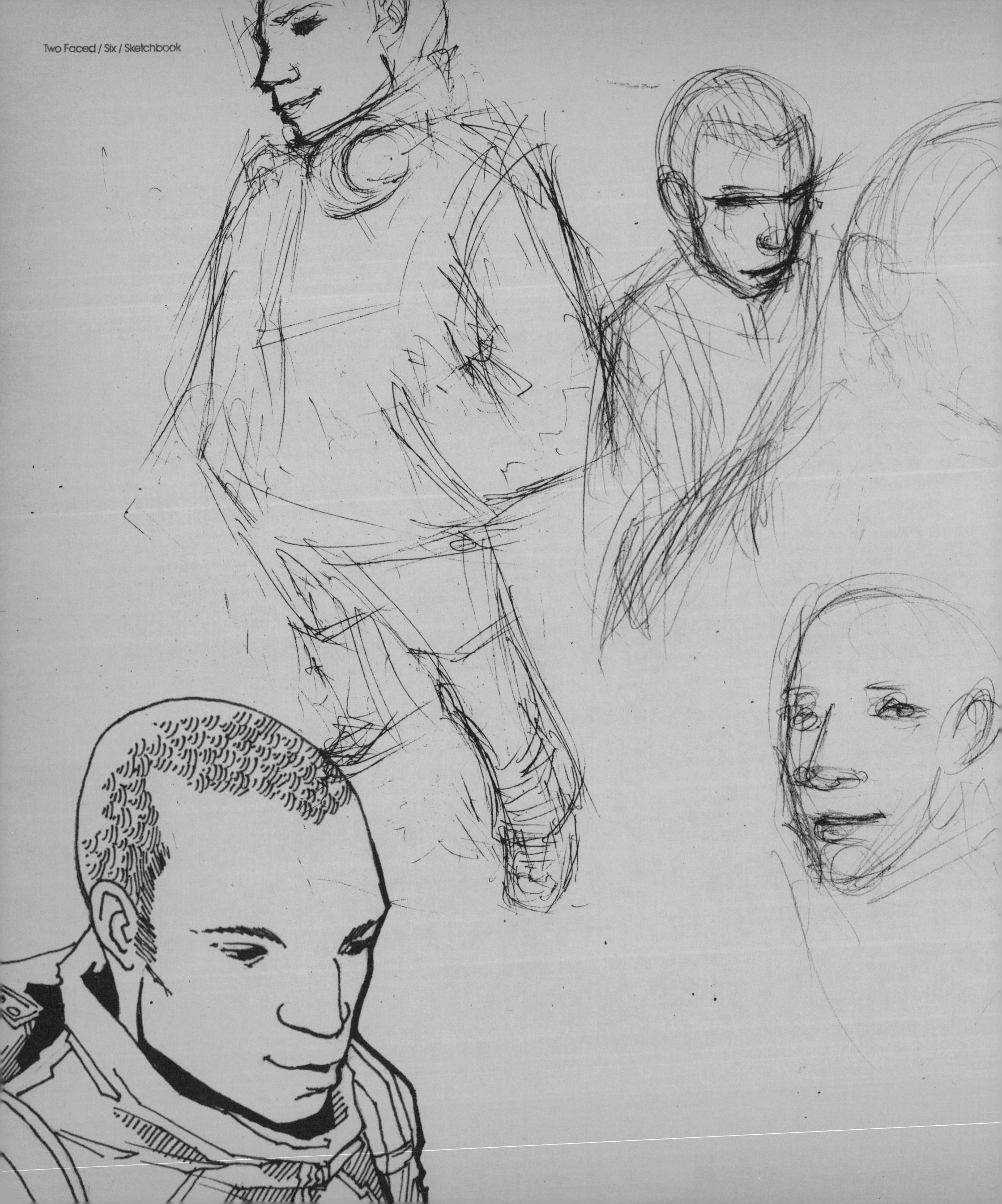

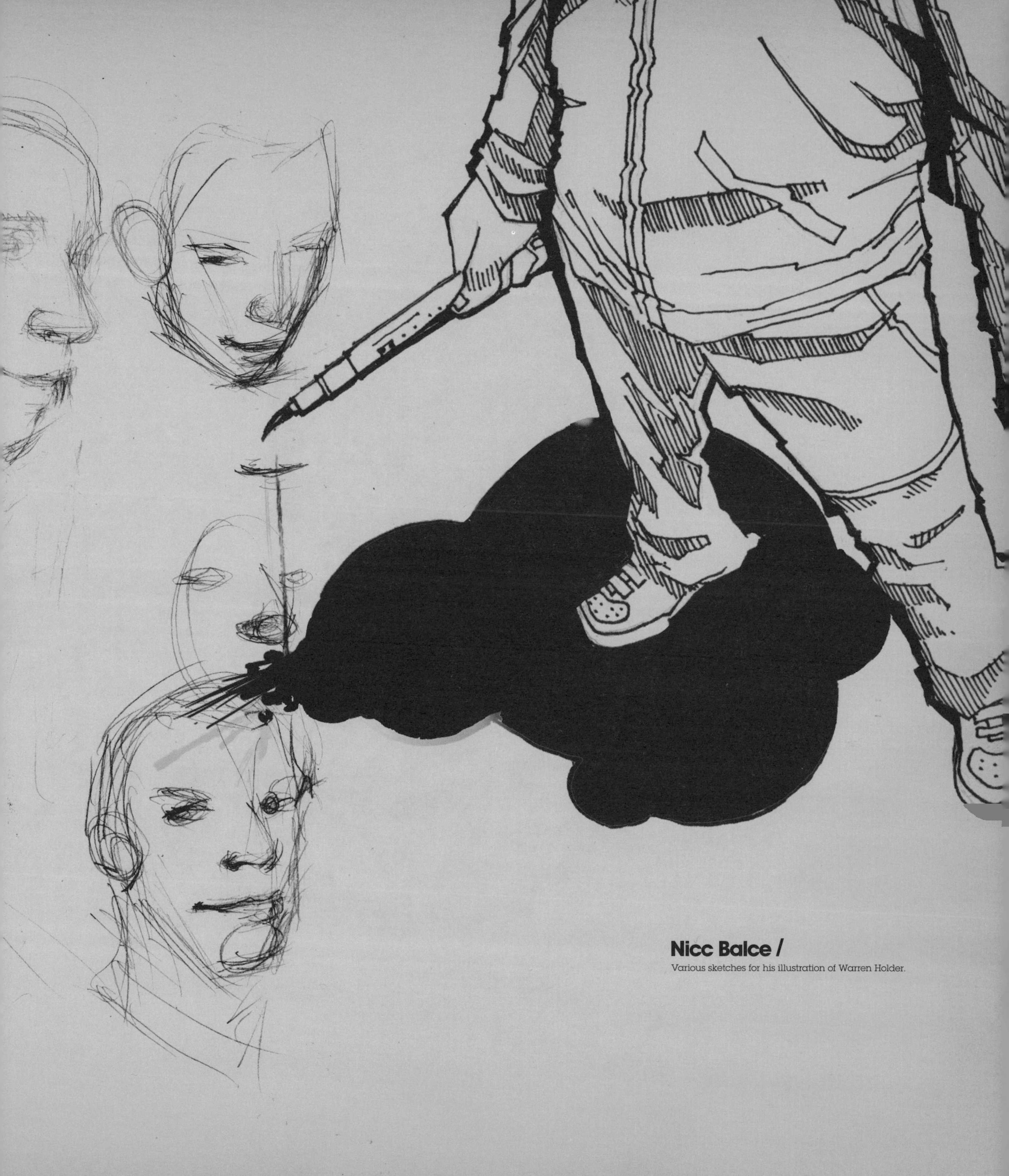

Nicc Balce /

Various sketches for his illustration of Warren Holder.

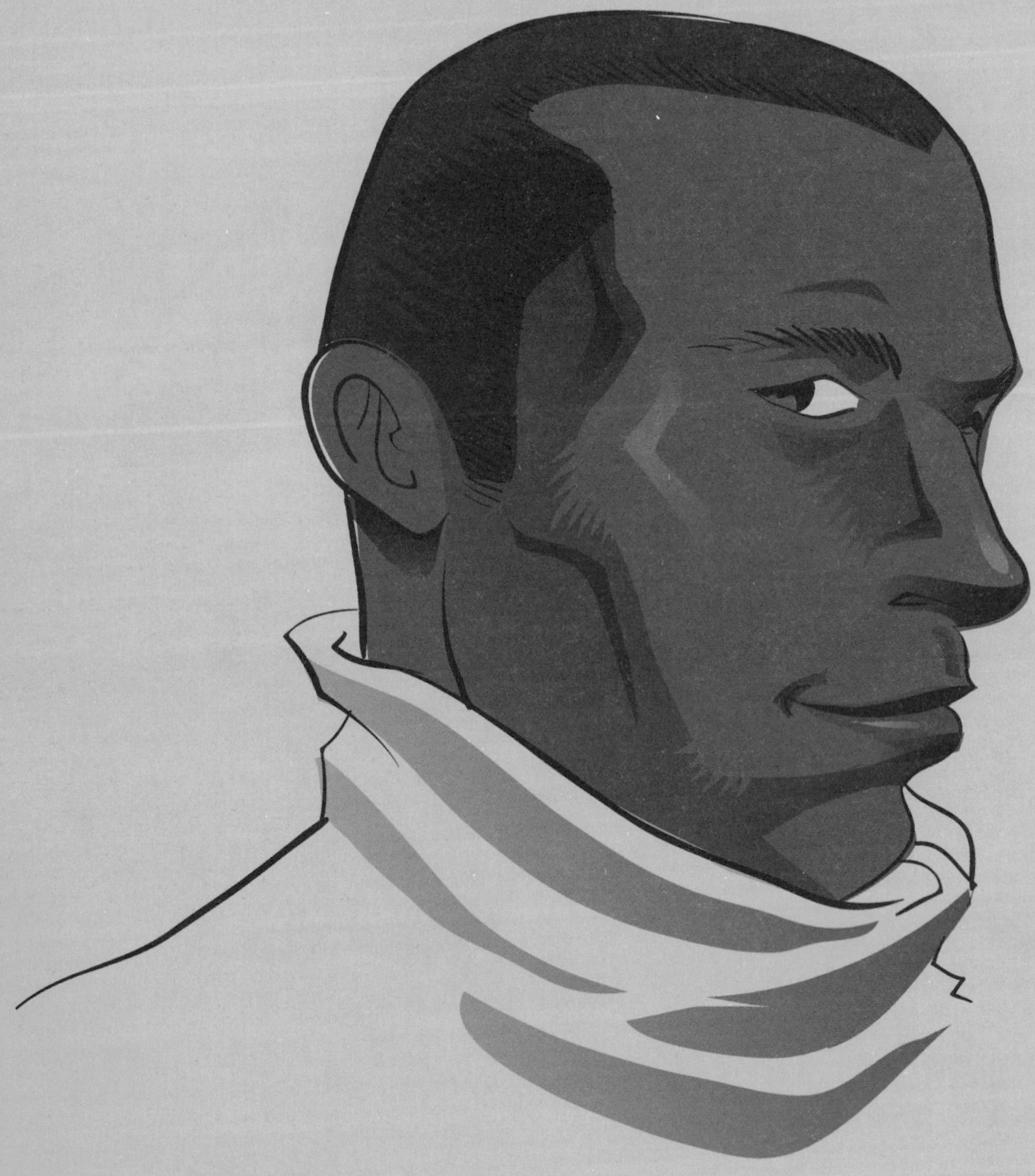

Nicc Balce /

Alternative vector version of Warren Holder.

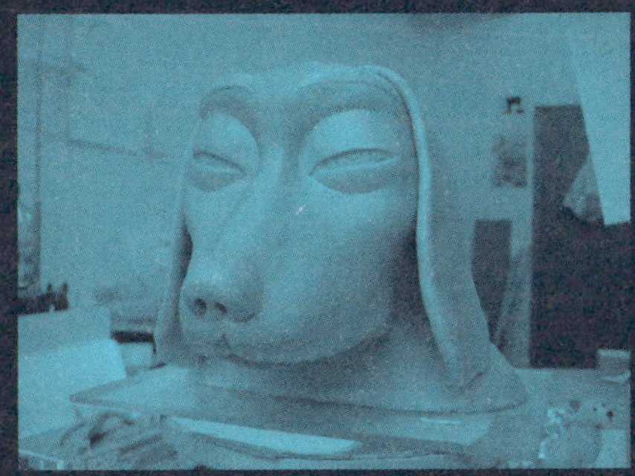

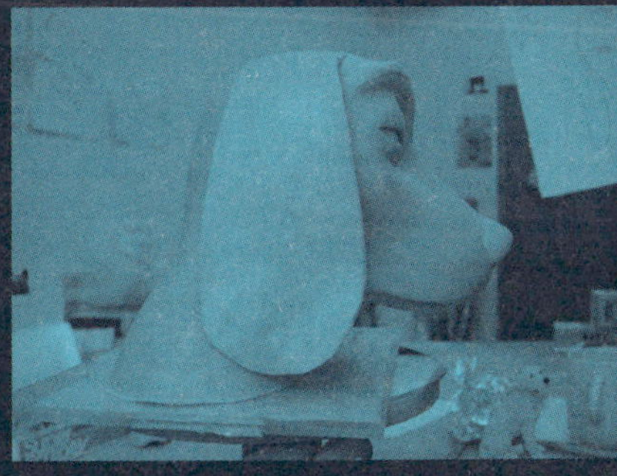

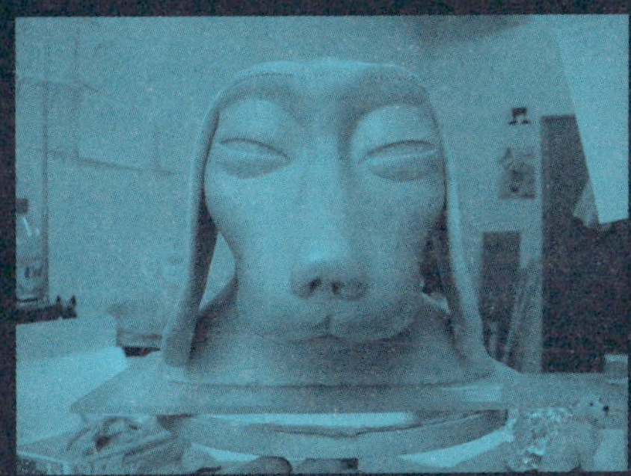

Wilfred Wood /

Early progressions of Shibuya sculpture.

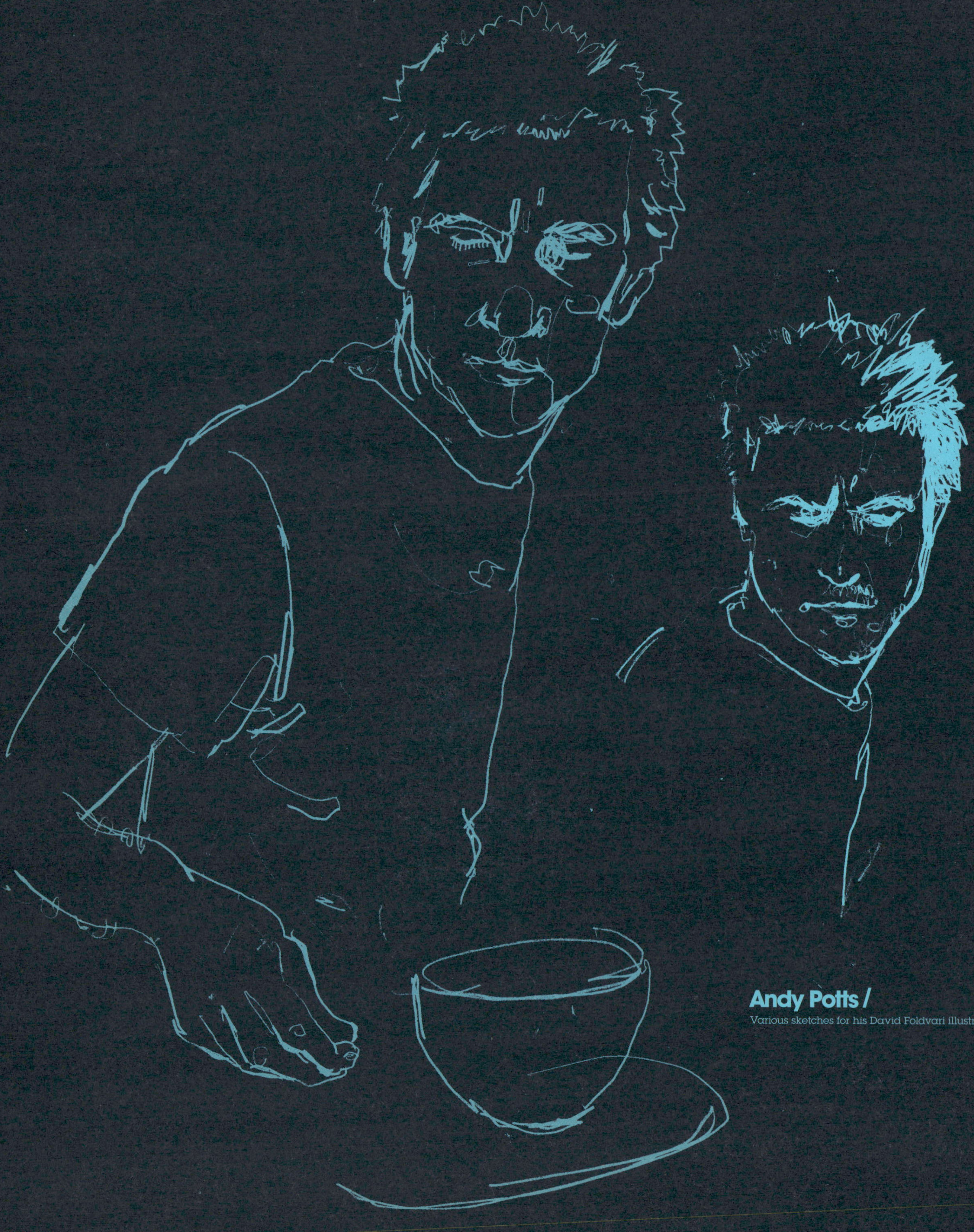

Andy Potts /

Various sketches for his David Foldvari illustration.

Neil Mcfarland /

Original sketch of Matt Sewell.

Kinsey /

Original sketch of Ben Tour.

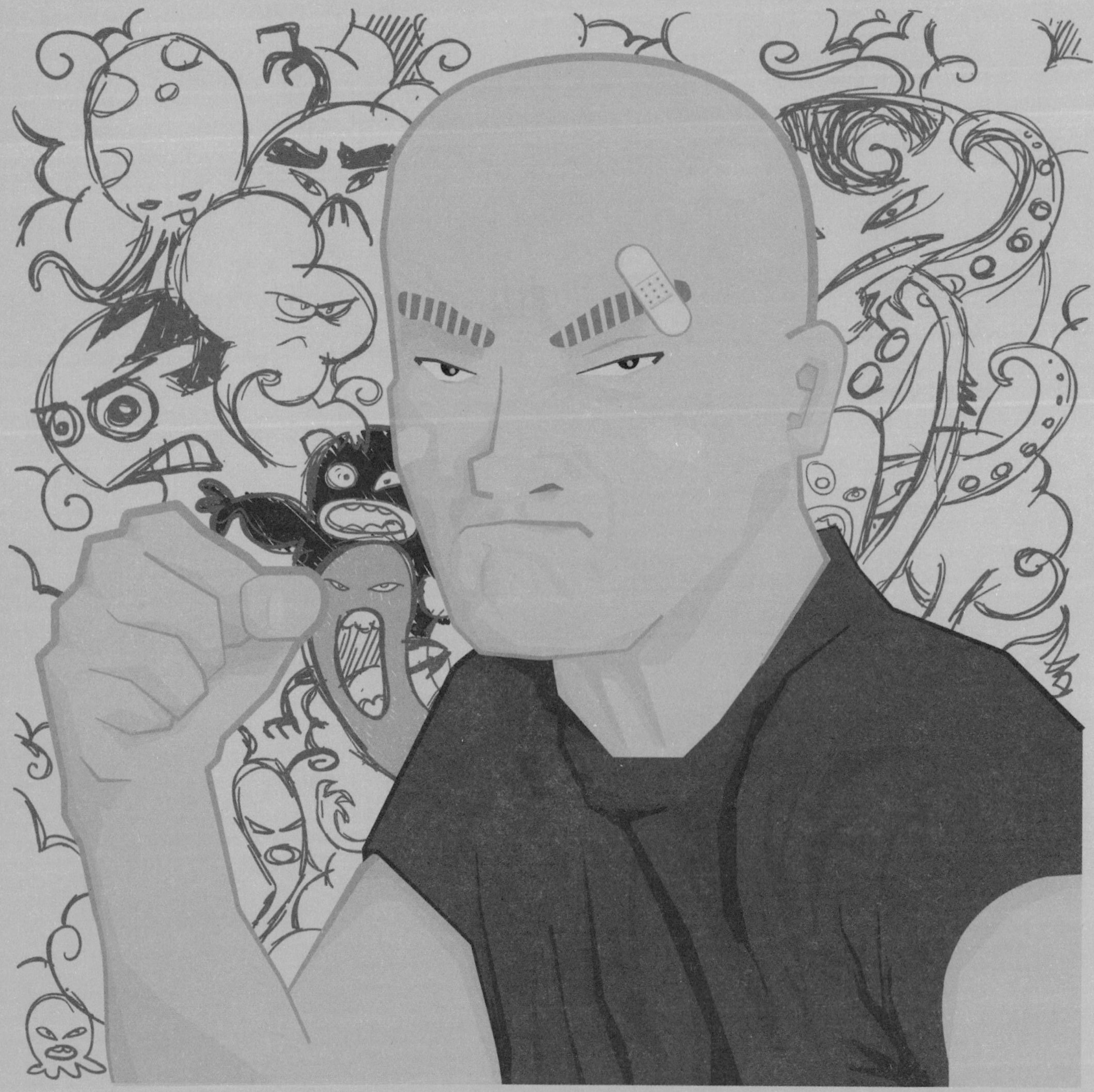

Gabriel Suchowolski /

Early progressions of his illustration of Trevor Van Meter.

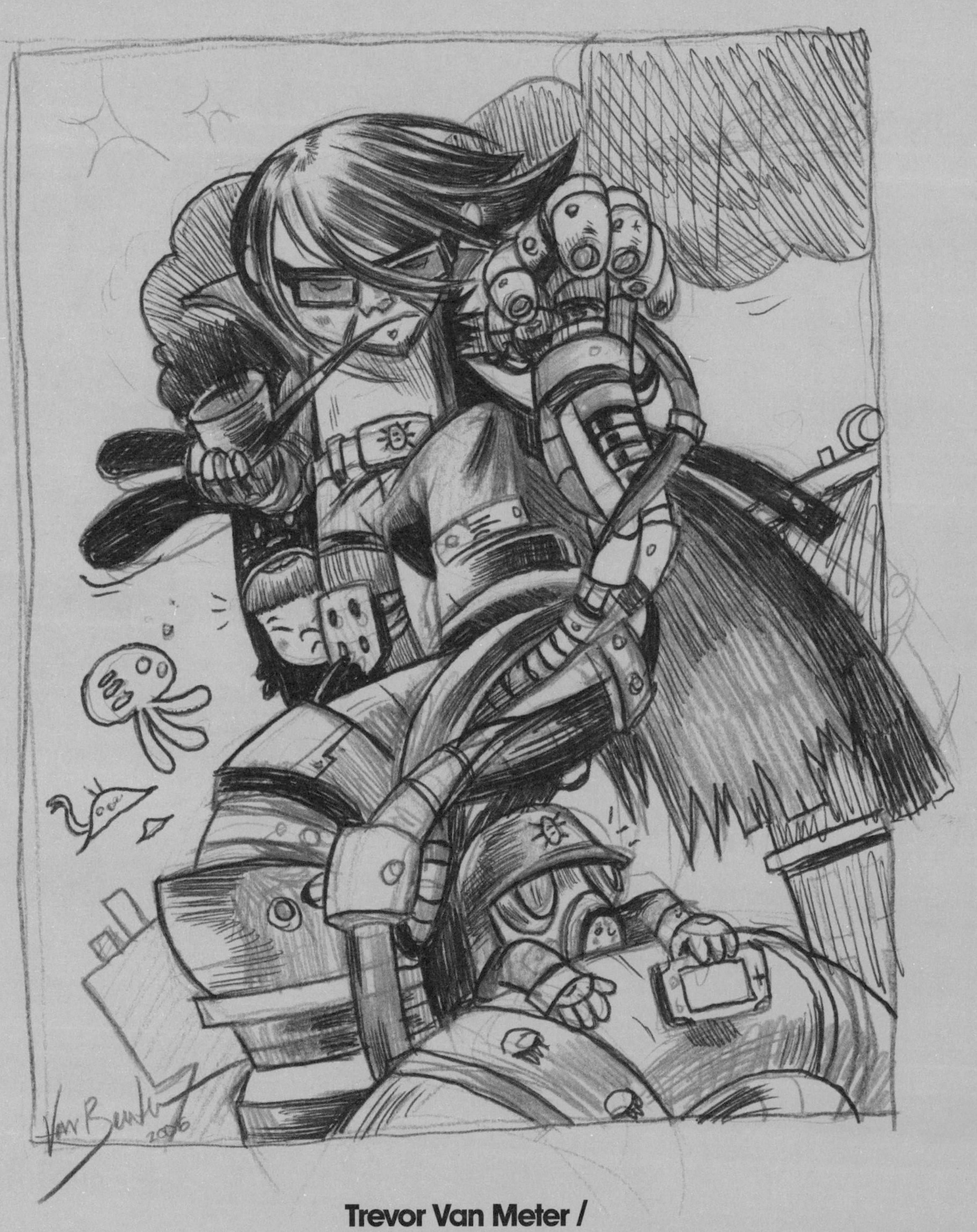

Trevor Van Meter /

Original sketch of Gabriel Suchowolski.

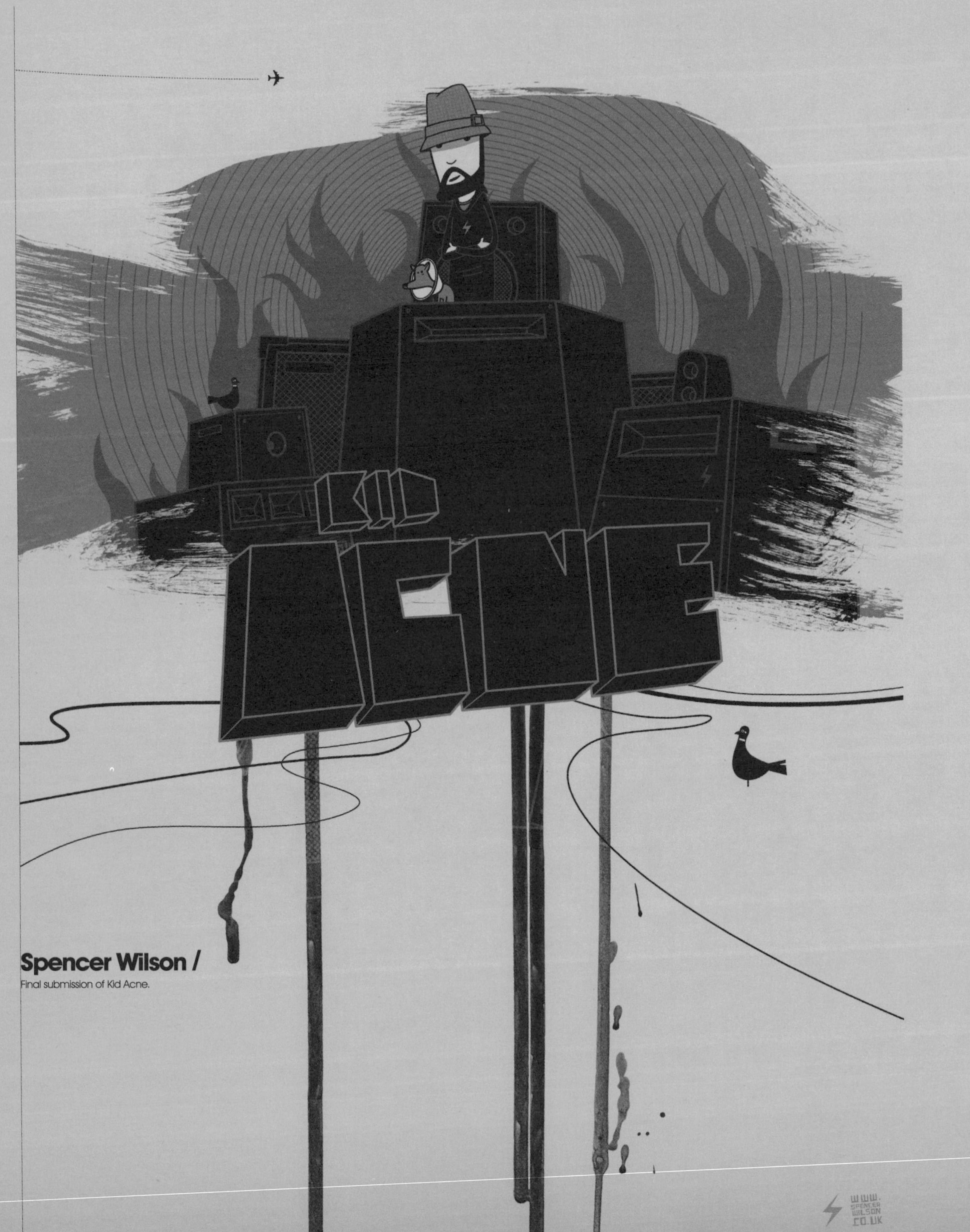

Spencer Wilson /

Final submission of Kid Acne.

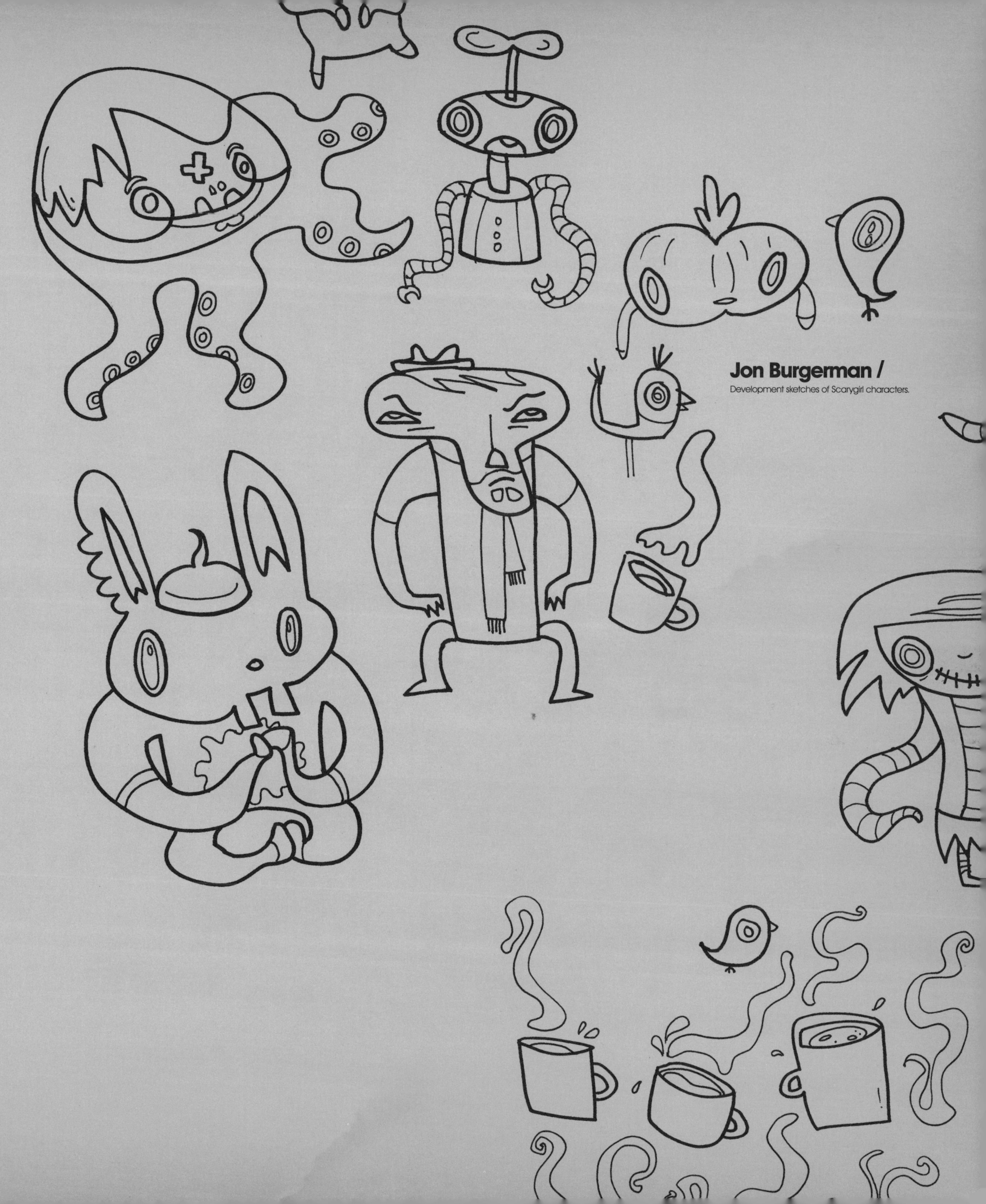

Jon Burgerman /

Development sketches of Scarygirl characters.

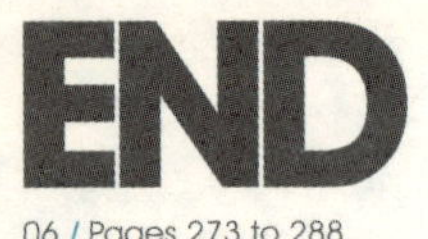
END
06 / Pages 273 to 288

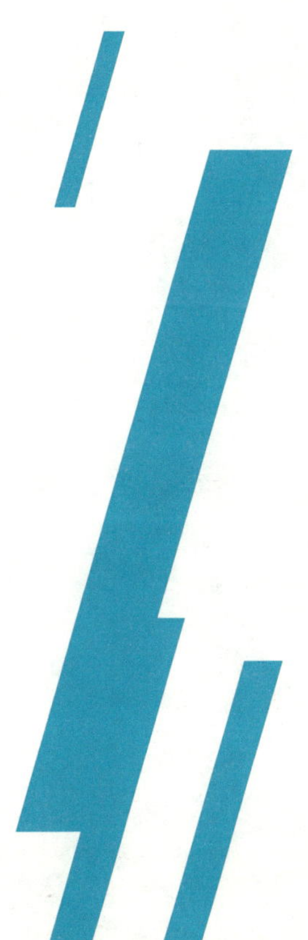

START

07 / Pages 289 to 296

SEVEN

/ BLANK CANVAS

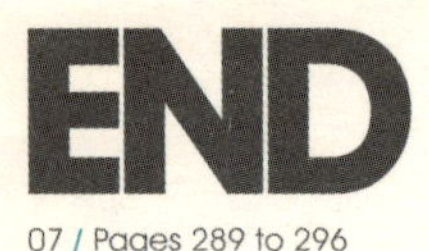

07 / Pages 289 to 296

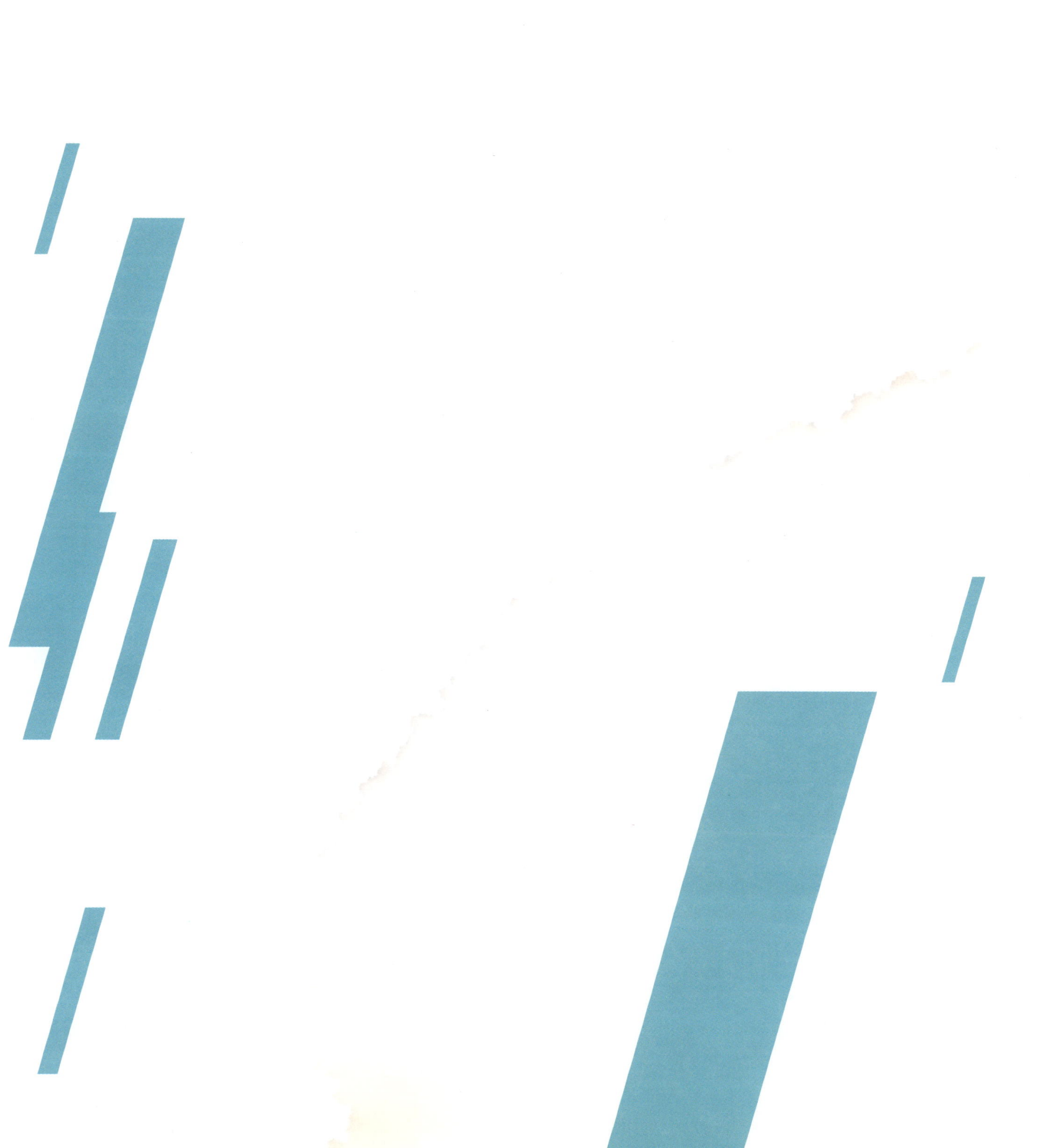

EIGHT /APPENDIX

_In Alphabetical Order

_Names A / E

123klan
www.123klan.com

Adam Pointer
www.adampointer.com

Adrian Shaughnessy
www.thisisrealart.com

Alexei Tylevich_Logan
www.hellologan.com

Amy Sol
www.amysol.com

Andy Potts
www.andy-potts.com

Anna Fowler
www.strawberrysucker.com

Anthony Burrill
www.anthonyburrill.com

Antoine + Manuel
www.antoineetmanuel.com

Armsrock
www.flickr.com/photos/tags/armsrock

Arno
www.debutart.com

Audrey Kawasaki
www.audrey-kawasaki.com

Autumn Whitehurst
www.art-dept.com/illustration/whitehurst

Ben Frost
www.benfrostisdead.com

A / E

_Names F / J

F / J

Ben Tour
www.thetourshow.com

Beci Orpin
www.beciorpin.com

Buggy
www.dutchuncle.co.uk

Charlotta Havh
www.chalet.se

Chris Kasch
www.chriskasch.co.uk

Chris Pyle
www.chrispyleillustration.com

Cyan D
www.machikoedmondson.com

Darren Firth
www.keepsmesane.co.uk

David Foldvari
www.davidfoldvari.co.uk

David Shrigley
www.davidshrigley.com

David Stewart
www.dhstewart.com

Dragon
www.dutchuncle.co.uk

Dustin Hostetler - Upso
www.dustinameryhostetler.com

Eboy
http://hello.eboy.com/eboy

Farmerbob
www.farmerbobsfarm.com

Fawn Gehweiler
www.nocandy.org

FL@33
www.flat33.com

Fons Schiedon
www.fonztv.nl

Friends With You
www.friendswithyou.com

Gabriel Suchowolski - Microbians
www.microbians.com

Geoff Mcfetridge
www.championdontstop.com

Grandpeople
www.grandpeople.org

Gregory Gilbert-Lodge
www.gilbert-lodge.com

Harmen Liemburg
http://harmenliemburg.nl

Hellobard
www.hellobard.com

Hellovon
www.hellovon.com

Herakut
www.maclaim.de

Hillman Curtis
www.hillmancurtis.com

Hope Gangloff
www.hopegangloff.com

Ian Stevenson
www.ilikedrawing.co.uk

Ian Wright
www.mrianwright.co.uk

James Jean
http://jamesjean.com

James Joyce
www.one-fine-day.co.uk

Jasper Goodall
www.jaspergoodall.com

Jason Arber
www.childrenoffinland.com

Jean Duprez
www.duprezdolores.com

Jesse Seppi_ Tronic
www.tronicstudio.com

Jeremyville
www.jeremyville.com

John Gray
www.johngrayart.com

Johnny Hardstaff
www.johnnyhardstaff.com

Jon Burgerman
www.jonburgerman.com

Jonathan Ellery
www.brownsdesign.com

F / J

_Names K / O

K / O

Joost Korngold
www.renascent.nl

Joshua Davis
www.joshuadavis.com

Josie McCoy
http://www.josiemccoy.co.uk/

Julia Sonmi
http://sonmisonmi.com

Karen Oxman
www.dutchuncle.co.uk

Ken Orvidas
www.orvidas.com

Kinsey
www.kinseyvisual.com

Klaus Haapaniemi
www.klaush.com

Kris Lewis
www.krislewisart.com

Kustaa Saksi
www.kustaasaksi.com

Marc Atlan
www.marcatlan.com

Marion Deuchars
www.mariondeuchars.co.uk

Mark Blamire
www.neuelaboratories.com

Matt Owens
www.volumeone.com

Matt Sewell
www.mattsewell.co.uk

Maureen Gubia
http://gubia.neurasthenic.net

Mauro Gatti
www.thebrainbox.com

Maya Hayuk
www.mayahayuk.com

Mcfaul
www.mcfaul.net

Michael C Place
www.designbybuild.com

Michael Gillette
www.michaelgillette.com

Mike Thompson
www.miketartworks.com

Mi-Zo
www.mi-zo.com

Morten Laursen
www.mortenlaursen.com

Nate Williams
www.n8w.com

Nathan Fox
www.foxnathan.com

Nathan Gale
www.intercitydesign.com

Nathan Jurevicius - Scarygirl
http://www.nathanj.com.au

Neil Mcfarland
www.parishair.com

Nicc Balce
www.the-null.com

Nico
www.dutchuncle.co.uk

Olaf Hajek
www.olafhajek.com

_Names P / T

Patrick Morgan
www.patrickmorgan.co.uk

Paul Davis
www.copyrightdavis.com

Paul Insect
www.insect.co.uk

Paul Willoughby
www.paulwilloughby.com

Rachel Domm
http://rdomm.com

Rachel Salomon
www.rachelsalomon.com

Rankin
www.rankin.co.uk

Rinzen
www.rinzen.com

Robert Lindstrom
www.designchapel.com

Saiman Chow
www.saimanchow.com

Samuel Cochetel
http://s.cochetel.free.fr

Seb Jarnot
www.sebjarnot.com

Scott Scheidly
www.flounderart.com

Shibuya
www.dutchuncle.co.uk

P / T

Shirana Shabazi
www.bobvanorsouw.ch

Simon Henwood
www.simonhenwood.com

Stefan Sagmeister
www.sagmeister.com

Stella Vine
www.stellavine.com

Stina Persson
www.stinapersson.com

Stuntkid
www.stuntkid.com

Sylvia Ji
www.sylviaji.com

Shynola
www.shynola.com

Syrup Helsinki
www.syruphelsinki.com

Tado
www.tado.co.uk

Terry Rodgers
www.terryrodgers.com

The Boy Fitz Hammond
www.tbfh.com

The Little Friends of Printmaking
http://thelittlefriendsofprintmaking.com

Thomas Kuhlenbeck
www.larkworthy.com

P / T

Thymann
www.thymann.com

Tim Marrs
www.timmarrs.co.uk

Timothy Saccenti
www.timothysaccenti.com

Toby Neilan
www.tobyneilan.com

Tom Bagshaw
www.mostlywanted.com

Tom Muller
www.hellomuller.com

Trevor Jackson
www.trevorjackson.org

Trevor Van Meter
www.trevorvanmeter.com

_Names U / Z

Vasava
www.vasava.es

Warren Holder
http://warrenholder.com

Wayne Hemingway
www.hemingwaydesign.co.uk

Wilfred Wood
http://wilfridwood.com

WWFT
www.weworkforthem.com

Yuck
http://schizoidbrain.free.fr

_Related Links

Art Department
www.art-dept.com

Blanka
www.blanka.co.uk

Computer Arts
www.computerarts.co.uk

Creative Review
www.creativereview.co.uk

Debut Art
www.debutart.com

Dutch Uncle
www.dutchuncle.co.uk

IdN
www.idnworld.com

Jeremyville
www.jeremyville.com

Kinsey Visual
www.kinseyvisual.com

Rankin
www.rankin.co.uk

This Is Real Art
www.thisisrealart.com

Un.titled
www.un.titled.co.uk

Webber Represents
www.webberrepresents.com

/ THANKYOU

_A massive thanks to

Emily Hall / Bruno / Emma Warner, Chris and Jonathan at *IdN*, Adrian Shaughnessy / Sam Renwick at ThisIsRealArt, Caterina at Webber Represents, Jane Finigan at Debut Art, Koko at CWC International, Christine Cavallomago at Art-Dept, Dan Bull / Jim Cochrane at Un.titled, Dan Chrichlow / Helen Cowley at Dutch Uncle, Gavin Lucas at Creative Review, Jeremy at Jeremyville, Nick at Scuffdept, Jana at Kinsey Visual, Blam at Blanka, Paul Newman / Tom Dennis at *Computer Arts*, Vivian Rosenthal at Tronic, Rachel Veniard at Browns Design, Zoe Tomlinson / Matt Doyle / Liza Barber at Rankin.

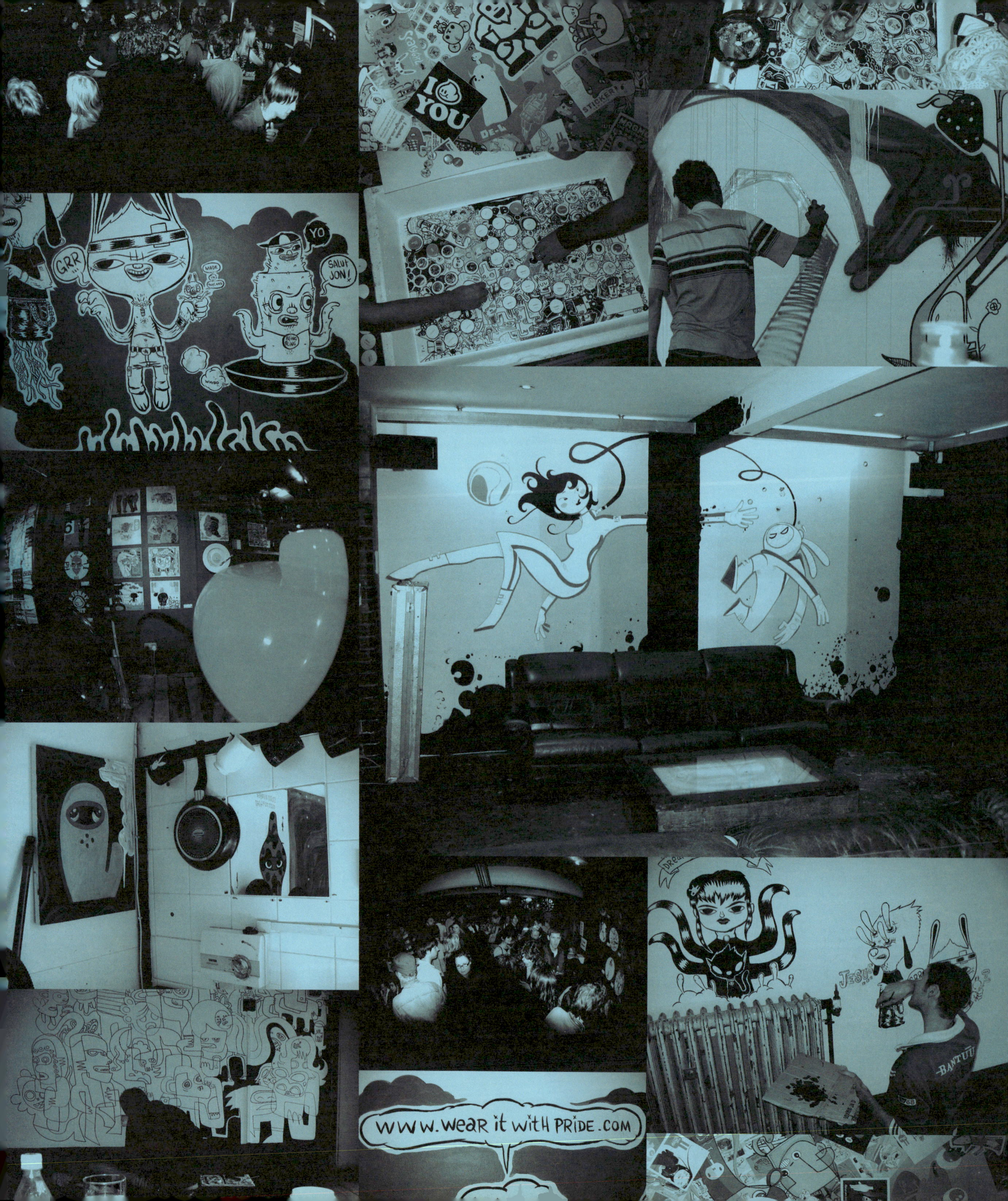
I ♥ YOU
GRR
YO
SALUT JON!
www.wear it with PRIDE.com

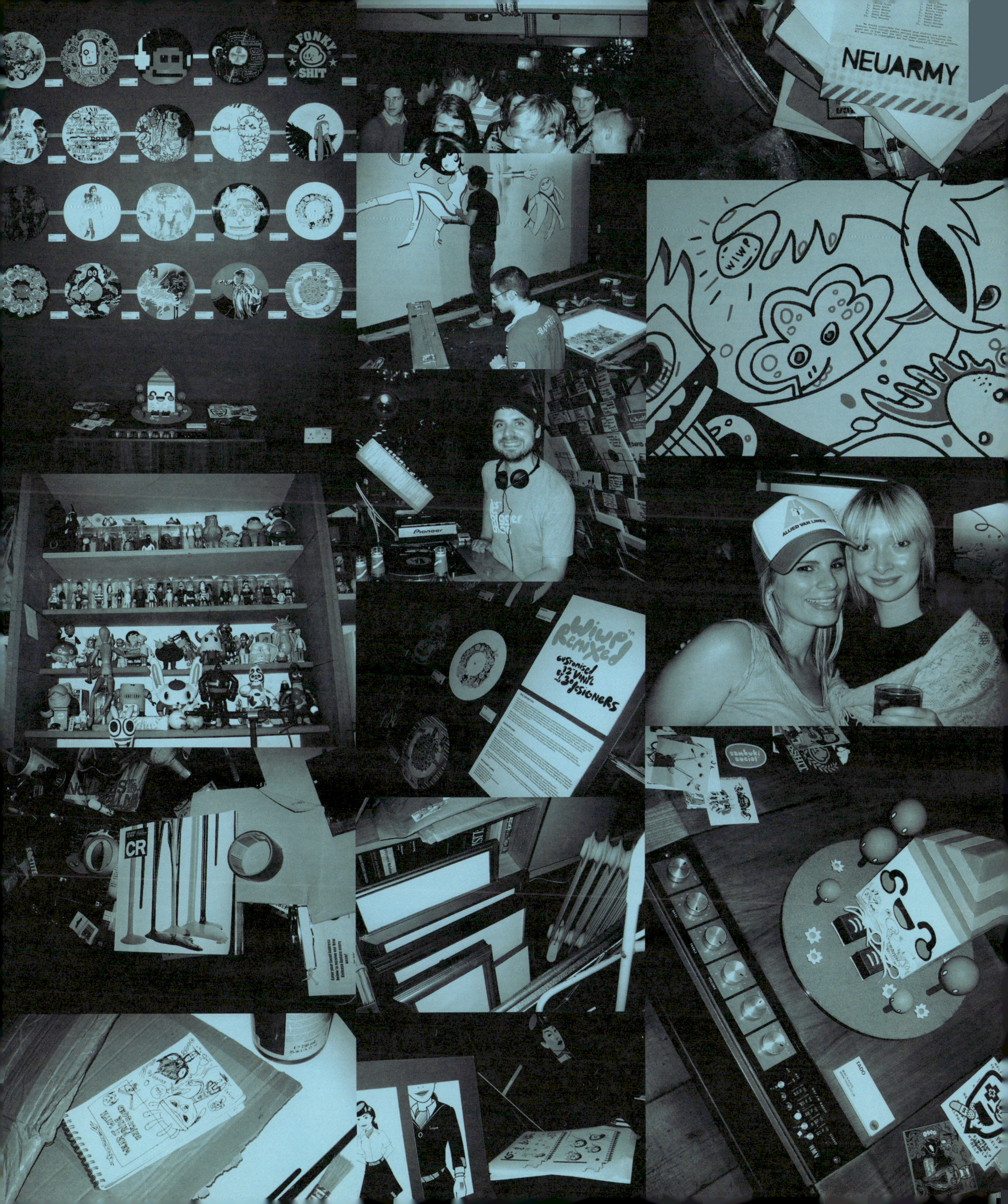
A FONKY SHIT
NEUARMY
Pioneer
ALLIED VAN LINES
WIWP Remixed
customised 12" vinyl by 30 designers
CR
sanbuki social

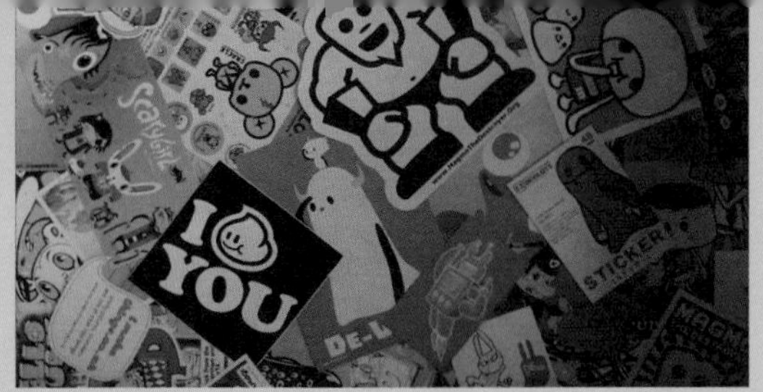

01

01 / Wearitwithpride Unplugged.
Stickers from numerous contributors.
Year_2004

02 / Wearitwithpride Unplugged.
Wall illustration by Jon Burgerman.
Year_2004

03 / Wearitwithpride Remixed.
Customised 12" Vinyl.
Year_2005

_About WIWP

WIWP is a creative collective of over 100 of the most talented and internationally renowned Illustrators and Designers. It was established in September 2003 by Darren Firth and Tim McKnight and after a year of running had over 100,000 hits and a solid user base of around 3,000. What started off as a humble badge design site has now evolved into a global platform, promoting artist collaboration through various online activities, competition's and exhibitions, becoming a great source for inspiration and artist information. It has attracted attention from the Design Council and its projects have been featured in numerous printed publications including MTV, *The Guardian, Elle, Creative Review, Design Week, Computer Arts and Metro* as well as online presences such as MTV Switched-on, Yahoo Picks, WGSN and Pixelsurgeon.

Its members range from famous illustrators and toy makers such as "Scarygirl" (Nathan J), Jeremyville and "Uglydolls" (David Horvath) to accomplished design set-ups such as Insect, Build and Ded Ass associates.

As individuals the group has worked with a wealth of prestigious clients including BBC, Adidas, Orange, Motorola, Nike, MTV, Cartoon Network and Puma; the list goes on.

02

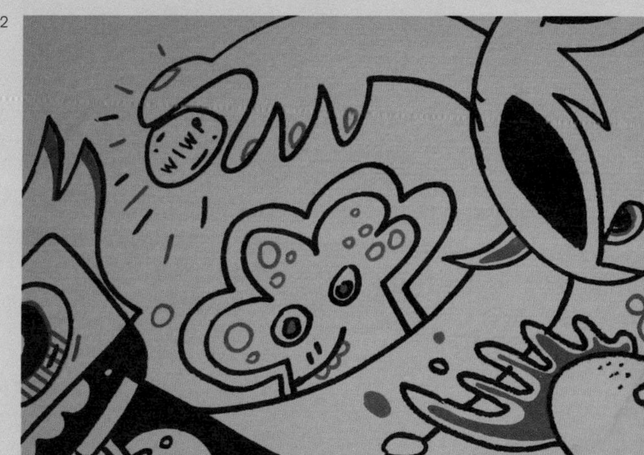

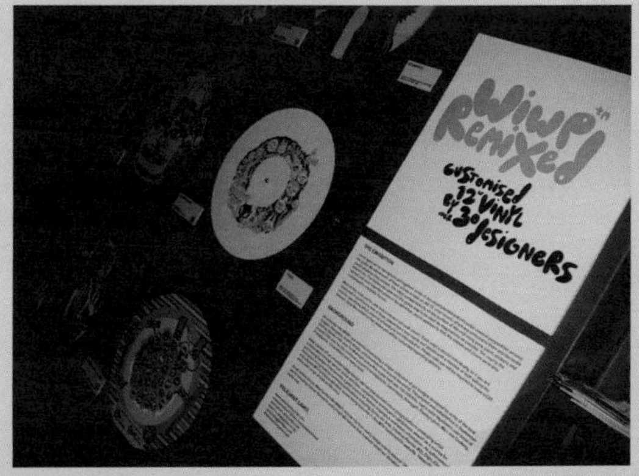

03

A PROJECT BY WIWP

Email: Darren@wearitwithpride.com
URL: www.wearitwithpride.com

_Designers

_Darren Firth /

Darren Firth, the original founder of Wearitwithpride (now know as WIWP) has managed the Brand and all its associated activities since its launch in 2003; from collaborative projects and promotions to full scale exhibitions and shows. Aside from these duties, Darren works as a Designer/Illustrator; and in his role as Senior Designer at Un.titled, has worked closely with brands such as Ben Sherman, Puma, Nike, Boxfresh, Lee Cooper and Clarks Originals. Darren's personal work (under the name Keepsmesane) is an eclectic mix of preferred styles, and has been featured in numerous international publications and exhibitions.

He is a member and Co-Founder of the collective "Sambuki Social", part of the Graphics team at the *Royal Magazine* and a regular contributer to *Computer Arts*, Pixelsurgeon and Lounge 72.

www.keepsmesane.co.uk

_Iain Follett /

Iain Follett, Senior Designer at Un.titled has worked closely with brands such as Puma, Speedo, John Smedley, Keenpac, and Portsmouth FC. Iain is also the founder of creative brand Adapt or Die under which his personal work is showcased.

He divides his time between the Midlands and London.

www.adapt-or-die.co.uk

A Project by /
Darren Firth (WIWP)

Layout and Design /
Keepsmesane & Adapt or Die

Cover Design /
Keepsmesane & Adapt or Die

Cover Artwork /
"Oh God Mother!" By Gregory Gilbert-Lodge

Foreword by /
Gavin Lucas

"Portrait of the Designer" by /
Adrian Shaughnessy

Logo Font /
ITC Avant Garde Gothic BT Bold

Contacts / General Enquiries
http://www.idnworld.com
http://www.wearitwithpride.com

2007 First Edition Published by /
Systems Design Limited
Publisher of *IdN* Magazine
4/F., Jonsim Place, 228 Queen's Road East,
Wanchai, Hong Kong
Tel: (852) 2528 5744
Fax: (852) 2529 1296
Email: info@idnworld.com
URL: www.idnworld.com

ISBN-13: 978-988-98992-5-7
ISBN-10: 988-98992-5-6

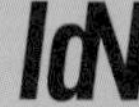

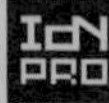

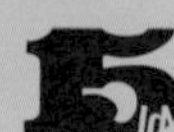

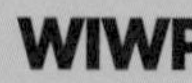

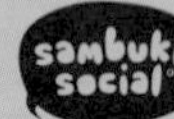